The French Contract Law Reform

A Source of Inspiration?

Editors:
S. Stijns & S. Jansen

The French Contract Law Reform

A Source of Inspiration?

intersentia

METRO

Ius Commune Europaeum

Intersentia Ltd
Sheraton House | Castle Park
Cambridge | CB3 0AX | United Kingdom
Tel.: +44 1223 370 170 | Fax: +44 1223 370 169
Email: mail@intersentia.co.uk
www.intersentia.com | www.intersentia.co.uk

Distribution for the UK and Ireland:
NBN International
Airport Business Centre, 10 Thornbury Road
Plymouth, PL6 7 PP
United Kingdom
Tel.: +44 1752 202 301 | Fax: +44 1752 202 331
Email: orders@nbninternational.com

Distribution for Europe and all other countries:
Intersentia Publishing nv
Groenstraat 31
2640 Mortsel
Belgium
Tel.: +32 3 680 15 50 | Fax: +32 3 658 71 21
Email: mail@intersentia.be

Distribution for the USA and Canada:
International Specialized Book Services
920 NE 58th Ave. Suite 300
Portland, OR 97213
USA
Tel.: +1 800 944 6190 (toll free) | Fax: +1 503 280 8832
Email: info@isbs.com

The French Contract Law Reform: A Source of Inspiration?

ISBN 978-1-78068-419-2
D/2016/7849/106
NUR 822

British Library Cataloguing in Publication Data. A catalogue record for this book is available from the British Library.

CONTENTS

Sophie Stijns
Sanne Jansen

INTRODUCTION

1. This book is the result of the Contract Law Workshop of the 20th Ius Commune Conference held 26–27 November 2015. The theme of this Workshop was: 'The French Contract Law Reform: a Source of Inspiration?' This theme was carefully chosen after the French *projet d'ordonnance* about contract law, the general regime of obligations and the proof of obligations appeared in February 2015. A few months after our workshop, in February 2016, the final version of the *ordonnance* was published. The contributions in this book are the proceedings of the presentations of this conference. Since the conference in November 2015, all authors have incorporated comments on the final version of the *ordonnance*. Whereas Van Loock briefly sketches the antecedents and the outcome of the reform, the other authors tackle each specific topics of the reform that surprised and/or excited the legal community. In what follows, we will introduce the contributions of Van Loock, Pannebakker, Peeraer, Leone, Lutzi, Oosterhuis, Jansen, Verkempinck, Storme, and Mahé to the reader.

2. As already mentioned, the contribution of Van Loock gives a broad overview of the pathway of the French reform. Firstly, it scrutinises the historical antecedents of the reform, the incentives for reform and the first reform projects (the Catala project, the Terré project and a governmental reform proposal). Furthermore, the author discusses and questions the legitimacy and the practicability of the choice to carry out the reform by way of an *ordonnance* (which involved a significant delegation of the legislative competences to the government) instead of going through the ordinary parliamentary procedure. The contribution also gives a short overview and appreciation of various innovations of the (*projet d'*) *ordonnance*. Moreover, he points out the differences between the draft and the final version of the articles, showing that the drafters of the final *ordonnance* have taken into account propositions received during the public consultation period. He concludes with lessons for a possible Belgian reform of the law of obligations. Indeed, the lessons learnt from the French reform will probably have to be taken into account soon. The Belgian Minister of Justice, Koen Geens indicated in his 'Justice Plan' (*Justitieplan*) of March 2015 and in his 'Policy Declaration' (*Beleidsnota*) of November 2015 that he is considering the reform of large parts of the Belgian Civil Code,

among which the law of obligations. The author remarks appropriately: "*Quand il pleut à Paris, il bruine à Bruxelles*".[1]

3. Pannebakker tackles the issue of the attractiveness of the new French rules about the pre-contractual phase for international commercial transactions. The first part of her contribution addresses the proposed new rules of the *ordonnance* (drawing inspiration from case law and e.g. the Unidroit Principles and the Principles of European Contract Law), while the second part focuses on the attractiveness of the new rules taking into account two factors: legal certainty and flexibility. Contrary to the original Civil Code, the new *ordonnance* proposes specific rules for the pre-contractual phase. More specifically, the drafters introduce rules about the process of negotiations (freedom of negotiation, the requirement to negotiate in good faith and information in negotiations) and about two instruments that parties may use in the course of negotiations (the pre-emption agreement and the unilateral promise). Some of those rules (such as an express limit of liability in the course of negotiations and the acknowledgement of *avant-contrats*) might, according to the author, enhance legal certainty. Nevertheless, she also points out some drawbacks of such a detailed regulations which might "encase living legal developments and block flexibility".

4. The contribution of Peeraer focuses on the complex doctrine of nullity in the new *ordonnance*. After giving an overview of the *ordonnance*'s provisions dealing with nullity, the author explores the concept of nullity in the new French rules. He points out (and criticises) that the scope of nullity is still the contract (and not the juridical act), that judicial intervention to enforce nullity is still necessary and that the claims for restitution after nullity are governed by a *sui generis* regime. He deplores that the *ordonnance* does not refer to the aim of the infringed norm and proportionality of the response (except with regard to its extent). Furthermore, he criticises the "oversimplified" codified distinction between absolute and relative nullity. The author is also very critical of the article introducing a partial nullity. He questions for example the choice of the drafters to restrict partial nullity to the situation where the ground of avoidance affects one or more terms of the contract, without extending it to the situation when the ground of avoidance only requires that some consequences of a single term are not recognised by the legal order. He also observes, one the one hand, a disproportionate use of the remedy of nullity because of its drastic results, and, on the other hand, situations where inopposability should have been replaced by nullity. Furthermore, the author suggests with regard to prescription to distinguish between the declaratory action in nullity (not subject to prescription) and the constitutive restitutionary action (subject to prescription). The overall conclusion of Peeraer's contribution is that the drafters of the *ordonnance* have not taken into account the complexity of the doctrine of nullity, and instead, favoured an oversimplified, coherent-looking system.

1 E. Dirix and P. Wéry, "Pour une modernisation du Code civil", *JT* 2015, (625) 625. See also: inaugural speech S. Stijns, Chaire Francqui, Facultés Saint Louis, 3 March 2016, *JT* 2016, no. 6647, (305) 305–311.

5. Leone explores in her contribution the potential impact of Article 1171 of the new *ordonnance* – introducing a general remedy against significantly imbalanced terms in non-negotiated contracts – on the judicial control of employment contracts. She first examines the meaning of the notion of non-negotiated contracts ("*contrats d'adhésion*") in new Article 1110. She then compares the substance of Article 1171 with the already existing parallel provisions in consumer contract law and competition law. She concludes that the drafters seemed to have in mind a mechanism not so far removed from the one already in place in consumer law. The provision on "significant imbalance" is also studied taking into account the delimitation with so-called "neighbouring" provisions such as the limitation of freedom of contract by public order and the "chronopost" codification in new Article 1170 in case of far-reaching liability exemption terms. The second part of the contribution deals with the transplantation of the "significant imbalance" provision in labour law contracts. The author starts by addressing mechanisms already used in order to deal with imbalanced terms in the labour law context (such as fundamental rights control, the principle invalidity of variation clauses and judge-made solutions to deal with for example non-competition clauses and clauses of *dédit-formation*[2]). According to the author, these alternative controlling mechanisms (with an exception to the fundamental rights control, which implies the violation of a right external to the contract) can probably be absorbed and reorganised under the new "significant imbalance" test.

6. In his contribution, Lutzi discusses the much-debated provision that introduces the theory of *imprévision* (change of circumstances) into French contract law. He starts his contribution by explaining the historical evolution of (and the existing exceptions to) the *pacta sunt servanda* principle. He then explores the current approaches to *imprévision* in French (no recognition, at least by civil courts), English (extension of the existing exception for impossibility) and German law (recognition of a separate exception based upon the principle of good faith). The latter approach has been adopted in many other legal systems (such as Italy and the Netherlands) and instruments (such as the Draft Common Frame of Reference and the Unidroit Principles). Also the drafters of the French *ordonnance* were convinced that the rigid attachment to the *pacta sunt servanda* principle should yield to the theory of *imprévision*. The author explains that the implementation of this theory in the 2015 project not only provoked positive reactions, but also some severe criticism. Practitioners were of the opinion that the provision would give too much power to the judge, whereas academics thought that it did not go far enough (requiring the consent of both parties to enable a judge to adapt the contract). In the final *ordonnance* the second paragraph was changed to address the criticism of the academics: in the event of a lack of an agreement between both parties, one party can ask for a judicial modification of the contract. Nevertheless, the author nuances this criticism to the initial 2015 proposal by stating that the mere prospect of judicial termination could have provided a significant incentive for the parties to jointly amend the contract or to agree upon a judicial

2 Terms requiring the restitution of in-work education costs in case of early termination of the employment contract.

adaptation. A final assessment of the new provision in the *ordonnance*, in comparison to its German counterpart, makes clear that it may appear as the more progressive one, because it implements a requirement to renegotiate.

7. Oosterhuis's contribution responds to the previous contribution, also dealing with the new Article 1195 introducing *imprévision* into French contract law. He mainly criticises Lutzi's (implicit) arguments to prefer the German system above the other approaches to *imprévision* (such as the French *projet d'ordonnance* of February 2015 and the English system). One of Oosterhuis's main arguments is that the English and former French system leave control over the contracts in the hands of the parties, whilst the German and the new French system would give away this control to a judge, who would have the possibility to reshape the contract. Under the first systems, the judge can only upheld or terminate the contract, or parties can negotiate and agree to amend their contract. Under the second system, a judge might be given the power to reshape the contract. According to him, a judge will not always be up to the task to amend a contract when parties do not reach a negotiated agreement. He also argues that the "legal transplant" of the theory of *imprévision* has not worked as well in the Netherlands compared to Germany (which has experienced massive economic upheaval), resulting in very little case law about *imprévision* in the Netherlands. Oosterhuis therefore criticises the fact that the new Article 1195 introduces a German-like 'open' remedy (allowing the judge, under certain circumstances, to adapt to contract when only one party requests him to do so) instead of the former proposal which introduced a 'closed remedy' (requiring the consent of both parties to enable the judge to adapt the contract). Finally, the author assesses the practical implications and the efficiency of the different policy options. He concludes that it is difficult to assess whether the benefits of the judge adjusting the contract in accordance with the preferences of the parties will exceed the losses of wrongly adjusted contracts.

8. The contribution by Jansen delves deeper into the (new) remedy of price reduction. Although price reduction was only recognised in a scattered way in French contract law, the *ordonnance* recognises it as a general remedy in Article 1223. It is a proportional remedy keeping to the middle between, on the one hand, termination of the contract, and, on the other hand, performance of the contract. Although the author applauds and welcomes the introduction of this remedy, she is of the opinion that important aspects of the price reduction remedy have not been fleshed out by the drafters of the *ordonnance* (for example its applicability in case of *force majeure*, the necessity of a notification duty in the event the creditor has already paid, what is meant by a "price", the way price reduction fits into the hierarchy of remedies, its extrajudicial application, etc.). She criticises the hasty introduction of the price reduction remedy without clarity about its relationship with other remedies, the conditions for its application, and the role of the judge and the parties.

9. Verkempinck explores in his contribution the measure of damages in the French contract law reform. He therefore boldly compares the new provisions with for example the Moldovan, Slovene, Czech, Hungarian, Italian, Spanish, US, and German legal systems. The author is fairly disappointed by the new French provisions which carry – according to him – "nothing more than the fingerprints of Napoléon's drafting committee". For example, the new *ordonnance* disregards the theories on the prominence of expectation damages and the subsidiary target position of reliance interest. Moreover, its provisions do not codify the leading principle of full compensation for the aggrieved party nor the date of assessment of the loss. Thirdly, the *ordonnance* does not include rules on the recoverability of non-pecuniary loss and lost chances. Furthermore, the provisions do not foresee the possibility of allowing equitable assessment of contractual damages and do not prescribe the duty to mitigate damages. The author examines the alleged shortcomings of the French *ordonnance* and proposes for each shortcoming a solution for the Belgian legislator, based on an impressive comparative study.

10. Storme argues in his contribution that the new rules on set-off in the *ordonnance* are a missed opportunity, although he also points out that some interesting innovations can be observed. He criticises for example the choice to define "set-off" and the incompleteness of this definition because the security function of set-off is completely missing. With regard to the requirements of set-off, the proposal fails to distinguish between the requirements for the *active* and the *passive* claim. According to the author, there is no reason why the passive claim should be "ascertained" or should be "due" (it is sufficient that it is already "payable"). He also criticises the fact that the French reform did not provide for set-off by declaration as soon as the passive claim is, although not due, already payable. Finally, the author points out the lack of rules about proprietary questions with regard to set-off. Many proprietary aspects are hidden behind a vague and too generally formulated rule prescribing that set-off cannot prejudice the rights of third parties.

11. Mahé struggles with the difficult question of why the final version of the *ordonnance* omitted the issue of interpersonal effects of fundamental rights on contractual freedom, which was previously been dealt with explicitly by Article 1102. She explains that under current French contract law the contractual violation of public policy rules is forbidden, but a general prohibition of contractual infringement of fundamental rights does not exist. The lack of a coherent framework and approach (e.g. different treatment depending on the fundamental right that is at stake) and the uncertainty of the consequences of contractual infringements of fundamental rights (e.g. incoherencies in applying the proportionality and necessity test) argue, according to the author, in favour of a codification taking into account the motives of the current reform (e.g. readability and predictability of the law). Moreover she adds that – notwithstanding the existing inconsistencies – the legislator and courts uphold the common view that fundamental rights have horizontal effect, contributing to the momentum for such a codification. Nevertheless, she also points out that the wording of former Article 1102 also implied the exclusion of direct (and indirect) interpersonal application of fundamental rights, because it merely recognised the protection of fundamental rights acknowledged by a provision (the so-called 'privatised fundamental rights'). In sum, she regrets that Article 1102 of the project was not improved in line with Article 4 of the Terré project, recognising direct interpersonal effects of fundamental rights in general.

Sander Van Loock*

THE REFORM OF THE FRENCH LAW OF OBLIGATIONS: HOW LONG WILL THE BELGIANS REMAIN NAPOLEON'S MOST LOYAL SUBJECTS?

1. Introduction

1. Exiled to the desolate island of Saint Helena, Napoleon Bonaparte pondered on one September evening in 1816: "*Waterloo will wipe out the memory of my forty victories; but that which nothing can wipe out is my Civil Code. That will live forever.*"[1] These thoughts have proven to be visionary. His Civil Code is not only still applicable in France, Belgium and Luxembourg, it has also influenced codifications all over the world.[2] Now, 200 years after his dramatic defeat in the Battle of Waterloo, the law of obligations as reflected in the French Civil Code will be modernised. This modernization is necessary as the law of obligations in the Civil Code has been left virtually unchanged since its adoption in 1804. The reform will not, however, put the Code's vocation to eternity to rest. On the contrary, its purpose is rather to re-establish the prestige of the French Civil Code as the cornerstone of French private law and a model for other jurisdictions.

2. On 11 February 2016, just a few days before the constitutional deadline, *ordonnance n° 2016-131 portant réforme du droit des contrats, du regime general et de la preuve des obligations* was published. With this ordinance, the French government modified the law of obligations in the French Civil Code. The authority to modify the Civil Code was

* LLM (Cantab), Bursary of the Agency for Innovation through Innovation (IWT), Institute for the Law of Obligations, KU Leuven, Belgium. The drafting of this contribution was finished on 12 February 2016. This contribution is largely based on S. Van Loock, "De hervorming van het Franse verbintenissenrecht: Le jour de gloire, est-il arrivé?", *RW* 2014–2015, 1562–1572.

1 According to one contemporary, Napoleon Bonaparte would have said: "*Ma gloire n'est pas d'avoir gagné quarante batailles et d'avoir fait la loi aux rois qui osèrent défendre au peuple français de changer la forme de son gouvernement. Waterloo effacera le souvenir de tant de victoires; c'est comme le dernier acte qui fait oublier les premiers. Mais ce que rien n'effacera, ce qui vivra éternellement, c'est mon code civil; ce sont les procès-verbaux de mon conseil d'État; ce sont les recueils de ma correspondance avec mes ministres; c'est enfin tout le bien que j'ai fait comme administrateur, comme réorganisateur de la grande famille française.*" See: C. Montholon, *Récits de la captivité de l'Empereur Napoléon*, I, Paris, Paulin, 1847, 470.

2 C. Grimaldi, "L'exportation du Code civil", *Pouvoirs* 2005, (80) 80–96; K. Zweigert and H. Kötz, *Einführung in die Rechtsvergleichung*, Tübingen, Mohr Siebeck, 1994, 96–117.

awarded by Parliament through the *Loi nr. 2015–177 relative à la modernisation et à la simplification du droit et des procédures dans les domaines de la justice et des affaires intérieures*, which was published on 17 February 2015. This act was adopted after a long procedural stand-off between the French government and the National Assembly on the one hand, and the Senate on the other hand. Pursuant to Article 8 of that act, the French government could by ordinance change the law in book III of the Civil Code in order to *"moderniser, de simplifier, d'améliorer la lisibilité, de renforcer l'accessibilité du droit commun des contrats, du régime des obligations et du droit de la preuve, de garantir la sécurité juridique et l'efficacité de la norme."*

3. Although a reform had been discussed before (Chapter 2), it would take until the turn of the millennium until the call for reform finally gained momentum. The motives which led to this change of hearts were not purely national, but came from a European and international level (Chapter 3). Chapter 4 describes the parliamentary procedure which has led to the adoption of Act nr. 2015–117. Chapter 5 provides a short overview of the content of the reform project. It will furthermore provide a brief discussion of the project in comparison with modern codifications, such as the Dutch and the German Civil Code, as well as with the *Draft Common Frame of Reference*. This discussion takes place in the light of the objectives formulated by the government to support the modernization. This introductory contribution will conclude with a discussion of the situation in Belgium (Chapter 6) and some brief lessons from the French reform (Chapter 7).

2. Historical antecedents

4. It is remarkable that it took more than 200 years to finally reform the law of obligations in the French Civil Code. This is all the more the case, as it is inherent to every codification that it begins to grow old from the day of its adoption.[3] No codification, even if it crystallises the existing law after its adoption, can stop the course of time indefinitely.[4] In the last sentence of his famous *Discours Préliminaire*, Portalis indicated that future legislatures might have to amend the Civil Code.[5] As early as the 1830s, legal

[3] R. Cabrillac, "Recodifier", *RTD civ.* 2001, (833) 834: *"Les codes ne vivent pleinement qu'un temps. Bref, pourrait-on dire avec un brin de pessimisme. En rupture avec l'ancien droit, les codes commencent à vieillir dès leur adoption."*; P. Rossi, "Observations sur le droit civil français" in *Mélanges d'économie politique d'histoire et de philosophie*, II, Paris, Guillaumin, 1857, (1) 17: *"(L)e Code, image fidèle d'abord de la société rajeunie, perd tous les jours un peu de cette parfaite ressemblance."* Portalis expressed a similar sentiment in his *Discours préliminaire*: *"Car les lois, une fois rédigées, demeurent telles qu'elles ont été écrites. Les hommes, au contraire, ne se reposent jamais; ils agissent toujours."* (J. Portalis, "Discours préliminaire" in Fenet, *Recueil Complet des Travaux préparatoires du Code Civil*, I, Paris, Videcoq, 1836, (463) 469).

[4] R. Cabrillac, "D'un code à l'autre, les difficultés d'une recodification" in *Mélanges en l'honneur du doyen Georges Wiederkehr*, Paris, Dalloz, 2009, (53) 63: *"Toute codification, même si elle opère après son adoption une cristallisation du droit existant, ne peut arrêter indéfiniment le cours du temps. Les plus solides et splendides monuments ont besoin de ravalement voire de restauration: les recodifications semblent indispensables à la survie des codes."*

[5] J. Portalis, "Discours préliminaire" in Fenet, *Recueil Complet des Travaux préparatoires du Code Civil*, I, Paris, Videcoq, 1836, (463) 525.

scholars began to argue that such a reform of the French Civil Code was necessary.[6] Committees to prepare a reform were set up in 1866 and in 1889 but proved unsuccessful. At the centennial anniversary of the Civil Code in 1904, the call for a reform grew stronger, as some scholars considered that the Civil Code had become obsolete.[7] This sentiment was reinforced through the comparison with the more modern German Civil Code, which had entered into force in 1900.[8] Planiol, however, was a generally known opponent of a complete revision of the Civil Code. As many others scholars, he preferred a more cautious and partial approach.[9] Another reform commission was established, but this project remained unsuccessful as well.

5. In the 1920s, a project for a Franco-Italian Code of Obligations and Contracts was initiated. The initiative came from the Italian author Scialoja, who presented the idea during a conference at the Sorbonne in 1918. The innovative project was published in 1927, but during the 1930s, support for the project faltered and it was abandoned. It has nevertheless influenced the Polish Code of Obligations (1937), the Romanian Civil Code (1940) and the Italian Civil Code (1942).[10] After the Second World War, another project was set up under the presidency of Julliot de la Morandière, which for some time ran parallel to the activities of Meijers in the Netherlands. The project did not succeed either.

6 P. Rossi, "Observations sur le droit civil français" in *Mélanges d'économie politique d'histoire et de philosophie*, II, Paris, Guillaumin, 1857, (1) 1–23 (reprint of a 1837 article).

7 F. Larnaude, "Le Code civil et la nécessité de sa Revision" in *Le Code civil 1804–1904 Livre du Centenaire*, II, Paris, Rousseau, 1904, (899) 891 ff; E Pilon, "Réforme du Code civil par voie de Revision générale" in *Le Code civil 1804–1904 Livre du Centenaire*, II, Paris, Rousseau, 1904, 933–951.

8 R. Saleilles, *Introduction à l'étude du droit civil allemand*, Paris, Pichon, 1904, 123: *"Le temps est donc venu de rédiger l'Édit. L'œuvre de la jurisprudence française de tout un siècle exige sa codification."* A century later, a similar thought was expressed with respect to the German *Schuldrechtsmodernisierung*: *"La réforme allemande est un bel exemple d'une révision partielle d'un code ancien qui retrouve son lustre mis à mal par des textes législatifs laissés en marge du BGB et des institutions prétoriennes qui s'étaient développées hors du code."* (C. Witz, "Pourquoi la réforme et pourquoi s'y intéresser en France", *Revue internationale de droit comparé (RIDC)* 2002, (935) 940). See for Belgium: *"Le Code allemand constituera une source précieuse de réflexion non seulement pour la transposition des directives européennes en droit civil mais certes également pour une possible révision de notre Code civil bicentenaire."* (D. Philippe, "La réforme du Code civil allemand: une source d'inspiration pour une révision du Code Napoléon" in A. Wijffels (ed.), *Le Code civil entre* ius commune *et droit privé européen*, Brussels, Bruylant, 2005, (93) 116).

9 M. Planiol, "Inutilité d'une Revision générale du Code civil" in *Le Code civil 1804–1904 Livre du Centenaire*, II, Paris, Rousseau, 1904, (953) 960 and 963. See also: E. Gaudemet, "Les Codifications récentes et la Revision du Code civil" in *Le Code civil 1804–1904 Livre du Centenaire*, II, Paris, Rousseau, 1904, (965) 986: *"Que ce Code soit aujourd'hui l'un des plus vieux du monde, il nous importe peu, si l'exemple des législations jeunes nous montre la vitalité de ses principes essentiels, si la science renouvelée de l'interprétation sait faire largement circuler sous l'écorce antique la sève vivifiante. (...) Le droit privé en France n'a pas besoin d'un Code nouveau."* See already: P. Rossi, "Observations sur le droit civil français" in *Mélanges d'économie politique d'histoire et de philosophie*, II, Paris, Guillaumin, 1857, (1) 23: *"Nul ne songe à porter la sape et le marteau dans ce vaste et beau monument que le génie français a élevé à la France nouvelle, pour en assurer la gloire et en attester la puissance. Quelques lois partielles qui puissent s'encadrer dans ce grand ensemble suffisent au besoin des temps."*

10 About the project: C. Witz, "Longue gestation d'un code européen de contrats", *RTD civ.* 2003, (447) 448–451.

The only proposals it produced, dealing with family law, were never submitted in Parliament.[11]

3. Incentives for the reform and the first reform projects

3.1. Incentives

6. France had to wait until the turn of the millennium for this situation to finally change. The incentives for the reform consist of a trinity which grew in the early 2000s and culminated around the *bicentennaire* of the Civil Code in 2004. Before discussing those in more detail, it is interesting to note that these motives are predominantly related to evolutions on an European and an international level, rather than to national evolutions. This tendency could also explain the defensive stance taken by some of the drafters of the initial reform projects, which will be discussed further.

7. A first incentive for the reform was initiated by the European Union. In 2001, the European Commission published its *Communication on European Contract Law* and launched a public consultation.[12] One year later, von Bar, as president of the *Study Group on a European Civil Code*, presented the project for a European Civil Code in the French *Cour de cassation*. This presentation, held in English in the centre of the French legal universe, sent an unprecedented shockwave through the French legal community and caused uproar in legal doctrine. Many French legal scholars were surprised by the progress made by the study group and felt that the French legal tradition was underrepresented in the project. Some French scholars reacted vehemently against the idea of a European codification of contract law. Legrand considered the project as *"politically complicitous, inherently oppressive, and fundamentally antihumanistic."*[13] Lequette, in turn, compared it to the identity politics of Nazi Germany and the Soviet Union.[14] Other scholarly

11 J. Lokin and W. Zwalve, *Hoofdstukken uit de Europese Codificatiegeschiedenis*, The Hague, Boom, 2014, 263. About the project: L. Julliot de la Morandière, "La réforme du Code civil", *D* 1948, 117–124; L. Julliot de la Morandière, "The Reform of the French Civil Code", *U.Pa.L.Rev.* 1948, 1–21; R. Houin, "Les travaux de la commission de réforme du code civil", *RTD civ.* 1951, 34–50.

12 *Communication from the Commission to the Council and the European Parliament on European contract law*, COM (2001) 398 final, OJ C 13 September 2001, 255. This communication was followed by an action plan: *Communication from the Commission to the European Parliament and the Council - A more coherent European contract law - An action plan*, COM (2003) 68 final, OJ C 15 March 2003, 63. The European Parliament had already called on the preparation of a European Code of Private Law: *Resolution of 26 May 1989 on action to bring into line the private law of the Member States*, OJ C 26 June 1989, 158, p. 400 and *Resolution of 6 May 1994 on the harmonisation of certain sectors of the private law of the Member States*, OJ C 25 July 1994, 205, p. 518.

13 P. Legrand, "Antivonbar", *JCL* 2005, (13) 27.

14 Y. Lequette, "Quelques remarques à propos du projet de code civil européen de M. von Bar", *D* 2002, (2202) 2212, no. 23. *Adde:* Y. Lequette, "Vers un code civil européen?", *Pouvoirs* 2003, 97–126. See further about these reactions: R. Michaels, "Code vs Code. Nationalist and Internationalist Images of the Code Civil in the French Resistance to a European Codification", *ERCL* 2012, 277–295 and R. Sefton-Green, "French and English crypto-nationalism and European private law", *ERCL* 2012, 260–276. However, as early as the 1940s, some French scholars have advocated a European codification:

reactions were more nuanced.[15] Cabrillac, *e.g.*, did not consider the project as a threat to the French Civil Code, but rather as an intellectual stimulus and a source of inspiration.[16] The work of the Study Group would *i.a.* result in the *Draft Common Frame of Reference*.[17]

8. A second incentive came from the World Bank in New York, which ranked the French legal system at the 44th place worldwide (*i.e.* after Jamaica, Botswana and Tonga) in its 2004 Doing Business Report. According to the report, the French legal tradition is one of the least likely to promote economic development. Although the methodology applied and its basic assumptions can be criticised,[18] the report nevertheless put a finger on France's weak spot as it reflected the decline or eclipse of the influence of the French Civil Code on the global legal stage.[19] A strong counteroffensive was set up fast. The French government created a programme on the *"Attractivité économique du droit"* and legal scholars went on the barricades. The

"L'Europe ne sera vraiment unie que si, à côté d'une unification politique et économique, on poursuit une unification juridique, même sur le terrain du droit privé. (...) Il y a, pour faciliter les relations économiques, à unifier le droit des échanges; il y a à prévoir des règles communes de conflits de lois. (...) Et ainsi nous ferons ensemble ce premier pas vers une Europe juridiquement organisée, c'est-à-dire vers l'Europe, au sens vrai du mot." (L. Julliot de la Morandière, "La réforme du Code civil", *D* 1948, 117). See also: *"En préparant dès maintenant l'unification de ce droit [des contrats et des obligations], les juristes ne se livreront pas à une anticipation hasardeuse; mais ils apporteront une base utile à la construction européenne"* (R. Houin, "Pour une codification européenne du droit des contrats et des obligations" in *Études juridiques offertes à Julliot de la Morandière*, Paris, Dalloz, 1964, (223) 231).

15 B. Fauvarque-Cosson, "Faut-il un Code civil européen?", *RTD civ.* 2002, 463–480; J. Huet, "Nous faut-il un "euro" droit civil?", *D* 2002, 2611–2614; P. Malaurie, "Le code civil européen des obligations et des contrats", *JCP G* 2002, 281–285; P. Malinvaud, "Réponse – hors délai – à la Commission européenne à propos d'un Code européen des contrats", *D* 2002, 2542–2551. In favour of a European codification: J. Ghestin, "Le futur: exemples étrangers. Le Code civil en France aujourd'hui", *Revue des contrats (RDC)* 2004, (1152) no. 10; D. Tallon, "Grandeur et décadence du Code civil français" in *Liber amicorum Marcel Fontaine*, Brussels, Larcier, 2003, (279) 291–294.

16 R. Cabrillac, "L'avenir du code civil", *JCP G* 2004, (547) 551, no. 11.

17 H. Eidenmüller, F. Faust, H.C. Grigoleit, N. Jansen, G. Wagner and R. Zimmermann, "Der Gemeinsame Referenzrahmen für das Europäische Privatrecht", *JZ* 2008, 529–550; J. Mance, "The Common Frame of Reference", *ZEuP* 2010, 457–462; W. Van Gerven and S. Lierman, *Algemeen Deel. Veertig jaar later* in *Beginselen van Belgisch Privaatrecht*, Antwerp, Kluwer, 2010, 187–189, no. 68.

18 *E.g.* C. Kern, "Doing-Business-Reports der Weltbank – fragwürdige Quantifizierung rechterlicher Qualität?", *JZ* 2009, 498–504; M. Siems, "The End of Comparative Law", *JCL* 2007, (133) 143–145; M. Renaudin, The role of the economic efficiency paradigm in commercial law reforms: a French perspective, *JBL* 2015, 472–483; M. Siems, *Comparative Law*, Cambridge, Cambridge University Press, 2014, 182–186. A more positive stance is taken by B. du Marais, "Attractivité économique du droit; le droit français peut-il survivre dans la compétition internationale", *D&P* 2008, (38) 41–45; C. Menard, and B. du Marais, "Can We Rank Legal Systems According to Their Economy Efficiency?", *Washington University Journal of Law & Policy* 2008, 55–88 and R. Michaels, "Comparative law by numbers", *American Journal of Comparative Law* 2009, 765–795.

19 C. Champalaune, "Les grand traits de la réforme" in P. Stoffel-Munck (ed.), *Réforme du droit des contrats et pratique des affaires*, Paris, Dalloz, 2015, (7) 8; M. Renaudin, The role of the economic efficiency paradigm in commercial law reforms: a French perspective, *JBL* 2015, (472) 476, calls the report "an important wake-up call for France"; R. Sefton-Green, "DCFR, the Avant-Projet Catala and French Legal Scholars A Story of Cat and Mouse", *Edin.L.R.* 2008, (351) 353.

Association Henri Capitant most notably defended the French legal tradition in two publications.[20]

9. A third incentive can be traced back to the *bicentennaire* of the Civil Code itself in 2004, which left French legal doctrine with mixed feelings. On the one hand, there was a sense of pride in celebrating the 200th anniversary of the *"Constitution civile de la France"*, which has served as a model for many codifications. On the other hand, many legal scholars considered the French Civil Code to be out of date and in dire need of modernization.[21] In the words of the *Assocation Henri Capitant*, at the occasion of the current ordinance: *"Construit en contemplation d'une France des champs et préindustrielle, il* [the Civil Code] *doit être modernisé et adapté à une France des villes, largement postindustrielle et tertiaire."*[22]

3.2. Initial reform projects

10. The initial reactions also consisted of three elements: two academic projects and one governmental project.

11. A first academic reaction was the Catala project, published in 2005 (*Avant-Projet de Réforme de Droit des Obligations et du Droit de la Prescription*).[23] The aim of the project was not only to reaffirm the tradition of the French Civil Code, against a felt European threat, but also to play a more important role on a European level.[24] In France, the project

[20] B. Fauvarque-Cosson, B. and A.-J. Kerhuel, "Is Law an Economic Contest? French Reactions to the Doing Business World Bank Report and Economic Analysis of the Law", *AJCL* 2009, 811–830. See further: L. Usunier, "Le rapport Doing Business 2012, la concurrence des systèmes juridiques et l'attractivité du droit français des contrats", *RDC* 2012, 575 ff.

[21] J.-L. Aubert, "La recodification et l'éclatement du droit civil hors le code civil" in *Le Code civil 1804–2004: Livre du Bicentenaire*, Paris, Dalloz, 2004, (123) 137–140; F. Barrière, "Le code civil français aujourd'hui: influences" in J.-P. Dunand and B. Winiger (eds.), *Le code civil français dans le droit européen*, Brussels, Bruylant, 2005, (95) 112–113, nos. 42–43 and 117–118, no. 49; J. Ghestin, "Le futur: exemples étrangers. Le Code civil en France aujourd'hui", *RDC* 2004, (1152) no. 3; M. Grimaldi, "L'exportation du Code civil", *Pouvoirs* 2003, (80) 93; J. Huet, "Nous faut-il un "euro" droit civil?", *D* 2002, (2611) 2614; P. Malinvaud, "Réponse – hors délai – à la Commission européenne à propos d'un Code européen des contrats", *D* 2002, (2542) 2551. *Contra:* A. Sériaux, "Vanitas vanitatum. De l'inanité d'une refonte du livre III du titre III du Code civil", *RDC* 2004, (1187), no. 3.

[22] *Réponse de l'Association Henri Capitant à la consultation relative au projet d'ordonnance portant réforme du droit des contrats, du régime général et de la preuve des obligations du 25 février 2015*, Paris, 30 April 2015, 1.

[23] Www.henricapitant.org/sites/default/files/Avant-projet_de_reforme_du_droit_des_obligations_et_de_la_prescription_et_expose_des_motifs.pdf.

[24] P. Catala, "Au-delà du bicentenaire", *RDC* 2004, (1145) no. 10; B. Fauvarque-Cosson and D. Mazeaud, "L'avant-projet français de réforme du droit des obligations et du droit de la prescription", *Unif. L.R.* 2006, (103) 105–106, no. 5; J. Lokin and W. Zwalve, *Hoofdstukken uit de Europese Codificatiegeschiedenis*, The Hague, Boom, 2014, 263. This defence stance is clearly present in P. Catala, "L'avant-projet de réforme des obligations et le droit des affaires" in V. Sagaert (ed.), *La réforme du droit privé en France*, Brussels, De Boeck, 2009 (85) 85. According to Catala one should not minimise the necessity of a reform with the argument that everything is good the way it is. With a reference to the Second World

was largely met with approval, although it was justifiably criticised for being rather *franco-français* and conservative.[25] The absence of (thorough) comparative legal input was highly criticised. The influence of comparative law on the different parts nevertheless differed greatly, as each of the 34 authors had written their own part of the project. Although the direct cause for the project was a conference where the Principles of European Contract Law were compared with French law, it hardly took into account any developments on a European or international level. The project therefore remained to a large extent loyal to the *Code civil* of 1804. The decision to maintain the *cause* as a validity requirement for legal acts, and even to even enlarge its role, was controversial.[26] The *Avant-Projet* of Catala consists of three parts: general law of obligations, law of prescription and tort law. The part on prescription was written by Malaurie and was heavily influenced by the *Principles of European Contract Law* and the German reform. It was used in 2008 to modernise the law of prescription in the Civil Code.[27] The part on tort law, which was under the aegis of Viney and Durry, was innovative as well. It might lead to a modernization of tort law in the future.[28] This modernization could take place soon. Together with the publication of the ordinance on the law of obligations, the government announced that a proposal on tort law was drafted in parallel.[29] On 29 April 2016, the French Minister of Justice presented a draft bill on the reform of civil liability ("*Avant-projet de loi. Réforme de la responsabilité civile*")[30] and launched a public consultation.

12. A second academic reaction was the Terré project, which was published by the *Académie des sciences morales et politiques* in 2009 (*Pour une réforme du droit des*

War, he remarks: "*Ma génération sait que cette chanson était sur toutes les lèvres à la vieille du désastre de 40.*"

25 D. Tallon, "Teneur et valeur du projet appréhendé dans une perspective comparative", *RDC* 2006, (131) 131; E. Hondius, "The Two Faces of the Catala Project – Towards a New General Part of the French Law of Obligations", *ERPL* 2007, (835) 837, no. 3; D. Mazeaud, "Observations conclusives", *RDC* 2006, (177) no. 2; R. Sefton-Green, "DCFR, the Avant-Projet Catala and French Legal Scholars A Story of Cat and Mouse", *Edin.L.R.* 2008, (351) 359–361. Very critical is E. Descheemaeker, "Review J. Cartwright, S. Vogenauer and S. Whittaker (eds), Reforming the French Law of Obligations, Hart, 2009", *MLR* 2010, 1086–1089, who speaks of "*a parochialism of thought.*"

26 B. Fauvarque-Cosson, "La réforme du droit français des contrats: perspective comparative", *RDC* 2006, (147) I.B.; B. Fauvarque-Cosson and D. Mazeaud, "L'avant-projet français de réforme du droit des obligations et du droit de la prescription", *Unif. L.R.* 2006, (103) 125–126, no. 38; M. Latina, "Contrat (généralités)" in *Rép.civ. Dalloz*, 2014, 36, no. 131.

27 Loi no. 2008–561 du 17 juin 2008 portant réforme de la prescription en matière civile, *JO* 18 June 2008, 9856. See: A.M. Leroyer, "Réforme de la prescription civile", *RTD Civ.* 2008, 563, ff. and P. Malaurie, "La réforme de la prescription civile", *Defrénois* 2008, no. 38842.

28 See further: E. Hondius, "The Two Faces of the Catala Project – Towards a New General Part of the French Law of Obligations", *ERPL* 2007, (835) 837–838, no. 4; D. Mazeaud, "Les projets français de réforme du droit de la responsabilité civile", *Petites Affiches* 13 March 2014, 8 ff. Recently: G. Viney, "Après la réforme du contrat, la nécessaire réforme des textes du Code civil relatifs à la responsabilité", *JCP* 2016, 99 ff.

29 *Rapport au Président relatif à l'ordonnance n° 2016–131,: "La réforme de la responsabilité civile contractuelle et extracontractuelle fera l'objet d'un projet de loi ultérieur qui sera débattu devant le Parlement, en raison des enjeux politiques et sociaux qui sont liés à ce domaine du droit."*

30 See: www.textes.justice.gouv.fr/art_pix/avpjl-reponsabilite-civile.pdf.

contrats).[31] This project is much more modern, as it took into account the developments on an international and European level. Whereas the Catala project was mainly a reaffirmation of the French tradition, the Terré project was in many respects very innovative and meant a breach with that tradition.[32] The *cause* was abandoned as a validity requirement,[33] and the role of the judge was strengthened, *i.a.* by introducing rules on change of circumstances and a general prohibition on unfair contract.[34]

13. A third reaction came from the French government itself. In 2008 it published a reform proposal, based on both the Catala and the Terré project. It was submitted to a public consultation and amended several times in the course of the following years.[35] In February 2014, a proposal was leaked on the website of *lesechos.fr*. The current ordinance is based on these earlier versions.

4. Chronicle of a Reform Foretold

4.1. Reform by ordinance

14. The reform of the law obligations had a slow start. The reason was a division between the Senate on the one hand, and the National Assembly and the government on the other hand as to the procedure to be taken for the reform. Where the former wanted the reform to take place in Parliament, the latter preferred a reform through ordinance (*ordonnance*).

15. The government submitted the proposal for an authorization act (*loi d'habilitation*) in the Senate in November 2013. Pursuant to its then Article 3 (its current Article 8), the government is authorised to modify the law of obligations in the Civil Code by way of ordinance.[36] Although the senators were in favour of a reform of the Civil Code, they

31 F. Terré (ed.), *Pour une réforme du droit des contrats*, Paris, Dalloz, 2009, 310 p.

32 D. Mazeaud, "Une nouvelle rhapsodie doctrinale pour une réforme du droit des contrats", *RDC* 2009, (1364) no. 3.

33 D. Houtcieff, "Le contenu du contrat" in F. Terré (ed.), *Pour une réforme du droit des contrats*, Paris, Dalloz, 2009, (183) 198–203.

34 J. Flour, J.-L. Aubert and E. Savaux, *Droit civil. Les obligations. 1. L'acte juridique*, Paris, Sirey, 2014, 61, no. 77–1; M. Latina, "Contrat (généralités)" in *Rép.civ. Dalloz*, 2014, 37–38.

35 See: P. Ancel, P. Brun, V. Forray, O. Gout, G. Pignarre and S. Pimont, "Points de vue convergents sur le projet de réforme du droit des contrats", *JCP G* 2008, I, 213; R. Cabrillac, "Le projet de réforme du droit des contrats", *JCP G* 2008, I, 190, 17 ff.; A. Ghozi and Y. Lequette, "La réforme du droit des contrats: brèves observations sur le projet de la chancellerie", *D* 2008, 2609 ff.; M. Fabre-Magnan, "Réforme du droit des contrats: "Un très bon projet"", *JCP G* 2008, I, 199; D. Mainguy, "Défense, critique et illustration de certains points du projet de réforme du droit des contrats", *D* 2009, 308 ff.; P. Malaurie, "Petite note sur le projet de réforme du droit des contrats", *JCP G* 2008, no. 204; D. Mazeaud, "La réforme du droit français des contrats", *Revue Juridique Themis* 2010, 243–257.

36 Pursuant to Article 38 of the French Constitution, Parliament can authorise the government in a "*loi d'habilitation*" to amend legislation by way of ordinance during a limited period of time. The normal parliamentary procedure is not followed, but in order to become law, the ordinance has to be ratified afterwards by Parliament. See: L. Favoreu, P. Gaïa *et al.*, *Droit constitutionnel*, Paris, Dalloz, 2014, 876–886.

were hostile to a reform of the French *"Constitution civile"* through ordinance. According to the Senate, a reform of such magnitude and importance should be discussed in Parliament.[37] Moreover, the reform is not a purely technical issue, as was sometimes put forward by the government, but also involved important policy questions, such as the scope of party autonomy, the protection of weaker parties, the role of the judge *etc*. The perspective of a ratification was not a sufficient guarantee in the eyes of the Senate. The Senate moreover doubted, whether the reliance on an ordinance would really gain time.[38]

16. The Senate adopted the proposal at the end of January 2014 without the aforementioned Article 3 and transmitted it to the National Assembly. There, Article 3 was reintroduced into the proposal. The decisive argument to do so was the concern to complete the reform during the current parliamentary term. Because of this division, the proposal was sent back and forth multiple times between both chambers of Parliament. On 28 January 2015, the National Assembly ended this *navette parlementaire* and finally adopted the authorization act. A group of senators challenged the act in a (symbolic?) rear-guard combat before the Constitutional Council. The Council dismissed their principled objections and ruled that Article 8 was in conformity with the French Constitution.[39]

17. The text of the reform proposal was published online at the end of February 2015 and subjected to a public consultation, which took place until the end of April. The text was submitted in parallel to various law faculties, interest groups and governmental bodies.[40] In parallel, the results of this consultation were analysed and the proposal was modified in collaboration with members of Parliament. The Council of State (*Conseil d'État*) had until December 2015 to evaluate the proposal. On 25 January 2016, two days before her resignation, the French Minister of Justice, Taubira, tweeted: *"Nous avons pu réformer le droit des contrats. Nous avons actualisé des textes vieux de 210 ans"*, indicating that the final drafting of the ordinance had been finished. After some uncertainty following her resignation, the ordinance was discussed on 10 February 2016 in the Council of Ministers and published the day afterwards. This publication took place just in time, the authorization of the government ending on 16 February 2017. The ordinance

37 Also critical: J.-L. Harouel, G. Teboul and O. Tournafond, "Le droit des contrats réformé par *ordonnance*?", *D* 2014, 1099–1100. More positive: F. Rome, "Droit des contrats: la réforme maudite?", *D* 2014, (1033) 1033. The French legislature has been relucted in the past to reform the Civil Code by ordinance. It has only done so twice before: for the reform of family law (2005) and the reform of the law on security interests (2006). Critical: R. Libchaber, "Le parlementarisme: acte de décès?", *RTD civ.* 2001, 695–698; D. Martin, "Le Code civil à saute-mouton", *D* 2005, 1577–1578. Asserts that *ordonnances* can play a complementary role to acts: M. Guillaume, "Les *ordonnances*: tuer ou sauver la loi?", *Pouvoirs* 2005, 117–129.

38 *Rapport par T.S. Soilihi*, Sénat 15 January 2014, no. 288, 19 – 24.

39 Constitutional Council 12 February 2015, n° 2015–710 DC, www.conseil-constitutionnel.fr/decision/2015/2015710dc.htm.

40 See *i.a.* the responses by the *Assocation Henri Capitant* (www.henricapitant.org/node/104568) and the CCI Paris Île-de-France (www.cci-paris-idf.fr/sites/default/files/etudes/pdf/documents/reforme-droit-des-contrats-fou1505.pdf).

is to be ratified by Parliament during the first semester of 2016. Pursuant to Article 9 of the ordinance, the changes will enter into force on 1 October 2016, but only for contracts made after this date. However, the three Articles which provide in interrogatory actions (Articles 1123, 1158 and 1183) will enter into force on 1 October 2016.

4.2. *Criticism*

18. One can question the choice of procedure which was followed to reform the Civil Code. In the National Assembly, the division between the proponents and the opponents was all too simplistically presented as a choice between realism and principles.[41] The choice for an ordinance would demonstrate a sense of realism and pragmatism, as the normal parliamentary procedure was considered too slow. The rapporteur in the National Assembly even admitted that they lack the time to undertake such an important project.[42] It is startling to see how the legislature is prepared to give up and delegate such an important part of its legislative competences to the government and to limit its role to the ratification of the ordinance afterwards. The concession that some members of parliament will be involved in the final drafting of the ordinance, is nothing but a scant consolation. Van Gerven and Lierman argue that a codification in a contemporary society must take place in accordance with democratic procedures. This is especially the case where fundamental policy questions have to be addressed. It is necessary to give this codification a clear foundation and coherence.[43] Contrary to what the government argued, a reform of the Civil Code is not a mere technical issue, but raises many questions of policy where a balance needs to be sought between the various interests involved.[44] Those issues merit and necessitate a public and parliamentary debate. This discussion can moreover provide guidance when these rules have to be applied afterwards.[45] Van Gerven and Lierman are somewhat doubtful whether a Parliament which now primarily focusses on its political controlling task, is still capable of playing a determining role in an important codification project.[46] The (recent) experience with the Code of International Private Law and the Act on Security Interests on Movables, nevertheless demonstrate that the Belgian Parliament, with considerable academic support, is still able to successfully accomplish a (re) codification. According to Erauw, one of the academic fathers of the proposal on a Code

41 P. Deumier and P. Puig, "Le code civil, la loi et l'*ordonnance*", *RTD civ.*2014, (597) 598.

42 *Rapport par C. Capdevielle Projet de loi relatif à la modernisation et à la simplification du droit et des procédures dans les domaines de la justice et des affaires intérieures*, Commission paritaire mixte, 13 May 2014, Assemblée Nationale no. 1933, 3–4.

43 W. Van Gerven and S. Lierman, *Algemeen Deel. Veertig jaar later* in *Beginselen van Belgisch Privaatrecht*, Antwerp, Kluwer, 2010, 189–190, no. 69. See also: E. Terryn, "Codificatie in het economisch recht en de rol van de nationale wetgever", *TPR* 2009, (105) 110, no. 7.

44 See: J.-P. Chazal, "Quel programme idéologique pour la réforme du droit des contrats?", *D* 2015, (673) 673.

45 *Adde*: J.-L. Harouel, G. Teboul and O. Tournafond, "Le droit des contrats réformé par *ordonnance*?", *D* 2014, (1099) 1099–1100.

46 W. Van Gerven and S. Lierman, *Algemeen Deel. Veertig jaar later* in *Beginselen van Belgisch Privaatrecht*, Antwerp, Kluwer, 2010, 192, no. 69.

of International Private Law, the parliamentary discussion has improved the quality of the text.[47]

19. Apart from issues of principle, there are also practical issues. The competences which are delegated by Parliament to the government must be described with precision. The government can thus not go beyond the limits of this delegation. Now, Barbier has argued that the ordinance is exactly doing this in consideration of the rules concerning non-performance. According to Article 8, the government is not authorised to modernise or modify the current law concerning non-performance, but can merely regroup the rules. According to this author, innovations such as price reduction and the limitation of the right of specific performance can therefore not be adopted.[48]

5. Overview

5.1. Incentives and aims of the reform

20. The incentives mentioned above can be traced back into the motives of the current reform.[49] In the first place, the reform seeks to reconcile the current law of obligations with the Civil Code and bring it up to date. Secondly, it wants to enhance the competitiveness of the French economy by improving the readability of the law and the predictability of economic transactions. Thirdly, it seeks to render the French legal tradition attractive again on the European and international level. One can question whether this will be achieved, as the ordinance still remains deeply embedded in the French legal tradition and is mainly a codification *à droit constant.*

21. The government's explicit aim is to modernise the law of obligations in order to promote economic transactions, while at the same time ensuring protection for weaker parties.[50] The ordinance is therefore a difficult balancing act between those often

47 J. Erauw, "Het aankomende wetboek IPR en de nieuwe minister en de senaat" in *Gandaius Actueel*, IX, Mechelen, Kluwer, 2004, (255) 262–263, nos. 19–20. *Adde*: D. Heirbaut, "Codificatie in België en Nederland: een voorbeeld van het (niet) moet?", *TPR* 2006, (1683) 1706–1707, no. 12.

48 H. Barbier, "Remarques introductives: étude de la conformité de l'*ordonnance* à l'habilitation législative", *Petites Affiches* 4 September 2015, (12) 12 ff.

49 *Exposé de Motifs*, Sénat 27 Novembre 2013, no. 175, 8: *"Si le texte propose de moderniser le droit des obligations en introduisant de nouvelles dispositions, une grande partie du projet vise à consolider les acquis en consacrant à droit constant dans le code civil des solutions dégagées depuis plusieurs années par la jurisprudence, et connues par les praticiens. Il s'agit essentiellement de répondre à l'objectif constitutionnel d'intelligibilité de la loi, de renforcer la sécurité juridique, tout en contribuant au rayonnement et à l'attractivité du système juridique français."* See also: *Rapport par T.S. Soilihi*, Sénat 15 January 2014, no. 288, 17–18; P. Stoffel-Munck, "Les enjeux majeurs de la réforme "Attractivité, Sécurité, Justice"" in P. Stoffel-Munck (ed.), *Réforme du droit des contrats et pratique des affaires*, Paris, Dalloz, 2015, (16) 15–26.

50 *Étude d'impact, Projet de loi relatif à la modernisation et à la simplification du droit et des procédures dans les domaines de la justice et des affaires intérieures*, 26 Novembre 2013: *"Il est donc nécessaire, non pas de refondre totalement ces matières, mais de les moderniser, en conservant l'esprit du code civil,*

opposing aims. Economic transactions and legal certainty and stability should, according to the government, be achieved by abolishing the *cause* as validity requirement for contracts, by regulating the precontractual phase and by allowing the extrajudicial termination of contract. The protection of weaker parties is to be ensured for instance by inserting a general prohibition on unfair contract terms, by introducing economic duress as a defect of consent and by introducing rules on change of circumstances.[51]

5.2. *General overview*

22. This introduction is not the place to provide a detailed overview of the ordinance. For an in-depth analysis, reference is made to the other papers in this book and to stream of publications devoted to the reform.[52] I will only focus on some general modifications and innovations. Where it is relevant, I will refer to the original drafting of the Article as it was rendered public in February 2015. Comparison with the original proposal demonstrates that the definitive ordinance was modified on several accounts, taking into account the comments, propositions and criticisms received during the public consultation.

23. An interesting innovation, as for the precontractual phase, is the introduction of a whole section on the dynamic conclusion of contract (Article 1112–1127–8). It is mainly a detailed codification of case-law, and one can wonder whether such a comprehensive regulation is necessary. Article 1112 confirms the principle of freedom to initiate, continue and break off negotiations. However, they must take place in accordance with the requirements of good faith. Importantly, Article 1112–1 introduces a general information duty. If a party has information which is decisive for the consent of the other party, it has a duty to disclose this information, if the other party legitimately does not have this information or relies on that party.[53] This information duty does not exist in

favorable à un consensualisme propice aux échanges économiques, tout en assurant la protection des plus faibles."

51 See for a discussion: C. Pavillon, "Een nieuw contractenrecht voor Frankrijk", *NTBR* 2015, (77) 78–86.

52 *E.g.* A. Aynès (ed.), "Dossier. Réforme du droit des contrats: le débat", *D&P* 2014, no. 240, 37–71; J. Ghestin, *et al.*, "Dossier – Projet d'*ordonnance*, Réforme de droit des contrats", *Petites Affiches* 4 September 2015, no. 177; M. Latina and G. Chantepie (eds.), *Projet de réforme du droit des contrats, du régime général et de la preuve des obligations*, Paris, Dalloz, 2015, 138 p.; P. Stoffel-Munck (ed.), *Réforme du droit des contrats et pratique des affaires*, Paris, Dalloz, 2015, 170 p; X., "Projet d'*ordonnance* portant réforme du droit des contrats, du régime général et de la preuve des obligations. Observation et propositions de modifications", *JCP G* 2015, Supplément au n° 21.
For international perspectives: J. Cartwright, "Un regard anglais sur les forces et faiblesses du droit français des contrats", *RDC* 2015, 691 ff.; M. Graziadei, "Le contrat au tournant de la réforme: les choix du juriste français et le précédent italien", *RDC* 2015, 720 ff.; J. Kleinschmidt and D. Groß, "La réforme du droit des contrats: perspective allemande sur la balance délicate entre liberté contractuelle et pouvoirs du juge", *RDC* 2015, 674 ff.; B. Moore, "Libres propos d'un juriste québécois concernant le projet de réforme des contrats", *RDC* 2015, 728 ff; C. Pavillon, "Een nieuw contractenrecht voor Frankrijk", *NTBR* 2015, (77) 78–86; S. Van Loock, "De hervorming van het Franse verbintenissenrecht: Le jour de gloire, est-il arrivé?", *RW* 2014–2015, 1562–1572.

53 J. Ghestin, "Observations générales", *Petites Affiches* 4 September 2015, (17) under Article 1129. In favour of its deletion or at least a restriction of its scope: Y. Fouchet (ed.), "Réponse de la CCI Paris Île-

respect of the value of the performance. Contrary to the original version,[54] the Article now explains that information is decisive when it has a direct and necessary connection with the content of the contract or the quality of the parties. Failure to disclose the necessary information gives rise to extracontractual liability and may lead to the annulment of the contract if this failure constitutes a defect of consent. Pursuant to Article 1112-1, fifth limb, parties cannot limit or exclude this information duty. It is questionable whether such a heavy information duty is strictly necessary, taking into account the information duties which exist already in consumer protection law. Moreover, it does not expressly contain a duty for a party to inform itself, although one could deduce such a duty from the fact that the ignorance of the party must be legitimate.[55] In contrast, Portalis interestingly held that *"Un homme qui traite avec un autre homme, doit être attentif et sage; il doit veiller à son intérêt, prendre les informations convenables, et ne pas négliger ce qui est utile. L'office de la loi est de nous protéger contre la fraude d'autrui, mais non pas de nous dispenser de faire usage de notre propre raison."*[56]

24. The ordinance introduces a new defect of consent (Article 1143), economic duress (*violence économique*). According to this Article, a contract is null, where one party exploits the other's state of necessity or dependence, in order to obtain an undertaking to which the latter would not have agreed if he had not been in that situation of weakness and has obtained an excessive benefit. In its original form and contrary to other jurisdictions, this Article did not contain the requirement of an excessive benefit.[57] It was therefore criticised as its wide protective scope gave rise to uncertainty.[58] It was considered as a general protection of weaker parties, rather than a protection against

de-France à la consultation ouverte par la Chancellerie", Paris, 2015, 11–12. The DCFR provides for an information duty for businesses in its Articles II-3:101 ff.

54 For criticism in this regard: N. Molfessis, "La formation du contrat", *JCP G* 2015, Suppl. no. 221, (6) no. 6.

55 In favour of a modification in that sense: J. Ghestin, "Observations générales", *Petites Affiches* 4 September 2015, (17) under Article 1129; J.-F. Hamelin, "Les devoirs de se renseigner et d'information (Projet, art. 1129)" in M. Latina and G. Chantepie (eds.), *Projet de réforme du droit des contrats, du régime général et de la preuve des obligations*, Paris, Dalloz, 2015, (25) 25–27: *"En outre, ne consacrer que le devoir d'information serait paradoxal. Comment admettre qu'un contractant soit tenu d'informer l'autre, s'il ne doit pas s'informer lui-même?"*

56 J. Portalis, "Discours préliminaire" in Fenet, *Recueil Complet des Travaux préparatoires du Code Civil*, I, Paris, Videcoq, 1836, (463) 512.

57 H. Barbier, "Le vice du consentement pur cause de violence économique", *D&P* 2014, (50) 50; J. Klein, "Le consentement", *JCP G* 2015, Suppl. no. 221, (14) 18, no. 9. In favour of the introduction of such a requirement: *Réponse de l'Association Henri Capitant à la consultation relative au projet d'ordonnance portant réforme du droit des contrats, du régime général et de la preuve des obligations du 25 février 2015*, Paris, 30 April 2015, 14–15; M. Latina, "La violence (Projet, art. 1139 à 1142)" in M. Latina and G. Chantepie (eds.), *Projet de réforme du droit des contrats, du régime général et de la preuve des obligations*, Paris, Dalloz, 2015, (35) 36. The Belgian Court of cassation requires a manifest disproportion: Cass. 9 November 2012, *Pas.* 2012, 2178 (2 cases). See further: Article 3:44(4) Dutch Civil Code, §138 II BGB, Article II-7:207(1) DCFR.

58 J.-P. Chazal, "Violence économique ou abus de faiblesse", *D&P* 2014, vol. 240, (47) 48–49. In favour of its deletion: Y. Fouchet (ed.), "Réponse de la CCI Paris Île-de-France à la consultation ouverte par la Chancellerie", Paris, 2015, 12–13.

unfair exploitation.[59] Moreover, the sanction is a relative nullity, which means that the weaker party cannot request the court to uphold the contract with modifications.[60] Following the criticism in legal doctrine and in business circles, its scope was reduced by adding the requirement that the other party had obtained an excessive benefit.

25. As for the conclusion of contract, the *cause* as a requirement for the validity of a contract has been abandoned. Several applications, however, have been codified.[61] A contract's content or purpose cannot derogate from public policy (Article 1102, second limb and Article 1162). The *Chronopost* case-law is codified in Article 1170, which considers any contract term which deprives a debtor's essential obligation of its substance, not written.

26. The introduction of a general prohibition on unfair contract terms (Article 1171), inspired by consumer contract law, is controversial.[62] Any contract term of a standard contract which creates a significant imbalance in the rights and obligations of the parties to the contract is considered to be not written. Contrary to other jurisdictions,[63] the original version of this article did not limit the judicial control of contract terms to standard terms, which gave the article an extremely wide scope. Stoffel-Munck therefore dubbed it the *"poison pill"* of the reform project, as it risked to lead to a lot of uncertainty in legal practice.[64] Leveneur saw it as the antithesis of legal certainty.[65] Considering the storm of criticism, it is not surprising that a restriction to standard contracts was introduced in the article. The article nevertheless still has a wide scope. Taking into

59 G. Loiseau, "La consécration de la violence économique" in P. Stoffel-Munck (ed.), *Réforme du droit des contrats et pratique des affaires*, Paris, Dalloz, 2015, (33) 35.

60 In favour of the introduction of this possibility: P. Ancel, "Article 1142: violence économique", *RDC* 2015, 747; J.-P. Chazal, "Violence économique ou abus de faiblesse", *D&P* 2014, vol. 240, (47) 49. See further: Article 3:54 Dutch Civil Code, Article II-7:207(2)(3) DCFR.

61 L. Leveneur, "La réforme du droit des obligations: incidences sur la pratique notariale", JCP N 2015, (1236) no. 19: *"supprimer le mot... tout en conservant la chose."*

62 Largely in favour of the introduction of such a general prohibition: G. Chantepie, "Obligation essentielle et clauses abusives (Projet, art. 1168 et 1169)" in M. Latina and G. Chantepie (eds.), *Projet de réforme du droit des contrats, du régime général et de la preuve des obligations*, Paris, Dalloz, 2015, (47) 47–49; N. Disseaux, "Les clauses abusives", *D&P* 2014, (53) 54; D. Mazeaud, "Droit des contrats: réforme à l'horizon", *D* 2014, (291) 297–298, no. 18. In favour of a limitation to standard contracts: *Réponse de l'Association Henri Capitant à la consultation relative au projet d'ordonnance portant réforme du droit des contrats, du régime général et de la preuve des obligations du 25 février 2015*, Paris, 30 April 2015, 17; R. Boffa, "Juste cause (et injuste clause)", *D* 2015, (335) no. 18; Y. Fouchet (ed.), "Réponse de la CCI Paris Île-de-France à la consultation ouverte par la Chancellerie", Paris, 2015, 15–18; M. Chagny, "La généralisation des clauses abusives (articles 1168 et 1169 du Code civil)" in P. Stoffel-Munck (ed.), *Réforme du droit des contrats et pratique des affaires*, Paris, Dalloz, 2015, (47) 55–56, no. 16; P. Dupichot, "Regards (bienveillants) sur le projet de réforme du droit français des contrats", *D&P* 2014, (32) 46; Gratton, L., "Les clauses abusives en droit commun des contrats", D 2016, (22) I; É. Savaux, "Le contenu du contrat", *JCP G* 2015, Suppl. No. 221, (20) 25, no. 14.

63 Article 6:231 Dutch Civil Code, §305 BGB and Article II-9:403–405 DCFR.

64 P. Stoffel-Munck, "Les clauses abusives: on attendait Grouchy", *D&P* 2014, (56) 59.

65 L. Leveneur, "La réforme du droit des obligations: incidences sur la pratique notariale", JCP N 2015, (1236) no. 21.

account the definition of standard contracts in 1110, second limb, it seems that if a contract consists of standard terms and negotiated terms, all contract terms are subjected to judicial control. The article is furthermore applicable irrespective the quality of the parties (consumer or professional). The only limitation is the subject-matter of the contract or the adequacy of the price (Article 1171, second limb).

27. As to the contractual phase, the ordinance contains a cautious provision on change of circumstances (Article 1195), which clearly illustrates the way in which the French legal tradition[66] weighs on the ordinance. In case of a change of circumstances, unforeseeable at the time of the conclusion of the contract, which renders performance excessively onerous for a party who had not accepted the risk of such a change, that party may ask the other contracting party to renegotiate the contract. In the original version of the Article, in case of refusal or failure of renegotiations, parties could by common agreement ask the court to modify the contract. Otherwise, a party could ask the court to terminate the contract. In contrast to the Netherlands, Germany and the DCFR, a court could only modify the content of the contract at the request of both parties.[67] In its current form, the article provides for such a possibility, albeit in a heavily regulated fashion. According to Article 1195, second limb, after a refusal or failure of renegotiations, parties can agree to terminate the contract or to ask the court to modify the contract. Only when such an agreement has not been reached within a reasonable time, one of the parties can ask the court to revise or terminate the contract. This provision is discussed in depth in the contributions of Tobias Lutzi (pp. 89 ff.) and Janwillem Oosterhuis (pp. 113 ff.).

28. The ordinance lists the remedies for non-performance in Article 1217. The ordinance *i.a.* codifies the *exceptio non adimpleti contractus* (Article 1219) and the *exceptio timoris* (Article 1220). The anticipatory breach, however, is not introduced.[68] The ordinance confirms performance in kind as the primary remedy for non-performance (Article 1221). A creditor can, however, not invoke it, where such performance is impossible or where the costs for the debtor are manifestly disproportionate to the interests of the creditor. This latter limitation to the creditor's rights was phrased differently in the previous form of this Article and only referred to manifestly disproportionate costs. It was highly controversial,[69] as it marks a deviation from the

66 See the *Canal de Craponne* decision: Cass.civ. 6 March 1876, *S* 1876, I, 161.

67 Article 6:258 Dutch Civil Code, §313 BGB and Article III-1:110 DCFR. See comparatively: H. Kötz, *Europäisches Vertragsrecht*, Tübingen, Mohr Siebeck, 2015, 407–425.

68 Article 6:80 Dutch Civil Code, §323 IV BGB, Article III-3:504 DCFR.

69 Proponents were: *Réponse de l'Association Henri Capitant à la consultation relative au projet d'ordonnance portant réforme du droit des contrats, du régime général et de la preuve des obligations du 25 février 2015*, Paris, 30 April 2015, 18 (proposes to replace the reference to the costs by a reference to an abusive exercise of the creditor's rights); Y.-M. Laithier, "Les règles relatives à l'inexécution des obligations contractuelles", *JCP G* 2015, Suppl. no. 221, (47) 52, no. 14; J. Le Bourg and C., Quézel-Ambrunaz, "Article 1221: l'exécution forcée en nature des obligations", *RDC* 2015, (782) III (propose to specify that the disproportion relates to the prejudice of the creditor); P. Lemay, "L'inexécution du contrat: l'exécution forcée en nature (Projet, art. 1221)" in M. Latina and G. Chantepie (eds.), *Projet de*

current law, which still remains firmly attached to the right of performance in kind, even where this is economically non-viable.[70] The question has furthermore been raised whether it fell within the delegation of the Parliament.[71]

29. Another innovation, which is expressly mentioned by the authorization act, is the extrajudicial termination of contract by way of notice (Article 1226). This Article is to some extent a codification of case-law.[72] It remains, however, heavily regulated.[73] A creditor may, at his own risk, terminate the contract by notice. He can only do so after giving notice to the debtor of his default (*mise en demeure*) and granting the debtor a reasonable time to perform. This notice must furthermore clearly indicate that the creditor will have the right to terminate the contract if the debtor fails to perform his obligations. If the debtor still fails to perform, the creditor can terminate the contract by

réforme du droit des contrats, du régime général et de la preuve des obligations, Paris, Dalloz, 2015, (76) 77; D. Mainguy, "Du coût manifestement déraisonnable" à la reconnaissance d'un "droit d'option"", *D&P* 2014, 60–62; D. Mazeaud, "Droit des contrats: réforme à l'horizon", *D* 2014, (291) 293, no. 7 (considers it to be an application of the prohibition of abuse). Opponents were: T. Génicon, "Contre l'introduction du "coût manifestement déraisonnable" comme exception à l'exécution forcée en nature", *D&P* 2014, (63) 65–66; L. Leveneur, "La réforme du droit des obligations: incidences sur la pratique notariale", JCP N 2015, (1236) no. 24: *"Le texte projeté est en contradiction frontale avec la force obligatoire du contrat."*

70 Cass.civ. III 11 May 2005, *Bull.* 2005, III, no. 103 (a house lacking 33 centimeters in height): "La partie envers laquelle l'engagement n'a point été exécuté peut forcer l'autre à l'exécution de la convention lorsqu'elle est possible."; J. Flour, J.-L. Aubert and É. Savaux, *Droit civil. Les obligations. 3. Le rapport d'obligation*, Paris, Sirey, 2014, 131–132, no. 151. Critical views on this decision: B. Fauvarque-Cosson, "Regards comparatistes sur l'exécution forcée en nature", *RDC* 2006, (529) 529 ff; D. Mazeaud, "Exécution forcée de l'obligation contractuelle de faire", *RDC* 2006, 323 ff. Interestingly, the third civil chamber of the *Cour de cassation* recently squashed a judgment concerning the effects of the annulment of a construction contract, which did not assess whether the demolition of the building *"constituait une sanction proportionnée à la gravité des désordres et des nonconformités qui l'affectaient."* See: Cass.civ. 15 October 2015, *D* 2015, 2423, note C. Dubois, *JCP G* 2016, 51, note M. Behar-Touchais.
Under Belgian law, a creditor cannot enforce specific performance where it is impossible or constitutes an abuse of rights (Cass. 6 January 2011, *Pas.* 2011, 44, concl. Henkes, *TBBR* 2012, 388, note P. Bazier); S. Stijns, *Verbintenissenrecht. Leerboek 1*, Bruges, die Keure, 2005, 172–173, no. 243; P. Wéry, *Droit des obligations*, Brussels, Larcier, 2011, 487–488, no. 507). In the Netherlands, the choice for the creditor between performance in kind and damages is subject to the requirement of good faith (*redelijkheid en billijkheid*), according to which the legitimate interests of the other party are *i.a.* taken into account: HR 5 January 2001, *NJ* 2001, 79, no. 3.5. Under German law, a debtor may refuse performance where that performance requires costs and efforts which, taking into account the subject matter of the obligation and the requirements of good faith (*Treu und Glauben*), is grossly disproportionate to the interest in performance of the creditor (§275 II BGB). According to Article III-3:302(3)(b) DCFR, specific performance cannot be enforced, where performance would be unreasonably burdensome or expensive. See comparatively: H. Kötz, *Europäisches Vertragsrecht*, Tübingen, Mohr Siebeck, 2015, 303–304.

71 H. Barbier, "Remarques introductives: étude de la conformité de l'*ordonnance* à l'habilitation législative", *Petites Affiches* 4 September 2015, (12) 12 ff; P. Grosser, "Observations. Section 4: L'inexécution du contrat", *Petites Affiches* 4 September 2015, vol. 177, (78) *v°* Article 1220.

72 *E.g.* Cass.civ. I 13 October 1998, *Bull.civ.* 1998, I, no. 300.

73 J. Kleinschmidt and D. Groß, "La réforme du droit des contrats: perspective allemande sur la balance délicate entre liberté contractuelle et pouvoirs du juge", *RDC* 2015, (674) II.B.2.a.

giving the debtor notice of the termination and the reasons on which it is based. At any time, the debtor may bring proceedings before a court to challenge such a termination. In comparison with other jurisdictions,[74] it is clear that termination is still considered as a judicial remedy, to which the extrajudicial termination constitutes a mere exception.[75]

5.3. *Appreciation*

30. The aim of the government is to modernise the law of obligations in order to promote economic transactions, while ensuring protection for weaker parties. Therefore, the ordinance seeks to perform a difficult balancing act between legal certainty and contractual fairness. This makes the ordinance to some extent inherently contradictory. These aims are hard to reconcile, but also risk to neutralise each other and produce incoherence.[76] The intention to provide strong protection to weaker parties, by *i.a.* introducing a general prohibition on unfair contract terms and economic duress, poses risks for legal certainty and may endanger the envisaged aim to promote economic transactions. However, the most far-reaching consequences of these protective provisions have been limited in comparison with the previous version of the ordinance. One can also question whether the aim of creating more legal certainty and simplicity by eliminating the requirement of *la cause*, is not compromised by the codification of many of its applications.[77]

31. Whether the reform will render French law more attractive for international contracts, remains to be seen. The issue of choice of law predominantly arises in B2B transactions. Therefore, if the aim of the reform is to make French law more attractive, businesses are the first which need to be convinced of its merits.[78] Only time will tell whether businesses find the reformed law more attractive than the current law.

32. The government wants to promote the French legal tradition and restore the prestige and influence of the French civil code on a European and international level. It is doubtful whether this reform will restore the influence the Civil Code had at the beginning of the XIXth century. Not only the inherent contradictions in the ordinance, but especially the lack of sufficiently taking into account modern developments may

74 Article 6:267 Dutch Civil Code, §323 ff BGB, Article III-3:501 ff DCFR.

75 J. Kleinschmidt and D. Groß, "La réforme du droit des contrats: perspective allemande sur la balance délicate entre liberté contractuelle et pouvoirs du juge", *RDC* 2015, (674) II.B.2.a: *"Il paraît que le projet de réforme soit réticent face à ses propres innovations, à savoir l'introduction de la résolution unilatérale."*

76 C. Pavillon, "Een nieuw contractenrecht voor Frankrijk", *NTBR* 2015, (77) 85, no. 24.

77 See: L. Leveneur, "La réforme du droit des obligations: incidences sur la pratique notariale", JCP N 2015, (1236) no. 19; M.-P. Weller, "Die französische causa-Lehre. Ende eines Mythos?" in C. Stumpf, F. Kainer and C. Baldus (eds.) *Privatinitiative und Gemeinwohlhorizonte in der europäische Integration. Festschrift Peter-Christian Müller-Graff*, Baden-Baden, Nomos, 2015, (109) 116–117.

78 P. Stoffel-Munck, "Les enjeux majeurs de la réforme "Attractivité, Sécurité, Justice"" in P. Stoffel-Munck (ed.), *Réforme du droit des contrats et pratique des affaires*, Paris, Dalloz, 2015, (16) 20.

render this ambition hard to achieve. The ordinance is still rather conservative and *franco-français*, which may inhibit its export abroad.

6. Belgium

33. As a jurisdiction which still has the same Civil Code, the reform in France is an important development for Belgium as well. The Belgians have been called *"Napoleons most loyal subjects"*,[79] as changes to the Civil Code have only been limited, especially in the field of the law of obligations and contract law. In light of the reform in France, the question arose whether this situation would remain the same for much longer.

34. The arguments which are raised in France to support a reform, are equally valid for the Belgian law of obligations and contract law. First of all, the law in the Civil Code has not been *"le reflet fidèle et sincère de la lettre et de l'esprit du droit contractuel contemporain"* for many years.[80] According to Fontaine, the Civil Code is reduced to a phantom: *"La codification n'en est plus une."*[81] As the law of obligations in the Civil Code has barely been changed, the courts (and especially the Court of cassation) had to perform its creative task in order to keep the law up to date and in line with societal, social and economic evolutions.[82] This had as a result that the current Belgian law of obligations *de lege lata* is no longer truthfully reflected in the Civil Code. This state of affairs is not only problematic from a constitutional perspective, but also reduces the accessibility and readability of the law, legal certainty and the coherence of private law as a whole. Secondly, the Civil Code has lost much of its value as cornerstone of private law, notably

79 D. Heirbaut, "Napoleons trouwste onderdanen, of waarom de *Code civil* na tweehonderd jaar nog steeds overeind staat in België" in D. Heirbaut en G. Martyn (eds.), *Napoleons nalatenschap. Tweehonderd jaar Burgerlijk Wetboek in België*, Mechelen, Kluwer, 2005, 77–95.

80 D. Mazeaud, "Droit des contrats: réforme à l'horizon", *D* 2014, (291) 291, no. 2. In a similar sense for Belgium: M. Fontaine and P. Wéry, "Libres propos sur le droit des obligations contractuelles au lendemain du bicentenaire du Code civil", *ADL* 2004, (357) 357–358 no. 2.

81 M. Fontaine, "Les obligations contractuelles: 1804–1904–2004 et l'avenir", in P. Wéry (ed.), *Le droit des obligations contractuelles et le bicentenaire du code civil*, Brussels, La Charte, 2004, (1) 17, no. 32.

82 E. Dirix, "Het nut van de Nederlandse ervaringen voor België: een Belgisch standpunt" in D. Heirbaut and G. Martyn (eds.), *Napoleons nalatenschap. Tweehonderd jaar Burgerlijk Wetboek in België*, Mechelen, Kluwer, 2005, (365) 368–369. *Adde*: M. Fontaine en P. Wéry, "Libres propos sur le droit des obligations contractuelles au lendemain du bicentenaire du Code civil", *ADL* 2004, (357) 358–365; A. Van Oevelen, "Hoofdlijnen in de ontwikkeling van het algemene verbintenissen- en overeenkomstenrecht 1964–2000", *TPR* 2001, (313) 355, no. 43; P. van Ommeslaghe, "Les grandes tendances de l'évolution du droit des obligations conventionnelles lors de trente-cinq dernières années", *TPR* 2001, (357) 357, no. 1. Some consider the judiciary as a supplementary legislature: W. Van Gerven and S. Lierman, *Algemeen Deel. Veertig jaar later* in *Beginselen van Belgisch Privaatrecht*, Antwerp, Kluwer, 2010, 119, no. 44. Voor Frankrijk: G. Cornu, "La lettre du Code à l'épreuve du temps" in *Mélanges offerts à René Savatier*, Paris, Dalloz, 1965, (157) 168.
Case-law can also contribute to a converging of the laws in the different member states of the European Union: W. Van Gerven, "Privaatrechtelijk *ius commune* en Europese integratie" in D. Heirbaut and G. Martyn (eds.), *Napoleons nalatenschap. Tweehonderd jaar Burgerlijk Wetboek in België*, Mechelen, Kluwer, 2005, (423) 427–429.

because of the proliferation of special acts and regimes outside of the Civil Code. This could result in the Civil Code being reduced to a mere residuary regime, which is only applicable to activities which the legislature has "forgotten" in his special legislation.[83] This fragmentation[84] is especially due to the unthoughtful manner in which the Belgian legislation ordinarily transposes European directives into Belgian law.[85] A modern law of obligations or a code of private law should correct this. It is remarkable that the French drafters of the ordinance only want to update the Civil Code and not go as far as to integrate various private law directives, such as the German and the Dutch legislature have done.[86] The Belgian legislature could be more ambitious on this subject.[87]

35. The call for a reform of the Belgian Civil Code goes back to the independence of Belgium. Pursuant to the Constitution of 1831, new codes were to be drafted *"dans le plus court délai possible."* Although Laurent prepared a reform proposal in the 1880s, the law of obligations and contract law in the Belgian Civil Code have been left virtually unchanged. The idea of reform has nevertheless remained present in Belgian legal doctrine. Recently, at the occasion of the recent codification of economic law in the Code of Economic Law, the idea of a modern law of obligations has arisen again.[88] In the coalition agreement of the current federal government, there is a cautious mentioning of a reform.

36. It has not come as a complete surprise when the Minister of Justice, Koen Geens, announced in Parliament in November 2015 that he had set up six committees in order to modernise the Belgian Civil Code. There are committees for the law of obligations, law of evidence, tort law, property law, the law of lending and credit and personal security rights. The law of specific contracts will be dealt with in a second stage.[89]

83 B. Bouckaert, "De herziening van het Burgerlijk Wetboek: Een tweede adem voor de rechtsstaat?" in J. Erauw *et al.*, *Liber Memorialis François Laurent*, Brussels, Story-Scientia, 1989, (215) 226.

84 W. Van Gerven, "Verkokering van het privaatrecht", *TPR* 1991, 1021–1023. *Adde*: H. Bocken, "Wat wij zelf doen, doen wij beter?", *TPR* 1991, (277) 277–279, nrs.1–2.

85 See about the private law outside of the Civil Code: A. Van Oevelen, "Het burgerlijk recht buiten het Burgerlijk Wetboek" in D. Heirbaut and G. Martyn (eds.), *Napoleons nalatenschap. Tweehonderd jaar Burgerlijk Wetboek in België*, Mechelen, Kluwer, 2005, 235–251. This process is even aggravated by the fact that the European legislature itself is not always very coherent: E. Terryn, "Codificatie in het economisch recht en de rol van de nationale wetgever", *TPR* 2009, (105) 116–117, no. 18.

86 M. Lehmann, "Le projet Catala et le droit allemand", *RDC* 2007, (1427) I.B.

87 See already: E. Dirix, "Het nut van de Nederlandse ervaringen voor België: een Belgisch standpunt" in D. Heirbaut and G. Martyn (eds.), *Napoleons nalatenschap. Tweehonderd jaar Burgerlijk Wetboek in België*, Mechelen, Kluwer, 2005, (365) 372.

88 B. Demarsin, "Het Wetboek van Economisch recht en zijn band met het Burgerlijk Wetboek" in E. Terryn and B. Keirsbilck (eds.), *Het Wetboek Economisch Recht*, Antwerp, Intersentia, 2014, (361) 396–397, no. 22; B. Keirsbilck, "Boeken VI & XIV. Marktpraktijken en consumentenbescherming, ook voor vrije beroepen" in E. Terryn and B. Keirsbilck (eds.), *Het Wetboek Economisch Recht*, Antwerp, Intersentia, 2014, (129) 201, no. 91; E. Terryn, "Codificatie in het economisch recht en de rol van de nationale wetgever", *TPR* 2009, (105) 134, no. 42; S. Van Loock, "De hervorming van het Franse verbintenissenrecht: Le jour de gloire, est-il arrivé?", *RW* 2014–2015, 1562–1572.

89 Doc. Parliament, 54, 1428/008, 44.

7. Conclusion: Brief lessons from the French reform

37. It has to be applauded that the reform in Belgium is a matter of Parliament. The Minister of Justice has set up academic committees to draft reform proposals, but these proposals will be submitted and discussed in Parliament. This combination where academics assist the legislature has proven to be fruitful in the past. It has recently been used for the Code of International Private Law and the Law on Security Interests on Movables.

38. As to the content itself, one should be cautious to codify too much case-law. First of all, a too detailed codification of case-law could threaten the flexibility of the law and hinder further legal development and the freedom of parties. It is probably unnecessary to regulate the precontractual phase as detailed as in the French ordinance. Portalis already warned that *"(o)n gouverne mal, quand on gouverne trop"*[90] and that *"l'esprit de moderation est le veritable esprit du législateur."*[91] Secondly, the codification project should be seized as an opportunity to finally modernise the current law of obligations and should not restrict itself to a mere recodification. A reform which does not go further than a mere recodification of case-law, is a missed opportunity.

39. Inspiration for such a modernization should be drawn from the many (more or less) recent national and supranational codifications. Although the French ordinance is a valuable instrument, it remains nevertheless strongly embedded in the French legal tradition and is still rather conservative in many aspects. One therefore hopes that the drafters of reform proposals will adopt a more modern and a more widely comparative approach. To name but a few, they can draw interesting lessons from reforms in the Netherlands, Germany and Switzerland, but also from the DCFR and the UNIDROIT Principles.

40. The French reform is to a large extent meant as a reaffirmation of the French legal tradition on the European and international legal stage. From this defensive stance, it is mainly a codification *à droit constant*. It is, however, doubtful whether it will really contribute to restoring the prestige and influence of the Civil Code worldwide, as it is precisely so strong embedded in the French legal tradition. A look into the Memorandum of Motives to the Act on Security Interests on Movables is illustrative as to another potential approach. There, the hope is also expressed to contribute to a future harmonization of the law in Europe. In order to do so, however, the legislature expressly indicates that a comparative approach is taken and contact is sought with recent developments abroad.[92] This openness for comparative influences could appear more successful in the end to contribute to the prestige, influence and attractiveness of Belgian law.

90 J. Portalis, "Discours préliminaire" in Fenet, *Recueil Complet des Travaux préparatoires du Code Civil*, I, Paris, Videcoq, 1836, (463) 514.

91 J. Portalis, *Discours, rapports et travaux inédits sur Code civil*, Paris, Joubert, 844, 99.

92 Doc. Parliament 53, 2463/001 en 2464/001, 10–11.

41. Hopefully, the drafters will demonstrate the kind of openness of Belgian lawyers for lessons from comparative law, as compared to their French counterparts, which was noticed by Simont:

> *"Cette différence s'explique sans doute d'abord par le caractère pragmatique du juriste belge, qui réunit souvent les qualités de juriste de faculté et de praticien, ensuite par le fait que citoyen d'un petit pays place au Carrefour de deux cultures, française et germanique, le juriste belge, comme le juriste Suisse, est traditionnellement ouvert aux leçons du droit comparé."*[93]

93 L. Simont, "L'engagement unilatéral" in *Les obligations en droit français et en droit belge: convergences et divergences*, Brussels, Bruylant, 1994, (17) 17.

Ekaterina
Pannebakker*

PRE-CONTRACTUAL PHASE: REFLECTIONS ON THE ATTRACTIVENESS OF THE NEW FRENCH RULES FOR THE PARTIES TO INTERNATIONAL COMMERCIAL TRANSACTIONS

1. Introduction

This paper addresses the new rules on the pre-contractual phase and reflects upon the following question. To what extent do these rules contribute to the attractiveness of the French law for parties to international commercial transactions?

The *ordonnance* for the reform of the law of contract, the general regime of obligations, and proof of obligations[1] (the *ordonnance*) modernises French law. The reform aims inter alia to make the French legal system more influential and attractive at international level.[2] Recent empirical findings on the choice of law applicable to contract have

* Doctoral candidate and lecturer, Erasmus University Rotterdam, School of Law.

1 *Ordonnance no 2016-131 du 10 février 2016 portant réforme du droit des contrats, du régime général et de la preuve des obligations* JORF 0035 of 11 February 2016. See also Draft *ordonnance* for the reform of the law of contract, the general regime of obligations, and proof of obligations (draft *ordonnance*) available at www.justice.gouv.fr/publication/j21_projet_ord_reforme_contrats_2015.pdf.
The English translation of the main concepts in this paper follows the official translation of the draft *ordonnance* by J. Cartwright, B. Fauvarque-Cosson and S. Whittaker available at www.textes.justice.gouv.fr/art_pix/Draft-*ordonnance*-for-the-Reform-of-the-Civil-Codepdf.pdf. The draft *ordonnance* has been also translated into Spanish and Portuguese, see www.justice.gouv.fr/art_pix/Projet_reforme_contrats_2015_ESPAGNOL.pdf; www.justice.gouv.fr/art_pix/Projet_reforme_contrats_2015_PORTUGAIS.pdf.
The on-line resources referred to in this paper were last visited on 01 March 2016.

2 See *Objectifs de la Reforme*, in *Rapport au Président de la République relatif à l'ordonnance no 2016-131 du 10 février 2016 portant réforme du droit des contrats, du régime général et de la preuve des obligations*, JORF 0035 of 11 February 2016. See also *Exposé des motifs in the Projet de loi du 27 novembre 2013 relatif à la modernisation et à la simplification du droit et des procédures dans les domaines de la justice et des affaires intérieures* available at www.senat.fr/leg/pjl13-175.pdf.
See also D. Mazeaud, 'Le Droit Français, Modèle pour les Projets Européens de Droit des Contrats (Quel Avenir pour le Modèle Juridique Français?)', in R. Cabrillac (ed.), *Quel Avenir pour le Modèle Juridique Français dans le Monde?*, Paris: Economica, 2011 (23) 23 ff. Generally, on the aims of several countries, including France, to increase the attractiveness of their own law in the international legal landscape, see generally X.E. Kramer, 'Competitie in de Europese Civiele Rechtsruimte. Een Spanningsveld in de Grensoverschrijdende Geschillenbeslechting?', 51 *Tijdschrift voor Privaatrecht*, 2014, (1745) para 2 and 3.

contended, indeed, that French law is not the regime most favoured by parties to international commercial transactions.[3]

The regulation of contractual negotiations, namely Articles 1112, 1112-1, 1112-2, 1123 and 1124 of the *ordonnance*, is one of the areas subject to modernisation.[4] The provisions established by the *Code Napoleon* of 1804 were underpinned by the model of simple, discrete transactions and, therefore, did not expressly deal with the contractual negotiations. By contrast, the *ordonnance* establishes a more sophisticated system of regulation.

This sophistication reflects firstly, the evolution of French case law. Since the adoption of the Napoleonic Code two centuries ago, French courts have come some distance in interpreting its provisions in the context of practical changes. Over the years of application and interpretation of the *Code civil*, French courts have developed standards of conduct to be respected by the parties during negotiations. The second point underpinning the *ordonnance* is the complexity of contract formation in practice. Legal scholars, pioneered by the US relational contract theorists at the end of the last century, have described the increasing gap between legal theory and practice. Their arguments have not gone unheard in France. However, many of these legal writings have been criticised for offering few sufficiently pragmatic legislative solutions. Thirdly, the *ordonnance* draws some inspiration from the existing international soft law instruments. In contrast to the more theoretical ideas of the relational contract scholars, modern soft law instruments offer concrete rules that may be applied to solve disputes. Two soft law instruments can be used as reference and illustration: the UNIDROIT Principles of International Commercial Contracts 2010 (UPICC)[5] and the Principles of European Contract Law (PECL).[6] This background to the *ordonnance* provides the main elements of the framework for a reflection on the attractiveness of the new rules at international level.

However, in order to ascertain the attractiveness of a given national rule for international transactions, reference should be made to the factors that may determine (or measure) such attractiveness. This paper will ascertain this attractiveness primarily from the perspective of the contracting parties (rather than from that of policymakers), in particular, parties to international commercial transactions.[7]

3 G. Cuniberti, 'The International Market for Contracts: The Most Attractive Contract Laws', 34 *Northwestern Journal of International Law & Business*, 2014 (455).

4 B. Fauvarque-Cosson, 'Towards an Important Reform of the French Civil Code', *Montesquieu Law Review*, 2015, (2) 2; B. Fauvarque-Cosson, 'The French Contract Law Reform in a European Context', *ELTE Law Journal*, 2014, (59) 62; C. Asfar-Cazenave, 'La Réforme du Droit Français des Contrats', *Revue Juridique Thémis de l'Université de Montréal*, 2016 (forthcoming). See also R. Schulze, G. Wicker, G. Mäsch and D. Mazeaud (eds.), *La Réforme du Droit des Obligations en France: 5èmes Journées Franco-Allemandes*, Paris: Société de Législation Comparée, 2015; M. Latina and G. Chantepie (eds.) *Supplément au Code civil 2016 Édition Limitée – Livret sur le Projet de Réforme du Droit des Obligations*, Paris: Dalloz, 2015.

5 Available at www.unilex.info.

6 O. Lando and H. Beale (eds.), *The Principles of European Contract Law. Parts I and II*, The Hague; London: Kluwer Law International, 2000.

7 Despite the adoption of the *Code de commerce*, the *Code civil* applies to relations between businesses if no specific regulation is established by the *Code de commerce*. In this way, the general part of the law obligations including the *ordonnance*, remains relevant for commercial transactions.

It is worth noting that the factors which effectively determine the choice of law in an international transaction still lead to complex unanswered questions.[8] A recent worldwide survey on international sale contracts has shed light on various reasons for choosing a particular law according to parties. Two factors were reported as being the most important legal reasons for the choice of law: legal certainty and flexibility of a concrete national law.[9] Legal certainty means that the outcome of the application of a legal rule is easily predictable. Flexibility here means the ability of a legal framework to enable private parties to shape their legal relations to fit their practical needs. These two factors were expressly put forward in the discussions of the *ordonnance* in France and were mentioned when the reforms were presented for public consultation. These two factors have also played a major role in the drafting of soft law instruments.[10]

For these reasons, the reflection will focus on two factors of attractiveness: legal certainty and flexibility of the new rules. In this way, the choice of these two factors deliberately disregards a number of other reasons that may also play a role in the choice of law, including the costs of litigation, the availability of effective court procedures and other practical, cultural, and psychological reasons.

The reflection will be structured in two parts. The first part will address the proposed new rules on contract negotiations, namely Articles 1112, 1112–1, 1112–2, 1123 and 1124 of the *ordonnance*, and their background (section 2). The second part will consider the new rules in the light of the aim of making them more attractive to parties by discussing two factors of attractiveness: their legal certainty and flexibility (section 3). Finally, concluding remarks will be provided (section 4).

2. Pre-contractual phase in the *ordonnance*

While the *Code civil* contains no specific provisions on contract negotiations, the *ordonnance* proposes new rules on the pre-contractual phase (2.1). Their background is formed primarily by the evolution of the national case law, and some provisions echo international soft law instruments and scholarship (2.2).

2.1. The new rules

The *ordonnance* contains two kinds of provisions on the pre-contractual phase. First, it provides the general legal regime governing the process of negotiations. Second, it

8 For recent studies, see S. Vogenauer and Ch. Hodges (eds.), *Civil Justice Systems in Europe Implications for Choice of Forum and Choice of Contract Law*, Oxford: Hart Publishing, 2014; G. Cuniberti, 'The International Market for Contracts: The Most Attractive Contract Laws' 34 *Northwestern Journal of International Law & Business*, 2014, (455) 459.

9 L. G. Meira Moser, 'Parties' Preferences in International Sales Contracts: An Empirical Analysis of the Choice of Law', 20 *Uniform Law Review*, 2015, (19) 26.

10 S. Vogenauer 'Introduction', in S. Vogenauer (ed.), *Commentary on the UNIDROIT Principles of International Commercial Contracts (PICC)*, 2nd ed., Oxford: Oxford University Press, 2015, (1) 17; O. Lando and H. Beale, 'Introduction', in O. Lando and H. Beale (eds.), *The Principles of European Contract Law. Parts I and II*, The Hague; London: Kluwer Law International, 2000, (xxi) xxiii-xxiv.

introduces the regulation of two instruments which may be created by the negotiating parties in the course of negotiations: the pre-emption agreement and the unilateral promise.

The first element of the general regime of negotiations is formulated in Article 1112 of the *ordonnance*. It starts by emphasising freedom of negotiations: the commencement, continuation and breaking-off of negotiations may be exercised freely. This freedom is counter-balanced by the requirement to negotiate in good faith. Freedom of negotiations, including the manner in which negotiations are conducted and broken off, should be exercised in compliance with the requirement of good faith. The second element of the general regime of negotiations is provided in the second part of Article 1112. It places an explicit limit on recovery for fault in negotiations: it is not possible to recover loss of profits which were expected from the negotiated but non-concluded contract. The third element is provided in Article 1112–1. It establishes the duty of information in negotiations. This provision links the regulation of negotiations to the regulation of defect of consent – a closely related field of regulation. Breach of Article 1112–1 is sanctioned by annulment of the concluded contract. Article 1112–2 contains the fourth element of the general regime of negotiations. It relates to the use of information exchanged during negotiations. The party using without permission confidential information obtained in the course of negotiations incurs liability.

In contrast to the general regime of negotiations, which is based essentially on non-contractual regulation, the rules on the pre-emption agreement and unilateral promise stem from contract law. These instruments emanate from the French conceptual framework of *avant-contrat*, covering preliminary agreements that mark a stage between the mere process of negotiations and the final contract.

Article 1123 of the *ordonnance* introduces the concept of pre-emption agreement. It is 'a contract by which a party undertakes that, in the event that he decides to enter into a contract, he will make the first proposal for that contract to the beneficiary of the pre-emption agreement.'[11] The pre-emption agreement represents a contract in itself. The definition does not specify whether pre-emption is supposed to be limited in time. In light of the case law, it may be said that the right can be given for a definite or indefinite term.[12] A further requirement is the debtor's decision to form the final contract, in which case he should first make a proposal to the beneficiary.

The provision also defines the consequences of breach of a pre-emption agreement. If a contract is concluded with third party who knows about the existence of the pre-emption, the beneficiary of the pre-emption right may claim damages, and in addition to this, has a right to make two further claims. Firstly, the beneficiary may make a claim for nullity of the contract which has been concluded between the debtor and the third party. If nullity is declared, the debtor and the third party are returned to the positions they were in before the conclusion of the contract. Secondly, the beneficiary may require that he be substituted for the third party in the contract concluded between the debtor and third party. In this way, the claimant may enter into the contract in the place of the third party.

11 Article 1123 *ordonnance*.

12 Cass 3 civ 15 January 2003 No. 01–03700 Bulletin 2003 III no. 9 p. 9.

The two latter remedies can be granted only if the third party was aware of both the existence of the pre-emption agreement and of the beneficiary's intention to exercise the pre-emption right.[13] These remedies require the court to address the role of the third party (or parties) in the breach of the pre-emption agreement. Furthermore, such claims may have important consequences for third parties. Article 1123 solves most of the practical issues revealed by case law and literature. As a general rule, contracts in French law may have effects for those third parties who are aware of their existence (*opposabilité du contrat aux tiers*).[14]

As Article 1123 relates directly to such third party effectiveness, it also contains a mechanism for a third party to prevent the claim in nullity. It states as follows: 'A third party may give written notice to the beneficiary requiring him to confirm within a fixed period which has to be reasonable the existence of a pre-emption agreement and his intention to exercise the pre-emption right.'[15] In this way, a party aware of any parallel negotiations may, in principle, ensure that these are merely negotiations, and no consent for the final contract is given (by a pre-emption agreement). It is worth noting in this regard that parties to advanced negotiations may have a duty to inform their counterpart of any parallel negotiations. This duty has been implied by French courts under the umbrella of good faith in negotiations.[16] Furthermore, parties may also agree on a contractual obligation of sincerity (*clause de sincérité*) covering the period of negotiations.[17]

Still, how practical is the exercise of the right to confirm the existence of pre-emption? Article 1123 aims to streamline the parties' approach in practice by prescribing the content of the notice. It goes on by stating: 'Such a written notice must state that if he does not reply, the beneficiary of the pre-emption agreement will no longer have the right to claim either to be substituted in any contract concluded with the third party, or nullity of the contract'.[18] The question as to whether the absence of reply effectively leads to the impossibility to claim nullity remains open.[19]

Article 1124 of the *ordonnance* defines the unilateral promise. It is 'a contract by which one party, the promisor, gives another, the beneficiary, a right, for a certain time, to have the option to conclude a contract whose essential elements are determined, and for the formation of which only the consent of the beneficiary is missing.'[20] The definition contains several elements. First, in the same way as the pre-emption agreement, the unilateral promise represents a contract in itself. Second, the option right that may be

13 See Article 1123 *ordonnance*.

14 See Articles 1199 ff. *ordonnance*. See also inter alia J. Ghestin and G. Viney, *Traité de Droit Civil. Introduction à la Responsabilité*, 3rd ed., Paris: L.G.D.J, 2008, para 202 and 207–3.

15 Article 1123 *ordonnance*. Compare with Article 1125 draft *ordonnance*: 'Where a third party believes that there may be a pre-emption agreement, he may give written notice to the beneficiary within a reasonable period requiring him to confirm it.'

16 Further on this provision, see section 2.2.1 below.

17 B. Fages, 'Étude 115. Les Accords de Pourparlers' (May 2011), in B. Fages (ed.), *Lamy Droit du Contrat*, Paris: Wolters Kluwer France, 2012, para 115–61.

18 Article 1123 *ordonnance*.

19 Further on this provision, see 3.2.1 below.

20 Article 1124 *ordonnance*.

provided is supposed to be limited in time. Third, the beneficiary's right relates to a contract, the negotiations for which have already set out the essential elements of the future agreement. Fourth, only the consent of the beneficiary to the final contract is absent, whereas the promisor's consent to the final contract is in place during the period for which the option right is given. The last element is related to the revocability of the unilateral promise. Even if the promise is revoked during the specified period, the contract will still be formed.

Furthermore, Article 1124 defines the consequences of breach of a unilateral promise. It leads to nullity of the contract concluded with a third party, provided that the third party knew of the existence of the promise. Nullity must be declared by the court unless the parties mutually agree to it.[21] Generally, the parties to a contract which has been declared a nullity are returned to the positions they were in before the conclusion of the contract.

2.2. *The background of the new rules*

The *ordonnance* is based on the considerable evolution of the French case law (2.2.1). It also draws inspiration from international soft law instruments and scholarship (2.2.2).

2.2.1. Evolution of case law

The new rules on the pre-contractual phase reflect first and foremost the evolution of French case law. Over the years of application and interpretation of the *Code civil*, French courts have developed standards of conduct to be respected by the parties during negotiations. This increasingly detailed regulation of the manner in which negotiations must be conducted and broken off has been called a 'particularly rigorous ethics of negotiations'.[22]

The ethics of negotiations in Article 1112 of the *ordonnance* come under the umbrella of the requirement of good faith. The genesis of their content and liability for breach is based on two articles of the *Code civil*. First, Article 1382 *Code civil* – the general provision on tort underpinned the concept of pre-contractual liability, shaped as the liability in tort (for *faute*).[23] Second, Article 1134 *Code civil* on the requirement of good faith in the execution of conventions (e.g. contracts)[24] became the basis of the 'ethics of negotiations'.[25] The *Code civil* established a duty of good faith only for the execution of contracts, but not

21 Article 1178 *ordonnance*. On nullity in the *ordonnance*, see the contribution of F. Peeraer in this volume.

22 D. Mazeaud, 'Mystères et Paradoxes de la Période Précontractuelle', in *Le Contrat au Début du XXIe Siècle: Études Offertes à Jacques Ghestin*, Paris: L.G.D.J., 2001, (637) 640.

23 J. Ghestin, 'La Responsabilité Délictuelle pour Rupture Abusive des Pourparlers, *La Semaine Juridique Edition Générale* no. 20, 16 May 2007, I 155 (15); J. Ghestin, 'Les Dommages Réparables à la Suite de la Rupture Abusive des Pourparlers', *La Semaine Juridique Edition Générale* no. 22, 30 May 2007, I 157 (19).

24 Article 1134 paragraph 3 *Code civil*.

25 D. Mazeaud, 'Mystères et Paradoxes de la Période Précontractuelle', in *Le Contrat au Début du XXIe Siècle: Études Offertes à Jacques Ghestin*, Paris: L.G.D.J., 2001, (637) 640.

for their formation.[26] However, the Cour de cassation has a long history of broad interpretation of this provision. It has progressively extended the scope of the duty of good faith to the pre-contractual phase.[27] Legal scholarship in France was generally supportive of this approach.[28] The extension of the contractual duty of good faith to cover the pre-contractual phase falls generally under the tendency of 'moralisation of the contemporary contract law'[29] in France.

The requirement of pre-contractual good faith in Article 1112 of the *ordonnance* is an open norm. At the same time, considerable case law provides a solid background and guidelines for its practical interpretation. The main 'ethics of negotiations' counterbalancing the freedom of negotiation include loyalty (sanction of conduct with an intention to harm),[30] consistency of conduct (requirement on each party to conduct negotiations in a manner consistent with his own previous behaviour and precluding 'fraudulent gambits'),[31] and transparency (requiring parties to exchange information crucial to the decision on the negotiated contract).[32] The approach to transparency in negotiations is developed in Article 1112–1. The clear difference between this provision and the regulation of negotiations relates to the nature of liability. Whereas the breach of good faith may constitute fault in negotiations and entails liability in tort, breach of the provisions on information leads primarily to invalidity of the concluded contract (due to vitiation of consent).

The new rules on the pre-emption agreement and unilateral promise are also primarily case law based. During the last few decades, French judges and scholars have become receptive to the practice of creating various pre-contractual documents.[33] Drawing on the general provisions of contract law, they have recognised a plethora of

26 The draft of the French civil code (*Code civil de l'an VIII*) stated that 'conventions have to be made and executed in good faith', but this redaction has not been adopted. See F. Terré, Ph. Simler and Y. Lequette, *Droit Civil: Les Obligations,* 10th ed., Paris: Dalloz, 2009, para 43.

27 See for an overview of the approach of the Cour de cassation Ch. Larroumet, *Les Obligations. Tome 3, Le Contrat,* 4th ed., Paris: Economica, 1998, para 239; B. Fages, 'Étude 105. L'entrée en Pourparler' (May 2011), in B. Fages (ed.), *Lamy Droit du Contrat,* Paris: Wolters Kluwer France, 2012; Ch. Jarrosson, 'La Bonne Foi, Instrument de Moralisation des Relations Économiques Internationales', in *L'éthique dans les Relations Économiques Internationales: En Hommage à Philippe Fouchard,* Paris: Pedone, 2006, (185) 197–198; D. Mazeaud, 'Mystères et Paradoxes de la Période Précontractuelle', in *Le Contrat au Début du XXIe Siècle: Études Offertes à Jacques Ghestin,* Paris: L.G.D.J., 2001, (637) 638.

28 Previous projects of reform have also included the duty of good faith in the formation of conventions. See for a synthetic note on the projects D. Mazeaud, 'La Réforme du Droit Français des Contrats: Trois Projets en Concurrence', in S. Bros and B. Mallet-Bricout (eds.), *Liber Amicorum Christian Larroumet,* Paris: Economica, 2009 (329).

29 D. Mazeaud 'La Réforme du Droit Français des Contrats: Trois Projets en Concurrence', in S. Bros and B. Mallet-Bricout (eds.), *Liber Amicorum Christian Larroumet,* Paris: Economica, 2009, (329) para. 15.

30 Cass 1 civ 14 June 2000 No. 98–17494 Unpublished; see also CA Versailles 10 September 2009 no. 08/04982 ('obligation de rectitude et loyauté').

31 Cass comm 3 October 1978 no. 77–10915 Bulletin Cass comm no. 208 p. 176.

32 See inter alia Cass 3 civ 18 February 2004 no. 02–17523 Unpublished.

33 See for example B. Fages (ed.), *Lamy Droit du Contrat,* Paris: Wolters Kluwer France, 2011, Part I 'Négociations'; O. Deshayes (ed.), *L'Avant-contrat: Actualité du Processus de Formation des Contrats,* Paris: Presses Universitaires de France, 2008; J. M. Mousseron, M. Guibal and D. Mainguy, *L'Avant-*

avant-contrats, including the project of contract, agreement in principle, pre-emption agreement, promise to contract and others.[34] The validity of these documents is underpinned by the distinction made in French scholarship and case law between the future contract and the mere process of negotiations preparing this contract. It is the process of negotiations that is privatised by contractual obligations. These preliminary agreements prepare for the creation of a contract in the future and may bind parties with contractual obligations before the negotiated contract is concluded. From the plethora of instruments used in practice and discussed in literature, the *ordonnance* defines two: the pre-emption agreement (Article 1123) and the unilateral promise (Article 1124).

The definitions reflect as well the choices made as a result of scholarly debates. One of the main debates related to the revocability of a unilateral promise. The *ordonnance* takes a position in this relatively long standing debate between the Cour de cassation and French scholars. Since 1993, the Cour de cassation has found that the promise may be revoked, and this revocation would lead to the situation where the final contract is not formed for the lack of consent of one of the parties.[35] According to the Cour de cassation, the only possible recovery was the reparation of damage. This position was underpinned essentially by the principle of freedom of contract. By contrast, several commentators have noted that the debtor should have no right to revoke his promise for the entire duration of the promise. According to them, this is the only solution that may logically flow from conceptualising the unilateral promise as a contract. More concretely, if a unilateral promise is regarded as a contract concluded for a definite term, it should be taken into account that such contracts may not be unilaterally withdrawn.[36] The *ordonnance* adopts the point of view advocated by many French scholars.

Another important debate related to the nullity of a contract concluded in breach of the pre-emption agreement. The discussions have been primarily related to the practicality of the remedy,[37] to the interests of third parties, and more generally to the extent to which an *avant-contrat* may have effects for third parties aware of its existence.[38]

contrat, Paris: Éditions Francis Levebvre, 2001; *La Formation du Contrat: L'Avant-contrat – Congrès des Notaires de France*, Lyon: Imprimerie A. Rey, 1964.

34 On the translation, see footnote 1. The translation of other terms not included in the draft *ordonnance* follows the translation by J. Cartwright and S. Whittaker of *P. Catala, Avant-Projet de Réforme du Droit des Obligations et de la Prescription*, Paris: Documentation Française, 2006, available at: www.justice.gouv.fr/art_pix/rapportcatatla0905-anglais.pdf (English version); www.justice.gouv.fr/art_pix/RAPPORTCATALASEPTEMBRE2005.pdf (original in French).

35 Cass 2 civ no. 91–10199 Bulletin 1993 III no. 174 p. 115. See also M. Fabre-Magnan, 'L'engagement du Promettant – Engagement au Contrat Préparatoire', 2 *Revue des Contrats*, 2012 (633) (approving the position of the Cour de cassation).

36 G. Wicker' 'L'engagement du Promettant: Engagement au Contrat Définitif', 2 *Revue des contrats*, 2012 (649); D. Mainguy, 'L'efficacité de l'Efficacité de la Rétractation de la Promesse Unilatérale de Contracter', *Recueil Dalloz*, 2011 (1460) (both disagreeing with the position of the Cour de cassation).

37 For an overview of the debate see Y.-M. Laithier and D. Mazeaud, 'La Nature de la Sanction: Satisfaction du Bénéficiaire par des Dommages-Intérêts ou Primauté de l'Exécution Forcée en Nature?', 2 *Revue des Contrats*, 2012 (681).

38 J. Schmidt-Szalewski, 'La Force Obligatoire à l'Épreuve des Avant-contrats', *Revue Trimestrielle de Droit Civil*, 2000 (25); J. Mestre, 'La Prudence Est Toujours de Rigueur… Pour la Cour de Cassation

The availability of this remedy was rather emphatically confirmed by the Cour de cassation in 2006,[39] and the *ordonnance* follows this approach.

2.2.2. International influence

In addition to reflecting the evolution of case law, the *ordonnance* draws inspiration from the harmonisation of contract law at the global and European levels. The proposed new rules on negotiations clearly take inspiration from international soft law instruments.[40]

For instance, Article 1112 of the *ordonnance* resembles the approaches of the PECL and the UPICC. Both soft law instruments contain specific provisions dedicated to contractual negotiations. The PECL establish a broad general requirement of good faith and fair dealing in negotiations.[41] The UPICC require parties to negotiate contracts in compliance with good faith and fair dealing in international trade.[42]

Another provision that can be traced back to international soft law instruments is Article 1112–2 of the *ordonnance* on confidential information provided in the course of negotiations. The manner of dealing with data exchanged by the parties in the course of negotiations can become highly relevant when negotiators exchange business-sensitive information. The most relevant issues relate to information marked as confidential, but which is not protected in any other way, for example by intellectual property rights. Both the UPICC[43] and the PECL[44] specifically address the issue of confidentiality in negotiations; the provisions of both instruments are more detailed than the rules of the *ordonnance*.

The UPICC state as follows:

> Where information is given as confidential by one party in the course of negotiations, the other party is under a duty not to disclose that information or to use it improperly for its own purposes, whether or not a contract is subsequently concluded. Where appropriate, the remedy for breach of that duty may include compensation based on the benefit received by the other party.[45]

dans la Sanction des Pactes de Préférence' *Revue Trimestrielle de Droit Civil*, 1998 (98); J.-P. Désidéri, *La Préférence dans les Relations Contractuelles*, PU Aix-Marseille, 1997.

39 Cass mix 26 May 2006 N° 03–19376 Bulletin 2006 Mixt. no. 4 p. 13.

40 No influence of the United Nations Convention on Contracts for the International Sale of Goods, Vienna, 1980 (CISG) is in place. Strictly speaking, the pre-contractual phase falls outside the scope of the Convention, and the *Travaux Preparatoires* to the CISG reflect a strong disagreement at the diplomatic conference on the question whether the CISG should regulate the process of contractual negotiations. For an argument that the CISG might be applicable to the pre-contractual phase see M. J. Bonell, 'Vertragsverhandlungen und Culpa in Contrahendo nach dem Wiener Kaufrechts-übereinkommen', 36 *Recht der Internationalen Wirtschaft*, 1990, (693) 699.

41 Article 2:301 PECL.

42 Article 2.1.15 UPICC.

43 Article 2.1.16 UPICC.

44 Article 2:302 PECL.

45 Article 2.1.16 UPICC.

In the UPICC, the starting point is the absence of a general duty of confidentiality.[46] Only information disclosed with an indication of its confidential (privileged) character should be treated as confidential. The receipt of such information is regarded as an implicit agreement to observe its confidentiality.[47] This provision is applicable to both the non-disclosure of the information exchanged in negotiations and the secrecy of the very fact that negotiations take place. Other information received in negotiations may be freely used, independently of the outcome of negotiations.

At the same time, the UPICC provide an exception to the absence of a general duty of confidentiality. In certain cases, confidentiality can be implied even for information disclosed with no indication of its privileged character.[48] The implication can be drawn from the nature of information or the professional activity of the receiving party. In the UPICC, the Illustration 3 to Article 2.1.16 UPICC provides an example. It describes negotiations of a joint venture agreement between two car manufacturers. In the course of negotiations, one party discloses to the other a design of a new car. The disclosure is made without mention of the privileged character of the design. Despite this, the receiving party should treat this information as confidential: in particular, it may not use the design in its own production or make it known to any third parties. According to the Official Comment included in Article 2.1.16 UPICC, confidentiality is implied into the relations between the two car manufacturers, because the information about a design of a new car goes to the core of the commercial activity of both parties. In this example, both the nature of the disclosed information and the parties' professional activity point therefore to the need to regard this information as business sensitive and consequently confidential. The UPICC also make a reference to the general duty of good faith and fair dealing, stating that treating such information as non-confidential may be contrary to this duty.[49]

The PECL deal with the issue of confidentiality in negotiations in Article 2:302. It is formulated along the same lines as the UPICC. The PECL impose no general duty of confidentiality in negotiations.[50] Only information expressly marked as secret when it is disclosed in the course of negotiations is required to be kept confidential.[51] Other information may be used by the receiving party for its own purpose or disclosed to third parties. Next to this, according to Article 2:302 PECL, confidentiality can be implied[52] if the 'special character' of information disclosed in negotiations or the parties' 'professional status' so dictate.[53] This provision covers the disclosure of highly business sensitive information relating to the core of the parties' business activity. To illustrate such

46 Official Comment 1 to Article 2.1.16 UPICC; M. J. Bonell (ed.), *The UNIDROIT Principles in Practice: Caselaw and Bibliography on the UNIDROIT Principles of Commercial Contracts*, 2nd ed., Ardsley, NY: Transnational Publishers, 2006, 141.

47 Official Comment 1 to Article 2.1.16 UPICC.

48 Official Comment 2 to Article 2.1.16 UPICC, para 2.

49 Official Comment 2 to Article 2.1.16 UPICC.

50 Article 2:302 PECL.

51 Comment A to Article 2:302 PECL.

52 Comment B to Article 2:302 PECL.

53 Id.

information the PECL mention know-how.[54] According to the PECL, it has to be treated as confidential even if no note on its confidential (privileged) character is made at the moment of disclosure.

Unlike the provisions on good faith and confidentiality in negotiations, the *ordonnance*'s articles on the pre-emption agreement and unilateral promise cannot be traced back to the PECL or UPICC.[55] These rules represent a specificity of the French approach to negotiations and possibly have another basis. The increase in the attention of French case law to *avant-contrat* has corresponded in time with the development of an important body of scholarship juxtaposing the law in the books and the law in practice. This was primarily the subject of scrutiny in US literature. For instance, a US scholar, Macneil, has called the back and forth of opinions and progressive development of the parties' relationship during negotiations a 'relational' aspect of contract.[56] He has submitted that contract law should have different (varying) rules depending on the degree to which the relational aspect is present in a relationship. In order to achieve this, he suggested using a framework of 'norms' for analysing a contract.[57] Another US lawyer, Feinman, has pleaded in favour of creating a flexible 'framework for parties who engage in business planning'.[58] This would allow parties 'to create relations, to determine their content, to avoid them altogether.'[59] It is to be noted, however, that Macneil's and Feinman's theories have faced criticism themselves. In particular, Macneil's views have been criticised mainly for not having proposed rules that would be sufficiently predictable and certain to replace the doctrines currently used.[60]

The relational contract theorists have not gone unheard in France.[61] Nonetheless, the solutions of the *ordonnance* are not explicitly motivated by the relational contract theory. Direct references to relational contract theory in case law are very infrequent.

54 Id.

55 To the author's knowledge nor can they be traced back to any other international soft law or uniform law.

56 Macneil has elaborated a contract theory often referred to as 'relational'. The theory covers contract formation and the execution of contracts, especially the execution of long-term contracts – happening in stages, over several years when the contractual relations evolve in time. See inter alia D. Campbell (ed.), *The Relational Theory of Contract: Selected Works of Ian Macneil*, London: Sweet & Maxwell, 2001.

57 These norms are 'role integrity', 'reciprocity', 'implementation and planning', 'effectuation of consent', 'flexibility', 'contractual solidarity', 'restitution, reliance and expectation interests', 'creation and restraint of power', 'propriety of means', 'harmonisation with the social matrix' and the 'relational' norms 'preservation of the relation' and 'harmonisation of relational conflict'. See D. Campbell (ed.), *The Relational Theory of Contract: Selected Works of Ian Macneil*, London: Sweet & Maxwell, 2001 (125).

58 J. M. Feinman, 'The Significance of Contract Theory', 58 *University of Cincinnati Law Review*, 1990, (1283) 1288.

59 J. M. Feinman, 'The Significance of Contract Theory', 58 *University of Cincinnati Law Review* 1990, (1283) 1288. See also D.K. Hart, 'Contract Formation and the Entrenchment of Power', 41 *Loyola University of Chicago Law Journal*, 2009 (1).

60 See for an overview of the critique (including Collins, Eisenberg, Posner) P. Vincent-Jones, 'The reception of Ian Macneil's work on contracts in the UK', in D. Campbell (ed.), *The Relational Theory of Contract: Selected Works of Ian Macneil*, London: Sweet & Maxwell, 2001, (67) 67–86. See also C. Mitchell, 'Narrativising Contract Law', 29 *Legal Studies*, 2009, (1) 21–22.

61 See inter alia with further references C. Boismain, *Les Contrats Relationnels*, Aix-Marseille: PUAM, 2005; A.-S. Courdier-Cuisinier, *Le Solidarisme Contractuel*, Paris: LexisNexis-Litec, 2006.

Nevertheless, it may be said that the *ordonnance* follows the spirit of the relational contract theory, because the *ordonnance* acknowledges instruments having a contractual nature and created in the course of negotiations. These aim to legally frame an intermediate situation between the domain of negotiations and the proper domain of contract. Furthermore, the reinforced underpinning of solidarity in contract law reflected in the *ordonnance* generally[62] echoes Macneil's elaboration of the norm of 'contractual solidarity'.[63]

3. Assessing the attractiveness of the new provisions

Having considered the content of the proposed new rules and their genesis, the paper now turns to an assessment of their attractiveness from the perspective of a party negotiating an international contract. Two important factors of attractiveness will be discussed – legal certainty (3.1) and flexibility (3.2) of the new rules.

3.1. Legal certainty

Three arguments point to a potential increase in legal certainty under the new rules, compared to the *Code Napoleon*. These include the express limit of liability (3.1.1), inspiration from the international soft law (3.1.2), and acknowledgment of the *avant-contrat* (3.1.3). These arguments will be advanced in turn and accompanied by the reservations that are worth making.

3.1.1. Express limit of liability

The express limit placed on liability in the course of negotiations can contribute to legal certainty, because it allows parties to estimate early the financial risks of a transaction and places a limit on the margin of judicial appreciation.

The approach summarises the settled French case law on liability for fault in the course of negotiations. Faced with disparities in the approaches adopted by the courts, the Cour de cassation has explicitly stated in the *Manoukian* case (2003)[64] that a victim of a pre-contractual fault was not entitled to recover the amount of money it could potentially earn if the negotiated contract had been concluded. The Cour de cassation explained that 'in the absence of firm and final agreement', the loss of chance of being awarded a contract cannot be recovered, because 'a fault committed in the exercise a right of unilateral withdrawal from pre-contractual negotiations is not the cause of damage consisting in the loss of chance to make a profit possibly expected from

62 B. Fauvarque-Cosson, 'Towards an Important Reform of the French Civil Code', *Montesquieu Law Review*, 2015, (2) 3.

63 D. Campbell, 'Ian Macneil and the Relational Theory of Contract', in D. Campbell (ed.), *The Relational Theory of Contract: Selected Works of Ian Macneil*, London: Sweet & Maxwell, 2001, (3) 9 ff.

64 Cass com 26 November 2003 no. 00-10243 00-10949 Bulletin 2003 IV no. 186 p. 206.

conclusion of a contract.'[65] According to the Cour de cassation, the fact of breaking off negotiations as such does not automatically lead to liability; a fault in tort and the elements of tort liability should also be in place. Furthermore, expectations raised in negotiations are protected by French law to a lesser extent than expectations arising from an existing contract. The Cour de cassation has strictly followed this approach in its later decisions.[66]

Having said this, three reservations should be made. First, as has been mentioned, the limit of liability in Article 1112 facilitates the estimation of risks related to negotiations. However, it enables a precise estimation of only part of the risks. Article 1112 covers only liability for acting contrary to the requirement of good faith. By contrast, no such limit is placed on liability for the unauthorised use of confidential information obtained in the course of negotiations (Article 1112–2). Future case law may follow different paths. One possibility is that the limit in Article 1112 can be interpreted broadly and extended to the liability of Article 1112–2. However, this option eventually goes against the intention of the drafters of the *ordonnance*, who have separated the provisions on *bona fide* and treatment of confidential information. Alternatively, the interpretation can follow the approach adopted in international soft law instruments. These provide a remedy which may go as far as the recovery of benefits obtained as a result of the misuse of confidential information (disgorgement of profits). Though, the precise cases when it can be applied are not extensively elaborated by the drafters of the UPICC and PECL.[67] It may be also noted that such liability is perhaps a too far-reaching solution for French law.

Second, the *ordonnance* leaves open another question debated since the *Manoukian* case. The reasoning of the Cour de cassation in this case has cast doubts on the possibility of recovering a loss of chance to conclude a contract with third party. This recovery relates to the fact that negotiations may impede the exploration of other potential contract opportunities. French scholars have expressed the view that the *Manoukian* approach precluded the recovery of any loss of chance.[68]

Third, the provision on liability for unauthorised use of confidential information in the *ordonnance* does not mention the possibility of implying a duty of confidentiality. Potentially, the implication of such a duty may be drawn from the requirement of good faith in negotiations. However, the *ordonnance* provides no guidance on the kind of information and situations that may lead to such an implication.[69]

65 Id.

66 Cass 3 civ 28 June 2006 no. 04–20040 Bulletin 2006 III no. 164 p. 136; Cass 3 civ 7 January 2009 no. 07–20783 Bulletin 2009 III no. 5; Cass 3 civ 3 June 2009 no. 08–16813; Cass com 18 September 2012 no. 11–19629 Bulletin 2012, IV, no. 163; Cass 3 civ 19 September 2012 no. 11–10532 Unpublished.

67 I. Zuloaga Rios, 'Article 2.1.16 (Duty of Confidentiality)', in S. Vogenauer (ed.), *Commentary on the UNIDROIT Principles of International Commercial Contracts (PICC)*, 2nd ed., Oxford: Oxford University Press, 2015, (364) 370.

68 D. Mazeaud, 'Réparation des Préjudices Précontractuels: Toujours Moins...?', *Recueil Dalloz* 2006, (2963) 2963 ff.

69 See in the same vein C. Asfar-Cazenave, 'La Réforme du Droit Français des Contrats' (2016) *Revue Juridique Thémis de l'Université de Montréal* (forthcoming).

3.1.2. Inspiration from the international soft law

Adopting an approach suggested in international soft law contributes to legal certainty, because the existing soft law instruments are known by legal practitioners in general and parties to international contracts in particular.[70] For example, the open norm of good faith in negotiations is a frequent vehicle of rules applied for tailoring an appropriate award in international arbitration.[71]

Nonetheless, the consequences of the resemblance between the formulations of the *ordonnance*, the PECL, and the UPICC are somewhat delicate. The provisions of the two soft law instruments appear to point to different interpretations of the *bona fide* concept. More concretely, the PECL adopt a broad concept of good faith and fair dealing.[72] This corresponds to the scope of the PECL: general contract law including contracts with consumers and commercial contracts. By contrast, the UPICC expressly refer to good faith and fair dealing in international trade, thereby keeping a distance from national interpretations of *bona fide*. This is in line with the scope of the UPICC which is limited to commercial contracts. As a consequence, liability for the breach of this duty is arguably triggered in the UPICC by more limited types of conduct than in the PECL. The UPICC confine liability to conduct in bad faith, which implies a higher threshold for liability than good faith and fair dealing in the PECL. This suggests that the concept of 'bad faith' in negotiations is confined in the UPICC to the concrete conduct described in Article 2.1.15 (2),(3) UPICC, and the provision should be interpreted restrictively. In this way, the rules of the PECL and the UPICC are not identical. Coming back to Article 1112 of the *ordonnance*, it may be recalled that this provision is based primarily on the genesis of national case law. In this way, the content of the *bona fide* requirement has a clear domestic specificity – the ethics of negotiations discussed earlier. Therefore, the mere requirement resembles the one in the international soft law instruments, but its content is different.

Furthermore, the provisions on pre-contractual bargaining in soft law are close to the approach of civil law traditions. For example, European continental legal systems are familiar with the requirement of good faith in negotiations and the general concept of pre-contractual liability. However, this is not shared in England and Wales. In this view, even if the *ordonnance* clarifies the French law approach to negotiations and demonstrates its resemblance to international instruments, the approach is not new in essence

70 See inter alia S. Lake, 'An Empirical Study of the UNIDROIT Principles – International and British Responses', 16 *Uniform Law Review*, 2011, (669), 696 ff.; S. Vogenauer, 'The UNIDROIT Principles of International Commercial Contracts at Twenty: Experiences to Date, the 2010 Edition, and Future Prospects', 19 *Uniform Law Review*, 2014 (480); see earlier inter alia E. Cashin Ritaine and E. Lein (eds.), *The UNIDROIT Principles 2004: Their Impact on Contractual Practice, Jurisprudence and Codification. Reports of the ISDC Colloquium (8/9 June 2006)*, Zürich: Schulthess, 2007.

71 C. Asfar-Cazenave, 'La Réforme du Droit Français des Contrats', *Revue Juridique Thémis de l'Université de Montréal*, 2016 (forthcoming).

72 For a debate on this, see O. Lando, 'Is Good Faith an Over-arching General Clause in the Principles of European Contract Law?', in M. Andenas, S. Diaz Alabart, Sir B. Markesinis, H. Micklitz and N. Pasquini (eds.), *Liber Amicorum Guido Alpa: Private Law Beyond the National Systems*, London: British Institute of International and Comparative Law, 2007 (601).

compared to the previous French solution. This means that the parties who would rather opt for the English law approach to negotiations would not find in the *ordonnance* substantially new alternatives. The solutions are very similar to the previous ones based on the *Code civil* and case law.

3.1.3. Definitions of preliminary agreements

French scholars have generally welcomed the inclusion in the draft *ordonnance* of the provisions on two preliminary agreements, because these give a legal basis to the instruments frequently used in practice.[73] As noted earlier, the *Code civil* is silent on the framework of *avant-contrat*. Given the fact that codified law is the primary source of law in France, the provisions on unilateral promise and pre-emption agreement acknowledge the development of law that has *de facto* already taken place.

The provisions have been welcomed primarily for ensuring the enforceability of these preliminary agreements and clarifying the remedies for their breach. This clarification would decrease uncertainty in disputes as to whether *avant-contrats* can have legal effects before the formation of the final contract. Furthermore, fewer doubts would arise as to the measure of liability, while some fifty years ago, such doubts were very sound.[74]

However, the positive attitude of French scholars is nuanced. The fact of providing definitions of preliminary agreements has been criticised for encasing living and developing trade usages related to *avant-contrat* in 'rigid legal moulds'.[75] This critique might explain why the *ordonnance* does not include an entire inventory of the preliminary agreements frequently used in practice,[76] but is limited to the two most salient ones.[77] This critique can also be seen from a broader perspective of the reactivity of law, namely the question as to whether the developments in law follow the changes in practice with a certain delay or, on the contrary, the law shapes the development in practice. From this perspective, the new rules on the unilateral promise and pre-emption agreement seem to underline current developments of jurisprudence, rather than innovate with the aim of reaching new results.

[73] B. Fages, 'Rapport Français – Le Processus de Formation du Contrat', in R. Schulze, G. Wicker, G. Mäsch and D. Mazeaud (eds.), *La Réforme du Droit des Obligations en France: 5èmes Journées Franco-Allemandes*, Paris: Société de Législation Comparée, 2015 (41); B. Fages, 'La Promesse Unilatérale et le Pacte de Préférence dans le Projet d'*ordonnance* de Réforme du Droit des Obligations', 240 *Droit et Patrimoine*, 2014 (42); D. Mainguy, 'Promesse Unilatérale et Pacte de Préférence: Des Définitions Inopérantes', 240 *Droit et Patrimoine*, 2014 (44).

[74] *La Formation du Contrat: L'avant-contrat – Congrès des Notaires de France*, Lyon: Imprimerie A. Rey, 1964; J. Schmidt-Szalewski, 'La Force Obligatoire à l'Épreuve des Avant-contrats', *Revue Trimestrielle de Droit Civil*, 2000 (25).

[75] B. Fages, 'La Promesse Unilatérale et le Pacte de Préférence dans le Projet d'*ordonnance* de Réforme du Droit des Obligations', 240 *Droit et Patrimoine*, 2014 (42); D. Mainguy, 'Promesse Unilatérale et Pacte de Préférence: Des Définitions Inopérantes', 240 *Droit et Patrimoine*, 2014 (44).

[76] See section 2.2.1 above.

[77] According to S. Bernheim-Desvaux, not including other *avant-contrats* in the Draft *ordonnance* is indeed a voluntary omission. See S. Bernheim-Desvaux, 'Les Négociations', in M. Latina and G. Chantepie (eds.) *Supplément au Code civil 2016 Édition Limitée – Livret sur le Projet de Réforme du Droit des Obligations*, Paris: Dalloz, 2015, (8) 9.

3.2. *(In)flexibility*

Two arguments point to the potential of the *ordonnance* to increase flexibility of the rules applicable to negotiations of contract, compared to the *Code Napoleon*. These relate to the effects of the *avant-contrat* (3.2.1) and the characterisation of liability that may arise in the course of negotiations (3.2.2). Both arguments also include important reservations.

3.2.1. Effects of preliminary agreements

The *ordonnance* clarifies the measure of liability for breach of the unilateral promise and pre-emption agreement. In both cases, the remedy may consist in nullity of a contract concluded with a third party in breach of the preliminary agreement. Furthermore, breach of the pre-emption agreement gives the beneficiary the right to be substituted for the third party in the concluded contract. This remedy amounts to a specific performance of the pre-emption agreement. In this regard, it should be noted that according to the *ordonnance*, specific performance may not be granted if it is impossible or if its cost for the debtor is manifestly disproportionate to its benefit for the creditor.[78]

From the internal perspective of the development of French law, the provision is not unusual. The extent of liability is based on the development of French case law, and the measure of liability follows the affirmation by the *ordonnance* of specific performance as one of the main remedies for breach of contract.[79] Besides this, French law generally admits that a contract may have effects for third parties aware of its existence.[80]

However, the remedy may undermine the flexibility of the framework, because specific performance may have a far-reaching effect related to third parties. The impact may be illustrated by considering the following example. A Publishing house negotiates a contract with a company *A* for the organisation of promotion of the books published by the Publishing house. The parties sign a pre-emption agreement, in which *A* is the beneficiary. However, the Publishing house breaches the pre-emption agreement and concludes a contract for promotion with *B*. Suppose *B* is aware that *A* conducts parallel negotiations, but does not enter into details of the matter due to lack of time. *A* learns about the concluded contract, and establishes a claim. *A* asks the judge to be substituted and come instead of *B* into the concluded contract. The result of the application of the rules on liability for breach of the pre-emption agreement may be as follows. As a result of the substitution, the Publishing house would find itself in a contract with *A* (with whom the Publishing house has decided not to conclude the final contract). *B* would lose the client, because the client (the Publishing house) breached the pre-emption agreement.

One may argue that the reasons for breaching the pre-emption agreement are relevant (these would, for instance, matter for breach of good faith). However, French law generally

[78] Article 1221 *ordonnance*.

[79] See Article 1217 *ordonnance*.

[80] J. Ghestin and G. Viney, *Traité de Droit Civil. Introduction à la Responsabilité*, 3rd ed., Paris: L.G.D.J, 2008, para 202 and 207–3.

does not follow the theory of efficient breach of contract.[81] Furthermore, B's attitude to the breach of the pre-emption agreement by the Publishing house may matter together with other factors assessed in estimating the effects of a preliminary agreement for third parties.[82] This assessment implies a complex inquiry to be made by the court.

As follows from this example, this measure of liability may undermine the flexibility of the new framework for the following reasons. It entails risks related to the possibility that a party in a contract is substituted for another one. The actual commercial impact of such sanction may be difficult to estimate. It may also imply the need to verify in a transaction whether a counterpart to negotiations is not bound by a pre-emption. The practical importance of such verification is correlated to the total amount at stake and other possible consequences related to facing a substituted party. Furthermore, doubts are still raised as to the practicality of the mechanism Article 1123 provides to third parties in order to make sure they commit no breach of a pre-emption agreement. For instance, the absence of reply from the supposed beneficiary offers no shield from nullity. Besides this, a situation where one addresses a competitor with the question suggested by the Article does not arise easily in commercial reality.

Therefore, whereas the provision is welcomed and logical from the internal perspective of French law, there are doubts as to whether it contributes to the flexibility of the framework of rules applicable to negotiations.

3.2.2. Characterisation of liability

The *ordonnance* characterises the nature of liability that may arise in the course of negotiations. The draft *ordonnance* did so in a straightforward manner. It stated that the breach of the requirement of good faith and the unauthorised use of confidential information entail extra-contractual liability[83] that is, liability in tort.[84] The *ordonnance* adopts the same approach, but the characterisation of liability is implicit. The provisions limiting possible recovery refer to liability for 'fault committed in negotiations',[85] and this is a reference to liability in tort. Furthermore, since the unilateral promise and pre-emption agreement are defined as contracts, fewer doubts arise as to the nature of liability for their breach.[86] The breach of the unilateral promise and pre-emption agreement leads to contractual liability.

This characterisation may contribute to the flexibility of the new framework, because it offers a possibility for the negotiating parties to influence – by creating a preliminary

81 M. van Kogelenberg, 'Deliberate Breach of Contract and Consequences for Remedies: Exploration of a Neglected Area in the Law of Contract' 21 *Maastricht Journal of European and Comparative law*, 2014 (141).

82 See on inventory of such factors L. M. van Bochove, *Betrokkenheid van Derden bij Contractbreuk*, Oisterwijk: Wolf Legal Publishers, 2013, Chapter 5.

83 See Articles 1111 and 1112 draft *ordonnance*.

84 Articles 1240 ff. *ordonnance*.

85 Article 1112 *ordonnance*.

86 See for ealier doubts J. Schmidt-Szalewski, 'La Force Obligatoire à l'Épreuve des Avant-contrats', *Revue Trimestrielle de Droit Civil*, 2000 (25).

agreement – the measure and the scope of liability that they may potentially incur. This influence is, of course, subject to the limitations placed on the possibility to modify or waive ('privatise') concrete rules. In particular, the provisions on tort are regarded in French law as part of *ordre public*. These may not be changed by the parties' agreement. By contrast, relations that may be framed by contract, including the now codified concepts, may be to a large extent modified or concretised by contractual provisions. French courts have been generally willing to uphold the obligations provided in the pre-emption agreement almost literally. Judges have held to be valid conditions specifying the moment, the form, and the content of the notification to be addressed to the beneficiary. They have also upheld provisions indicating the period of time during which the beneficiary has to react to the notification.[87] At the same time, the question as to what extent parties may 'privatise' the relationship that is otherwise regulated by tort remains difficult.

In this light, more flexibility might have been provided by the *ordonnance* by articulating the relation between the fields of law relevant for the pre-contractual phase. It is also worth noting that contract and tort law are not the only fields of law applicable to the pre-contractual phase in French law. Unjustified enrichment may play a role in the recovery of the anticipated performance made at the stage of negotiations,[88] even if the role is limited due to the subsidiary character of the claim in unjustified enrichment in French law. The applicability of this field of law appears to remain in place, on the basis of case law, but is not expressly mentioned in the Draft *ordonnance*. Clarification may still be provided by the reform of tort law, which is one of the next steps in codification in France in the near future.[89]

4. Conclusion

To conclude the reflections on the attractiveness of the proposed new rules on the pre-contractual phase for parties to international commercial transactions, the following may be noted.

France follows the recent 'wave'[90] of codifications in Europe. During the last twenty years, reforms of the law of obligations have taken place in the Netherlands, Germany, and several countries of Eastern Europe. The changes were made for various reasons, however the aim of increasing the attractiveness of domestic law at the international level was not the main cause.[91]

87 B. Fages, 'Étude 120. Le Pacte de Préférence' (June 2012), in B. Fages (ed.), *Lamy Droit du Contrat*, Paris: Wolters Kluwer France, 2012, para 120.40; see also Cass 1 civ 3 October 2006 no. 05-14099 Bulletin 2006 I no. 422 p. 364.

88 Cass 1 civ 13 July 2004 no. 01-03608 Bulletin 2004 I no. 208 p. 174; Cass com 9 July 2013 no. 12-17434 Unpublished.

89 B. Fauvarque-Cosson, 'Towards an Important Reform of the French Civil Code', *Montesquieu Law Review*, 2015, (2) 4.

90 R. Schulze and F. Zoll (eds.), *The Law of Obligations in Europe: A New Wave of Codifications*, Munich: Sellier European Law Publishers, 2013.

91 Though, the impetus for the reforms in Eastern European countries was undoubtedly international integration.

In France, the express aim of contributing to the influence of national law beyond its borders can only subtly be traced back to the *ordonnance*. The new rules on the pre-contractual phase are certainly innovative in comparison with the *Code civil*. However, they do not amount to innovation in comparison with the contemporary case law. To a much greater extent, the *ordonnance* reiterates the solutions settled in the judge-made law. The provision on liability for fault in negotiations and the nature of liability are examples of this relative innovation. Furthermore, the proposed new rules seek to clarify the main scholarly debates. This has been done by the choice and clarification of the approach to the revocability of the pre-emption agreement and to damages recoverable for fault in negotiations.

The codification of case law on the pre-contractual phase appears to be a logical development, because France is a civil law tradition, where codified law is assumed to be more readily accessible (ideally for everyone but essentially for lawyers) and less contradictory than judge-made law. The judicial interpretation of the *Code civil* has created a gap between the code and the case law regarding the pre-contractual stage, and the time is ripe for codification.

In essence, the new rules on the pre-contractual phase do not provide parties with any substantially new solutions that would sharply contrast with the *Code civil* as interpreted by the extensive existing case law.

Frederik Peeraer*

NULLITY IN THE *ORDONNANCE*

1. Introduction

1. For the past two centuries, French legal doctrine has tried to elaborate a comprehensive theory of nullity to remedy the absence of such a framework in the *Code civil*. Due to the variety of sources in the *Ancien Régime*, the rules regarding nullity formed an intricate whole prior to the enactment of the *Code civil*.[1] Still largely inspired by those rules, the *Code civil* did not attempt to clarify the situation.[2] Up until now, both in France and in Belgium, the doctrine of nullity is regarded as one of the most obscure and impenetrable theories in private law.[3] Notwithstanding an unremitting interest in the matter,[4] scholarship has not sufficiently demystified the concept of nullity and the way it operates in private law. The announced revision of large parts of the *Code civil* offers a unique chance to elucidate the matter at hand and to boldly go where the *Code civil* has not gone before.

2. This paper will scrutinise whether the *ordonnance* has indeed seized the opportunity. First, this paper will give a brief overview of the *ordonnance*'s approach to nullity (2). Since the different aspects of nullity are too multifarious to deal with in a single paper, the scope of the research will be limited to the concept of nullity (3), its use (4), and its

* Teaching assistant and junior researcher (PhD student) KU Leuven, institute for the law of obligations. Articles mentioned without an indication of a specific statute are articles of the *ordonnance n° 2016-131 du 10 février 2016 portant réforme du droit des contrats, du régime général et de la preuve des obligations* (hereinafter *ordonnance*).

1 Cumyn, *La validité du contrat suivant le droit strict ou l'équité: étude historique et comparée des nullités contractuelles* (LGDJ 2002), 12–3, no. 30.

2 Picod, 'Nullité', in *Rep.civ.Dalloz* 2013, no. 7.

3 For Belgium, see e.g. De Page, *Traité élémentaire de droit civil belge*, II, *Les incapables – Les obligations* (Bruylant 1964), 141, no. 96. For France, *cf.* Japiot, *Des nullités en matière d'actes juridiques – Essai d'une théorie nouvelle* (A. Rousseau 1909), 112 and Posez, 'La théorie des nullités – Le centenaire d'une mystification', *RTD Civ.* 2011, 647 *et seq.*

4 In the past years, several authors have conducted penetrating inquiries into the topic. See e.g. Al Khoury, *Des nullités en matière civile – Essai de reconstitution d'une théorie en droit français et libanais en considération des perspectives européennes et internationales* (PhD-thesis Montpellier 2011); Posez (n 3), 647 *et seq.*; Sadi, *Essai sur un critère de distinction des nullités en droit privé* (Mare & Martin 2015). A comprehensive overview of the actual regime of nullity can be found in Ghestin/ Loiseau/Serinet, *La formation du contrat*, II, *L'objet et la cause – Les nullités* (LGDJ 2013), 697–1605, nos. 2001–2955.

enforcement (5) in the *ordonnance*. As a consequence, the grounds of invalidity and the consequences of nullity (such as restitutions and potential liability connected to avoidance) will not be examined. Since the *Draft Common Frame of Reference* (*DCFR*) and the Dutch *Burgerlijk Wetboek* of 1992[5] have reconsidered the analysis of nullity, the *ordonnance*'s propositions will be compared to those solutions in order to see whether the *ordonnance* offers state-of-the-art solutions. The results of those comparisons will demonstrate to what extent the *ordonnance* can be a source of inspiration for the further development of the Belgian and Dutch law regarding nullity.

2. Overview of the *ordonnance*'s approach

3. The *ordonnance* dedicates an independent paragraph to the remedy of nullity (Articles 1178–85), whereas the *Code civil* only contains scarce and dispersed rules in this regard.[6] Since the majority of the relevant rules are to be found in that passage, those articles will occupy a prominent role in this paper. Article 1178 starts with a description of nullity, its enforcement, and its consequences. The following articles (Articles 1179–81) codify the classic distinction between absolute and relative nullity and its consequences (which relate to the difference regarding the parties allowed to invoke nullity and the possibility to confirm the null contract), with confirmation itself being described in the subsequent Article 1182. Article 1183 offers a party the possibility to impose a choice on the party entitled to avoid the contract between the nullity and the validity of the contract. The following Article 1184 comprises a general recognition of the so-called 'partial nullity' and the maintenance of the contract if the law deems a specific clause unwritten ('*réputée non écrite*') or if the aim of the violated rule requires its maintenance. Ultimately, Article 1185 codifies the so-called exception of nullity. Since the way the *ordonnance* makes use of nullity can only be revealed by other, specific provisions, those other rules will also be taken into account.

The choice to regulate nullity in a specific chapter is not entirely innovative. Previous projects, such as the *Avant-Projet Catala*,[7] the *Projet Terré*,[8] the *Projet de la Chancellerie*[9] and the recent *Projet d'ordonnance*,[10] also bundled several aspects of nullity in a specific part of the text.[11] As the *ordonnance* is to a large extent indebted to those projects, the comments on those previous propositions may elucidate the content of the *ordonnance* and will therefore be scrutinised as well.

5 Hereinafter Dutch civil code or DCC.

6 See Ghestin et al. (n 4), 697–9, no. 2002.

7 Avant-Projet de réforme du droit des obligations (Articles 1101 à 1386 du Code civil) et du droit de la prescription (Articles 2234 à 2281 du Code civil) – Rapport à Monsieur Pascal Clément, Garde des Sceaux, Ministre de la Justice – 22 September 2005.

8 Terré (ed.), *Pour une réforme du droit des contrats* (Dalloz 2009).

9 Projet de réforme du droit des contrats, juillet 2008.

10 Projet d'*ordonnance* portant réforme du droit des contrats, du régime général et de la preuve des obligations.

11 *Avant-Projet Catala*: Articles 1129 – 1130-3; *Projet Terré*: Articles 78–88; *Projet de la Chancellerie*: Articles 90–100.

3. The concept of nullity

3.1. Essential aspects and distinction with other remedies

4. Like the *Code civil*, the *ordonnance* does not provide for an explicit definition of the concept of nullity. Nevertheless, the first article dedicated to nullity (Article 1178) is particularly revealing of the way it is perceived by the drafters. According to the first three paragraphs of that article, "*Un contrat qui ne remplit pas les conditions requises pour sa validité est nul. La nullité doit être prononcée par le juge, à moins que les parties ne la constatent d'un commun accord.*

"*Le contrat annulé est censé n'avoir jamais existé.*

"*Les prestations exécutées donnent lieu à restitution dans les conditions prévues aux articles 1352 à 1352-9.*"

5. With that description, the *ordonnance* follows in the footsteps of earlier projects[12] and largely adheres to the predominant view on nullity in French scholarship. The only difference – but a very meaningful one – concerns the scope of nullity. Contrary to various authors, who apply nullity to every juridical act,[13] the *ordonnance* only discusses nullity in the context of contracts. This should not come as a surprise, since the drafters did not opt for a different level of abstraction than the *Code civil*. Thus, contracts – and not juridical acts or declarations of will – remain the focal point of the regulation in French private law. With regard to other aspects of the notion of nullity, the *ordonnance* aligns with the prevalent views in French scholarship. The *ordonnance*, as well as the traditional doctrine, identifies nullity as a remedy for contracts/juridical acts which (at the time of their formation) do not comply with all legal requirements.[14] As a result of that invalidity, the contract/juridical act is deprived of its effects.[15] Both the *ordonnance* and legal scholarship consider a judicial intervention necessary to enforce nullity: as long as the judge has not declared the nullity of the invalid juridical act, that act still produces its legal effects (unless parties agree on the nullity of the contract).[16] Like the majoritarian view,[17] the *ordonnance* does not require a judicial decision if the parties to the contract recognise its nullity and the subsequent presence of restitutionary claims. Finally, the *ordonnance* only confirms the prevailing analysis in French law when it refers to a specific regime for those claims. Although the *Code civil* contains specific rules regarding undue payment (Articles 1375–81) and case-law has recognised the general principle prohibiting

12 Earlier projects contained a comparable description of nullity. Yet, in those projects, the necessity of a judicial intervention was regulated in a separate article. See Articles 1129 and 1130-1 *Avant-Projet Catala*; Articles 78 and 85 *Projet Terré*, and Articles 90 and 98 *Projet de la Chancellerie*.

13 See e.g. Picod (n 2), no. 1.

14 See Terré/Simler/Lequette, *Droit civil – les obligations* (Dalloz 2013), 109, no. 82.

15 See the reference to Ponsard and Blondel in Ghestin et al. (n 4), 707, no. 2007, note 2. See *ibid.* for slightly different descriptions; Terré et al. (n 14), 109, nos. 81–2.

16 Ghestin et al. (n 4), 995 *et seq.*, no. 2286 *et seq.*; Picod (n 2), no. 31; Terré et al. (n 14), 437, no. 390. For an alternative view, see Posez (n 3), 647 *et seq.*

17 Ghestin et al. (n 4), 1000–2, no. 2291; Picod (n 2), no. 32; Terré et al. (n 14), 437, no. 389.

unjustified enrichment,[18] those rules are deemed unsuitable for the restitution after nullity. Consequently, according to the prevailing view, restitutionary claims are governed by an autonomous legal basis and a regime *sui generis*.[19] The *ordonnance* codifies this view by dedicating a specific chapter to restitutionary claims (Articles 1352–1352-9), which has not been integrated in the rules on undue payment (Articles 1302–1302-3) or unjustified enrichment (Articles 1303–1303-4).

6. For the purpose of this paper,[20] nullity must be distinguished from the concepts of inopposability (*inopposabilité*) and termination (*résolution*). In French law, opposability is viewed as the necessary complement to the obligatory effect a contract has between parties. It is described as the phenomenon that tends to make third parties acknowledge the existence of a contractual relationship. When a contract is '*inopposable*', (some) third parties are allowed to ignore the contract and to behave without having regard to the contract.[21] In this respect, a distinction is made between the 'internal' and the 'external' effects of a contract. 'Internal effects' can be described as the juridical effects directly affecting the parties to that contract, for example by imposing obligations on them; 'external effects' as the sole duty to acknowledge the existence of a contract and its influence on the juridical positions of the parties to that contract.[22] The distinction between termination and nullity is primarily connected to the types of defects justifying those remedies. In contrast to nullity, termination can be used as a remedy for fundamental non-performance. Consequently, while nullity relates to defects in the formation of juridical acts, termination can only be triggered by posterior circumstances.[23] Regarding the applicable regime, both remedies converge to a large extent. The most fundamental difference can be found in the powers of the judge: as opposed to his duty[24] to pronounce nullity when he is asked to do so, he has a large margin of appreciation

18 See the *Boudier* judgment, Req. 15 June 1892, *DP* 1892, 1596, *S* 1893, I, 281. For the subsequent evolution, see Terré et al. (n 14), 1113, no. 1065.

19 Cass. 24 September 2002, *Bull.civ.* I, no. 218, *D.* 2003, 369, note Aubert, *RTD Civ.* 2003, 284, obs. Mestre/Fages, *Defrénois* 2003, Article 37664, note Aubert. See Ghestin et al. (n 4), 1537, no. 2883. In Belgium, a similar opinion prevails. See Baeck, *Restitutie na vernietiging of ontbinding van overeenkomsten* (Intersentia 2012), 39 *et seq.* Others advocate the use of the rules on undue payment: e.g. Flour/Aubert/Savaux, *Droit civil – Les obligations – 1. L'acte juridique* (Dalloz 2014), 379, no. 362.

20 In the following parts, I will argue that the *ordonnance* sometimes seems to confuse nullity with inopposability, which is detrimental for an appropriate use of those concepts (see 4.2). Moreover, the *ordonnance* does not use the same methods for enforcing nullity and termination. Regarding one method, that differentiation does not appear to be based on solid arguments (see *infra* 5.1.2).

21 Ghestin et al. (n 4), 785, no. 2076 and the references therein; Terré et al. (n 14), 542 and 547, nos. 483 and 490. The same distinction is made in Belgian law: see *inter alia* Wéry, *Droit des obligations – Volume 1: Théorie générale du contrat* (Larcier 2011), 863 *et seq.*, no. 922 *et seq.* The difference between nullity and inopposability is not to be exaggerated: in the end, the dichotomy between those notions only concerns their extent, and not their nature: Japiot (n 3), 33.

22 *Cf.* Fontaine, 'Les effets "internes" et les effets "externes" des contrats', in Fontaine/Ghestin (eds.), *Les effets du contrat à l'égard des tiers* (LGDJ 1992), 40–66.

23 Ghestin et al. (n 4), 780 *et seq*, no. 2073 *et seq.*; Picod (n 2), no. 16; Terré et al. (n 14), 110, no. 82.

24 On some occasions, judges have discretion to decide whether or not to pronounce nullity. In those cases, the nullity is called 'facultative'. Regarding 'facultative nullities', see Ghestin et al. (n 4), 1042 *et seq.*, no. 2339 *et seq.*

when considering the opportunity of terminating the contract.[25] In the use of those notions, the *ordonnance* does not deviate from the generally accepted doctrinal analysis.

7. Although the aforementioned proposition is widely accepted in French scholarship, it does not offer a state-of-the-art solution. The proposition lacks any reference to the purpose of the infringed norm, despite its crucial importance for shaping and using nullity. The requirements for the validity of a contract consist of the consent of the parties, their capacity, and a licit and certain content (Article 1128). Article 1162 explains that a contract may not derogate from the public order (*ordre public*), whether it be by means of its content or its goal. Regrettably, the project does not specify in what circumstances the content (or goal) of a contract would derogate from the public order. In what circumstances does the infringement of a rule entail such a prohibited derogation?

In multiple modern codifications and doctrinal codes, the essence of nullity is not only found in a defect of the requirements for the validity of juridical acts, but also in a proportionate response to the infringement of a norm. Thus, several codes and projects put the aim of the infringed norm in the centre of attention. They mention the impact an infringement can have on juridical acts and contain a provision clarifying that not every violation of a mandatory norm entails the nullity of the juridical act.[26] Whether or not a certain infringement of a rule influences the validity of the juridical act depends on the goal of the infringed norm and the sanctions that can be used to realise that goal. Often, the purpose of a rule can be achieved more adequately by other remedies than nullity (for example by criminal or administrative sanctions).[27] The absence of a similar provision in the *Code civil* is unfortunately not remedied in the *ordonnance*. Although Article 1184 para 2 *in fine* does mention the goal of the infringed norm, the relevance of the purpose of the rule seems limited to the *extent* of nullity. Since it is located in Article 1184, it does not seem to answer the question whether or not the infringement of a norm entails nullity, but appears limited to the question whether or not the nullity of a term will affect the entire contract.

3.2. *The summa divisio between absolute and relative nullity*

8. In line with the first article of the *ordonnance* on nullity, the following three articles represent the view of the prevalent scholarly opinions in France and have their roots in

25 Ghestin et al. (n 4), 782–784, no. 2075.

26 E.g. §134 BGB ("*A juridical act that violates a statutory prohibition is void, unless the statute leads to a different conclusion.*"); Article 3:40 para 3 DCC ("*The previous paragraph does not concern statutory provisions that do not purport to make a conflicting juridical act invalid.*"); Article II.–7:302 DCFR.

27 *Cf.* Comment E ('Sanctions already incurred') on Article II.–7:302 DCFR, von Bar/Clive/Schulte-Nölke (eds.), *Principles, Definitions and Model Rules of European Private Law – Draft Common Frame of Reference (DCFR) – Full Edition* (2009), 568: "*If the rule in question provides for a criminal or administrative sanction against the wrongdoer, the imposition of that sanction may be enough to deter the conduct in question without adding the nullity of the contract. The goal of deterrence is usually better achieved through such criminal or administrative sanctions than by way of private law. Often such sanctions will take into account the degree of blameworthiness of the party concerned, and this may be a more appropriate response to the conduct than avoiding the contract in whole or in part.*"

the preceding projects.[28] Article 1179 contains the *summa divisio* in French private law between 'absolute' and 'relative' nullity. As stated in that article, the nullity is denominated 'absolute' when the transgressed rule aims to safeguard the general interest and 'relative' when it aims to safeguard a private interest. Pursuant to Articles 1180 and 1181[29], the two fundamental differences between those nullities concern (1) the parties authorised to invoke the nullity and (2) the possibility to remedy that nullity by confirming the contract. An absolute nullity can be invoked by everybody having an interest in doing so, including the *ministère public*, but cannot be remedied by confirmation. In contrast, a relative nullity can only be invoked by the party that the law intends to protect, but can be remedied by confirmation. Although the distinction between absolute and relative nullity is well established in scholarship,[30] its explicit recognition and description in black letter rules is remarkable.

9. From a theoretical point of view, it remains doubtful whether a private law codification should ossify such a purely dogmatic distinction. The absence of a similar distinction in the *Code civil* offered scholars the necessary flexibility to create new concepts in order to deal with unexpected questions and/or societal changes. By rigidifying the *summa division* between absolute and relative nullity, the *ordonnance* might rather hamper the further development of the law than support it.

10. Even if there were no theoretical drawbacks, there remain several reasons why Articles 1179–81 seem a rather unfortunate and oversimplified representation of nullity and its different varieties.

First, according to the *ordonnance*, absolute and relative nullities seem to be the only varieties. That appearance is contradicted by the actual French positive law. Although many of the nineteenth-century distinctions have dissipated,[31] the differences between for example textual and virtual nullities[32], and facultative and obligatory nullities[33] remain part of the French legal system. By concealing the existence of those nullities, the *ordonnance* lacks the fastidiousness that is indispensable for a code which aims to (among other things) modernise, improve the legibility and the accessibility of the general law of contracts and obligations, and guarantee legal certainty and the efficacy of

28 See Articles 1129–1 and 1129–3 *Avant-Projet Catala*; Articles 79–81 *Projet Terré*, and Articles 91–93 *Projet de la Chancellerie*.

29 Similar provisions were present in earlier projects: see Articles 1129–2 – 1129–3 *Avant-Projet Catala*; Articles 80–81 *Projet Terré*, and Articles 92–93 *Projet de la Chancellerie*.

30 See Flour et al. (n 19), 332 *et seq.*, no. 324 *et seq.*; Ghestin et al. (n 4), 789 *et seq.*, no. 2091 *et seq.*; Picod (n 2), nos. 23–8; Terré et al. (n 14), 109 *et seq.*, no. 81 *et seq.*

31 E.g. the difference between statutory and natural nullities, peremptory and comminatory nullities, permanent and transitory nullities, and extrinsic and intrinsic nullities: see Posez (n 3), no. 3 and the references therein.

32 The explicit recognition of the virtual nullity (i.e. a nullity which is not expressly proscribed by a statute) could remedy the absence of a provision similar to §134 BGB, Article 3:40 para 3 DCC or Article II.–7:302 DCFR. See *supra*, 3.1 *in fine*. For these nullities, see e.g. Ghestin et al. (n 4), 716 *et seq.*, no. 2018 *et seq.*

33 For these nullities, see e.g. Ghestin et al. (n 4), 1042 *et seq.*, no. 2339 *et seq.*

legal norms.[34] Consequently, the *ordonnance*'s oversimplification can frustrate nuanced solutions in private law.

This can be illustrated by Article 1169. According to that article, an onerous contract is null when, at the moment of its formation, what is agreed on as a counterpart for the benefit of the person who took on an obligation, is illusory or derisory. This is for example the case when the insured 'risk' in an insurance contract does not exist (anymore) when the contract is concluded.[35] In the *ordonnance*, that nullity must be either an absolute or a relative nullity: which one can be determined by investigating the specific protective goal of the infringed rule. Yet, the nullity of Article 1169 cannot easily be analysed in terms of 'protection'. Does that rule exist for the benefit of private individuals, or for the benefit of the general interest? Unsurprisingly, both positions have been defended by French scholarship.[36] In reality, and contrary to what the *ordonnance* states, nullity is not always about protection. In this case, for instance, arguments related to the protective aim of the infringed rule are intrinsically maladjusted. The legal order does not require the presence of a risk in order to 'protect' certain parties or the general interest, but to maintain the vital coherence of the concept of an insurance contract.[37] An insurance contract without a risk is just as inconceivable as a sales contract without a price. The solution for this problem can be found in the regrettably forgotten[38] distinction between natural and legal nullities. In earlier times, the applicable type of nullity to such problems was neither absolute nor relative, but 'natural' (this is pertaining to the 'nature' of the used concepts). As a result, the irrelevant question of the protective aim of the infringed rule was not raised. The *ordonnance*, however, will force legal practitioners to ask the wrong questions, thus increasing the risk of unjustifiable solutions.

Second, the legal consequences connected to the distinction between absolute and relative nullity are not accurately represented.

34 See Article 8 *Loi n° 2015-177 relatif à la modernisation et à la simplification du droit et des procédures dans le domaines de la justice et des affaires intérieures*: "*Dans les conditions prévues à l'article 38 de la Constitution, le Gouvernement est autorisé à prendre par voie d'ordonnance les mesures relevant du domaine de la loi nécessaires pour modifier la structure et le contenu du livre III du code civil, afin de moderniser, de simplifier, d'améliorer la lisibilité, de renforcer l'accessibilité du droit commun des contrats, du régime des obligations et du droit de la preuve, de garantir la sécurité juridique et l'efficacité de la norme*" (emphasis added).

35 Traditionally, these problems are situations where the 'cause' of the obligation was absent.

36 For an overview, see Flour et al. (n 19), 344–346; Ghestin et al. (n 4), 854 *et seq.*, no. 2157 *et seq.*; Sadi (n 4), 146–162, nos. 99–109.

37 *Cf.* Japiot (n 3), 602–603: "*Nous rencontrons ici les nullités sanctionnant certaines règles qui, à la différence de toutes autres, ne sont pas à considérer comme des règles protectrices* [...]. *S'il y a inefficacité dans ces hypothèses, c'est seulement parce qu'il est matériellement impossible qu'il en soit autrement* [...]. *De même, on considère qu'il est nécessaire ou naturel de reconnaître l'inefficacité des actes dont l'objet ou la cause font entièrement défaut, ou sont d'une importance trop minime pour entrer en ligne de compte* [...]. *Si l'assurance contractée après la réalisation du sinistre et la destruction de la chose assurée est nulle en principe, c'est que l'assurance ne se comprend pas sans un risque.*"

38 Luckily, some authors have recently discovered those nullities. See e.g. Sadi (n 4), 160 *et seq.*, no. 108 *et seq.*

Regarding the persons authorised to invoke the nullity of the contract, the *ordonnance* creates the illusion of an undeniable difference. In reality, it is hard to say whether there exists any distinction at all in this matter.[39] First, the authority for the *ministère public* to invoke the absolute nullity seems misplaced. Similar to Belgian law,[40] French law provides for that possibility when the public order is or is threatened to be endangered.[41] There is no one-to-one relationship between that 'endangerment' and the presence of an absolute nullity. Not every absolute nullity leads to an endangerment of the public order, and conversely, an absolute nullity is not required for the public order to become endangered. Second, a general, unspecified interest does not suffice for a party to provoke the absolute nullity of the contract; instead, a specific personal interest is required.[42] Third, the party that the law intends to protect is not always the only one authorised to rely on a relative nullity. Sometimes, representatives of the protected party or specific third parties (for example creditors) can also invoke such a nullity.[43] In this matter, the difference between the types of nullity is rather attributable to the specific aims of the norm. In my opinion, the purpose of the norm that provides for a nullity will always determine who can invoke that nullity. When the protection only exists for the benefit of one of the contracting parties, the absence of a possibility for the other party to rely on nullity must not be explained by the categorisation of the concerned 'type' of nullity, but by an interpretation of the aim of the relevant norm.

In the same vein, it is too simple to state that absolute nullities, contrary to relative nullities, can never be confirmed. Again, the statement that an absolute nullity cannot be confirmed is not as undisputed as the *ordonnance* and its predecessors suggest. Although the prevalent opinion shares that view, several contemporary authors mention specific situations in which absolute nullities can be confirmed as well.[44] In earlier times, scholars argued that every nullity, even an absolute nullity, can be confirmed in principle.[45] Article 931–1, which is an exact copy of Article 1340 *Code civil*, illustrates that a general impossibility to confirm an absolute[46] nullity is not tenable. According to that paragraph, the heirs or successors of a donor can confirm the nullity of a gift after the death of the donor. During his lifetime, the donor cannot confirm the null act, but must repeat the gift. Scholarship adhering to the prevalent view struggles with the

39 *Cf.* Ghestin et al. (n 4), 925, no. 2214: "*Entre les deux espèces, les différences de régime ont sans doute aujourd'hui perdu beaucoup de leur acuité*".

40 Article 138*bis*, §1 *Code judiciaire*: "*Le ministère public agit d'office dans les cas spécifiés par la loi et en outre chaque fois que l'ordre public exige son intervention.*"

41 See Article 423 *Code de procédure civile*: "[...] *il peut agir pour la défense de l'ordre public à l'occasion des faits qui portent atteinte à celui-ci.*"

42 Ghestin et al. (n 4), 970–6, nos. 2255–6.

43 For an overview of the parties authorised to invoke a relative nullity, see Flour et al. (n 19), 352 *et seq.*, no. 339 *et seq.*; Ghestin et al. (n 4), 927 *et seq.*, no. 2216 *et seq.*; Picod (n 2), no. 43–5; Terré et al. (n 14), 441 *et seq.*, no. 395 *et seq.*

44 See Flour et al. (n 19), 362, no. 348; Ghestin et al. (n 4), 1156–63, nos. 2470–3.

45 See e.g. Aubry/Rau, *Cours de droit civil français d'après l'ouvrage allemand de C.-S. Zachariae*, III (Cosse 1856), §337, 187, note 6; Japiot (n 3), 716.

46 Scholarship equates Article 1340 *Code civil* with an absolute nullity. See e.g. Sana-Chaillé de Néré, 'Articles 1338 à 1340 – Fasc. 10', in *JCl.-Civ.* 2008, no. 95.

classification of that provision and analyses its content as a 'paradox'.[47] In this situation as well, whether or not a null contract can be confirmed depends on the aim of the infringed norm and the specific circumstances in which the confirmation takes place. In my opinion, confirmation should be allowed each time it does not contravene the aim of the infringed norm at the time the confirmation ought to produce its effects. In this view, the rule of Article 931–1 can easily be explained: during the life of the donor, confirmation would contradict the aim of that provision (this is to protect the donor against a rash decision to donate); after his death, that aim does not preclude his heirs (or successors) from confirming the null donation.

3.3. *The recognition of partial nullity*

11. The *Code civil* of 1804 does not contain a general provision regulating the possibility to restrict nullity to specific effects of the contract. Scholarship however started from the particular Articles 900 and 1172 *Code civil*[48] to elaborate a more comprising theory concerning partial nullity.[49] In line with previous projects,[50] the *ordonnance* codifies that idea in one article (Article 1184): "*Lorsque la cause de nullité n'affecte qu'une ou plusieurs clauses du contrat, elle n'emporte nullité de l'acte tout entier que si cette ou ces clauses ont constitué un élément déterminant de l'engagement des parties ou de l'une d'elles.*".[51] Like the other articles dedicated to nullity, this article can be criticised on multiple grounds. The most important reasons concern the requirements the article imposes to restrict the effect of nullity and the scope of the article.

3.3.1. Requirements

12. Regarding the earlier *Projet d'ordonnance*, a first remark could have been that the 'decisiveness' of the terms affected by nullity seems to be the only relevant factor in determining whether or not the nullity of those terms affects the complete contract. Opposite to Article 1130–2 *Avant-Projet Catala*, Article 86 *Projet Terré*, and Article 99 *Projet de la Chancellerie*, the *Projet d'ordonnance* did not contain any reference to the purpose of the infringed norm. Though it is undisputed in French law that the extent of nullity is determined by those aims,[52] the *Projet d'ordonnance* suggested that such goals are irrelevant. Luckily, Article 1184 has been amended in the *ordonnance* to remedy the

[47] In this vein, e.g., Sana-Chaillé de Néré (n 46), no. 93.

[48] Article 900 *Code civil*: "*Dans toute disposition entre vifs ou testamentaire, les conditions impossibles, celles qui sont contraires aux lois ou aux mœurs, seront réputées non écrites.*"; Article 1172 *Code civil*: "*Toute condition d'une chose impossible, ou contraire aux bonnes mœurs, ou prohibée par la loi est nulle, et rend nulle la convention qui en dépend.*"

[49] See e.g. Simler, *La nullité partielle des actes juridiques* (LGDJ 1969). See Ghestin et al. (n 4), 1247 *et seq.*, no. 2575 *et seq.*

[50] Article 1130–2 *Avant-Projet Catala*; Article 86 *Projet Terré* and Article 99 *Projet de la Chancellerie*.

[51] "*Where a ground of nullity affects only one or more terms of the contract, it only entails the nullity of the whole act if this term or these terms constituted a decisive factor for the commitment of the parties, or of one of them.*"

[52] See Ghestin et al. (n 4), 1249 and 1309 *et seq.*, nos. 2577 and 2626 *et seq.*

unfortunate absence of any reference to the purpose of the infringed norm. At present, Article 1184 para 2 *in fine* states that the contract is maintained when the purpose of the infringed norm requires so.

13. Notwithstanding that welcome addition, a second point of critique is not dealt with by the *ordonnance*. Like in the *Projet d'ordonnance*, the nullity of a term will only entail the nullity of the entire contract if the term affected by nullity was 'decisive' ('*déterminant*') for the commitment of the parties. French scholars interpret that criterion as purely voluntarist or psychological[53] and focus of the intention of the parties to determine the extent of nullity. Nullity will affect the entire contract if the affected term has been the impulsive and determining condition for at least one party to enter into the agreement.[54] That reference to the 'intention' of the parties obfuscates the normative nature of the decision a judge has to take to determine the extent of nullity. What parties really agreed upon, was the (null) contract. What they would have agreed upon if they knew about the ground of nullity has never actually been agreed upon. Denying the actual powers of judges in this matter inhibits a proper understanding of the source, guiding principles, and limits of those powers. In my opinion, the debate on partial nullity can only benefit from recognising the normative task judges have in this matter. Thus, a criterion focusing on the different interests of all related parties seems preferable to a criterion that stresses the subjective intention of the parties.[55]

3.3.2. Scope

14. Another questionable choice can be found in the scope of Article 1184. The aforementioned article only regulates the situation where the ground of avoidance affects one or more terms of the contract. Unfortunately, it does not extend that approach to situations where the ground of avoidance only requires that some consequences of a single term are not recognised by the legal order. Yet, the restriction of nullity in those situations is an established practice in current French positive law.[56] Perhaps one might argue that an extension of the scope of Article 1185 is superfluous, since an analogous application of Article 1184 could suffice. Although such an application *per analogiam* might indeed lead to a just solution in a particular case,[57] an extension of that article's

53 See e.g. Serinet, "Observations", *Petites Affiches* 2015, (59) II – "Sur art. 1185".

54 Ghestin et al. (n 4), 1254, no. 2584 and the references therein.

55 In the same vein for Belgium, see e.g. Tanghe, *Gedeeltelijke ontbinding en vernietiging van overeenkomsten* (Intersentia 2015), 225, no. 212. *Cf.* Article II.-7:214 DCFR: "*If a ground of avoidance under this Section affects only particular terms of a contract, the effect of an avoidance is limited to those terms unless, giving due consideration to all the circumstances of the case, it is unreasonable to uphold the remaining contract.*"

56 See Flour et al. (n 19), 377–8, no. 360; Ghestin et al. (n 4), 1363 *et seq.*, no. 2675 *et seq.*

57 In Germany, the prevalent opinion considers §139 BGB (partial nullity) to be applicable *per analogiam* to those situations. See e.g. Busche, 'BGB §139 Teilnichtigkeit', in Säcker (ed.), *Münchener Kommentar zum Bürgerlichen Gesetzbuch* (Beck 2012), no. 26; Dorn, '§§139–141. Nichtigkeit II', in Schmoeckel/Rückert/Zimmermann (eds.), *Historisch-kritischer Kommentar zum BGB*, I, *Allgemeiner Teil §§1–240* (Mohr Siebeck 2003), (753) 768, no. 16; Roth, '§139 Teilnichtigkeit', in Habermann (ed.), *J. von*

scope could only be beneficial for the accessibility and intelligibility of the *ordonnance*. Furthermore, the consequences that Article 1184 gives rise to seem unnecessarily limited. The current wording of Article 1184 suggests that the only alternative for the nullity of an entire act is to be found in the nullity of one or more terms. So, contrary to for example the Dutch civil code[58] and the German *BGB*[59], Article 1184 does not provide for the possibility to convert a null contract in another, valid contract of a different type ('conversion'). Since the concepts of partial nullity, reduction, and conversion are in essence only specific applications of a more fundamental principle favouring juridical acts (*favor negotii*),[60] the *ordonnance* misses out on the opportunity to codify those three concepts in one encompassing provision.[61] Such a single article would not only be a fundamental progression compared to the *Code civil*, it would also prevent futile discussions relating to the (merely pedagogical) differences between partial nullity, reduction, and conversion.[62]

4. The use of nullity

15. Throughout the *ordonnance* numerous articles decree the nullity of a contract if it does not comply with specific requirements, these are requirements that are generally not imposed for the validity of contracts (Article 1128). The following part will give a

Staudingers Kommentar zum Bürgerlichen Gesetzbuch: Staudinger BGB - Buch 1: Allgemeiner Teil - §§139–163 (Sellier 2010), no. 68. *Contra* Flume, *Allgemeiner Teil des Bürgerlichen Rechts*, II, *Das Rechtsgeschäft* (Springer 1965), 574, §32, no. 2, littera d).

58 Article 3:42 DCC: "*When the necessary implications of an invalid juridical act are in conformity with those of another - valid - juridical act and this in such a degree that it is presumable that this other juridical act would have been chosen instead of the invalid one if the acting party or parties would have been aware of the invalidity of the latter act, then this invalid juridical act shall be converted by operation of law into that other valid juridical act with all its normal legal effects, unless such a conversion would be unreasonable towards an interested person who has not participated as a party in the involved juridical act.*"

59 §140 BGB: "*If a void juridical act fulfils the requirements of another juridical act, then the latter is deemed to have been entered into, if it may be assumed that its validity would be intended if there were knowledge of the invalidity*".

60 That principle is well known in Italy and Spain. See e.g. (for Italy) Grasetti, 'Conservazione (principio di)', in *Enciclopedia del diritto*, IX (Giuffrè 1961), 173–5; Marseglia, *La conservazione degli effetti negoziali tra principi e clausole generale* (Università degli Studi di Trento 2010), 68 p; (for Spain) Delgado Echeverría/Parra Lucan, *Las nulidades de los contratos* (Dykinson 2005), 215 *et seq.*; Marín Padilla, *El principio general de conservación de los actos y negocios jurídicos - "utile per inutile non vitiatur"* (Bosch 1990); Serrano Acitores, 'El principio de conservación de los contratos frente a las figuras de la nulidad y la anulabilidad', *Noticias Jurídicas* 2010. Moreover, the *Principes directeurs du droit européen du contrat* and the DCFR explicitly mention that principle as a guiding principle for those projects. For the *Principes Directeurs*, see Article 0:204 and Fauvarque-Cosson/Mazeaud (eds.), *European Contract Law - Materials for a Common Frame of Reference: Terminology, Guiding Principles, Model Rules* (sellier 2008), 496–514; for the DCFR, see von Bar et al. (eds.) (n 27), 62.

61 In favour of such a general provision favouring juridical acts, see e.g. Van Schaick, *Contractsvrijheid en nietigheid* (Tjeenk Willink 1994), 279, no. 5.

62 *Cf.* Flume (n 57), §32, no. 9, littera a): "*Die Abgrenzung des §139* [partial nullity] *und des §140* [conversion] *stellt kein wesentliches Problem dar, weil die Regelung grundsätzlich die gleiche ist.*"

brief outlook on how the *ordonnance* utilises nullity as a remedy for contracts that infringe particular rules. The *ordonnance*'s use of nullity is comparable to the way it treats fundamental aspects of the concept of nullity, analysed in the previous part. Although nullity is generally used in concordance with the prevalent views in French scholarship, that remedy seems disproportionate in some situations. In contrast, inopposability is used on other occasions where nullity would seem more appropriate. In other words: on the one hand, there are too many applications of nullity (4.1); on the other hand, nullity is not used enough (4.2). The following critical remarks take nothing away from the merits of the *ordonnance* in opting for nullity as the applicable remedy for for example defects of consent (Articles 1129–1144), incapacity (Articles 1145–1152), and the violation of formal requirements (Article 1172 para 2).[63]

4.1. Too much nullity

16. Just like any other remedy, nullity should only be used when it is a proportionate reaction to the infringement of a norm. The severe consequences nullity entails are among the elements that need to be taken into account. In general, a null contract does not produce the desired legal effects. That drastic result signifies among other things that the parties to the contract are not protected for their expectation ('positive') interest, but only for their reliance ('negative') interest. Consequently, the decision to deny parties a protection equal to their expectation interest must be necessary in order to attain the goal of the infringed rule. If that goal can be achieved by means of less intrusive, but equally effective remedies, then those remedies must be preferred to nullity.

17. In Article 1123, Article 1124 para 3, and Article 1202, the *ordonnance* seems to use nullity in cases where the less intrusive remedy of inopposability is available. According to Article 1124 para 3, a contract that violates a unilateral promise is null if the third party with whom it was concluded, was aware of the unilateral promise. If that third party did not act with the sole intention to harm the promisee, nullity seems disproportionate. In most situations, the interests of the harmed promisee are equally protected by a mere inopposability. The difference can be found in the position of the third party: when the contract is null, the third party can only claim reliance damages, whereas he might be able to claim expectation damages if the contract is only 'inopposable' to the promisee. In the latter case, the contract with the third party remains valid *inter partes.* A similar remark can be made with regard to Article 1123. That article offers the beneficiary of a pre-emption agreement the right to invoke the nullity of a contract that infringes his right if the third party with whom the contract was concluded, was aware of his right. Again, in order to protect the beneficiary, a simple inopposability would suffice. There does not seem any reason to deny the third party the possibility to claim expectation damages in all circumstances. The same holds true for Article 1202. That provision, that has no equivalent in the previous projects, provides for the nullity of

63 Certainly concerning the latter, nullity can only be regarded as an adequate remedy if an automatic nullity is admitted.

contracts which aim for example to conceal a part of the price in a sale of immovable property. Also in respect to that article, nullity does not seem required. Why should a party to such an agreement have the possibility to withdraw from the agreement without any cost? In my opinion, the infringed tax norm could be enforced more effectively, more efficiently, and more proportionately by recovering the evaded tax and supplementary fines.[64]

4.2. *Not enough nullity*

18. A remarkable feat of the *ordonnance* is that it seems to confuse nullity and inopposability also the other way around. Article 1156 states that the contract concluded by an unauthorised representative is 'inopposable' to the principal. Yet, in this case, since the contract is in reality concluded between the principal and the third party, nullity is more appropriate – on the condition that an automatic nullity would be admitted. If a contract has no effects *vis-à-vis* the parties who concluded the contract, that contract is traditionally deemed 'null' in French law, and not merely 'inopposable' to those parties (or one of them).

5. The enforcement of nullity

19. For the purpose of this part, the 'enforcement' of nullity can be described as the pathway that needs to be followed in order for a juridical act to lack (this is to not produce) the intended legal effects. In general, three methods of enforcement are available. First, the legal order can automatically – *ipso iure* – not recognise the intended legal effects. In this case, the juridical act will not produce legal effects by force of law, thus without requiring any particular intervention. Second, a judicial intervention can be required. As long as nullity has not been decreed by a judge, the invalid juridical act still produces its legal effects. Third, nullity can be enforced via a unilateral, extrajudicial notification. It is sufficient that the authorised party declares to the other party that it relies on the nullity of the act, for the act to be deprived of its intended effects.

20. This part will investigate what types of enforcement are recognised in the French *ordonnance*. Although the explicit choice for the obligatory judicial intervention is shared by a majority of contemporary scholarship, the rejection of the two other possibilities is criticisable (5.1). Yet, the way nullity can be enforced does not tell anything about the circumstances that determine whether or not nullity can still be enforced in a particular situation. It might be possible that nullity must be invoked within a specified period of time, or that certain behaviour can preclude a party from relying on nullity. Therefore, the obstacles to the enforcement of nullity (prescription, confirmation, and regularisation) will be analysed as well (5.2).

64 For a similar position, see Court of Appeal Ghent 29 January 2013, *Nieuw Juridisch Weekblad* 2014, 357. *Cf.* Court of Appeal Ghent 7 October 2014, *Fiscoloog* 2015, 13.

5.1. *Judicial enforcement*

5.1.1. Principle

21. Confirming yet again the prevalent view in scholarship[65] but unlike other legal systems,[66] the *ordonnance* clings on to the necessity of a judicial intervention in order to deprive a contract of its intended effects. In comparison to the previous projects, the judicial enforcement of nullity is even more prominently present in the *ordonnance*. Whereas the requirement of a judgment was mentioned in one of the last articles on nullity in earlier projects, the *ordonnance* boilerplates it in the very first one.

In French legal literature, the most prominent[67] characteristic of the judicial enforcement of nullity is that an action in nullity is required for nullity to deprive a contract of its effects. That action must be introduced within five years after the conclusion of the contract.[68] When five years have passed, the contract cannot be avoided anymore. Nevertheless, a party allowed to invoke nullity can still invoke nullity as a defence. That so-called 'exception of nullity' is not subject to prescription and can be invoked *ad aeternam*, as long as the contract has not been performed (Article 1185).[69]

5.1.2. Criticism

22. The *ordonnance's* view does not leave room for a nullity which operates *ipso iure* and does not provide for the possibility to avoid a contract by unilateral notification. Both those consequences can be challenged: is it really justified to impose a judicial procedure for each and every nullity? First, the negation of an automatic nullity will be questioned; second, the choice to exclude a unilateral notification will be scrutinised.

23. Regarding the absence of an *ipso iure* enforcement, the following two objections can be raised.

First, this view obliges to create other, superfluous remedies in order to make up for the shortcomings of the 'judicial nullity'. The undebatable necessity of a judgment has resulted in the emergence of a 'different' and 'independent' remedy, by which clauses are

65 See Flour et al. (n 19), 341 *et seq.*, no. 332 *et seq.*; Ghestin et al. (n 4), 995 *et seq.*, no. 2286 *et seq.*; Picod (n 2), no. 31; Terré et al. (n 14), 437 *et seq.*, no. 390 *et seq.*

66 See e.g. the Dutch (Article 3:49 *et seq.* DCC) and German (§143 BGB) legal systems and the DCFR (Article II.-7:209).

67 Another characteristic relates to the constitutive nature of the judgment pronouncing nullity: Ghestin et al. (n 4), 1320, no. 2631; Gout, *Le juge et l'annulation du contrat* (Presses universitaires d'Aix-Marseille 1999), 95–96, no. 122. For criticism, see Flour et al. (n 19), 337, no. 329.

68 Article 2224 *Code civil*, as interpreted by the majority of French scholarship. See e.g. Flour et al. (n 19), 338, no. 331; Ghestin et al. (n 4), 1182 *et seq.*, no. 2519 *et seq.*; Picod (n 2), no. 63; Terré et al. (n 14), 109, no. 81.

69 See Flour et al. (n 19), 369 *et seq.*, no. 356 *et seq.*; Ghestin et al. (n 4), 1220 *et seq*, no. 2542 *et seq.*; Picod (n 2), no. 76; Terré et al. (n 14), 458 *et seq.*, no. 417 *et seq.*

'deemed unwritten' (*"réputée non écrite"*).[70, 71] In contrast to a clause which is 'null', a clause which is 'deemed unwritten' does not require a judicial intervention in order to be deprived of its effects. A possible judgment will only have a declaratory effect: the judgment will only investigate whether all requirements are fulfilled, and if that is the case, it will conclude that the clause has never produced any effect whatsoever. The most important difference with a 'judicial nullity' is to be found in the unlimited period of time a party can invoke that a clause is deemed unwritten. Even when the contract has been concluded for example twenty years ago, a party can still rely on the protection offered by that remedy. If the *ordonnance* had recognised the automatic enforcement of nullity, the same would have been true for nullity. Consequently, there would not have been any need to use the superfluous '*réputée non écrite*'.

Second, the refusal to acknowledge the existence of an automatically enforced nullity could be attributed to an imprecise analysis of the 'action in nullity' (*"action en nullité"*). Presently, the majoritarian view does not distinguish between a declaratory action to assess the nullity of an act (which is not subject to any prescription) and the constitutive action in restitution (which, in contrast, is subject to prescription). Yet, such a distinction could clarify that a judicial intervention is not required to deprive an act of its effects, but only to allow a subsequent restitutionary claim.[72] By ossifying the judicial nature of nullity, the aforementioned distinction might be overlooked.

24. In the same vein, there are at least four reasons why the impossibility to avoid a contract by notification should be reconsidered.[73]

First, the arguments in favour of an obligatory judicial intervention fail to convince. According to Simler, who wrote the explanatory statement of the *Avant-Projet Catala* concerning nullity, it seems more just to impose the initiative on the person who invokes nullity, rather than on the person who contests the nullity of the juridical act.[74] In my opinion, the grounds of invalidity are too diverse to justify such a general statement. Is it

70 On the relative autonomy of that remedy, see for example Ghestin et al. (n 4), 1318–21, no. 2631; Sadi (n 4), 597–604, nos. 513–22.

71 In the *ordonnance*, the 'réputée non écrite' is used in Articles 1170, 1184 para 2, 1231–5, and 1343–5.

72 In the same vein Hamelin, 'Le caractère judiciaire de la nullité à l'heure de la réforme du droit des contrats', *Petites affiches* 2014, issue 245, 4 *et seq*, no. 44 *et seq*. *Cf.* Posez (n 3), 647 *et seq*.; Sacco/De Nova, *Il Contratto*, II (UTET 1993), 483–4.

73 Various French authors raise similar objections. See Rezgui, 'L'annulation unilatérale du contrat', *Petites affiches* 2009, issue 130, 6 *et seq*.; Sadi (n 4), 586–91, nos. 498–506; Sautonie-Laguionie, 'Le rôle du juge et des parties dans l'anéantissement du contrat en droit français', *Revue des contrats* 2013, issue 4, 1643 *et seq*. For a recent PhD thesis related to this topic, see Jaouen, *La sanction prononcée par les parties au contrat* (Economica 2013).

74 Simler, 'Exposé des motifs – Sanctions (Articles 1129 à 1133)', in *Avant-Projet de réforme du droit des obligations* (n 7), (44) 45: *"A été écartée, au contraire, la possibilité d'une annulation unilatérale qui serait simplement notifiée à l'autre partie, celle-ci ayant alors la faculté de la contester. Une telle solution est proposée pour la résolution (Article 1158). Dès lors que la nullité n'a pas pu faire l'objet du constat mutuel ci-dessus évoqué, le contentieux est inévitable et il paraît alors plus juste d'en imposer l'initiative à celui qui demande la nullité qu'à celui qui la conteste."*. *Inter alia* Houtcieff shares his opinion: see 'Les sanctions des règles de formation des contrats', in Terré (ed.), *Pour une réforme du droit des contrats* (Dalloz 2009), (223) 228, no. 10).

really an equitable solution to impose a duty to start judicial proceedings on for example the victim of duress in order to deprive the contract of its binding effects? In reality, in remains unclear what reasons can justify such a solution.

Second, the obligatory judicial intervention seems incoherent. Why can a party opt for the validity of a null contract by an extrajudicial confirmation,[75] but not for the nullity of such a contract by a comparable notification?[76] If the *ordonnance* had made the aforementioned distinction between 'nullity' and 'restitution', it would have been clear that the recognition of an extrajudicial confirmation should be accompanied by the possibility to opt for the nullity of a contract by means of a (extrajudicial) notification.

Third, the *ordonnance* appears to make an unjustified distinction between nullity and termination for fundamental non-performance. In contrast to nullity, termination can be provoked by a unilateral notification (Article 1224 *et seq.*). Yet, it is difficult to see why a judicial intervention is intricately woven in the French conception of nullity, but not in the concept of termination.[77] Since judges have a large margin of appreciation when considering the opportunity of terminating the contract,[78] it would be more comprehensible if termination by notice was excluded.

Finally, in the actual proposition, excluding the possibility to avoid a contract by notification leads to undesirable effects. The *ordonnance* excludes avoidance by notice, but contains a peculiar rule which allows a party to impose a burden on the party entitled to avoid the contract (Article 1183).[79] According to that provision, a party is allowed to impose a choice on the party entitled to avoid the contract between the confirmation of the contract and the judicial avoidance of the contract. If the latter party does not start proceedings to annul the contract in the first six months after the other party has imposed that choice, the contract is deemed confirmed. Under the current proposition, the contract is deemed confirmed if the party entitled to avoid nullity does not start judicial proceedings within six months, even if that party has notified its intention to opt for nullity within that period. Otherwise, such a notification could have been analysed as an extrajudicial nullity. The project has not clarified why a timely notification of the choice to rely on nullity cannot suffice. Instead, a party entitled to nullity is now obliged to commence judicial proceedings in order to maintain its protection, although a simple notification seems equally effective. It does not come as a surprise that the Dutch civil code and the *Projet Terré*, which contain a similar option to impose a burden of choice in Article 3:55 para 2 and Article 83, only require a 'choice'. It is by no means necessary that the party which is entitled to nullity commences judicial proceedings in the system of the Dutch civil code or the *Projet Terré*. The additional requirement in the *ordonnance* to commence such proceedings does not seem justified; it is rather a cumbersome and superfluous burden.

75 See Articles 1182–1183.

76 See Sadi (n 4), 588, no. 502: "*De même, puisque la confirmation d'un acte peut avoir lieu par acte unilatéral, il serait logique que, par symétrie, il en soit de même pour l'annulation.*"

77 See Sadi (n 4), 588, no. 502: "*Or on voit mal en quoi la nullité est plus judiciaire que la résolution.*"

78 See *supra*, 3.1.

79 A comparable rule was proposed by the *Avant-Projet Catala* (Article 1129–5).

5.2. *Obstacles to the enforcement of nullity*

5.2.1. Prescription

25. In the *ordonnance*, no provision explicitly deals with the prescription of the so-called 'action in nullity'. In contrast, earlier projects contained a specific article on the prescription of that action.[80] The absence of a similar provision can be explained by the enactment of the Statute of 17 June 2008 on prescription.[81] Since scholarship accepts that the modified Article 2224 *Code civil* also imposes a five year time limit on each and every nullity,[82] a similar provision in the *ordonnance* would be excessive. Again, a more precise analysis of the action in nullity could nuance the prescription of the 'action in nullity'. With regard to a purely declaratory action to ascertain whether the discussed act is null or not, a time limit does not seem justified. In contrast, when the action in nullity must be regarded as a restitutionary action, the presence of a time limit is understandable.[83]

26. Notwithstanding the modification of the applicable time limits, the aforementioned Statute has not regulated the so-called 'exception of nullity'. According to French tradition, as long as the contract has not been executed, a party can still invoke nullity as an exception even if the time limit has expired.[84] Contrary to the previous *Projet d'ordonnance*, the *ordonnance* does mention that specific rule (Article 1185) – just like earlier projects.[85]

5.2.2. Confirmation

27. A second possible obstacle to enforce nullity can be found in the confirmation of the null contract. One of the novelties in the *ordonnance* with regard to confirmation is its definition: Article 1182 para 1 describes confirmation as an act by which a person entitled to invoke nullity renounces that right.[86] Like the *Code civil*[87], the *Avant-Projet Catala* and the *Projet Terré* did not contain a description of the notion of 'confirmation', or were at least less clear.[88-89] Apart from that definition, the article on confirmation can be regarded as a step backwards compared to Article 1338 *Code civil.*

80 *Avant-Projet Catala*: Article 1130 para 1; *Projet Terré*: Article 84 para 1; *Projet de la Chancellerie*: Article 97 para 1.

81 *Loi n° 2008-561 du 17 juin 2008 portant réforme de la prescription en matière civile.*

82 See 5.1.1 and the references in n 67.

83 *Cf.* Hamelin (n 72), no. 42 *et seq.*

84 See the references in n 68.

85 The three previous projects did contain a provision dedicated to the 'exception of nullity': *Avant-Projet Catala*: Article 1130 para 2; *Projet Terré*: Article 84 para 2; *Projet de la Chancellerie*: Article 97 para 2.

86 For a comparable definition, see Article 94 para 1 *Projet de la Chancellerie.*

87 Article 1338 *Code civil.*

88 The *Avant-projet Catala* did not define 'confirmation' in Article 1129–4, and the *Projet Terré* was more ambiguous in its Article 81 *et seq.*

89 See Wicker/Boucard, 'Les sanctions relatives à la formation du contrat', *JCP G* 2015, (32) no. 11.

First, it does not mention the concept of 'ratification' anymore, although that notion is still used throughout the project.[90] Consequently, one could be persuaded to think that confirmation and ratification are completely separate concepts, whereas Article 1338 *Code civil* demonstrates that they are quintessentially the same. They produce the same legal effect, this is the loss of the possibility to rely on nullity as a defence. It is hard to understand why one – and only one – of those concepts has been defined.

Second, in line with other articles concerning nullity, Article 1182 para 3 is an oversimplification.[91] According to the *ordonnance*, the voluntary performance of the contract amounts to confirmation if the performing party is aware of the ground of invalidity.[92] An exception is recognised in the following phrase of the article: in the case of duress, confirmation can only take place after the duress has ceased. It seems to limit grounds of invalidity to defects of consent, thus equating the awareness of a ground of invalidity with its cessation. That might be correct for duress, but not for for example incapacity. The awareness of an incapable party of its incapacity does not imply that its incapacity has suddenly ceased. A minor can be perfectly aware of its incapacity, but that realisation does not influence his incapacity. Consequently, a voluntary performance of a minor should not result in confirmation, contrary to what Article 1182 para 3 suggests. In this respect, Article 1338 (para 2) *Code civil* is more refined: in present-day French law, voluntary performance only entails confirmation if it takes place at a time when the obligation could be validly confirmed or ratified.[93]

5.2.3. Regularisation?

28. A third obstacle for the avoidance of a contract lies in the so-called regularisation. Ever since the ground-breaking thesis of Dupeyron[94], French scholars have debated the precise content of that notion.[95] According to Ghestin, Loiseau, and Serinet, regularisation can be defined as a juridical act, which is not regulatory nor legislative, which validates, retroactively and *vis-à-vis* everyone, an act that was initially null by adding the element, objective or subjective, which the act initially lacked.[96] Regularisation occurs for example when a party offers to repair the disadvantageous effects of the voidable act and results in the loss of the possibility to invoke nullity. Contrary to the *Code civil*, which does not recognise that concept, the *Projet d'ordonnance* made one specific application in Article 1183 para 2. According to that rule, in case of mistake, a party cannot invoke

90 See for example Articles 1156 para 3; 1161 para 2; 1204 para 3; 1301–3 and 1342–2 para 2.

91 See Wicker/Boucard (n 89), no. 13.

92 Article 1182 para 3.

93 "*A défaut d'acte de confirmation ou ratification, il suffit que l'obligation soit exécutée volontairement après l'époque à laquelle l'obligation pouvait être valablement confirmée ou ratifiée.*" *Cf.* Article II.-7:211 DCFR: "*If a party who is entitled to avoid a contract under this Section confirms it, expressly or impliedly, after the period of time for giving notice of avoidance has begun to run, avoidance is excluded.*".

94 Dupeyron, *La régularisation des actes nuls* (LGDJ 1973).

95 For an overview, see Ghestin et al. (n 4), 1053–71, nos. 2364–83; Picod (n 2), nos. 54–60.

96 Ghestin et al. (n 4), 1071, no. 2383: "*La régularisation se définit comme un acte juridique, ni réglementaire, ni législatif, qui valide, rétroactivement et à l'égard de tous, un acte initialement nul, en lui apportant l'élément, objectif ou subjectif, qui lui faisait défaut*".

nullity anymore when the other party has offered to perform the contract the way the mistaken party has understood the contract. Both the scope and the choice to codify that rule in Article 1183 can be criticised.

Regarding the scope, it remained vague why the project did not contain a more general provision concerning regularisation.[97] In contrast, the previous *Projet Terré* explicitly recognised that notion independent from confirmation and proposed the following, general Article 90: "*Sauf disposition légale contraire, la régularisation restitue son plein effet à un contrat par la suppression de l'imperfection qui l'affecte ou par l'accomplissement de la formalité requise.*"[98] Although the primary use of the article might be found in cases of mistake, it seems too radical to suppose that regularisation cannot play a role in other situations. If the disadvantageous effects caused by a ground of invalidity other than mistake are repaired by an offer made by the other party, why should the party entitled to invoke nullity still be able to invoke nullity?

A second debatable choice was the insertion of that rule in Article 1183 of the *Projet*. Since it was proposed as para 2 in that article, it might seem that the time limit of six months mentioned in paras 1 and 3 also applied to regularisation. In other words, the party entitled to invoke nullity might seem to have six months time to refuse the repairing offer. However, if the offer repairs the disadvantageous effects, a choice to refuse the offer seems unjustified.[99]

Hence, it does not come as a surprise that the *ordonnance* has struck out Article 1183 para 2. Yet, that does not imply that the notion of regularisation has been completely abandoned. Contrary to the *Projet d'ordonnance*, the *ordonnance* provides for the possibility to regularise contracts which are null due to the violation of a formal requirement (Article 1172 para 2). Unfortunately, the *ordonnance* remains cryptic regarding that possibility and does not clarify in what circumstances a regularisation could take place.

6. General appreciation

6.1. A textbook example of Begriffsjurisprudenz

29. In my opinion, the most fundamental critique with regard to the *ordonnance*'s rules on nullity can be found its lack of fastidiousness. The proposed set of rules concerning nullity reveals that the drafters had a stunningly narrow scope of cases in mind when drafting the rules, thereby denying the complexity of real-life situations. It seems only the easiest and least challenging situations have been taken into account.

97 The Dutch civil code, which only recognises a comparable rule to Article 1183 para 2 of the *Projet* for mistake and undue influence, has also been criticised for not containing a more general provision. See e.g. Hijma, *Nietigheid en vernietigbaarheid van rechtshandelingen* (Kluwer 1988), 188 *et seq*. Similarly, the DCFR offers the possibility to adapt the contract in case of mistake (Article II.-7:203) and unfair exploitation (Article II.-7:207).

98 "*Unless a statutory rule provides otherwise, the regularisation restitutes the full effect to a contract either by suppressing the imperfection that affected the contract or by fulfilling the required formality.*"

99 *Cf.* Wicker/Boucard (n 89), no. 17.

More problematic cases appear undervalued and dismissed as irrelevant exceptions to a beautiful and coherent system. Yet, in my opinion, such hard cases must not merely stand on equal footing with less defiant cases; they must be at the centre of attention when drafting a normative framework. The ability of a code to resist the ravages of time depends on it. There are only two solutions for hard cases when a newly elaborated code does not pay sufficient attention to them: one can either apply the rule as it is narrowly conceived, or give an extensive interpretation to the rule. None of those solutions are suitable. The first one will not provide for an adequate solution of hard cases; the second one will frustrate the aim of the *ordonnance* (that is – among other things – to modernise, ameliorate the legibility and the accessibility of the general law of contracts and obligations, and guarantee legal certainty and the efficacy of legal norms) since the legal practice will inevitably differ from the black letter rule. In other words: the preference of the *ordonnance* for concepts over interests is a dubious legislative choice.

30. The lack of fastidiousness also underlies the formal presentation of the discussed rules. One might say that Articles 1178–85 rather resemble a summary of a legal handbook than a codification. Due to the didactical aim of legal handbooks, a certain simplification is comprehensible: if an introduction to nullity would incorporate all nuances, readers (for example students) might not be able to acquire a sufficient insight in the basic structures. In my opinion, a codification must not focus on didactics, but predominantly on a well-balanced and insightful solution for possible problems. In that respect, scholarly definitions and distinctions might guide those solutions, but must not be confused with the solutions themselves.

By confusing the aim of handbooks with the aim of a codification, the proposed regulation regarding nullities is useless at best, harmful at worst. It is useless, since its content mainly[100] corresponds to the prevalent views in French legal literature. What is the use of a codification if it only restates what the dominant authors in French law already agree upon? But more importantly, the proposed regulation could, to a certain extent, frustrate its aim. As shown before, the concept, use, and enforcement of nullity in the *ordonnance* is not entirely reconcilable with the necessity to provide for a solution for hard cases: either the *ordonnance* does not enable an adequate solution, or the legal practice differs considerably from the black letter rule.

6.2. *Are there any lessons for Belgium and the Netherlands?*

31. Presently, Belgian law still uses the same black letter rules concerning nullity as French law. Nullity is not regulated in a general and comprising way, though some scarce (and unclear) provisions are present in the Belgian *Code civil*. If an overarching framework is deemed necessary, the *ordonnance* does not offer much suitable inspiration. In contrast, the *ordonnance* can be regarded as an unequivocal *caveat* for a future Belgian

100 One could mention Article 1183 as an exception. Yet, a similar result could presently be obtained by a specific use of the requirement of good faith and fair dealing.

revision.[101] The rather unfortunate draft of a general theory of nullity can warn Belgian drafters to avoid mistaking a summary of a legal handbook for a solid black letter codification. Since the *ordonnance*'s approach to regulating nullity should be reconsidered, a future revision of the Belgian *Code civil* must take a cautious approach and pay sufficient attention to the fundamental mechanisms determining equitable solutions when dealing with nullity.

32. Similarly, the answer to the question whether the *ordonnance* can be useful for the current Dutch approach is rather disappointing. Contrary to the *ordonnance*, the Dutch civil code has indeed (to some extent) reconsidered the concept, use, and enforcement of nullity, thus introducing regulation that is probably much more able to resist the ravages of time. In fact, it remains puzzling why none of the different French projects has considered using the Dutch civil code as a starting point, at least with respect of nullity. The actual provisions of the *ordonnance* do not seem able to suggest any amelioration of the current Dutch law. The concept of nullity (Article 3:40 DCC), however imperfect and criticisable it may be,[102] is still more suitable than Article 1178. The same holds true for the use and enforcement of nullity. Although the concept of '*relatieve nietigheid*' (used in for example Article 3:45 DCC) is less refined in my opinion than the French and Belgian concept of '*inopposabilité*', the Dutch civil code seems to use nullity in general more appropriately than the *ordonnance*. The Dutch civil code does not contain for example a similar provision to Articles 1123, 1124 para 3, or 1203.[103] With regard to the enforcement of nullity, the Dutch civil code recognises an automatic – *ipso iure* – nullity (for example Article 3:39–40 DCC) and allows avoidance by notification (Article 3:49 *et seq.* DCC). Contrary to the *ordonnance*, Article 3:54 DCC provides for a (more)[104] general provision allowing a party to regularise the voidable act by offering to repair its disadvantageous effects. Since Article 3:49 DCC recognises the possibility to avoid a juridical act by a

[101] Recently, the Policy Paper of the Ministry of Justice has announced the plan to reform certain parts of the Belgian *Code civil*: see Chambre of Representatives 2015–16, www.dekamer.be/FLWB/PDF/54/1428/54K1428008.pdf. See also Dirix/Wéry, 'Tijd voor een hercodificatie van het Burgerlijk Wetboek', *Rechtskundig Weekblad* 2015–16, 2.

[102] For an overview of the content and interpretation of Article 3:40 DCC, see Hartkamp/Sieburgh, *Verbintenissenrecht – Algemeen overeenkomstenrecht* in *Mr. C. Asser's Handleiding tot de beoefening van het Nederlands Burgerlijk Recht*, 6-III (Kluwer 2014), nos. 310–346; Hijma/van Dam/van Schendel/Valk, *Rechtshandeling en Overeenkomst* (Kluwer 2013), nos. 147–158. For a critical appreciation, see e.g. Hartkamp/Sieburgh (this note), nos. 347–347g; Hijma *et al.*(this note), no. 148: according to van Dam, "*de regeling van art. 3:40* [is] *geen schoolvoorbeeld van eenvoud. Het belangrijkste onderdeel van deze bepaling – de regeling van de rechtshandeling in strijd met de wet – spant in dit opzicht de kroon en kan worden beschouwd als één van de lelijkste eendjes van het BW.*" ("*The regulation of Article 3:40 is not a prime example of simplicity. The most important part of this provision – the regulation of the juridical act contrary to the law – takes in this regard the cake and can be regarded as one of the most ugly ducklings of the Dutch civil code*").

[103] For a brief presentation of those provisions, see *supra* 4.1.

[104] Article 3:54 DCC only regards abuse of circumstances. Article 6:230 DCC contains a similar rule for error. The limited scope of the possibility to regularise juridical acts this way has been criticised by e.g. Hijma (n 97), 188 *et seq.*

unilateral notification, the last point of criticism regarding Article 1183[105] does not apply to Dutch law.

7. Conclusion

33. This article has scrutinised whether the *ordonnance* has grasped the opportunity to boldly go where the *Code civil* has not gone before and to design a general framework for nullity.

In Article 1178–85, the *ordonnance* has indeed grasped the opportunity: in those articles, the *ordonnance* makes explicit choices regarding the concept of nullity and its enforcement (and obstacles) that were not made in the *Code civil*. However, that pronounced approach is not satisfactory. Several arguments plead against the proposed concept, use, and enforcement of nullity. Those points of criticism boil down to one single underlying objection regarding the chosen approach. Throughout the *ordonnance*, the articles related to nullity demonstrate the *ordonnance*'s preference of concepts over interests. The *ordonnance* seems more concerned with the recognition of French legal concepts (such as the distinction between absolute and relative nullity and the indispensable judicial intervention for nullity to have effect) than with a comprising, balanced, and transparent regulation of conflicting interests. In this regard, the analysed articles might even be considered as a textbook example of *Begriffsjurisprudenz*.[106] The articles on nullity have become the prisoner of artificial categorisation, itself the result of unsatisfactory distinctions: between judicial nullity and automatic '*réputée non écrite*', and between unconfirmable absolute nullity and confirmable relative nullity.[107] The lack of fastidiousness will either lead to a strict interpretation of the proposed provisions, thereby inhibiting an adequate solution, or to an extensive interpretation or application *in analogiam* of the available articles, thus frustrating the *ordonnance*'s goal to improve legal certainty and to make the general law of contracts and obligations more accessible and legible. Due to the debatable oversimplification in the proposition, the main lesson for Belgian law can only be that future drafters should be very cautious in designing a general framework, certainly if such a framework was deemed too controversial by the drafters of the *Code civil*. The French choice to mainly codify widely accepted doctrinal analyses precludes any progress in comparison to the regulation of nullity in the Dutch civil code. Consequently, with regard to nullity, the *ordonnance* does not offer any

105 See *supra* 5.1.2.

106 See von Jhering, *Scherz und Ernst in der Jurisprudenz* (Breikopf und Härtel 1904), 347: With Begriffsjurisprudenz is meant "*jene Verirrung unserer heutigen Jurisprudenz (...), welche, den praktischen Endzweck und die Bedingungen der Anwendbarkeit des Rechts außer Acht lassend, in demselben nur einen Gegenstand erblickt, an dem das sich selber überlassene, seinen Reiz und Zweck in sich selber tragende logische Denken sich erproben kann, – eine Arena für logische Evolutionen, für die Gymnastik des Geistes, in der dem größten Denkvirtuosen die Palme zufällt.*".

107 Paraphrase of the majority judgment in Cavendish Square Holding BV v Talal El Makdessi (Rev 3) [2015] UKSC 67, para 31, relating to the penalty rule: "*In our opinion, the law relating to penalties has become the prisoner of artificial categorisation, itself the result of unsatisfactory distinctions: between a penalty and genuine pre-estimate of loss, and between a genuine pre-estimate of loss and a deterrent.*"

innovation whatsoever for the further development of Dutch law. In general, the doctrinal French approach seems too self-contained and regards itself too much as an unparalleled expression of a specific legal culture, to serve as a fruitful basis for future codifications, at least concerning the remedies for invalid juridical acts.

Candida Leone*

A TALE OF NOVELTY AND CONTINUITY: EXPLORING THE FUTURE JUDICIAL CONTROL OF EMPLOYMENT CONTRACTS IN THE FRENCH CONTRACT LAW REFORM

1. Introduction

1. The reform of the law of obligations recently approved by the French government[1] introduces a *general* remedy against "significantly imbalanced" terms in non-negotiated contracts. According to proposed Article 1171 CC[2] "in a contract of adhesion, any term which creates a significant imbalance between the parties' rights and obligations is considered as never written". By virtue of its position, among the general rules on contractual content, the provision would apply to all non-negotiated contracts, including those which are not specifically regulated within the civil code.[3]

2. This chapter explores the new rule's potential impact on one specific domain, namely the judicial control of employment (and, potentially, employment-like) contracts. The rule echoes two existing provisions belonging to the specialised domains of consumer[4] and competition[5] law, but the application to labour law[6] that comes with its scope is unprecedented, and the option that the proposal embraces has not been discussed thoroughly in the French literature – although some authors, occasionally, had invoked[7]

* PhD candidate, Centre for the Study of European Contract Law, Amsterdam.

1 *Ordonnance* no. 2016-131 du 10 février 2016 portant réforme du droit des contrats, du régime général et de la preuve des obligations, available online at https://www.legifrance.gouv.fr/eli/*ordonnance*/2016/2/10/2016-131/jo/texte (last accessed 14 March 2016).

2 In the present chapter, the notation CC is used to designate provisions belonging to the *ordonnance* above or to its near antecedent, the Avant-projet published in 2015. Articles contained in the Code Napoleon in its current form are referred to with the extended notation of Article *** Code civil.

3 Thus its potential scope of application extends to commercial contracts as well as to contracts between private parties and all sorts of personal work contracts.

4 Article L. 132-1 Code de la consommation.

5 Article L. 442-6, I, 2° du Code de commerce.

6 The rules of general contract law, or *droit commun des contrats* are applicable to employment contracts, as confirmed by Article L. 1221-1 Code du travail.

7 Pélissier, Pour un droit des clauses du contrat de travail, *RJS* 7/2005, p. 499.

or foreshadowed[8] the possibility. At the same time, the paper will show, on occasion French courts already engage in activities that might resemble unfair terms control- be it by applying general contract law or labour law-specific tools.

3. If some form of control of specific terms in employment contracts under open norms is already in place in France, in order to assess the likely impact of the reform on this field, it is important to investigate the similarities and differences between the mechanisms in place and the one to come. Since, as said above, the proposed rule appears to resemble very strongly existing rules targeting unfair terms (*clauses abusives*) in consumer and commercial contracts, there may be reasons[9] to believe that some commonality is to be expected between all these mechanisms – the one formally in place in the special codes, the one to come with the reform, and the one(s) to be found in the law in practice as developed by French labour courts. The paper will then investigate to what extent the existing models, and especially the "original" device in place for consumer contracts, is likely to influence the way in which the new mechanism will be implemented. To this end, it is essential to keep in mind that the forms which "clauses control" takes in labour law nowadays are very diverse: courts have been making use of fundamental rights arguments, general clauses specific to labour law, as well as of pure contract law principles. Not all of these mechanisms will be suitable to be brought back to the idea of unfair terms control, so that the impact of the reform could also be differentiated.

4. In the rest of the paper, the argument is developed as follows: section 2 will provide an analysis of the provision on "significant imbalance" in the reform proposal with the aim of assessing its nature and possible workings. In order to do so, the provision will be (2.1) analysed and compared to similar rules already existing outside the Code Civil and (2.2) studied in light of relevant "neighbouring" provisions in the reform project, in particular the limitation of freedom of contract provided by public order and the codification of the so-called *Chronopost* rulings; section 3, then, will be devoted to the provision's potential impact on labour law, through a short recollection of the several devices already used to the ends of unfair terms control in employment contracts and a comparison between these and the existing model of unfair terms control; finally, section 4 will bring together the results from the previous parts to draw some conclusions.

8 Zabel, Clauses abusives et droit du travail: le concept issu du droit de la consommation pénètre-t-il le droit du travail? *Petites affiches* 184/2013, p. 6.

9 Reinforced by the Report to the President of the Republic accompanying the *ordonnance*, according to which "Les critères d'appréciation du déséquilibre sont déjà connus puisqu'ils sont inspirés de ceux fixés dans le code de la consommation et qu'ils résultent de la transposition de la directive 93/13/CEE du 5 avril 1993 sur les clauses abusives." The report is available online at https://www.legifrance.gouv.fr/affichTexte.do?cidTexte=JORFTEXT000032004539 (last accessed 14 March 2016).

2. What's new? The new Civil code provisions and the existing rules

5. The *ordonnance* contains several norms which are of potential interest to this analysis. As a matter of fact, the new provision on unfair terms[10] is best understood in light of its scope, as delimited by the definition of contract of adhesion, as well as of other mechanisms of judicial control. Such in-context analysis is necessary in order to identify the likely division of labour among the different provisions. In addition, the paragraph will briefly touch upon a missed chance, or the disappearance of fundamental rights as a possible ground of judicial control. This section addresses all these changes and, where appropriate, compares them to existing "twin" rules in special laws. The overall aim of this analysis will be to get an understanding of the nature of the proposed "significant imbalance" control.

2.1. *Clauses creating "a significant imbalance"*

6. The core novelty, from the point of view adopted here, is the introduction of an "unfair terms" rule in the first part of the book on obligations. According to the future Article 1171 CC:

> "Dans un contrat d'adhésion, toute clause qui crée un déséquilibre significatif entre les droits et obligations des parties au contrat est réputée non écrite.
>
> L'appréciation du déséquilibre significatif ne porte ni sur l'objet principal du contrat ni sur l'adéquation du prix à la prestation."[11]

7. The scope of the provision is determined by the notion of *contrat d'adhésion*, as defined in Article 1110 CC. According to that provision, a contract is *de gré à gré* when its terms have been freely negotiated between the parties; it is *d'adhésion* when its

10 The Gorvernment's online institutional communication presents the rule as a "mechanisme de lutte contre les clauses abusives dans les contrats d'adhésion": see www.justice.gouv.fr/le-garde-des-sceaux-10016/reforme-du-droit-des-contrats-28738.html, last accessed 11 March 2016. The wording *clauses abusives* never appears in the *ordonnance*, but features in the relevant provision from the Code de la consommation. When the 1978 *Loi Scrivener*, which introduced the first rules on unfair terms, it did so in a chapter devoted to "La protection des consommateurs contre les clauses abusives". The original prohibition applied to imbalanced terms which appeared to have been "imposed to the consumer though an abuse of economic power by the other party" (art 35 Loi no.78–23 du 10 janvier 1978 sur la protection et l'information des consommateurs de produits et de services). In this text, unfair terms and clauses abusives are used interchangeably as shortcut for "terms creating a significant imbalance", although the terminology betrays some confusion between the national and the European legal models.

11 "A contract term which creates a significant imbalance in the rights and obligations of the parties to the contract may be struck out by the court on the request of the party to the contract to whose detriment it is stipulated. The assessment of significant imbalance must not concern either the definition of the subject-matter of the contract nor the adequacy of the price in relation to the act of performance." Unless expressly mentioned, the paper follows the English translation realised by Bénédicte Fauvarque-Cosson, Simon Whittaker and John Cartwright at the request of the French ministry of justice (full text available online at www.justice.gouv.fr/art_pix/Projet_reforme_contrats_2015_EN.pdf).

"general conditions" have been determined by one of the parties, without prior negotiation.[12] The category of general conditions, to which the provision refers, is not defined in the text but is well-known to French law[13] as well as to other European legal systems.[14] The concept is also employed by the future Article 1119 CC, according to which general conditions can only be invoked when they have been brought to the attention of the non-drafting party and have been accepted by that party.[15] The text marks a shift in comparison with the similar provision contained in Article 1108 CC in the Taubira proposal, which based the classification of a contract as *d'adhésion* on the fact that the contract's *stipulations essentielles* had not been open to the parties' "free discussion".[16] This shift seems to be well-conceived, as the old formulation might have generated ambiguities in cases in which the contract's price, and nothing else, would have been open to some degree of negotiation – which is often the case in mass contracts.[17] The definition might be slightly redundant taking into account that general conditions are almost by definition non-negotiated, but this feeling is attenuated by the lack of a legislative definition of general conditions. It does not expressly address the case in which the contract terms have actually been drafted by a third party, but it seems reasonable to infer that this case would also be covered by the definition of non-negotiated contract if one of the parties alone has decided to adopt the pre-drafted terms.

8. The provisions of Articles 1110 and 1171 CC might bring an end to a discussion which had been open for a very long time. While the notion of *contrat d'adhésion* is over a century old,[18] it had so far not made its way into a legal provision. When unfair terms control was first introduced in France by the Loi Scrivener ignoring this much-debated concept, the choice was lamented by prominent scholars and mostly justified by the difficulty of defining a *contract of adhesion*. Should non-negotiation be the only benchmark, or should the parties' qualities play a role? And, was the legislator to make a difference between single- and multiple-use textwork? The wording was often

12 According to proposed Article 1110 CC, second paragraph "*Le contrat d'adhésion est celui dont les conditions générales, soustraites à la négotiation, sont determinées à l'avance par l'une des parties*".

13 See J. Calais-Auloy, H. Temple, Droit de la Consommation, 8th edition, Dalloz 2010, p. 195, defining them as "pre-drafted terms in contracts concluded by one person with a series of other persons".

14 Think of the German *allgemeine Geschäftsbedingungen*, the Dutch *algemene voorwaarden*, the Italian *condizioni generali di contratto...*

15 Article 1119 CC: (1) *Les conditions générales invoquées par une partie n'ont effet à l'égard de l'autre que si elles ont été portées à la connaissance de celle-ci et si elle les a acceptées. (2) En cas de discordance entre des conditions générales invoquées par l'une et l'autre des parties, les clauses incompatibles sont sans effet. (3) En cas de discordance entre des conditions générales et des conditions particulières, les secondes l'emportent sur les premières.*

16 Article 1108 CC under the the Taubira proposal read "*Le contrat d'adhésion est celui dont les stipulations essentielles, soustraites à la libre discussion, ont été déterminées par l'une des parties*".

17 The replacement of free discussion with the notion of negotiation, on the other hand, seems relatively irrelevant at the level of content, but brings a slight improvement from the point of view of form since it uses an existing legal concept rather than referring to a new notion.

18 Famously introduced into the French legal debate by Raymond Saleilles, the issue was already the topic of a PhD dissertation in 1912: see Pichon, *Des contrats d'adhésion: leur interpretation et leur nature*, La revue judiciaire 1912.

used, throughout the years, in academic texts and has been incorporated in the civil code of Quebec,[19] but the questions stayed unanswered. The text of the *ordonnance* doesn't expressly address all of them – for instance, while the reference to *general conditions* suggests that the main object of the rules are clauses regularly used by one of the parties, it will be up to courts to determine to what extent single-use, non-negotiated conditions can also be checked –, it provided a clear legal basis to address them.

9. As to the substance of the rule, Article 1171 CC resembles closely the language of two other provisions located outside the civil code, namely Article L. 132–1[20] Code de la consommation and Article L. 442–6, I, 2°[21] Code de commerce. Both articles deal with terms creating "a significant imbalance in the rights and obligation of the parties". The consumer law provision, however, has been in place for a longer time and is usually considered to have been a source of inspiration for the similar rule of the Code du commerce. It seems, therefore, that this provision will be the main point of reference to the ends of assessing whether other provisions resemble a mechanism of unfair terms control.[22]

10. Under French consumer law, the prohibition of unfair terms applies exclusively to contracts between a professional and a "non-professional or a consumer". This latter definition covers consumers in the strict sense as well as legal persons which are not conducting business, such as non-profit organisations. This restricted scope traditionally[23] characterises the French approach to unfair terms control *vis-à-vis*, for instance, the German choice to allow review of all non-negotiated contracts – including, thus, business to business transactions.

19 Thus under Article 1379 of the Civil Code of Quebec: *Le contrat est d'adhésion lorsque les stipulations essentielles qu'il comporte ont été imposées par l'une des parties ou rédigées par elle, pour son compte ou suivant ses instructions, et qu'elles ne pouvaient être librement discutées. Tout contrat qui n'est pas d'adhésion est de gré à gré.* Both the reference to "stipulations essentielles" and the notion of free discussion, which featured in the Taubira draft, might have been inspired by this provision.

20 Under Article L 132–1 Code de la consommation: "*Dans les contrats conclus entre professionnels et non-professionnels ou consommateurs, sont abusives les clauses qui ont pour objet ou pour effet de créer, au détriment du non-professionnel ou du consommateur, un déséquilibre significatif entre les droits et obligations des parties au contrat. [...]L'appréciation du caractère abusif des clauses au sens du premier alinéa ne porte ni sur la définition de l'objet principal du contrat ni sur l'adéquation du prix ou de la rémunération au bien vendu ou au service offert pour autant que les clauses soient rédigées de façon claire et compréhensible.*"

21 According to Article L 442–6 Code du Commerce: "*Engage la responsabilité de son auteur et l'oblige à réparer le préjudice causé le fait, par tout producteur, commerçant, industriel ou personne immatriculée au répertoire des métiers: [...] De soumettre ou de tenter de soumettre un partenaire commercial à des obligations créant un déséquilibre significatif dans les droits et obligations des parties*".

22 See in this respect fn 9 above.

23 See the standard reference contained in the EU consumer law compendium: Schulte-Nölke, Twigg-Flesner and Ebers, EC Consumer Law Compendium- Comparative Analysis (2007), available at http://ec.europa.eu/consumers/archive/cons_int/safe_shop/acquis/comp_analysis_en.pdf, in particular the categorisation at p. 337.

11. Parallel to the choice for a limited personal scope is the consumer law rules' applicability irrespective of the negotiated or non-negotiated nature of the terms considered, a point on which the French approach departs not only from the German model but also from the EU (minimum harmonisation) Unfair Terms directive.[24] The provision forbidding "unfair" terms was already in place before the Directive's adoption, but it is only after the latter's implementation[25] that it explicitly allows the judge to hold the imbalanced term for never written.[26] In deciding on a term's potential unfairness, the judge has to take into account the circumstances surrounding the contract's conclusion as well as all the other terms included in the contract.[27]

12. The new provision, as we have seen, will apply to all non-negotiated contracts-irrespective of the parties' qualities. The substantive test, thanks to the reference to a "substantive imbalance", seems very similar to the consumer law rule. Another striking similarity concerns the fact that the new provision, like both Article L 132-1 Code de la consommation and the Directive, exempt core and price terms from scrutiny. This is in alignment with the choices of other countries which have introduced specific rules for non-negotiated contracts.[28]

13. In contrast to the earlier version of the provision contained in the draft *ordonnance* published in 2015,[29] Article 1171 CC seems to leave room for an ex officio exercise of judicial control: whereas the draft opted for a mechanism which was clearly different to the one adopted in consumer law, requiring the aggrieved party's to ask for the term's invalidation, the current version adopts the language of "non-écrite" already to be found in the Code de la consommation. The latter sanction, which needs inter alia to be interpreted in light of the case law of the European Court of Justice on the Unfair Terms Directive, has to be considered as more similar to a special form of nullity than to voidability – in other words, it should not be conditional on the aggrieved party's request. This change seems in line with the decision to restrict judicial control to non-negotiated contracts: while requiring some self-reliance seems appropriate in the context of

24 See again the Compendium.

25 For a brief account, see Chazal, Clauses abusives, in *Répertoire du droit commercial*, Dalloz 2013, in particular par 5–6.

26 According to the sixth paragraph of Article L 132–1 "*Les clauses abusives sont réputées non écrites.*" But *Le contrat restera applicable dans toutes ses dispositions autres que celles jugées abusives s'il peut subsister sans lesdites clauses.*"

27 Article L 1321-1 Code de la consommation, fifth paragraph: "*Sans préjudice des règles d'interprétation prévues aux articles 1156 à 1161, 1163 et 1164 du code civil, le caractère abusif d'une clause s'apprécie en se référant, au moment de la conclusion du contrat, à toutes les circonstances qui entourent sa conclusion, de même qu'à toutes les autres clauses du contrat. Il s'apprécie également au regard de celles contenues dans un autre contrat lorsque la conclusion ou l'exécution de ces deux contrats dépendent juridiquement l'une de l'autre.*"

28 See for instance Article 6:231(a) of the Dutch Burgerlijk Wetboek.

29 According to the Taubira proposal's Article 1169 CC "*Une clause qui crée un déséquilibre significatif entre les droits et obligations des parties au contrat peut être supprimée par le juge à la demande du contractant au détriment duquel elle est stipulée.*" The proposal is still available online at the address www.justice.gouv.fr/publication/j21_projet_ord_reforme_contrats_2015.pdf.

"traditional" (i.e. negotiated) contracts, the threshold for protection can reasonably be set lower for parties to contracts of adhesion. In the latter context, the ex officio mechanism is supposed to compensate for the party's presumed weakness and guarantee the extirpation of unfair terms.

14. Analysing the competition law unfair terms provision seems to confirm what has been observed so far. Article L- 442–6 Code du commerce has been adopted more recently, signalling the expansion of the notion of *clause abusive* (unfair term) beyond the domain of consumer law.[30] Unlike both Article L 132–1 Code de la consommation and the coming Article 1171 CC, the competition law provision does not exclude terms defining the contract's object and the balance between price and performance from its scope. This difference is not surprising since price agreements are actually a typical subject of competition law. In the context of commercial relationships, however, the insertion of an unfair term had no consequence on the contract: it was merely sanctioned by means of damages- where damage could be proved.[31] This brief analysis reinforces, *a contrario*, the impression that the rule of Article 1171 CC bears a strong resemblance to the one of Article L 132–1 of the Code de la consummation – in other words, it seems that the new mechanism is likely to work in a way which is similar to what has been experienced so far in consumer law.

15. What kind of unfair terms control does the new rule foreshadow? We have seen that, compared to the corresponding rules within consumer law, the provision seems to have a similar scope – excluding terms defining the contract's object and the price-performance relationship –, similar standard and also a possibly similar functioning, as indicated by the choice to hold an imbalanced clause for *non-écrite*. One possible difference is to be found in the focus of the scrutiny to be effected by the courts, which in consumer contracts involves appreciating the circumstances of the case at hand and examining contentious terms against the rest of the contract.[32] The new provision, on the contrary, seems to concentrate the imbalance assessment on the individual term concerned.

16. The drafters, thus, seem to have in mind a mechanism not too far removed from the one already in place in consumer law. This mechanism appears to be centred on remedying the accepting party's inability to negotiate the contract by allowing judicial

30 See again Zabel, Clauses abusives et droit du travail: le concept issu du droit de la consommation pénètre-t-il le droit du travail? *Petites affiches* 184/2013.

31 With reference to commercial contracts, then, the main effect of the new provision will be in the remedies available to the non-drafting party, which in certain cases will be able to demand the unfair term to be declared void. But this is something which goes beyond the scope of this contribution.

32 As well as vis à vis other related contracts: see Article L 132–1 (4) Code de la consommation: *Sans préjudice des règles d'interprétation prévues aux articles 1156 à 1161,1163 et 1164 du code civil, le caractère abusif d'une clause s'apprécie en se référant, au moment de la conclusion du contrat, à toutes les circonstances qui entourent sa conclusion, de même qu'à toutes les autres clauses du contrat. Il s'apprécie également au regard de celles contenues dans un autre contrat lorsque la conclusion ou l'exécution de ces deux contrats dépendent juridiquement l'une de l'autre.*

scrutiny of the terms that the party has probably paid less attention to when deciding to enter the contract. The provisions seek to make sure that excessively imbalanced non-negotiated terms will not be enforced upon non-drafting parties by holding these terms as never written. As said above, it seems very likely that control under Article 1171 CC will take a shape similar to that of current-day consumer law control of clauses abusives.

2.2. *The penumbra of unfair terms control*

17. The conclusion above is again reinforced by an analysis of other provisions concerning contractual content and limitation to its admissibility in the *ordonnance.* Immediately after giving a definition of contracts (proposed Article 1101 CC), the project introduces a provision which for the first time expressly codifies freedom of contract and sets the scope of a general limitation thereto. According to Article 1102 CC, freedom of contract "*does not allow the parties to derogate from rules which are an expression of public policy.*"[33] This provision basically codifies the direct effect on contractual autonomy of Article 6 CC, which provides that private agreements cannot derogate from good morals and public order. The existence of such direct effect, in any case, had been established already some years ago by the Court of Cassation[34] – thus the reform does not innovate on this point.

18. Compared to the *Taubira* draft, it is interesting to take notice of the disappearance of what used to be the second part of this sentence: "[…] *nor to infringe fundamental rights and freedoms recognised by a provision which applies to relationships between private parties except where such infringement is indispensable to the protection of legitimate interests and proportionate to the intended purpose.*"[35] Fundamental rights would then be considered not as an absolute limit to contractual freedom, but as norms that tolerate to be compressed, as long as the restriction is justified by a legitimate interest.[36]

19. The disappeared provision echoed limitations that were already existing in the case-law of the Court of Court of Cassation.[37] Moreover, it closely resembled the fundamental rights control provision in labour law, Article L 1121–1 Code du Travail.[38] Within the draft proposal, the provision clarified that fundamental rights were not to become the domain of unfair terms control, which would have to concentrate on different interferences. The failure to incorporate the provision in the final version might entail a

33 The new Article 1162 CC further explains that neither the contract's terms *nor its objective* can be against public order: *Le contrat ne peut déroger à l'ordre public ni par ses stipulations, ni par son but, que ce dernier ait été connu ou non par toutes les parties.*

34 Cass. civ. 7 december 2004 no.01–11823.

35 Ses Article 1102 CC Taubira draft.

36 See Chantepie's recent contribution to the Dalloz blog dedicated to the reform: http://reforme-obligations.dalloz.fr/2016/02/16/la-liberte-contractuelle-back-to-basics/#more-200.

37 See Maurin, Contrat et droit fondamentaux, LGDJ 2013.

38 See *infra* para 3.1.

different articulation between provisions in and outside of labour law, where, as we just said, a similar rule is already in place. Alternatively, it seems possible to envisage that the protection of fundamental rights will just be taken up into the notion of "public order" consecrated by Article 1102 CC.[39]

20. In the later section on the contract's content, the proposed Article 1170 CC provides that "all terms depriving the debtor's essential obligation of its substance are considered as not written". The first provision, in essence, reproduces the well-known *Chronopost*[40] decision, in which the *Court of Cassation* had voided a term which limited a transporter's responsibility for failing to deliver in the promised time was severely limited, basically leaving the transporter's promise deprived of any meaningful sanction. This provision is one of the marks left by the abolition of the notion of *cause,* which the Court of Cassation had then controversially employed to invalidate the limitation of liability. At that time, the Court's intervention was arguably required by the absence of a rule allowing the invalidation of unfair terms outside the domain of consumer contracts. In this sense, the question may be raised whether a rule of this sort would still be necessary in view of the proposed Article 1171 CC. While the doubt may seem warranted at first glance, "blacklisting" this kind of terms might not be superabundant once the text of proposed Article 1171 CC is subjected to closer inspection. In the context of consumer contracts, terms such as those addressed by Article 1171 CC are taken care of by the Directive's (non-binding) annex and, in French law, by the 2009 regulations establishing the "black" and "grey" lists. In the context of general contract law, however, courts might have been tempted to give greater significance to the second part of Article 1171 CC, which excludes from control the contract's object and the relationship between price and performance. Considered that this relationship is precisely what is affected by exemption clauses, it is probably wise to have included a special provision to secure that they would not be exempted from control. This might, in turn, also provide a source of inspiration for courts dealing with similar, albeit less far-reaching provisions. Again, however, this contributes to shaping the contours of Article 1171 CC: it is not there to address those "extreme" cases of contractual imbalance, which will be taken care of by Article 1170 CC, or, in even more extreme cases, by Article 1169 CC. The latter provision, which also is reminiscent of the functions of *cause,* holds as invalid an onerous contract in which the counter-performance promised to the party undertaking an obligation is "illusory or derisory".[41]

21. To draw some preliminary conclusions, it seems that a first look at some neighbouring provisions confirms that the new rules will occupy in general contract law a space similar to the one taken by "consumer" unfair terms control. The object and price exemption differentiates it quite clearly from a "*laesio enormis*" rule. This is reinforced by

39 See Chantepie, above fn 36.

40 Cass. comm. 22 Octobre 1995, no. 93-18632.

41 This is an exception to the principle, stated in Article 1168 CC, that lack of equivalence between the promised performances does not affect the contract's validity.

the fact that the borderline case of extreme-reaching exemption terms is separately taken care of by Article 1170, and that of an illusory counter-performance by Article 1169 CC. The missed codification of a more clearly structured fundamental rights control will require courts some extra effort to articulate the boundaries between the new unfair terms control and the limitations imposed by public order.

22. As to the rules' application to labour contracts, the "transplant" of the provision will land on a series of mechanisms that we will briefly analyse in the second part of this paper. In particular, in interpreting the provisions, account will still need to be taken of the provision on fundamental rights which is already in force in that field. On the other hand, it seems that the domain, which is historically characterised by a presumption of inequality in negotiation between the parties, seems a particularly fertile terrain for this transplant.

3. Possible headings of unfair terms control in French labour law

Within the labour law debate, in spite of the wide personal scope of Article132–1 Code de la consommation, the applicability of the consumer unfair terms provision to employment and other work contracts has never really entered the picture. However, this situation does not leave courts entirely unequipped to perform a function similar to that of unfair terms control – albeit in different forms. We will see how several provisions have been mobilised and courts have themselves intervened in order to deal with one-sided terms.

3.1. The general provision of Article L. 1121–1 Code du Travail

23. First, it is appropriate to take a look at judicial control based on the protection of fundamental rights. Originally introduced in the Code du Travail in 1992 as then Article L 120–2, the wording of Article L 1121–1 is particularly general:

> *Nul ne peut apporter aux droits des personnes et aux libertés individuelles et collectives de restrictions qui ne seraient pas justifiées par la nature de la tâche à accomplir ni proportionnées au but recherché.*

24. The provision extends a limitation originally imposed on company regulations (*règlements d'atelier*) to all sorts of actions undertaken in the operation of a business. It applies, thus, to employment and other work contracts. What characterises the provision is, on the one hand, its reference to rights and liberties; on the other hand, the standard based on which the employer's actions are scrutinised, namely whether they are justified by the nature of the employee's task and proportionate to the objective pursued. While the second requirement is arguably close to the rationality of unfair terms control, this is hardly the case for the first. Talking of workers' "rights and liberties" is evidently not the same as referring to the balance between the rights and duties of both parties to the contract, as unfair terms provisions typically do. While the consumer provisions look at the rights established by the contract and their balance, Article 1121–1 Code du Travail relates to rights existing independent of the contract and protects them against different sorts of violations- including those which might take place by means of contract terms.

25. The focus on personal rights makes the provision at hand of limited use for the scrutiny of contractual terms, but court practice shows that it has found application with reference to different kinds of clauses. Terms that were liable to affect, for instance, the employee's occupational freedom (e.g. non-competition clauses) or her right to freely determine her residence have been scrutinised under Article 1121–1 Code du Travail. Thus, in the case of a term requiring a lawyer to establish her residence nearby her law firm, the employee's integration in the "local environment" of the firm's place of establishment was not considered a sufficient reason to interfere with her freedom to choose her place of residence.[42] Also the practice of requiring employees to return a bonus that they have received from the employer at the end of a year if they resign early during the following year is problematic under this provision, since it restricts the employee's occupational freedom.

26. The rule of Article 1121–1 Code du travail, then, bears significant differences and important similarities to unfair terms control. On the one hand it resembles the latter mechanism in its protective intent and, possibly, in the way it focuses on the employer's unilateral (contractual) activity. On the other hand, the requirement that rights *other than the ones created by the contract* are infringed upon both signifies a different rationale – with much simplification, the protection *of certain rights* rather than control of unilateral drafting – and makes the mechanism harder to invoke in a contractual context.

3.2. The regime of clauses de variation

27. Another mechanism worth considering is the regime to which the Court of Cassation has subjected different kinds of clauses allowing the employer to unilaterally modify the contract (*clauses de variation*, hence: modification clauses). These clauses can take very different forms and affect different elements in the exchange, but usually they are all aimed at allowing adjustments in case the employer's situation should change over time. Classical examples are terms allowing a change in the employee's place of work, in the working time or in the tasks assigned to the employee. Terms establishing a variable remuneration could also fall under this group.

28. The validity of these terms was questioned in a rather radical way by the Court of Cassation in 2001, with a decision according to which

> "(L)a clause par laquelle l'employeur se réserve le droit de modifier, en tout ou partie, le contrat de travail est nulle comme contraire aux dispositions de l'article 1134, alinéa 2, du Code civil, le salarié ne pouvant valablement renoncer aux droits qu'il tient de la loi".[43]

[42] Cass. soc.12 juillet 2005 n. 04–13342.
[43] Cass. soc. 27 février 2001, n. 99–40219.

29. Article 1134 of the code civil sanctions the binding force of contract. The provision's second paragraph, recalled in the decision, establishes the irrevocability of contracts, except for the case of mutual consent. This principle includes a prohibition for one party to impose a modification of the contract to the other party during the contract's execution. In this sense, the decision considers the modification clause void insomuch as it deprives the employee of her right to refuse a change to her contract's terms.

30. Notwithstanding this general statement, however, the Court of Cassation allows a number of modification clauses to deploy their effects – subject to conditions that depend on the object of the term considered. In particular, clauses establishing a variable remuneration are admitted when the variation is based on objective criteria which are independent of the employer's will, the variation is not such to shift the entrepreneurial risk onto the employee and the statutory and collective minima are preserved.[44] Terms called "of territorial mobility" (*clauses de mobilité géographique*) are also deemed legitimate[45] when they determine the size of the area to which they apply. It is not allowed to include a term that reserves the employer the possibility to modify the territorial domain to which the employee's mobility obligation applies.[46]

31. Modification clauses are arguably a sensible instrument for increasing the contract's resilience in the context of all long-term relationships. However, they undoubtedly introduce an element of uncertainty into the contract and usually their effects are mostly enjoyed by the drafter. They are also not unknown to consumer contracts, and indeed also in that context they are often the object of specific regulation. In the French system of unfair terms control in consumer contracts, terms of this kind are considered both in the "black" list of terms which are always unfair and in the presumptive "grey" list. The relatively wide wording in the black list, prohibiting all terms that "authorise the professional to unilaterally modify the contract's terms concerning its duration, the character of the goods or services to be delivered or their price"[47] does not mean that all variation clauses are inhibited. The lists, indeed, are followed by exemptions concerning certain long-term contracts.[48] For certain services, an explicit exception is carved out in the legislative part of the Code de la consommation. Thus, for instance, the Court of

44 "*Une clause du contrat de travail peut prévoir une variation de le rémuneration du salarié dès lors qu'elle est fondée sur des éléments objectifs indépendants de la volonté de l'employeur, ne fait pas porter le risque d'entreprise sur le salarié et n'a pas pour effet de réduire la rémunération en dessous des minima légaux et conventionnels*" Cass. soc. 2 juillet 2002, no. 00–13111; Cass. Soc. 4 mars 2003, no. 01–41864 et 20 avril 2005, no. 03–43696.

45 And effective. The Court of Cassation, indeed, has sometimes also refused to identify terms that were not sufficiently explicit. See Antonmattei, *Les clauses du contrat de travail*, Ed. Liaisons, 2009, p. 49–50.

46 Both requirements are articulated in Cass 7 Juin 2006, n. 04–45846.

47 Article R 132–1 Code de la consommation considers a term that "*autorise le professionnel à modifier unilatéralement les clauses du contrat relative à sa durée, aux caractéristiques ou au prix du bien à livrer ou du service à rendre*" always invalid. Furthermore, Article R 132–2 of the same code establishes a presumption of unfairness when a term "*réserve au professionnel le droit de modifier unilatéralement les clauses du contrat relatives aux droits et obligations des parties (autres que celles interdites)*".

48 See Article R132–2–1 Code de la Consommation.

Cassation recently granted avail to terms concerning the possible variation of overdraft interests in contracts for banking accounts.[49] The usual requirement for these terms to be valid, in consumer law, is that they must be connected to other mechanisms protecting the consumer's free determination – such as the possibility to terminate the contract without penalty – and, often, that they indicate under which conditions a variation will take place.[50]

32. The criteria used to identify acceptable variation clauses, then, seem rather similar in consumer and employment contracts. In both contexts it is necessary to strike a balance between the need for flexibility typical of long-term relationships and the preservation of a reasonable contractual equilibrium, preventing the consumer/employee from being abandoned to the other party's arbitrary will. In this respect, the indication of the parameters according to – or within which – the prerogative will be exercised represent both an instrument of transparency, hopefully allowing the accepting party to know what she can expect, and a substantive guarantee against capricious requests.

33. The differences which can be identified as to the regime to which certain terms are subject in the two domains do not seem to imply different approaches- in other words, the judicial control of variation clauses seems quite comparable to "consumer law" unfair terms control. In particular, it is interesting to observe that as far as the remuneration is concerned an additional guarantee is added – namely that salary variations have to be based on objective criteria. This requirement is absent in consumer contracts. Arguably, in that context more faith is put in competition: in case the consumer finds the modifications unreasonable, she is entrusted with disciplining the provider by terminating the contract; if a sufficient numbers of consumers react in the same way, it will be the market response that punishes the provider's arbitrary behaviour.[51] Relying on a similar mechanism in the domain of employment relations would be much more controversial.

3.3. *The judge-made regime of certain clauses*

34. Finally, it is important to mention that French courts have also developed specific regimes for certain terms, not necessarily based on general principles but as a more express form of judge-made law. Here we will consider in particular the case of non-competition clauses and of so-called "*clauses de dédit-formation*", terms requiring the restitution of in-work education costs in case of early termination of the employment contract.

49 See Cass 23 January 2013, no. 10–21177.

50 See Article 128–84 *Code de la consommation* and, in the same direction, the Court of Justice's interpretation of the transparency requirement laid down in Directive 93/13. In this respect, I will be forgiven for referring to my own comment: Leone, Transparency revisited – on the role of information in the recent case-law of the CJEU, *ERCL* 2014, p. 312.

51 This observation is confirmed by the fact that, where competition can more obviously not be relied on – as in the case of natural monopolies such as energy supply – the issue of prices becomes more salient and is sometimes subject to specific regulation.

35. The case of non-competition clauses is exemplary because of the strict principles developed and the fragmentary evolution that has led to the current legal framework. The Court of Cassation, indeed, started with requiring that the term be necessary for the protection of a legitimate interest of the employer and gradually added further requirements, such as the inclusion of a geographical and temporal delimitation. Only in 2002, finally, did the Court add that a non-competition obligation must be accompanied by the payment of an indemnity compensating the employee for the loss of chances that such obligation entails.[52]

36. As concerns the *clauses de dédit-formation*, it is generally considered that the possibility of using them has a value to both parties. The reasoning is that, by being able to secure (the return on) his investment through a restitution clause, the employer should be incentivised to offer employees valuable educational experiences, which may benefit both the employer and the employees. There is, however, a risk that the mechanism will turn into a mere device of employee retention.[53] In order to avoid this risk, the validity of these terms is again subjected to several conditions.

37. From a substantive point of view, the Court of Cassation requires: a) that the offered programme has imposed on the employer additional costs compared to those which were in any case due by law or collective agreements;[54] b) that the amount to be refunded is proportionate to the undergone expenses and in the duration of the training;[55] c) that the term does not result in depriving the employee of her ability to resign. This last requirement means that the "fidelity" obligation imposed on the employee should not be exceedingly long, while the proportionality prong suggests that the amount to be returned should decrease with time. However, neither of the two prongs seem to have been further specified by the highest court.[56]

38. As far as form is concerned, the obligation "has to be the object of a specific agreement entered into before the beginning of the training and which specifies the date, the nature, duration and actual cost to the employer of the training as well as the amount and mode of the reimbursement due by the employee". The "specific agreement"

52 This solution differs from the one retained for commercial agency contracts, where no compensation is required. See Article L. 134–14 Code du Commerce. The Cassation affirms that the provision's failure to require such compensation must be seen as an explicit choice of the legislator. See Cass. com., 4 December 2007, no. 06–15.137.

53 Antonmattei, p 80 uses as example the case of a logistics company specialised in the transportation of hydrocarbons which regularly hired drivers lacking the necessary licence and then asked them to undertake the indispensable training and a correlated obligation to remain with the company for 18 months. In this case, the objective was reducing personnel turnover in a sector whose working conditions were particularly challenging. This strategy represents an abuse of the *clause de dédit-formation*. The case is taken from Cass. soc. 4 juin 1987, n 84–43639.

54 Thus the costs have to be mentioned in the term, Cass. soc. 16 mai 2007, and have to be real (not already refunded to the company by the state), Cass. soc. 19 nov. 1997.

55 Cass. soc. 16 mai 2007, no. 05–16647 and 19 nov. 1997, no. 94–43195.

56 See Antonmattei, p 82. Cass. soc. 17 juill. 1991, no. 88–40201.

requirement is to be intended as imposing that the term should concern one particular training, so that the employee's consent is not given without actual knowledge of the deal's conditions. As to the consequences of incorrect drafting, in most cases a failure to meet all the mentioned requirements will entail the term's nullity. However, when the fidelity obligation stretches exceedingly far in time or the amount to be reimbursed is exceedingly high, it is possible for the judge to reduce the term instead of eradicating it. This is done under application of Article 1152 of the Civil Code, concerning penalty clauses.

39. Whereas non-competition covenants and terms of *dédit-formation* are subject to different standards, what they share is their nature of "collateral" agreements vis à vis the employment relationship. They both concern elements which are not part and parcel of the relationship, but get agreed between the parties due to some specific interest of one or both of them. Therefore, they cannot – or can only partially – be legitimised by reference to some other element in the relationship; they rather have to be *internally* balanced. Thus, the non-competition obligation needs to be granted separate compensation, and the restitution obligation has to relate to expenses freely incurred and must be structured in a fair way. In this sense, they might be relatively hard to fit within the standard paradigm of unfair terms control, which connects the assessment to the parties' rights and duties as arising from the contract as a whole.

40. At the same time, the concern with ensuring a sufficiently balanced content and with making sure that the effects of the clause are clearly identified – and delimited – resonates with what we have seen above. In both cases, finally, a background concern seems to exist with reference to the employee's fundamental rights; the highly specific validity regimes applied to these terms, however, seems to go beyond the control standard articulated by Article L 1121-1 Code du Travail – they look rather as attempts, by the Court, to concretise a fairness or balance requirement which is as closely associated with the relationship between the parties as it is with external (fundamental rights) concerns.

4. Conclusion

41. In the first part of the paper we have seen how the new provisions in the *ordonnance* issued in February 2016 seem to introduce into general contract law a mechanism of unfair terms control very similar to the one already in place in French consumer law. The mechanism, in fact, is so similar to the one of the Code de la consommation that it seems justified to infer that it has comparable aims. The conclusion appears warranted in light both of a comparison between the new unfair terms provisions and the "old" consumer law rules and of the likely division of labour among the different provisions concerning control of contractual content incorporated in the new Code civil.

42. As to the new provision's likely impact on unfair terms control in labour law, we have seen that courts already perform several – scattered – forms of control. Not all these forms can be assimilated to unfair terms control as understood in this paper, i.e. a "consumer law-like" control of contractual content. In particular, the differences between the control exercised under Article L 1121–1 Code du Travail protecting fundamental rights and liberties of workers and unfair terms control are to be highlighted. While there can be overlap between the two spheres, Article L 1121–1 presupposes the violation of a right *external* to the contract, whereas unfair terms control is first of all concerned with the rights and duties arising from the contract. The fact that the reform project simultaneously introduces a limitation based on fundamental rights and a form of generalised unfair terms control seems to confirm this observation.

43. The several different forms of control which courts exercise outside of Article L1121–1, on the other hand, could probably be absorbed and re-organised under the heading of unfair terms control. This would both reduce the existing complexity and contribute to a more clear articulation of the validity requirements imposed on certain terms – in particular, one may add, if the courts would be ready to make use of transparency requirements as applied in consumer law. Furthermore, the novelty will do away with the current uncertainty concerning the legal basis justifying the imposition of the said validity requirements, which is at times unclear and at times essentially non-existent.

44. All in all, it seems that one may be able to adapt a classical adagio and say that, with reference to labour law and judicial control of *clauses abusives*, everything needs to change, so most things can stay the same. The choice to restrict the scope of control to contracts of adhesion, besides allowing closing some loopholes, should have reassured at least some of those[57] who were particularly alarmed at the idea of generalised unfair control as foreseen by the Taubira draft. At least with reference to labour law, this contribution would like to submit, the most likely impact of the new rules will be a contribution to some classical values of civil law – accessibility and legal certainty. In addition to that, while holding a moderate potential in terms of (corrective) justice, they also seem unlikely to do much further harm to contractual autonomy.

[57] See for instance http://business.lesechos.fr/directions-juridiques/droit-des-affaires/contrats-et-clauses/02111428568-droit-des-contrats-la-reforme-qui-change-tout-ou-presque-110548.php.

Tobias Lutzi*

INTRODUCING *IMPRÉVISION* INTO FRENCH CONTRACT LAW – A PARADIGM SHIFT IN COMPARATIVE PERSPECTIVE

1. Introduction

1. 'Agreements lawfully entered into have the force of law for those who have made them.' The principle of *pacta sunt servanda* so famously enshrined in Article 1134, al 1, of the *Code civil* is regularly considered a cornerstone of French contract law – which has been repeatedly upheld by the *Cour de cassation* in the most uncompromising terms. Its decision to refuse any judicial intervention for *imprévision* to account for supervening circumstances, however severely they may have disturbed the contractual balance, is a particularly well-known example,[1] which has made the *Canal de Craponne* by far the best-known waterway amongst French law students.[2]

2. One of the reasons for the decision's notoriety stems from the fact that its rigour is almost unheard of in other European legal systems (arguably with the exception of Belgium).[3] It is therefore hardly surprising that it has not only instigated a seemingly endless stream of scholarly publications and academic discussion[4] – while also leaving room for the occasional decision to cast doubts on the court's otherwise strict adherence to the principle[5] – but has also been addressed in all recent reform projects as well as in

* MJur (Oxford); Diplom-Jurist (Cologne); LLM (Cologne/Paris 1); Maîtrise en droit (Paris 1). The author is indebted to Professors John Cartwright and Stefan Vogenauer, whose insightful seminars on European Contract Law have laid the groundwork for this paper; he is equally grateful to his friends Dr Thomas Coendet, MJur, and Cordt-Magnus van Geuns-Rosch, MJur, who have carried on the spirit of these seminars into evenings of stimulating discussion and who generously shared with him their critical thoughts on an earlier version of this paper. The text was amended in February 2016 to reflect the changes that *ordonnance n° 2016-131* has brought to that part of the reform that this paper discusses.

1 Cass civ, 6 March 1876, *Canal de Craponne*, D 1876 I, 193; for the details, see below, 3.1.

2 Cf similar remarks by Fauvarque-Cosson, 'Le changement de circonstances', *RDC* 2004, 67, para 1; Stoffel-Munck, 'La réforme en pratique – La résiliation pour imprévision', *AJCA* 2015, 262.

3 See below, n 51.

4 See below, 2.1.

5 See below, n 60 and 64.

loi n° 2015-177 du 16 février 2015, the respective *projet d'ordonnance*, and *ordonnance n° 2016-131 du 10 février 2016*.[6]

3. Reforming this area of law required the French legislator (who, in this case, was actually the French government) to strike a new balance between, on the one hand, the principle of *pacta sunt servanda* and the legal certainty that is usually ascribed to it and, on the other hand, the idea of contractual solidarity and fairness that lies at the foundation of every exception for *imprévision* admitted elsewhere. The controversial comments to which the proposed provision has given raise bear testimony to the difficulty of that task.

4. Yet, many other European systems have faced this challenge before, coming to a variety of different solutions, which has been described as 'revealing all the difficulties of the construction of a *ius commune* of contract'.[7] But the diversity of approaches does not only make *imprévision* one of the most interesting aspects of the French reform, especially for the present conference, the viable balance that has been found in many legal systems also seems to have provided useful guidance during the French reform process and will continue to enrich its academic discussion. This is particularly true for a comparitivist look at German law, which does not only offer a rich and relatively coherent body of case law but also the experience of its codification in a provision that is conceptually similar to what is about to become the new Article 1195 of the *Code civil*.

5. To provide a framework for such a comparison, the problem of *imprévision* will be described as a (potential) exception to the principle of *pacta sunt servanda* (2.). It will be shown that the respective solutions (currently) applied in French, English, and German law are the result of three fundamentally different approaches to such an exception (3.). The French reform, constituting a shift from one of these approaches to another, will then be critically assessed (4.), followed by some concluding remarks (5.).

2. *Imprévision* as an exception to *pacta sunt servanda*

6. Although it is widely regarded as a cornerstone of virtually all European systems of contract law, the principle of *pacta sunt servanda* has never been admitted without exceptions (1.). In order to discuss the French reform with regard to supervening circumstances, it will be useful to understand *imprévision* as one of these exceptions (2.).

2.1. The principle of pacta sunt servanda *and its exceptions*

7. Marking the transition from Roman law, where only some forms of promises (*contractus*) were actionable while others (*pacta nuda*) were not,[8] to the medieval

6 See below, 4.

7 Mekki, 'Hardship et révision des contrats 1. Quelle méthode au service d'une harmonisation entre les droits?', *JCP* 2010, 2291.

8 *D.* 2.14.7.4: '*nuda pactio obligationem non parit*'.

canonists who claimed that (nonetheless) all promises must be kept,[9] the principle of *pacta sunt servanda* is rightly considered as an essential ingredient to private autonomy and a cornerstone of virtually all European systems of contract law.[10] It is enshrined in Article 1134, al 1, of the French Civil Code, §241 of the German *Bürgerliches Gesetzbuch (BGB)*, and was authoritatively stated for English law in 1647.[11] *Pufendorf* described it as 'a most Sacred Command of the Law of Nature and what guides and governs not only the whole Method and Order but the whole Grace and Ornament of Human Life, that every Man keeps his Faith, or which amounts to the same that he fulfils his Contracts, and discharges his Promises'.[12]

8. Yet, despite its omnipresence in modern contract law, the principle of *pacta sunt servanda* has always been subject to exceptions, many of which are concessions to contractual fairness. While some of these exceptions go to the formation of the contract – absence of contractual requirements like a legal *cause* or a certain form,[13] vitiating factors like mistake or duress, or consumer rights to redress –, others concern its performance – such as, most importantly, the exception for impossibility.

9. In many legal systems, the contract is void or unenforceable if performance has been impossible before the contract was concluded – be it for lack of object,[14] common mistake,[15] or under a separate doctrine.[16] But the debtor[17] is also regularly discharged

9 Cf Landau, 'Pacta sunt servanda. Zu den kanonistischen Grundlagen der Privatautonomie', in Ascheri et al. (eds), *Ins Wasser geworfen und Ozeane durchquert. Festschrift für Knut Wolfgang Nörr* (Böhlau 2003), 457; Zimmermann, *The Law of Obligations. Roman Foundations of the Civilian Tradition* (Clarendon 1990), 542–44.

10 Maskow, 'Hardship and Force Majeure' (1992) 40 *AmJCompL* 657, 658; Hyland, 'Pacta Sunt Servanda: A Meditation' (1994) 34 *VJIL* 405, 406, 427–28; Weller, *Die Vertragstreue* (Mohr Siebeck 2009), 153–65, 274–75.

11 *Paradine v Jane* (1647) Aleyn 26; see generally Treitel, *Frustration and Force Majeure* (3rd edn, Sweet & Maxwell 2014), paras 2-001 to 2-009; McKendrick, *Contract Law – Text, Cases, and Materials* (6th edn, OUP 2014), 697–98.

12 Pufendorf, *De iure natura et gentium* (1672), III, ch IV, §§2, translation by Kennett (Lichfield 1703).

13 Although some of these requirements have historically evolved to counter-balance the principle of binding force of a contract, one may argue that they do not constitute exceptions but rather define what constitutes a *pactum* that is *servandum* (see also Thier in Hondius/Grigoleit (eds), *Unexpected Circumstances in European Contract Law* (CUP 2011), 19).

14 Cf, e.g., Cass com, 26 May 2009, pourvoi n° 08-12.691, Bull civ IV, no. 71 for French law.

15 Cf *Sheikh Brothers Ltd v Arnold Julius Ochsner* [1957] AC 136 and *Great Peace Shipping Ltd v Tsavliris Salvage (Int) Ltd (The Great Peace)* [2002] EWCA Civ 1407, paras 50–61, for English law.

16 Cf §311a BGB for German law. Note that the German doctrine of the disappearance (or disturbance) of the basis of the transaction, which will be discussed in the following, also covers cases of initial mistakes as to the basis of the transaction, now codified in §313(2) BGB; they lie beyond the scope of this paper.

17 In civil law systems, the provisions on impossibility only discharge the party whose performance has become impossible, while the other party to a contract is discharged as a consequence of the contractual synallagma (§326(1) BGB; Art. 1463 Codice civile; in French law, this results from Art. 1131 Code civil, the contract being devoid of a valid cause. In English law, however, frustration automatically discharges both parties (*Taylor v Caldwell* (1863) 3 B & S 826, 840; cf s 1(1) Law Reform (Frustrated Contracts) Act 1943)).

if performance becomes subsequently impossible, provided that the circumstances were unforeseeable and the debtor was not responsible for them or has contractually undertaken the risk.[18] In most legal systems, this results from a separate doctrine which can take a number of different forms[19] but is regularly formulated as an exception to *pacta sunt servanda*.[20]

10. The English doctrine of frustration, for instance, was expressly developed as an exception to the principle of absolute liability,[21] based on an implied condition that 'in contracts in which the performance depends on the continued existence of a given person or thing [...] the impossibility of performance arising from the perishing of the person or thing shall excuse the performance.'[22] And while the juristic basis of the doctrine seems to have shifted towards the 'true construction of the contract' in later cases,[23] its character as an exception to *pacta sunt servanda* has not changed.[24] By the same token, the French doctrine of *force majeure*[25] is codified in Article 1148 of the *Code civil*, which posits an exception to contractual liability set out in Article 1147; it has been developed by the courts, which have traditionally applied a remarkably high standard,

18 Most legal systems impose at least some of these requirements for a contract to be discharged; yet, they differ as to how these work in practice. For instance, frustration does not discharge the contract under English law if one party has undertaken the risk (cf *Taylor v Caldwell* (n 17), 833) or if frustration was self-imposed (cf *J Lauritzen A/S v Wijsmuller BV (The Super Servant Two)* [1990] 1 Lloyd's Rep 1, 10), but is not excluded if the event was foreseeable (cf *Edwinton Commercial Corp & Anor v Tsavliris Russ (Worldwide Salvage & Towage) Ltd (The Sea Angel)* [2007] EWCA Civ 547, paras 127–28); for French law, see n 27 below.

19 Cf Beale et al, *Cases, Materials and Text on Contract Law – Ius Commune Casebook for the Common Law of Europe* (2nd edn, Hart 2010), 1094–126. In addition to the examples given in the next paragraph, see §275 BGB for German law (which only excludes the 'primary' obligation, but leaves the contract otherwise intact).

20 Cf already *D.* 50.17.185: *impossibilium nulla obligatio*.

21 Cf McKendrick (n 11), 697–98. While it was not referred to in the judgment itself, the plaintiff in *Taylor v Caldwell* (n 17), 831 had expressly invoked the rule from *Paradine v Jane* (n 11) and Blackburn J (as he then was) had started his speech by stating that '[t]here seems no doubt that where there is a positive contract to do a thing, not in itself unlawful, the contractor must perform it or pay damages for not doing it, although in consequence of unforeseen accidents, the performance of his contract has become unexpectedly burthensome or even impossible.'

22 Blackburn J (as he then was) in *Taylor v Caldwell* (n 17), 839.

23 See *Davis Contractors Ltd v Fareham UDC* [1956] AC 696 (HL), 720–21; *National Carriers Ltd v Panalpina (Northern) Ltd* [1981] AC 675 (HL), 688 (including a discussion of the alternative theories that have been advanced).

24 See Bingham LJ in *The Super Servant Two* [1990] 1 *Lloyd's Rep* 1, 8: 'The doctrine of frustration was evolved to mitigate the rigour of the common law's insistence on literal performance of absolute promises. The object of the doctrine was to give effect to the demands of justice, to achieve a just and reasonable result, to do what is reasonable and fair, as an expedient to escape from injustice where such would result from enforcement of a contract in its literal terms after a significant change in circumstances.'

25 It has inspired a number of model laws and harmonization projects, which sometimes use the term 'impediment' to describe the concept, cf Art. 79 CISG, Art. 7.1.7 UNIDROIT PICC, Art. 8:108 PECL, and Art. III.–3:104 DCFR.

requiring the supervening event to have been irresistible, unforeseeable, and external,[26] but seem to have abolished the third requirement since two decisions of the *Cour de cassation*'s *Assemblée plénière* in 2006.[27]

2.2. The exception for imprévision

11. Legal systems tend to differ more strongly when it comes to circumstances that render performance more onerous rather than impossible. These are sometimes discussed under the descriptive, and therefore relatively neutral, headline of 'supervening' or 'unexpected circumstances',[28] even though this term technically covers cases of both mere hardship and (supervening) impossibility. Most French authors, however, refer to the particular situation where performance has been rendered more onerous as the problem, or theory, of *imprévision*.[29]

12. It has been argued that this terminology is imprecise since it is not the parties' failure to foresee (*prévoir*) the supervening circumstances but the effect these circumstances have on the contractual balance that gives rise to a potential judicial intervention.[30] Yet, legal systems tend to agree that there is no room for such an intervention if the circumstances have been foreseeable (let alone foreseen) at the conclusion of the contract. Therefore, and in view of the name of a similar doctrine in French administrative law,[31] to which the French government expressly referred in their *rapport* accompanying *ordonnance n° 2016-131 du 10 février 2016*,[32] the term *imprévision* will be used throughout this paper to describe the problem of unforeseeable supervening circumstances rendering performance considerably more onerous (but not impossible) for one party.

13. Whether the different remedies that legal systems provide in such cases should be understood as exceptions to *pacta sunt servanda* has also been subject to some discussion. It has been argued that remedies which are conceptually based on the construction of the contract or the parties' obligation to perform their obligations in good faith do not constitute such an exception as they only reduce (or transform) the ostensibly owed

26 Bénabent, *Droit civil - Les obligations* (13th edn, Montchrestien 2013), para 332.

27 As Plén, 14 April 2006, pourvoi n° 02-11.168, Bull civ AP n° 4; reaffirming, at the same time, that the conditions of irresistibility and unforeseeability need to be satisfied cumulatively.

28 Hondius/Grigoleit (n 13) ('Unexpected Circumstances'); Beale et al (n 19), 1091 ('Supervening Events'); Rodière (ed), *Les modiflcations du contrat aux cours de son execution en raison de circonstances nouvelles* (Pedone 1986).

29 Cf Bénabent (n 26), para 292; Souchon, in Rodière (n 28), 13, 14-18; Ghestin/Jamin/Billiau, *Les effets du contrat* (3rd edn, LGDJ 2001) para 290, however limiting it to monetary obligations.

30 Fauvarque-Cosson (n 2), para 2.

31 See below, 3.1.

32 See *Rapport au Président de la République relatif à l'ordonnance n° 2016-131 du 10 février 2016 portant réforme du droit des contrats, du régime général et de la preuve des obligations* (2016), 14: *'L'article 1195 constitue quant à lui l'une des innovations importantes de l'ordonnance, puisqu'il introduit l'imprévision dans le droit des contrats français, notion bien connue en jurisprudence administrative.'*

performance (in)to what has actually been promised.[33] But such an understanding fails to reflect the considerable impact these remedies have on the legal certainty that the principle of *pacta sunt servanda* is considered to promote.[34] Consequently, most authors rightly consider them as exceptions to the principle.[35] With regard to its practical effects, the question whether a judge may modify a contract in light of supervening circumstances that have drastically altered the initial contractual balance is as much a question of the scope of *pacta sunt servanda*[36] as the question whether the owner of a concert hall that has burned down is still under an obligation to lease it to the other party[37] or whether a manufacturer who became terminally ill and thus could not finish a machine only he was able to build was still under an obligation to deliver it when he died.[38] In all these cases, one party does not get what they initially expected to get, even if the reason for this may be dogmatically found in the initial contract itself.

3. Current approaches to *imprévision*

14. Conceptually, legal systems that already allow an exception to *pacta sunt servanda* for cases of impossibility may take one of three different approaches to cases of *imprévision*: they may not discharge the parties unless performance has become actually impossible; they may extend the existing exception for impossibility to (some of) these cases; or they may develop a separate exception.[39] These different approaches have been taken in French (1.), English (2.), and German law (3.), respectively.

3.1. The French approach: no exception for imprévision

15. The traditional French approach to *imprévision* is notorious for its uncompromising adherence to *pacta sunt servanda*. It is perfectly illustrated by the *Cour de cassation*'s

33 Medicus, 'Vertragsauslegung und Geschäftsgrundlage' in Jakobs et al (eds), *Festschrift für Werner Flume zum 70. Geburtstag* (Otto Schmidt 1978), 629, 631–32; Finkenauer, in *Münchener Kommentar zum BGB* (6th edn, Beck 2012), §313, paras 3–4; in the same direction Mekki (n 7), 1.A.2°.

34 Moreover, it would arguably even deny the English doctrine of frustration the status of an exception to *pacta sunt servanda* since it is regularly explained as the consequence of the 'true construction of the contract'.

35 Cf McKendrick (n 11) 697–98; Treitel (n 11), para 1-001; Hondius/Grigoleit, in Hondius/Grigoleit (n 13), 6; Markensis/Unberath/Johnston, *The German Law of Contract* (Hart 2006), 320; Grüneberg, in *Palandt* (4th edn, Beck 2015), §313, para 1; Weller (n 10), 297; Zimmermann (n 9): 'one of the most (…) dangerous inroads into *pacta sunt servanda*.' A similar approach is taken in contemporary literature on international treaties, cf Binder, *Die Grenzen der Vertragstreue im Völkerrecht am Beispiel der nachträglichen Änderung der Umstände* (Springer 2013).

36 Thus, the German *Bundesgerichtshof* requires 'very particular circumstances that justify to make an exception to the principle of *pacta sunt servanda*' before it modifies a contract based on the doctrine of the basis of the transaction (see BGH, 11 July 1958, *NJW* 1958, 1772; 25 May 1977, *NJW* 1977, 2262). Cf also Weller (n 10), 298.

37 Cf *Taylor v Caldwell* (n 17).

38 Cf As Plén, 14 April 2006 (n 27).

39 For a different classification of 'open' and 'closed' legal systems see Hondius/Grigoleit in Hondius/Grigoleit (n 13), 10–12; 643–44.

leading decision in *Canal de Craponne*,[40] where the owner of a channel asked the courts to increase the charges that were due to them by the adjoining owners in exchange for their obligation to maintain the channel under contracts concluded in 1560 and 1567, which had become entirely derisory in 1876. While the lower courts[41] allowed the claim and modified the contract, expressly admitting an exception to the principle of *pacta sunt servanda* for contracts that are executed over a certain period of time,[42] the *Cour de cassation* overruled the decision, pointing out that Article 1134 reproduces a general and *absolute* principle that applies to *all* contracts, including those entered into before the *Code civil* was enacted.[43] Thus, it was not the task of the courts, however fair they thought their decision to be, to modify a contract and replace freely negotiated terms.[44]

16. It is evident from this decision that the court understood Article 1134 *Code civil* in a way that its first two paragraphs, i.e. the principle of *pacta sunt servanda*, always[45] take precedent over the third paragraph, i.e. the principle of good faith. Freely stipulated contract terms become 'the law' for both the parties and the judge,[46] and *only* the parties themselves may alter it.

17. This understanding of Article 1134 had been repeatedly confirmed in subsequent decisions.[47] French authors who defend it regularly invoke the importance of legal certainty as well as the fact that it encourages parties to make provisions for supervening circumstances[48]). Moreover, they argue that the courts were not well placed to amend a

40 Cass civ, 6 March 1876 (n 1).

41 Tribunal civil d'Aix, 18 March 1841; Cour d'appel d'Aix, 31 December 1873.

42 Cour d'appel d'Aix, 31 December 1873: '*Attendu que si les conventions légalement formées tiennent lieu de loi aux parties et si elles ne peuvent être modifiées que du consentement commun, il n'en est pas de même pour les contrats qui ont un caractère successif.*'

43 Cass civ 6 March 1876 (n 1): '*[L]a disposition de cet article n'[est] que la reproduction des anciens principes constamment suivis en matière d'obligations conventionnelles, la circonstance que les contrats dont "exécution donne lieu au litige sont antérieurs à la promulgation du Code civil ne saurait être, dans l'espèce, un obstacle à l'application dudit article; [L]a règle qu'il consacre est générale, absolue, et régit les contrats dont l'exécution s'étend à des époques successives de même qu'à ceux de toute autre nature.*'

44 Ibid.: '*[D]ans aucun cas, il n'appartient aux tribunaux, quelque équitable que puisse leur paraître leur décision, de prendre en considération le temps et les circonstances pour modifier les conventions des parties et substituer des clauses nouvelles à celles qui ont été librement acceptées par les contractants.*'

45 For the different provisions that allow for judicial interventions in particular types of contract see Hondius/Grigoleit (n 13), 146; Souchon, in Rodière (n 28), 18–21; Bénabent (n 26), para 294.

46 Capitant/Terré/Lequette, *Les grands arrêts de la jurisprudence civile* (12th edn, Dalloz 2008), 183, para 2.

47 Cass civ, 6 June 1921, Bull civ, n° 95; Cass com, 18 January 1950, D 1950, 227; 18 December 1979, pourvoi n° 78–10.763, Bull civ IV, n° 339; civ 3, 30 May 1996, pourvoi n° 94–15.828, Contrats, conc, consom 1996, n° 185; com 18 Mar 2009, pourvoi n° 07–21.260, Bull civ III, n° 64.

48 Terré/Simler/Lequette, *Droit civil. Les obligations* (10th edn, Dalloz 2009), para 470; Fauvarque-Cosson (n 2), para 25; see also Souchon, in Rodière (n 28), 17; Mekki (n 7), 1.B.1°. The argument can also be found in many English decisions (see, e.g., *Paradine v Jane* (1647) Aleyn 26, [1558–1774] All ER Rep 172, 173: '[W]hen the party by his own contract creates a duty or charge upon himself he is bound to make it good, if he may, notwithstanding any accident by inevitable necessity *because he might have provided against it by his contract.*' (emphasis added); see also McKendrick, 'Force Majeure and Frustration – Their Relationship and a Comparative Assessment', in McKendrick (ed), *Force Majeure and Frustration*

contract.[49] Interestingly, the same arguments seem to have prevailed in Belgian law, where the problem is however often discussed (much like in English law)[50] as one of the scope of the *force majeure* exception.[51]

18. The French administrative courts have nevertheless refused to follow the decision in *Canal de Craponne* and repeatedly allowed a party for which the execution of a contract has become unexpectedly more onerous to demand a temporary[52] surcharge, which is to be fixed either by the parties or by the judge.[53] This divergence from the civil courts is usually attributed to the particular importance of a continued execution of contracts of a public law character,[54] but it should be noted that it considerably undermined the alleged increase in legal certainty gained from the civil courts' refusal to interfere with a contract where the nature of this contract is unclear or even in dispute.[55]

19. Moreover, a doctrinal current promoting the idea of 'contractual solidarism' (*solidarisme contractuel*) has gained considerable importance over the last decades.[56] It argues in favour of a new understanding of Article 1134 *Code civil* that gives the same weight to its third paragraph as is usually given to its first paragraph.[57] But although such an understanding would have provided a solid basis for a new approach to

(2nd edn, Routledge 2013), 43). One may of course question whether a default rule should be designed in a way to encourage the parties to prevent its application.

49 Capitant/Terré/Lequette (n 46), para 4; Fauvarque-Cosson (n 2), para 7; Stoffel-Munck (n 2), 263.

50 See below, 3.2.

51 See Herbots, *Contract Law in Belgium* (Kluwer/Bruylant 1995), paras 352 and 355; Hondius/Grigoleit (n 13), 158; Fouques-Duparc, in Rodière (n 28), 49–52; Cousin et al, 'Regards comparatistes sur l'avant-projet de réforme du droit des obligations', D 2015, 1115, II.B.2.

52 This '*théorie de l'imprévision*' only applies to temporary obstacles to the performance of the contract; if the obstacle is permanent, the contract will simply be discharged for *force majeure* (cf CE, 9 December 1932, *Compagnie des tramways de Cherbourg*, Rec 1050; 14 June 2000, *Commune de Staffelden*, Rec 227).

53 CE, 3 February 1905, *Ville de Paris*, Rec 105; 30 March 1916, *Compagnie générale d'éclairage de Bordeaux*, Rec 125; see also 30 October 1925, *Mas-Gayet*, Rec 836; 22 February 1963, *Ville d'Avignon*, Rec 115; Sect 12 Mar 1976, *Département des Hautes-Pyrenées*, Rec 155.

54 '*La continuité du service public*'; cf Nicholas, *The French Law of Contract* (2nd edn, Clarendon 1992), 209–10; Beale et al (n 19), 1130; Long et al, *Les grands arrêts de la jurisprudence administrative* (16th edn, Dalloz 2007), n° 31, paras 1 and 5–6. One may argue that this can hardly be the sole reason given that an indemnity can be awarded even after the contract has come to an end (CE 27 July 1951, *Commune de Montagnac*, Rec 439; Sect 12 March 1976, *Département des Hautes-Pyrenées* (n 53)).

55 This is illustrated by the facts of Cass civ 1, 16 March 2004, pourvoi n° 01–15.804, Bull civ I, n° 86, where the operation of a municipality's cafeteria was conceded to a private entity, which invoked the economic imbalance of the contract in front of the administrative courts; after the municipality (and another party) had seized the civil courts, the *Tribunal des conflits* authoritatively qualified the agreement as a private law contract.

56 Cf the important essay by Jamin, 'Révision ou intangibilité du contrat ou la double philosophie de l'article 1134 du Code civil', *Droit et Patrimoine* 1998, 46; see also Cédras, 'Le solidarisme contractuel en doctrine et devant la Cour de cassation', in *Rapport Cour de cassation 2003*; Mazeaud, D 2004, 1754, para 8.

57 Jamin (n 56), 49 and 54–57.

imprévision[58] – as the development of the German approach demonstrates[59] – it seems to have inspired only one very limited attenuation of the traditional approach. According to two decisions of the commercial chamber of the *Cour de cassation*, the refusal of one party to renegotiate the contract in light of supervening circumstances that have considerably altered the initial contractual balance may constitute a breach of its obligation to perform the contract in good faith.[60] Yet, a number of authors have argued that these decisions can be explained by the particular circumstances of the two cases and do not testify to a larger change of paradigm.[61] The fact that the consequence of a breach of the obligation to renegotiate is a damage award, and not the modification of the contract, seems to indicate that they are right. Besides, the approach of the commercial chamber is yet to be confirmed by other chambers of the *Cour de cassation*.[62]

20. Meanwhile, the commercial chamber had hinted towards a second device that could potentially accommodate cases of *imprévision*. In a decision from 2010, rendered via the so-called *procédure de référé* and inexplicably[63] not published in the *bulletin*, it quashed a decision for 'not having researched whether the evolution of economic circumstances [...] did not have the effect [...] of disequilibrating the general economy of the contract [...] and of depriving the obligation [of the defendant] of every counterpart',[64] possibly leaving it without a valid *cause*. But although a number of authors had already proposed to use the concept of *cause* in these cases,[65] the decision has been met mostly with criticism[66] and remained isolated.[67] Given that the concept of *cause* has finally been abolished by *ordonnance n° 2016-131*,[68] it is very likely to remain that way.

58 Cf Jamin (n 56), 49 and 54–57; Fauvarque-Cosson (n 2), para 19; Tallon, 'La révision du contrat pour imprévision au regard des enseignements récents du droit comparé', in *Études à la mémoire d'Alain Sayag* (Litec 1997), 403, 413.

59 See below, 3.3.1.

60 Cass com, 3 November 1992, *Huard*, pourvoi n° 90-18.547, Bull civ IV, n° 338; 24 November 1998, pourvoi n° 96-18.357, Bull civ IV, n° 277.

61 Renaud-Payen, JCP E 2004, 737.

62 While the language of the decision in Cass civ 1, 16 March 2004 (n 55) seemed to indicate that the first civil chamber adhered to the same approach, the appeal was dismissed because it was based on an initial imbalance of the contract rather than on supervening circumstances; thus, the part in question is nothing more than an *obiter dictum* (see Renaud-Payen, JCP E 2004, 737; Fages, *Droit des obligations* (2nd edn, LGDJ 2009), para 423, fn 26).

63 See the criticism by Le Gac-Pech, 'L'équilibre du contrat au travers de la cause: un substitut à la théorie de l'imprévision?', *La Semaine Juridique – Entreprise et affaires*, 2010, 2108.

64 Cass com, 29 June 2010, *Soffimat*, pourvoi n° 09-67.369, D 2010, 2481.

65 See, e.g., Fauvarque-Cosson (n 2), para 20; Capitant/Terré/Lequette (n 46), para 3; Souchon, in Rodière (n 28), 18.

66 Cf Le Gac-Pech (n 7); Fages, 'Le déséquilibre résultant d'une évolution des circonstances économiques peut-il rendre sérieusement contestable, au sens de l'article 873, alinéa 2, du code de procédure civile, l'obligation dont une partie sollicite l'exécution devant le juge des référés?', *RTD Civ* 2010, 782; Genicon, 'Théorie de l'imprévision... ou de l'imprévoyance?', D 2010, 2485; more welcoming Mekki (n 7); Savaux, 'Frémentissement en matière d'imprévision', *RDC* 2011, 34.

67 Cf Cass com, 18 March 2014, pourvoi n° 12-29.453, and the commentary by Laithier, 'La cause n'est pas un remède aux contrats non rentables', *RDC* 2014, 345.

68 Cf *ordonnance n° 2016-131 du 10 février 2016*, Art. 1128.

21. In practice, parties to a long-term contract were thus only protected if they entered specific provisions for the event of supervening circumstances into their contract – which is most usually done in the form of a hardship clause.[69] Otherwise, they risked to be stuck with 300-year-old contract terms stipulating prices in a currency that had long ceased to exist.

3.2. *The English approach: extension of the impossibility exception*

22. While the English doctrine of frustration was developed in a case involving impossibility,[70] which would presumably also have fallen under the exception for *force majeure* in French law, English judges did not see much of a problem to extend it to cases where performance had not become literally impossible[71] but would not serve the intended purpose or otherwise be something entirely different from what the parties had in mind when concluding the contract.[72] In the first such case,[73] Vaughan Williams LJ concluded that 'it is not essential to the application of the principle of *Taylor v Caldwell* that the direct subject of the contract should perish or fail to be in existence at the date of performance of the contract. It is sufficient if a state of things or condition expressed in the contract and essential to its performance perishes or fails to be in existence at that time.'[74]

23. Based on that reasoning, the English courts have applied the doctrine of frustration where supervening circumstances had rendered performance more burdensome to a degree that it would be fundamentally different from what was originally agreed.[75] And while the threshold for frustration in these cases is certainly very high as the courts do not want to allow the parties to escape from a bad bargain,[76] the decision in *Staffordshire Area Health Authority*[77], which was made in circumstances very similar to the French

69 Cf Beale et al (n 19), 1165–69. It has even been argued that the omnipresence of such clauses in international commerce supports the traditional French approach (as both ultimately exclude judicial interventions; Fauvarque-Cosson (n 2), paras 28–9). Note that these clauses can also be found in many administrative contracts, where they aim, but do not always succeed, to replace the *théorie de l'imprévision* (cf CE Sect, 5 November 1937, *Département des Côtes-du-Nord*, Rec 900 and *Ducos*, Rec 902).

70 *Taylor v Caldwell* (1863) 3 B & S 826.

71 It could be argued that performance had not become literally impossible in *Taylor v Caldwell* either since it would probably have been possible, in theory, to rebuild the concert hall (cf Treitel (n 11), para 6–001).

72 In addition, hardship also plays a role as a defence to a claim for certain remedies (see Peel, *Treitel. The Law of Contract* (14th edn, Sweet & Maxwell 2015), paras 3–146, 21–015, and 21–030).

73 *Krell v Henry* [1903] 2 KB 740 (CA).

74 ibid., 754.

75 Cf *Metropolitan Water Board v Dick Kerr* [1918] AC 119 (HL); see also *Bank Line v Arthur Capel & Co* [1919] AC 435 (HL).

76 Cf *Davis Contractors* [1956] AC 696 (HL); *Amalgamated Investments & Property Co Ltd v John Walker & Sons Ltd* [1977] 1 WLR 164 (CA); *Ocean Tramp Tankers Corporation v V/O Sovfracht (The Eugenia)* [1964] 2 QB 226 (CA).

77 *Staffordshire Area Health Authority v South Staffordshire Waterworks Co* [1978] 1 WLR 1387 (CA).

decision in *Canal de Craponne*, illustrates how the slightly wider doctrine of frustration can be used to come to a different result than the one French courts would find.[78]

24. Still, although impossibility and frustration of purpose are usually treated as two different types of frustration,[79] they are applications of the same doctrine.[80] As a consequence, none of the English decisions seems to be understood as an application of the *clausula rebus sic stantibus* doctrine,[81] even though the doctrine of frustration was originally also based on an implied term.[82] More importantly, as cases of impossibility and hardship fall under the same doctrine, the remedy is exactly the same in both situations: if the high threshold for frustration is fulfilled, both parties are automatically discharged, without any intervention of the parties or the courts,[83] and the Law Reform (Frustrated Contracts Act) 1943 applies to the respective liabilities of the parties.[84]

25. This approach has the advantage of not requiring a distinction between circumstances that render performance impossible and those that render performance more difficult.[85] But it may also be seen as one of the main reasons why English courts have been particularly reluctant to admit that a contract has been frustrated, which would extinguish it in its entirety without leaving any room for contractual modification.[86] Such an all-or-nothing approach may be justified for the all-or-nothing question of whether performance is still possible – but one may argue that it fails to accommodate the more subtle question of whether performance in the way originally agreed is still fair.

3.3. The German approach: development of a separate exception

26. The German approach to *imprévision* is radically different from both the English and the traditional French approach in that it is based on a doctrine which is entirely separate from the doctrine of impossibility (a.). It has inspired similar approaches in a number of other European legal systems and found its way into most harmonization

78 While the majority construed the contract as being concluded for an indefinite period of time and thus open to termination upon reasonable notice, Lord Denning considered it to have ceased to bind because 'the situation has changed so radically since the contract was made.' (ibid., 1398). See also Hondius/Grigoleit (n 13), 212–14.

79 Cf McKendrick (n 21), 723. Cases of illegality are usually distinguished as a third type.

80 Cf *Krell v Henry* (n 73), 749, where Vaughan Williams LJ even considered the contract to have become 'impossible of performance by reason of the non-existence of the state of things assumed by both contracting parties as the foundation of the contract'.

81 Cf Weir, 'Review of "Frustration of contract and clausula rebus sic stantibus"', (1988) 37(2) ICLQ 452.

82 See n 22 above.

83 McKendrick (n 48), 44–45; Treitel (n 11), para 15–002.

84 Treitel (n 11), paras 15–053 to 15–058.

85 For the problems this has caused in German law see below, 4.2.

86 While the Law Reform (Frustrated Contracts Act) 1943 gives the courts some flexibility with regard to the consequences of the discharge (cf Peel (n 72), paras 19–092 to 19–108), it should be noted that it has only been applied in a very limited number of reported cases.

projects and international instruments on contract law (b.). In 2002, the German legislator finally codified the doctrine (c.).

3.3.1. The doctrine of the basis of the transaction

27. Although they were aware of the concept of the *clausula rebus sic stantibus*,[87] as well as *Windscheid*'s theory of the 'precondition' (*Voraussetzung*),[88] the legislator of the *Bürgerliches Gesetzbuch* decided not to incorporate a general provision dealing with changing circumstances[89] in an effort not to undermine the principle of *pacta sunt servanda*.[90] As the German *Reichsgericht* (which was established 20 years earlier than the BGB entered into force) had never ascribed to the *clausula* theory anyway,[91] the court initially had little difficulty to honour the legislator's decision.[92]

28. However, in light of the hyperinflation that followed World War I, the German court – unlike the French *Cour de cassation*[93] – started to make exceptions. Interestingly, the court initially extended the already existing exception for impossibility to cases of 'economic impossibility'.[94] But it quickly put its reasoning on a different footing and invoked the principle of good faith (§§157, 242 BGB); first to allow parties to terminate contracts that they could not perform without a serious risk of bankruptcy,[95] then also to judicially modify such contracts.[96] In 1922, the court finally adopted the so-called doctrine of *Wegfall der Geschäftsgrundlage* (disappearance of the basis of the transaction),[97] which had been developed by *Oertmann*.[98]

87 Cf *Motive zu dem Entwurfe eines bürgerlichen Gesetzbuches für das Deutsche Reich* (Guttentag 1888), Vol II, 199; *Protokolle der Kommission für die zweite Lesung des Entwurfs des BGB* (Guttentag 1897–79), Vol II, 1264–65.

88 Cf *Motive* (n 87), Vol I, 249.

89 *Motive* (n 87), Vol I, 249; Vol II, 199. Exceptions were however admitted for loan agreements (§610 BGB; see Vol II, 314–15) and contracts where one party is obliged to perform in advance (§321 BGB; see *Protokolle* (n 87) II, 1264). Moreover, §812(1)(2) Alt 2 still contains a reminiscence to *Windscheid's* theory.

90 Wieacker, *Privatrechtsgeschichte der Neuzeit* (2nd edn, Vandenhoeck & Ruprecht 1967), 520; Finkenauer (n 33), para 21.

91 Cf RG 13 May 1889, *RGZ* 24, 169, 170.

92 Cf RG 11 April 1902, *RGZ* 50, 255, 257; 4 May 1915, *RGZ* 86, 397, 398.

93 Cf Cass civ, 6 June 1921 (n 47); 30 May 1922, D 1922, I, 69. These decisions may well be understood as a conscious rejection of the German approach, cf Fauvarque-Cosson (n 2), para 5.

94 RG 4 February 1916, *RGZ* 88, 71, 74; 15 October 1918, *RGZ* 94, 45, 47; 2 December 1919, *RGZ* 98, 18, 20–21. This approach is evidently very similar to the extension of the English doctrine of frustration to cases of hardship; just as the House of Lords in *Metropolitan Water Board v Dick Kerr* (n 75), the Reichsgericht limited the category of 'economic impossibility' to cases where performance had become completely different from what was promised.

95 RG 19 May 1920, *RGZ* 99, 115, 116; 8 July 1920, *RGZ* 99, 258, 259.

96 RG 21 September 1920, *RGZ* 100, 129, 131. The decision expressly invokes the *clausula* doctrine; according to the court, the interpretation given to the provisions on impossibility and good faith in the aforementioned decisions demonstrated that this doctrine could indeed be found in the BGB.

97 RG 3 February 1922, *RGZ* 103, 328.

98 Oertmann, *Die Geschäftsgrundlage. Ein neuer Rechtsbegriff* (Deichert 1921).

29. Aware of the risk for legal certainty,[99] the court initially defined the 'contractual foundation' narrowly as 'a belief as to the existence of certain essential circumstances held by the parties and apparent at the moment of the conclusion of the contract'.[100] Its disappearance discharged the party for which performance had become more onerous from its obligation unless the other party agreed to amend the contract.[101]

30. Over the following decades, the *Reichsgericht* and, subsequently, the *Bundesgerichtshof (BGH)* had numerous opportunities to uphold and develop the doctrine[102] and to clarify its ingredients.[103] Some of these decisions had to deal with very substantial changes of circumstances similar to the hyperinflation of the 1920s, such as the end of the Third Reich,[104] the 1948 Berlin blockade[105] and the German reunification[106], while others addressed relatively trivial situations. Thus, the court has considered the acquisition of a building licence as the 'basis' of a sales contract for a prefabricate house,[107] certain soil conditions as the 'basis' of a construction contract,[108] and the (non-)involvement of a professional football player in a match-fixing scandal as the 'basis' of a transfer contract between two football clubs.[109]

31. These decisions have been conceptualised into a three-prong test, requiring a factual element (i.e. a change of circumstances),[110] a hypothetical element (i.e. the parties would not have concluded the contract if they had been aware of this change),[111] and an equitable element (i.e. it would not be equitable for one party to deny the other party any amendment of the contract).[112] When these elements had been established, one party could demand from the other what the parties would have agreed if they had been aware of the risk and the contract had been amended accordingly;[113] (only) if the other party

99 Cf RG 3 February 1922 (n 97), 331.

100 ibid.

101 ibid., 333; unlike in RG 21 September 1920 (n 96), the court denied any judicial power to amend the contract.

102 In BGH 16 January 1953, *MDR* 53, 282, the court made clear that 'economic impossibility' is distinct from 'actual impossibility' and governed by §242 BGB, not §275 BGB. Cf also BGH 23 October 1957, *BGHZ* 25, 390, para 27.

103 For instance, the BGH immediately made clear that it might modify a contract, cf BGH 16 January 1953 (n 102).

104 BGH 29 May 1951, *BGHZ* 2, 237; 30 September 1952, *BGHZ* 7, 238.

105 BGH 16 January 1953 (n 96).

106 BGH 14 October 1992, *BGHZ* 120, 10.

107 BGH 23 March 1966, *JZ* 66, 409.

108 BGH 21 November 1968, *NJW* 69, 233.

109 BGH 13 November 1975, *NJW* 76, 565. In view of the court's decisive argument that the player had become useless for both parties (paras 23–24), the case would presumably be one of frustration of purpose in English law.

110 According to the BGH, this element needs to be construed narrowly (see next paragraph).

111 This element is missing if the parties have been aware of the risk, cf BGH 29 May 1951 (n 104), para 18; 30 September 1952 (n 104), para 11.

112 This element requires that the risk does not lie exclusively with one party, cf, e.g., BGH 10 March 1983, *BGHZ* 87, 112, para 13 (the risk not to obtain a credit lies with the debtor).

113 Cf BGH 23 March 1966 (n 107), paras 18–21; see BGH 14 October 1992 (n 106), para 40 for an exception.

refused this or an amendment were not possible, the party for which performance had become more onerous could terminate the contract.[114]

32. Both the requirements and the effects of the disappearance of the basis of the transaction are a direct consequence of the doctrine being an application of the principle of good faith.[115] It is not only evident in the 'equitable element' of the aforementioned test, but also the reason for the preference given to the adaptation of the contract over its termination.[116] Moreover, the courts have always emphasised the need for a narrow construction of the doctrine, despite the wide range of situations it is supposed to cover, given that it is an exception to the principle of *pacta sunt servanda*.[117] And while some authors have argued that such a narrow construction is misplaced as the doctrine is ultimately nothing else than an instance of contractual interpretation,[118] the *Bundesgerichtshof* has repeatedly confirmed it.[119]

3.3.2. Reception in other legal systems and instruments

33. Even before *Oertmann* had developed the German doctrine, the idea of a 'basis' or 'foundation of the contract' featured in English decisions on the doctrine of frustration.[120] But rather than serving as the underlying concept, it appears to have mainly been used to restrict the scope of the doctrine,[121] the contractual 'foundation' being understood considerably more narrowly than in German case law.[122]

34. After the German courts had started to regularly apply the doctrine of disappearance of the basis of the transaction, it was however adopted in a number of other European[123] legal systems, some of which had formerly adhered to the French concept of an immutable

114 Cf BGH 21 November 1968 (n 108), paras 31–34; 13 November 1975 (n 109), paras 32–33; BGH 15 December 1983, *BGHZ* 89, 226, para 60.

115 For the historical development of this reasoning see Wieacker (n 90), 520.

116 Cf BGH 23 October 1957 (n 102), para 27; 31 Januar 1967, *BGHZ* 47, 48, paras 12, 14.

117 Cf Markensis/Unberath/Johnston (n 35), 325–26; in the context of the recent 'financial crisis', see KG Berlin 5 November 2012, *NJW* 2013, 478 and Tröger, 'Das Vertragsrecht der Krise: Vertragstheorie und -dogmatik im Lichte der Finanzkrise' in Tröger/Karampatzos (eds), *Gestaltung und Anpassung von Verträgen in Krisenzeiten* (Mohr Siebeck 2014), 49, 56.

118 Finkenauer (n 33), paras 41–46; Medicus (n 33), 631–33. Given the reference to good faith in §157 BGB, such an understanding is easily reconcilable with the principle of good faith as the foundation of the doctrine.

119 Cf BGH 13 November 1975 (n 109), para 22.

120 Cf *Krell v Henry* (n 73), 750–51; see also *National Carriers Ltd v Panalpina (Northern) Ltd* (n 23), 688.

121 Thus, the contract to hire a steamship was not frustrated in *Herne Bay Steam Boat Co v Hutton* [1903] 2 KB 683 by the coronation of Edward VII being cancelled (which had however frustrated the contract for the hire of a room in *Krell v Henry* (n 73), decided by the same judges) because it was not the 'foundation of the contract' (ibid., 689). Cf also the example given by Vaughan Williams LJ in *Krell v Henry*, 750, of engaging a cabman to Epsom on Derby Day, which would not be frustrated even if the race would not take place because it would not be the 'foundation of the contract'.

122 Cf the decisions cited in n 107–09, none of which would amount to 'frustration' in English law.

123 A relatively similar doctrine also exists in US law, where a party can be discharged in cases of 'commercial impracticability' (cf Treitel (n 11), paras 6–002 to 6–020).

principle of *pacta sunt servanda*.[124] Thus, both the Italian *Codice civile* and the Dutch *Burgerlijk Wetboek* contain provisions[125] that have been inspired by the German case law[126] and allow the judge to either amend or terminate a contract if an unforeseeable change of circumstances has made performance considerably more onerous. Austrian and Swiss courts seem to apply a similar rule, without the legislators having codified it.[127]

35. Moreover, the German approach has been adopted in many[128] harmonization projects and international instruments of contract law.[129] Artt. 6:111 PECL[130], III.–1:110 DCFR[131], 89 CESL[132], and 6.2.3. UNIDROIT Principles of International Commercial Contracts (2010)[133] all allow the courts to amend or terminate a contract if 'performance becomes so onerous because of an exceptional change of circumstances that it would be manifestly unjust to hold the debtor to the obligation',[134] with preference given towards the amendment of the contract.[135] Yet, unlike the German case law,[136] they all require an attempt to renegotiate the contract before the courts may intervene.

3.3.3. The codification of 2002

36. When the German legislator reformed the law of obligations in 2002, they also codified the doctrine of the disappearance of the basis of the transaction, in order to give it a textual basis without changing its content.[137] Thus, the following §313 was introduced into the BGB:[138]

124 For further examples see Rodière (n 28); Finkenauer (n 33), paras 29–39; von Bar/Clive/Schulte-Nölke, *Principles, definitions and model rules of European private law. Draft Common Frame of Reference (DCFR)* (OUP 2010), 741–44.

125 Art. 1467 and 1468 Codice civile; Art. 6:258 Burgerlijk Wetboek.

126 Cf Beale et al (n 19), 1146; Tallon 'Hardship', in Hartkamp et al (eds), *Towards a European Civil Code* (3rd edn, Nijhoff 2004), 502; von Bar/Clive/Schulte-Nölke (n 124), 742; Hondius/Grigoleit (n 13), 118–19.

127 Finkenauer (n 33), paras 33–34; Fauvarque-Cosson (n 2), para 13.

128 A notable exception is the CISG, which only contains an exception for *force majeure* in Art. 79 CISG.

129 See generally Brunner, *Force majeure and hardship under general contract principles. Exemption for non-performance in international arbitration* (Kluwer 2009), 397–535.

130 Principles of European Contract Law, published in Lando/Beale, *Principles of European Contract Law (PECL), Parts I and II* (Kluwer 2000).

131 Draft Common Frame of Reference, published in von Bar/Clive/Schulte-Nölke (n 124).

132 Proposal for a Regulation of the European Parliament and the Council on a Common European Sales Law, COM(2011), 635 final.

133 International Institute for the Unification of Private Law, *UNIDROIT Principles of International Commercial Contracts* (2010).

134 Art. III.–1:110 DCFR. Interestingly, all of these provisions start by restating the principle of *pacta sunt servanda* and formulate the case of *imprévision* as a restrictive exception.

135 Cf, e.g., von Bar/Clive/Schulte-Nölke (n 124), 741; McKendrick, in Vogenauer (ed), Commentary on the UNIDROIT Principles of International Commercial Contracts (PICC) (2nd edn, OUP 2015), Art. 6.2.3., para 6.

136 See below, 3.3.3.

137 BT-Drucksache 14/6040, 93; 175, 176.

138 Translation provided by juris for the German Ministry of Justice <www.gesetze-im-internet.de/englisch_bgb/> last accessed 12 February 2016.

(1) If circumstances which became the basis of a contract have significantly changed since the contract was entered into and if the parties would not have entered into the contract or would have entered into it with different contents if they had foreseen this change, adaptation of the contract may be demanded to the extent that, taking account of all the circumstances of the specific case, in particular the contractual or statutory distribution of risk, one of the parties cannot reasonably be expected to uphold the contract without alteration.
(2) It is equivalent to a change of circumstances if material conceptions that have become the basis of the contract are found to be incorrect.
(3) If adaptation of the contract is not possible or one party cannot reasonably be expected to accept it, the disadvantaged party may revoke the contract. In the case of continuing obligations, the right to terminate takes the place of the right to revoke.

37. Although the new provision is formulated in very broad and open terms,[139] it is largely considered as an adequate restatement of the former case law.[140] It only differs from the latter insofar as it cannot be applied *ex officio*; instead, a party who wants the contract to be amended or terminated has to invoke the provision.[141] Of course, this digression may well be seen as an additional safeguard against judicial interventionism.

38. In general, there can be little doubt that the codification of the doctrine succeeded. Although §313 BGB seems to be more and more frequently invoked in litigation,[142] the courts seem to have largely respected the legislator's intention and refrained from applying the provision beyond the previous case law. The few cases where the §313 BGB has been applied although §242 had not[143] do not seem to be a consequence of the reform but rather appear to be instances of 'regular' change in the courts' jurisprudence. As a consequence, neither German[144] nor foreign[145] commentators consider the doctrine of the disappearance of the basis of the transaction as codified in §313 BGB as undermining legal certainty.

39. Uncertainties have however arisen out of the overlap with other newly modified provisions, most importantly with §275 BGB (governing impossibility). While it was clear, before 2002, that the doctrine of the disappearance of the basis of the transaction had no role to play where performance had become impossible,[146] many authors argue

139 Cf Markensis/Unberath/Johnston (n 35), 324; Finkenauer (n 33), para 7.
140 Cf Finkenauer (n 33), para 26; Grüneberg (n 35), para 1.
141 Cf Grüneberg (n 35), paras 1 and 41.
142 See, e.g., BGH 11 November 2010, NJW-RR 2011, 916, where a party invoked the provision in order to terminate a two-year internet provider contract after having moved away six months after its conclusion.
143 E.g. to gifts by parents-in-law to their son-in-law (BGH 3 December 2014, *NJW* 2015, 1014).
144 Cf Finkenauer (n 33), paras 3–6, 41–46, 52; surprisingly critical: Zweigert and Kötz, *An Introduction to Comparative Law* (3rd edn, OUP 1998), 535, 536.
145 Cf Beale et al (n 19), 1146; Markensis/Unberath/Johnston (n 35), 325–6; Tallon (n 126), 504.
146 BGH 17 February 1995, *NJW-RR* 95, 854, para 13; see also BT-Drucksache 14/6040, 176.

that it may be invoked in cases that fall under the new exception for 'factual impossibility' in §275(2) BGB, provided that the requirements of both provisions are met.[147]

40. Moreover, it may be seen as a downside to the legislator's otherwise strict adherence to the existing case law that they have not introduced an obligation to renegotiate,[148] which can be found in virtually all international model rules.[149] Thus, authors have remained divided as to whether an attempt to renegotiate is a requirement to modification or termination of the contract and what the consequences of the other party's refusal to negotiate are.[150] Meanwhile, the *Bundesgerichtshof* has held that §313 entails a duty to renegotiate, the breach of which may not only make termination available as a remedy even if the contract can be modified but also may itself be remedied by damages.[151]

4. The French reform

41. Under the impression of the international success of provisions on *imprévision*, many French authors[152] had argued for a long time that the decision in *Canal de Craponne* and the subsequent case law should be abolished – a position especially popular amongst those who generally advocated to give greater importance to the principle of good faith in contract law and more competences to the judge.[153] Yet, although Article 1134, al 3, of the *Code civil* would arguably have provided a solid textual basis for such a *revirement de jurisprudence*,[154] the impact of this movement seems to have been limited to the two decisions of the *Chambre de commerce* cited above.[155]

42. Still, it is hardly surprising that all projects for a reform of the *Code civil* contained some provisions that would overrule the decision in *Canal de Craponne*. While the *avant-projet Catala* allowed the courts to order renegotiation of a contract in case of supervening circumstances, failure of which would give both parties a right to terminate

147 Ernst (n 71), para 23; Finkenauer (n 33), para 164.

148 It was only stated in the reform materials that the parties 'should' renegotiate before seizing the courts (BT-Drucksache 14/6040, 176).

149 See above, 3.3.2.

150 Cf Finkenauer (n 33), para 122; for the same debate in Dutch law cf Busch, in Busch et al (eds), *The Principles of European Contract Law and Dutch Law. A Commentary* (Kluwer 2002), 289.

151 BGH 30 September 2011, *BGHZ* 191, 139, paras 27–28 and 33–34 (for critical comment see Teichmann, JZ 2012, 421). Concerning the availability of damages for a violation of the duty to renegotiate, the decision interestingly comes very close to the French judgment in *Huard* (n 60).

152 Cf, e.g., Philippe, *Changement de circonstances et bouleversement de l'économie contractuelle* (Bruylant 1986), 620–59; Fauvarque-Cosson (n 2), paras 8–25; Souchon, in Rodière (n 28), 17–18. See also Bell/Boyron/Whittaker, *Principles of French Law* (2nd edn, OUP 2008), 346.

153 See above, n 56.

154 See above, n 58; Philippe (n 152), 621–24; see also Fauvarque-Cosson (n 2), para 20, Capitant/Terré/Lequette (n 46), para 3, and Souchon, in Rodière (n 28), 17–18, all also pointing to other potential bases.

155 Above, n 60.

the contract,[156] both the *projet Terré*[157] and the Ministry of Justice's proposal[158] also gave the courts the power to amend the contract in such a situation.

43. Accordingly, *loi n° 2015-177 du 16 février 2015*, which authorised the government to 'modernise, simplify, and improve' *livre III* of the *Code civil*, also included a mandate 'to specify the rules concerning the effects of the contracts between the parties and for third persons by confirming their right to adapt their contract in the case of unforeseeable change of circumstances.'[159]

44. Thus, Article 1196[160] of the corresponding *projet d'ordonnance* stated that,[161]

> (1) If a change of circumstances unforeseeable at the conclusion of the contract renders its execution excessively onerous for one party that has not accepted to assume that risk, that party can demand a renegotiation of the contract. The party has to continue to perform their obligation during the renegotiation.
> (2) In the case of refusal or failure of the renegotiations, the parties may demand, by mutual agreement, a judge to proceed to adapt the contract. Failing this, a party may demand the judge to end the contract at the date and under the conditions that [the judge] fixes.

45. But although many authors seemed to welcome the general idea of codifying a provision for supervening circumstances,[162] the initial proposal was met with criticism:

156 Avant-projet de réforme du droit des obligations (2005), Art. 1135-1 to 1135-3.

157 Terré, *Pour une réforme du droit des contrats* (Dalloz 2008), Art. 92.

158 Ministère de la Justice, *Projet de réforme du droit des* contrats (2008), Art. 136; translations of all three texts can be found in Beale et al (n 19), 1134–35.

159 *Loi n° 2015-177 du 16 février 2015 relative à la modernisation et à la simplification du droit et des procédures dans les domaines de la justice et des affaires intérieures*, Art. 8: '*[L]e Gouvernement est autorisé à prendre par voie d'ordonnance les mesures [...] nécessaires pour modifier la structure et le contenu du livre III du code civil, afin de moderniser, de simplifier [et] d'améliorer la lisibilité [...], et, à cette fin [...] 6° Préciser les règles relatives aux effets du contrat entre les parties et à l'égard des tiers, en consacrant la possibilité pour celles-ci d'adapter leur contrat en cas de changement imprévisible de circonstances.*'

160 According to the official presentation of the *projet*, the provision is part of those seeking a better protection of the weaker party (cf Ministère de la Justice, *Presentation de l'avant-projet d'ordonnance en Conseil des ministres le 25 février 2015* <www.justice.gouv.fr/publication/j21_dp_projet_ord_reforme_contrats_2015.pdf> last accessed 12 February 2016.

161 *Projet d'ordonnance portant réforme du droit des contrats, du régime général et de la preuve des obligations* (2015), Art. 1196: '*(1) Si un changement de circonstances imprévisible lors de la conclusion du contrat rend l'exécution excessivement onéreuse pour une partie qui n'avait pas accepté d'en assumer le risque, celle-ci peut demander une renégociation du contrat à son cocontractant. Elle continue à exécuter ses obligations durant la renégociation. (2) En cas de refus ou d'échec de la renégociation, les parties peuvent demander d'un commun accord au juge de procéder à l'adaptation du contrat. A défaut, une partie peut demander au juge d'y mettre fin, à la date et aux conditions qu'il fixe.*'

162 Cf Alpa, 'Projet francais de réforme du droit des contrats', *Rev int de dr comp* 2015, 877, 893; Desaché/Dupichot/Dondero, 'Droit des contrats: la réforme (enfin) engagée', *Capital Finance*, 22 June 2015, 23; Stoffel-Munck (n 2), 263; Latina, 'L'imprévision', in *Dalloz Blog Réforme du droit des obligations*,

at the same time, it was criticised by practitioners for giving too much power to the judge[163] and by academics for not going quite far enough.[164]

46. In *ordonnance n° 2016-131*, paragraph (2) was changed to state that,[165]

> (2) In the case of refusal or failure of the renegotiations, the parties may agree to dissolve the contract at the date and under the conditions that they determine, or demand, by mutual agreement, a judge to proceed to adapt the contract. Failing an agreement within a reasonable delay, the judge can, at the request of a party, revise the contract or end it at the date and under the conditions that [the judge] fixes.

47. This amendment seems to be a reaction to (some of) the criticism that was levelled at the reform proposal. While the significance of the paradigm shift marked by the reform (1.) did arguably allow to put some of this criticism into perspective (2.), the provision that was finally adopted seems to be an even stronger reflection of these comparativist arguments (3.).

4.1. The doctrinal importance of the French reform

48. The importance of the French reform, which openly admits to be 'inspired by comparative law',[166] clearly lies in its doctrinal dimension. It puts the uncompromising adherence of French law to a sacrosanct principle of *pacta sunt servanda* to an end and finally provides an escape route for parties that have not, and could not, foresee a

23 March 2015 <http://reforme-obligations.dalloz.fr/2015/03/23/limprevision/> last accessed 12 February 2016.

163 Cf Cousin et al (n 51), II B 1; Rocher, 'La réforme du droit des contrats: quelles conséquences pour les contrats de construction?', Point de vue, moniteur.fr, 2 July 2015 <www.lemoniteur.fr/article/point-de-vue-la-reforme-du-droit-des-contrats-quelles-consequences-pour-les-contrats-de-construction-28959918> last accessed 12 February 2016; see also Sidier/Niel, 'Le contrat ne fera bientôt plus vraiment la loi des parties: introduction de l'imprévision dans le Code Civil', finyear.com, 8 June 2015 <www.finyear.com/Le-contrat-ne-fera-bientot-plus-vraiment-la-loi-des-parties-introduction-de-l-imprevision-dans-le-Code-Civil_a33204.html> last accessed 12 February 2016, criticising that the provision will allow parties to escape from the obligation to perform in good faith by simply refusing to renegotiate.

164 Chagny, 'Vent de réforme: du contrat à la concurrence et vice versa', AJ Contrats d'affaires, Concurrence, Distribution 2015, 145; see also Latina (n 162); Latina, 'L'attractivité du droit des contrats: l'efficacité économique du droit des contrats', in *Dalloz Blog Réforme du droit des obligations*, 8 September 2015 <http://reforme-obligations.dalloz.fr/2015/09/08/lattractivite-du-droit-des-contrats-lefficacite-economique-du-droit-des-contrats/> last accessed 12 February 2016.

165 *Ordonnance n° 2016-131 du 10 février 2016 portant réforme du droit des contrats, du régime général et de la preuve des obligations*, Art. 1195: '*(2) En cas de refus ou d'échec de la renégociation, les parties peuvent convenir de la résolution du contrat, à la date et aux conditions qu'elles déterminent, ou demander d'un commun accord au juge de procéder à son adaptation. A défaut d'accord dans un délai raisonnable, le juge peut, à la demande d'une partie, réviser le contrat ou y mettre fin, à la date et aux conditions qu'il fixe.*'

166 See above, n 150.

particular change of circumstances. Following the example of other legal systems,[167] the French government opted against merely redefining an existing doctrine like *force majeure* or using one of the other existing devices that have been proposed for such a reform[168] and instead created a separate exception to *pacta sunt servanda.*

49. Within the conceptual framework established above, this puts French law very close to German law. Still, the reform proposal was not entirely clear on whether the new French provision would be rooted in the principle of good faith as much as the German §313 BGB. While the latter emerged from case law explicitly based on §242 BGB, giving preference to amending the contract over terminating it, the proposed French provision, to be introduced without indication of its conceptual basis, would be a bit more ambivalent. Its first paragraph could certainly be linked to the aforementioned decisions of the commercial chamber[169] establishing a duty to renegotiate based on Article 1134, al 3, *Code civil.*[170] According to its second paragraph, however, the usual remedy in cases of *imprévision* would have been the termination of the contract, a judicial modification being only possible where both parties had agreed on it, putting the proposed provision conceptually closer to the reasoning underlying the *force majeure* exception. Making adaptation available to each party under the same conditions as termination, *ordonnance n° 2016–131* has however clarified that the new provision will indeed be rooted in the principle of good faith.[171]

50. But even in the form that was originally proposed, the introduction of the new exception for *imprévision* would have had undeniable benefits for French law. First, it would have put an end to the confusing plurality of exceptions to the principle expressed in *Canal de Craponne,*[172] which include the positions of the administrative courts as well as the commercial chamber's ambiguous decisions in *Huard* and *Soffimat.*[173] This should have been considered as an important contribution to legal certainty in itself.

51. Second, the introduction of an exception that is distinct from the doctrine of *force majeure* would have nuanced the approach French law applied to supervening circumstances and allowed the courts to award a much more adequate remedy than the automatic discharge of the parties.[174] The fact that English courts do not enjoy this liberty has been shown to be one of the reasons for their very restrictive approach to the doctrine of frustration of purpose.[175]

[167] Cf Fages (n 77), para 423; Fauvarque-Cosson (n 2), paras 13–15; Stoffel-Munck (n 2), 262.

[168] See above, n 150.

[169] Above, n 60.

[170] As far as an obligation to renegotiate is admitted in German law, it is also inferred from §242 BGB, see above, para. 40.

[171] See below, 4.3.

[172] According to Bénabent (n 26), para 293, the amount of exceptions has rendered the principle 'an empty shell'.

[173] See above, 3.1.

[174] Cf von Bar/Clive/Schulte-Nölke (n 124), 738, for a similar consideration.

[175] See above, para. 25.

4.2. The practical shortcomings of the reform proposal

52. In view of these general advantages that a separate exception for *imprévision* would have for French contract law, some of the arguments that had been put forward against the originally proposed provision and, especially, its practical effects, had to be put into perspective. A comparison to the conceptually similar approach of German law, for instance, could not only disprove the general concern that judicial intervention would unduly decrease legal certainty[176] but also allowed to address some of the more nuanced comments made by French authors.

53. In this regard, a first point of criticism concerned the fact that the provision was drafted in very broad and imprecise terms, which could create uncertainty concerning, in particular, the threshold of *imprévision* and its relationship to the doctrine of *force majeure*.[177] While the fact that the same uncertainty seems to surround the equally broadly formulated[178] German §313 BGB,[179] even though the provision was drafted on the back of 80 years of case law, might have indicated that this would indeed be a problem, there were a number of reasons not to overstate this risk. French courts do not only have considerable experience in fleshing out important doctrines and legal concepts (such as the doctrine *force majeure*)[180] on the basis of open and imprecisely formulated provisions, they could also draw from the impressive body of academic writing on the *théorie de l'imprévision*, the case law regarding types of contracts for which it is already admitted[181] and, most importantly, the case law of the administrative courts which have applied it alongside the doctrine of *force majeure* ever since the decision in *Gaz de Bordeaux*.[182]

54. While this criticism remains valid in light of the provision ultimately adopted, paragraph (1) of which has remained unchanged from the *projet d'ordonnance*, the fact that the *rapport* accompanying the final *ordonnance* expressly refers to *imprévision* as 'a notion well-known in administrative law'[183] makes it even more likely that the courts will adopt the distinction between *force majeure* and *imprévision* developed by the administrative courts, drawing a line between supervening events that are irresistible and those that are not.[184]

176 Cf Tallon (n 58), 410–12; Terré/Simler/Lequette (n 48), para 471; see also von Bar/Clive/Schulte-Nölke (n 124), 741.

177 Cf Dissaux/Jamin, *Projet de réforme du droit des contrats, du régime général et de la preuve des obligations rendu public le 25 février 2015. Commentaire article par article* (Dalloz 2015), Art. 1034, C; Bridier, 'Encore des critiques sur la réforme du droit des contrats', actuel-direction-juridique.fr, 22 July 2015 <www.actuel-direction-juridique.fr/content/encore-des-critiques-sur-la-reformes-du-droit-des-contrats> last accessed 12 February 2016.

178 Cf Finkenauer (n 33), para 7.

179 See above, n 39.

180 As to the development of which see Nicholas, 'Force Majeure in French Law', in McKendrick (n 48), 21.

181 See above, n 45.

182 Above, n 53.

183 See above, n 32.

184 Cf Cousin et al (n 51), II B 2; Fauvarque-Cosson (n 2), paras 10, 23.

55. A second point of criticism went to the relatively tame remedies offered to the party for which performance had become more onerous.[185] While it is not uncommon to impose a duty to renegotiate the contract on that party,[186] the proposed French provision appeared as particularly weak insofar as it restricted judicial modification of the contract to cases where both parties had agreed to it if such renegotiation failed. To a certain degree, this could be explained by an awareness of many practitioners' hostility towards judicial interventionism. Yet, contractual parties had arguably always been free to demand a judge to amend their contract by common agreement.[187] As a consequence, the proposal would have changed the law only insofar as it allowed the judge to end the contract at the application of one of the parties if renegotiations were unsuccessful.[188]

56. While this perceived weakness has been remedied by *ordonnance n° 2016–131*,[189] it was arguably less problematic than many commentators seemed to think. In fact, the mere prospect of judicial termination could well have provided a significant incentive for the parties to either amend the contract themselves or agree on a judicial modification.[190] The fact that commercial parties regularly include hardship clauses into complex long-term contracts regardless of whether the applicable law provides for a remedy in cases of *imprévision* or not[191] seems to indicate that parties do indeed often want to uphold their contracts and remain in charge of potential modifications, rather than losing it altogether.[192]

57. Moreover, the practical impact of the proposed provision would have highly depended on how the courts would have interpreted the powers conferred upon them. Again, it should be borne in mind that the French courts have considerable experience in refining broadly formulated doctrines.[193] Just as the German courts have applied the solution developed during the hyperinflation of the 1920s to a myriad of other situations and legal problems,[194] there would have been a good chance that the French courts would have made use of their experience in developing and refining legal doctrines when interpreting the text of the new provision.

58. The proposed provision would have been open to such interpretation in at least two regards. First, the courts would have had to define the scope and content of the requirement to renegotiate the contract before it could be terminated; by considering an

185 See above, n 160.
186 See above, paras 35 (for international model rules) and 40 (for German law).
187 Latina (n 162).
188 Cousin et al (n 51), II B 1.
189 See below, 4.
190 Cf Rocher (n 163). See also *Rapport au Président de la République* (n 32), 14.
191 See above, n 69. In German law, these clauses usually also contain an obligation to renegotiate before the courts can be seized (see Finkenauer (n 33), para 123). For English law see Treitel (n 11), ch 12.
192 For a law-and-economics perspective on this point cf Cenini/Luppi/Parisi, in Hondius/Grigoleit (n 13), 37.
193 See above, at n 180.
194 See above, 3.3.1.

offer made by the party seeking termination as unsatisfactory, they could have directly influenced the negotiations and the content of the potentially amended contract. Second, paragraph two of the proposal would have allowed the judge 'to end the contract at the date and under the conditions that [the judge] fixes'; again, it would have been up to the courts to determine what shape these conditions may take.[195]

59. The perceived weakness of the remedies provided in the reform proposal might thus have been counterbalanced, at least to a certain degree, by the room left to the courts by the wording of the proposal and the absence of a coherent body of former case law. Of course, there were still good reasons to doubt that this would have been sufficient to realise the beneficial economic effects usually ascribed to provisions on *imprévision*, i.e. to decrease transactions costs by reducing the need for *force majeure* and hardship clauses.[196]

4.3. *The provision finally adopted*

60. The provision ultimately adopted in *ordonnance n° 2016-131 du 10 février 2016* has rendered part of this discussion obsolete. The new Article 1195 does not only clarify that the parties are free to dissolve their contract if their renegotiations remain fruitless, it also allows each of them individually to seek a judicial adaptation of the contract. As a consequence, the courts will not be limited to 'end the contract at the date and under the conditions that [they] fix' but may also modify the contract at the request of one of the parties.

61. The French government seems to have taken into account the criticism regarding the perceived weakness of the originally proposed provision and has considerably strengthened both the party for which performance has become more onerous and the courts' role as guardians of the fairness of the contract. As a consequence, there does not remain much doubt that Article 1195 is an application of the principles of good faith in performance and contractual fairness, inspired by considerations of comparative law.[197]

62. The new provision, which will enter into force on 1 October 2016, now looks strikingly similar to its German counter-part. Two differences seem to remain: First, §313 BGB stipulates a clear hierarchy between its two remedies – adaptation and termination – which cannot be found in Article 1195.[198] Second, the text of §313 BGB

195 Cf Stoffel-Munck (n 2), 265; Alpa (n 162), 894. For a well-known example from English law for a court setting aside a contract 'on terms' (due to a common mistake), see *Solle v Butcher* [1950] 1 KB 671, 696–97.

196 Cf McKendrick (n 48), 43.

197 See also *Rapport au Président de la République* (n 32), 14: *'Cette consécration inspirée du droit comparé comme des projets d'harmonisation européens, permet de lutter contre les déséquilibres contractuels majeurs qui surviennent en cours d'exécution, conformément à l'objectif de justice contractuelle poursuivi par l'ordonnance.'*

198 See above, 3.3.3.

does not contain a requirement to renegotiate, which however features quite prominently in Article 1195. In light of the ongoing debate among German scholars whether such a requirement can be found somewhere in the provision,[199] the recent decision by the *Bundesgerichtshof*,[200] and the fact that renegotiations are a requirement of virtually all provisions on *imprévision* in international harmonisation projects,[201] Article 1195 may even appear as the more progressive of the two provisions in this regard.

5. Conclusion

63. Over the last century, the different European legal systems have adopted a number of approaches to the problem of *imprévision*. While some have not admitted any exception to *pacta sunt servanda*, or merely extended the existing exception for impossibility, many legal systems have adopted a separate doctrine to accommodate these cases and to reconcile the principle of *pacta sunt servanda* with the doctrine of good faith.

64. Against this backdrop, the French reform should first and foremost be praised for the paradigm shift that it marks; it is submitted that it will increase both legal certainty and contractual fairness. Given the amendments that have been made to what appeared as a somewhat underwhelming reform proposal, there remains little doubt that the new Article 1195 of the *Code civil* will have a very positive impact on French law in practice.

65. Hopefully, this will extent to the economic effects of the provision. While it puts a greater emphasis on prior renegotiations than its German counterpart – clearly reflecting its roots in the principle of good faith – Article 1195 should be equally able to reduce transaction costs for commercial parties by minimising the need for hardship clauses.

199 ibid.
200 Above, n 151.
201 See above, 3.3.2.

Janwillem (Pim)
Oosterhuis*

COMMERCIAL IMPRACTICABILITY AND THE MISSED OPPORTUNITY OF THE FRENCH CONTRACT LAW REFORM: DOCTRINAL, HISTORICAL AND LAW AND ECONOMICS ARGUMENTS – COMMENT ON LUTZI'S INTRODUCING *IMPRÉVISION* INTO FRENCH CONTRACT LAW

1. Introduction

1. Unforeseen circumstances pose one of the perennial dilemmas of private law: if due to unforseen circumstances performance becomes impracticable or even impossible, is a non-performing party then still liable out of the contract? Or might he be excused? In other words, should precedence be given to rules based on the adage *pacta sunt servanda*, or rather to excuses based on *clausula rebus sic stantibus* or other good faith principles?[1] The French legislature clearly struggled with this dilemma in its recent adjustment of the *Code civil*, as can be seen from the *Projet d'ordonnance* of 2015[2] and the *ordonnance n° 2016-131* of 10 February 2016.[3] Before, a seemingly endless parade of scholars, both within and outside France, discussed the current solution in the *Code civil* to the problem

* Assistant Professor, Faculty of Law & Fellow, Maastricht Private Law Institute, Maastricht University.
For critical remarks, I would like to thank Kristel de Smedt and Niels Philipsen. An earlier version of this paper was presented at the Workshop on Contract Law of the Ius Commune Conference, Leuven, 26 November 2015, and I wish to thank Jacques du Plessis, Stellenbosch, and Tobias Lutzi, Oxford, for their critical comments during the discussion. The text was amended in March 2016 as a result of the introduction of *ordonnance n° 2016-131*.

1 A discussion of the relation between the adage *pacta sunt servanda* and impracticability excuses is closely connected to the more general discussion of the role of specific performance as a contractual remedy. On the (in)efficiency of specific performance in contract law, see e.g. S. Shavell, Specific Performance versus Damages for Breach of Contract: An Economic Analysis, 84 *Texas Law Review* (2006), 831–876. On the historical development of specific performance until the 20th century, see e.g. J. Oosterhuis, *Specific Peformance in German, French and Dutch Law in the Nineteenth Century: Remedies in an Age of Fundamental Rights and Industrialisation*, Leiden 2011.

2 *Projet d'ordonnance portant réforme du droit des contrats, du régime général et de la preuve des obligations* (2015), Art 1196.

3 *Ordonnance n° 2016-131 du 10 février 2016 portant réforme du droit des contrats, du régime général et de la preuve des obligations*, Art. 1195: The provisions of *ordonnance n° 2016-131* are effective as of 1 October 2016.

of unforeseen circumstances,[4] but also the solutions proposed in various drafts, such as the Avant-projet Catala.[5]

2. In the previous contribution to this volume, *Introducing Imprévision into French Contract Law, A Paradigm Shift in Comparative Perspective*,[6] Tobias Lutzi not only analysed an impressive amount of French and foreign contemporary scholarship on – the traditional lack of – *imprévision* in French private law, but also assessed the current, proposed and recently adopted French solutions to commercial impracticability resulting from unforeseen circumstances.[7] For this assessment, he compared the English, German (in particular) and the current, proposed and new French solutions to unforeseen circumstances with each other, thereby highlighting lessons to be learned from the German solution. The focus of Lutzi's comparison is mainly at a conceptual level,[8] namely whether the systems compared offer an adequate exception to rules based on *pacta sunt servanda*[9] and he argues that the German solution to the problem of unforeseen circumstances – to which the new Article 1195 *Code civil* will be quite similar – is to be preferred over the English, and the current and previously proposed French solutions.[10]

3. Lutzi's line of argument runs more or less as follows: most legal systems adhere – explicitly or implicitly – to a rule that contracts always have to be performed, which is derived from the principle of *pacta sunt servanda*. Such rule is too strict in legal practice, not only in the event that performance has become impossible,[11] but also where performance has become commercially impracticable. To accommodate legal practice, legal systems should allow an exception to the rule that all obligations have to be performed. Otherwise, the coherence of a legal system will be jeopardised, which eventually will lead to legal uncertainty and thus to higher transaction costs.[12]

4. Conceptually – or dogmatically – Lutzi distinguishes between three solutions to commercial impracticability due to unforeseen circumstances, and in doing so also compares the French, English, and German legal systems: (i) no exception (the current French solution, which has led to piecemeal solutions in judicial practice and uncertainty in legal practice);[13] (ii) an exception whereby a contract will be discharged,

4 For references see the previous contribution to this volume, T. Lutzi, Introducing Imprévision into French Contract Law, A Paradigm Shift in Comparative Perspective, in S. Stijns & S. Jansen (eds), *The French Contract Law: Source of Inspiration?*, Cambridge 2016, [1–20].

5 See for example J. Cartwright, S. Vogenauer & S. Whittaker (eds), *Reforming the French Law of Obligations*, Oxford 2009.

6 Lutzi (n 4), 89–112.

7 Lutzi (n 4), 94–8 (nos 15–21), 105–12 (nos 41–62).

8 Lutzi (n 4), 94 (no 14).

9 Lutzi (n 4), 91–2 (nos 8–9).

10 Lutzi (n 4), for example 108 (no 49), 109 (no 53).

11 Lutzi (n 4), 91–2 (nos 8–9).

12 Lutzi (n 4), 93–4 (nos 11–3).

13 Lutzi (n 4), 94–98 (nos 15–21), 108 (nos 50–1).

basically by extending the impossibility excuse (the English system);[14] or (iii) a separate exception whereby a contract will be discharged or adjusted, ultimately based on the concept of good faith (the German system).[15] Now, according to Lutzi, the German solution is superior for essentially three reasons: (i) it is doctrinally or dogmatically superior;[16] (ii) its long use and widespread reception confirm this superiority;[17] and (iii) it works best in practice.[18] In this contribution I will comment critically on these arguments.

2. The German commercial impracticability excuse and legal doctrine

5. Admittedly, the most important standard Lutzi is applying in his paper is a legal-dogmatic or doctrinal standard. This is the standard of a coherent and clear legal system, that is whether rules fit well together in a contemporaneous legal system, and whether such system is accessible and workable.[19] Here I would like to distinguish between the exception or excuse as such, and a remedy (discharge, adjustment, or a combination of both) based on such exception. For the exception as such, I appreciate the argument Lutzi is making. He notices that exceptions necessarily have to be made to the rule that contracts always have to be performed, not only because of impossibility or *force majeure*, but also because of commercial impracticability or *imprévision*, and he points out that particularly for the latter situation the German solution is superior to the English and French ones – except for the new French solution. He considers the English solution to commercial impracticability to be a mere extension of the impossibility doctrine, and that for French private law a solution to commercial impracticability is essentially absent, resulting in a range of more or less obscure, haphazard exceptions to the rule that obligations always have to be performed. And here he is right: if one takes the coherence of a legal system as a standard, than indeed the German disappearance of the contractual basis, '*Wegfall der Geschäftsgrundlage*', ultimately based upon the principle of good faith, is to be preferred over piecemeal solutions. Because, as Lutzi points out quite clearly, the current French system seems to be rather unclear (when exactly is there an excuse?) and incoherent (why do we have *imprévision* in the first place, and what about the exceptions in case law?).[20] And indeed an impracticability excuse[21] as such can just as well be based on the principles of either good faith or *clausula rebus sic stantibus*.

14 Lutzi (n 4), 98–9 (nos 22–5).
15 Lutzi (n 4), 99–105 (nos 26–40).
16 Lutzi (n 4), 100–2 (nos 27–32).
17 Lutzi (n 4), 103–5 (nos 33–5).
18 Lutzi (n 4), 105–6 (nos 36–40), 109–11 (nos 52–9).
19 Recently on such legal-dogmatic standard, see J. Smits, *What is Legal Doctrine? On the aims and methods of legal-dogmatic research*, September 2015, M-EPLI Working Paper 2015/6 (http://papers.ssrn.com/sol3/papers.cfm?abstract_id=2644088), 5–7.
20 Lutzi (n 4), 94–8 (nos 15–21).
21 In this contribution I will use the term impracticability excuse instead of the more general term *imprévision*.

6. Admittedly, it is somewhat hard to compare dogmatic coherence if one compares civil and common law systems, because good faith does not play a large role in the common law system. Basing an excuse of impracticability upon this concept would be rather alien to the common law system, hence the English struggle with the implied condition and frustration of contract as a basis for such exception.[22] Nevertheless, the idea of a separate exception when performance has become impracticable, apart from the exception for impossible performance, seems to be plausible, because those are indeed conceptually separate situations.

7. Even so, if one looks at the remedy based on such an exception, I am less convinced that discharge or adjustment – an 'open' remedy – is doctrinally superior to renegotiation by the parties and/or discharge – a 'closed' remedy.[23] In the event of commercial impracticability, German courts can discharge or adjust a contract, giving discretion to the judiciary to possibly reshape the contract – the German legal system has therefore been characterised as an 'open' legal system in this respect.[24] Similarly, the new Article 1195 of the *Code civil* transforms the French legal system into an 'open' system: according to the new Article 1195, courts can eventually be authorised to discharge but also to adjust a contract.[25]

8. The English and both the current and formerly proposed French solutions to commercial impracticability, however, leave control over the contract in the hands of the parties, because in the event of commercial impracticability the contract simply has to be upheld (current French private law, more or less), is discharged (English law), or is discharged if parties fail to renegotiate the contract themselves (former French proposal of 2015[26]). These solutions do not give the judiciary any discretion to reshape a contract,

22 See A.W.B. Simpson, 'Innovation in Nineteenth Century Contract Law', in A.W.B. Simpson, *Legal Theory and Legal History*, London 1987, 171–202 (197); C. MacMillan, 'Taylor v Caldwell (1863)' in Ch. Mitchell & P. Mitchell (eds), *Landmark cases in the law of contract*, Oxford 2008, 167–203 (192–9); M. Lobban, 'Contract' in W.R. Cornish et al. (eds), *The Oxford History of the Laws of England, Volume XII 1820–1914*, Oxford 2010, 295–610 (512–21).

23 See on the classification in 'open' and 'closed' legal systems in respect of remedies for unexpected circumstances, E. Hondius & H.C. Grigoleit, 'Introduction: An approach to the issues and doctrines relating to unexpected circumstances' in E. Hondius & H.C. Grigoleit (eds), *Unexpected Circumstances in European Contract Law*, Cambridge 2011, 3–14 (11).

24 E. Hondius & H.C. Grigoleit (eds), *Unexpected Circumstances in European Contract Law*, Cambridge 2011, 11, 62–3.

25 See *ordonnance n° 2016-131* (n 3), Art. 1195: *(1) Si un changement de circonstances imprévisible lors de la conclusion du contrat rend l'exécution excessivement onéreuse pour une partie qui n'avait pas accepté d'en assumer le risque, celle-ci peut demander une renégociation du contrat à son cocontractant. Elle continue à exécuter ses obligations durant la renégociation. (2) En cas de refus ou d'échec de la renégociation, les parties peuvent convenir de la résolution du contrat, à la date et aux conditions qu'elles déterminent, ou demander d'un commun accord au juge de procéder à son adaptation. A défaut d'accord dans un délai raisonnable, le juge peut, à la demande d'une partie, réviser le contrat ou y mettre fin, à la date et aux conditions qu'il fixe.*

26 See *Projet d'ordonnance* (n 2), Art 1196: *(1) Si un changement de circonstances imprévisible lors de la conclusion du contrat rend l'exécution excessivement onéreuse pour une partie qui n'avait pas accepté d'en assumer le risque, celle-ci peut demander une renégociation du contrat à son cocontractant. Elle*

and the English and current French law and the former French proposal can therefore be characterised as 'closed' legal systems in this respect.[27]

9. In addition, the principle of *clausula rebus sic stantibus* is more in line with discharge, because 'the matters so standing' is generally thought of as a condition under which performance can be demanded.[28] If matters change, performance is no longer due. Discharge as a remedy for commercial impracticability due to unforeseen circumstances indeed fits well with English law, because the continued existence of a certain situation – and thus the non-occurrence of certain unforeseen circumstances fundamentally changing that situation – is thought of as an implied condition to the contract.[29] Problematically, this might result in discharging potentially still efficient contracts.[30]

10. Admittedly, the more general principle that parties should behave in good faith in a contractual relationship does not per se seem to dictate that a judge has to modify the contract as a result of unforeseen circumstances either. Theoretically, if performance is still efficient after unforeseen circumstances, the parties will renegotiate the contract (in the course of which they have to act in good faith) – and many systems, including the former French proposal of 2015 and the new Article 1195 of *Code civil*, include a duty to renegotiate. If performance is no longer efficient after the unforeseen circumstances, then they will not reach agreement and/or the contract will be discharged. However, in practice, renegotiating in good faith is hard to supervise and strategic behaviour might prevent the renegotiation of a contract that is still effective. Therefore, one might argue that the good faith in which the parties initially concluded the contract gives the court discretion to enforce this good faith upon the parties when performance of the contract is still effective after the unforeseen circumstances. However, the question is obviously whether courts are up to such a task. If so, then courts essentially have to establish a contract that would have been initially concluded by the parties, for which the courts need to know inter alia which party is the cheapest cost avoider,[31] the cheapest

continue à exécuter ses obligations durant la renégociation. (2) En cas de refus ou d'échec de la renégociation, les parties peuvent demander d'un commun accord au juge de procéder à l'adaptation du contrat. A défaut, une partie peut demander au juge d'y mettre fin, à la date et aux conditions qu'il fixe.

27 Hondius (n 24), 11, 144–9 (France), 163–6 (England).

28 For the historical development of the *clausula rebus sic stantibus* doctrine, and its decline in the 18th and 19th centuries, see R. Zimmermann, "Heard Melodies are sweet, but those unheard are sweeter' – Condicio tacita, implied condition und die Fortbildung des europäischen Vertragsrecht', 193 Archiv für die Civilistische Praxis (1993), 123–173 (135–6); A. Thier, 'Legal History' in Hondius (n 25), 15–32 (25–30); R. Meyer-Pritzl, '§§313–314: Störung der Geschäftsgrundlage. Kündigung von Dauerschuldverhältnisse aus wichtigen Grund' in M. Schmoeckel, J. Rückert & R. Zimmermann (eds), Historisch-Kritischer Kommentar zum BGB, Tübingen 2008, 1708–59 (II.4–5).

29 On the continental influences on this doctrine, via Pothier and Blackburn J., see Simpson (n 22), 194–5; MacMillan (n 22), 192–4; Lobban (n 22), 514.

30 This will be discussed below in chapter 4. Practical implications: which remedy is more efficient?, section 4.3. Reduction of transaction costs ex post: discharge or adjustment?, nos 38–9.

31 The cheapest cost avoider is the party who can avoid the event which causes the increase in costs, at the lowest cost. See H-B. Schäfer & C. Ott, *Lehrbuch der ökonomische Analyse des Zivilrechts*, Berlin 2012, 434–7.

insurer,[32] and the superior risk bearer.[33] These are more or less unobservable factors for courts or can only be observed at very high cost. It is very possible that a court will make errors in establishing such a contract.[34] Nevertheless, there indeed seems to be a dogmatic case for an 'open' remedy.

3. Long use and widespread reception: lessons from legal history

11. According to Lutzi, the long use and widespread reception of the German impracticability excuse confirm its superiority. His argument can be summarised as follows: an 'open' remedy has been used for quite a long time in Germany, and it worked quite well, so it must be a good remedy: moreover, many systems have taken over the German open remedy, which also proves that it is a good remedy. Or rather, history is used as a standard to compare and assess the impracticability excuses – or the lack thereof – in the various legal systems. However, explaining or understanding why exactly certain institutions worked in the past and in various places seems necessary before any conclusions can be drawn about the quality of these institutions.[35]

12. If in the past certain institutions worked in some places, we might infer that, given certain conditions, these institutions might also work in other places and in different times. 'Given certain conditions' is crucial. Institutions, including the '*Wegfall der Geschäftsgrundlage*', do not arise in vacuum, as Lutzi indicated very clearly for the German exception: the German courts developed this exception in response to the consequences of the hyperinflation in Germany after the First World War.[36] France and England, and also for instance the Netherlands, did not experience such an economic catastrophe: inflation was high, but not high enough to develop a separate exception, such as in Germany.[37]

[32] The cheapest insurer is the party who can insure an increase in costs at the lowest price. See Schäfer & Ott (n 31), 437–41.

[33] The superior risk bearer is the party who can bear the risk that the losses will occur at the lowest costs. See Schäfer & Ott (n 31), 442–4.

[34] Establishing a fully specified contract and allocating risks upon the occurrence of an unforeseen circumstance, will be discussed in more detail below, 4.3. Reduction of transaction costs ex post: discharge or adjustment?, nos 30–1. On the fundamental problem of access to information, or, who has better information, see S. Shavell, Liability for Harm versus Regulation of Safety, 13 *Journal of Legal Studies* (1984), 357–374 (359–60).

[35] On the complexity of explanation, see for example J. Elster, *Explaining Social Behaviour*, Cambridge 2007, 7–30.

[36] Lutzi (n 4), 100–1 (nos 28–30). See fundamentally J. Thiessen, The German Hyperinflation of the 1920s, in D. Fox & W. Ernst (eds), *Money in the Western Legal Tradition*, Oxford 2016, 735–69. See also J.P. Dawson, 'Effects of inflation on private contracts: Germany, 1914–1924', 33 *Mich. L. Rev.* (1934), 171–238 (175–7); H. Dörner, 'Erster Weltkrieg und Privatrecht', 17 *Rechtstheorie* (1986), 385–401 (385); S-R. Eiffler, 'Die "Feuertaufe" des BGB: Das Vertragsrecht des Bürgerlichen Gesctzbuchs und das Kriegswirtschaftsrecht des 1. Weltkriegs', 20 *Zeitschrift für Neuere Rechtsgeschichte* (1998), 238–55; J. Oosterhuis, Unexpected Circumstances arising from World War I and its Aftermath: 'Open' versus 'Closed' Legal Systems, 7(2) *Erasmus Law Review* (2014), 67–79 (76–7).

[37] See S. Renner, *Inflation and the enforcement of contracts*, Cheltenham 1999, 16–7, 25; Oosterhuis (n 36), 75–6.

Admittedly, only in legal systems that have experienced serious economic catastrophes – Austria, Italy, Greece – will the development or transplant of an 'open remedy' have a lasting effect.[38] The Netherlands is a case in point: in 1992, an open remedy was transplanted in article 6:258 of the *Burgerlijk Wetboek* – after the German example. However, in judicial practice, the Dutch legal system is 'closed' after all: the remedy is virtually a dead letter.[39] One could argue that this remedy has not yet been necessary, that is, there were no serious economic crises to trigger the use of such a remedy. Once the Netherlands is hit by significant economic upheaval, the remedy in article 6:258 of the *Burgerlijk Wetboek* might become a living institution after all. However, the excuse and remedy have been part of the Dutch legal system since 1992, so for more than two decades. Rather, already in 1976 the Dutch Supreme Court decided that under certain circumstances a court was indeed authorised to adjust a contract.[40] In the last two decades, and certainly since 1976, the Netherlands has experienced some serious economic crises, such as the second oil crisis in 1979, and the financial crisis since 2007. These were global crises, and their experience was shared with, amongst others, Germany: the financial crisis since 2007 has resulted in case law in Germany,[41] unlike in the Netherlands, as far as I am aware. This discrepancy in using available remedies confirms that legal transplants often develop in their own unique ways, independently and different from the original donor.[42]

13. In addition, the inclusion of the German impracticability excuse in various soft law instruments, that is, less binding instruments on international and European (commercial) contract law, such as the Principles of European Contract Law (PECL) (1995, 1999, 2003), the Draft Common Frame of Reference (DCFR) (2010), and the former proposal for a Common European Sales Law (CESL) (2011), do not by themselves indicate that the drafters were convinced by the superiority of an 'open' remedy: it might as well demonstrate a strong German influence during the drafting of these instruments.[43]

14. The codification of the *Allgemeines Deutsches Handelsgesetzbuch* of 1861 provides an example where political power was ultimately decisive for the adoption of the text of the code, not its quality as such. Here Prussia succeeded in having its already existing *Entwurf eines Handelsgesetzbuch für die Preussischen Staaten* of 1856 taken over almost in its entirety as the *Allgemeines Deutsches Handelsgesetzbuch*.[44] This example merely

38 See Oosterhuis (n 36), 79.

39 See Hondius (n 24), 643; Oosterhuis (n 36), 78.

40 HR, 16 December 1976, *NJ* 76, 136 (*Ziekenfonds*). See Oosterhuis (n 36), 78.

41 For example KG Berlin 5 November 2012, NJW 2013, 478, referred to by Lutzi (n 4), 102 (n 117).

42 See A. Watson, *Legal Transplants, An Approach to Comparative Law*, London 1993, 100.

43 On for example German influence on the DCFR, see M. Siems, *Comparative Law*, Cambridge 2014, 156.

44 See C. Bergfeld, Preußen und das Allgemeine Deutsche Handelsgesetzbuch, *Zeitschrift für Europäische Rechtsgeschichte* (*ZER*), Ius Commune XIV, Veröffentlichungen des Max-Planck-Instituts für Europäische Rechtsgeschichte, Frankfurt am Main 1987, 101–14 (108–10); A.J. Kanning, *Unifying Commercial Laws of Nation-States: Coordination of Legal Systems and Economic Growth*, Maastricht 2003, 79; J. Oosterhuis, Convergence and Unification of Nineteenth Century European Commercial Sales Law. Why the CESL might just be an Intermezzo in the Game of Unifying European Sales Law, 21(4) *European Review of Private Law* (2013), 991–1007 (1003–4).

aims to illustrate that the reception of certain institutions in another legal system may have various reasons, and not primarily or even only the high quality of certain rules – although they nevertheless can be of high quality and fit for their purpose, as the *Allgemeines Deutsches Handelsgesetzbuch* itself illustrates.[45]

15. Moreover, content-wise, PECL, DCFR and the former proposal for a CESL all have a preliminary duty to renegotiate, before a court may adjust a contract. So party autonomy still has a prominent place in these instruments. However, it is difficult to discern lasting effect of these less binding instruments on European legal practice. And as Lutzi himself points out, a more binding international instrument, the Vienna Convention on Contracts for the International Sale of Goods (CISG) (1980) – a commercial instrument *pur sang* – offers only an impossibility excuse, that is, it is a 'closed' legal regime.[46]

16. Therefore, I am not convinced by the superiority of the German 'open' remedy. Rather, comparative legal history suggests that the former French proposal – a 'closed' remedy – would have had better chances of survival than the transplant of an 'open' remedy via the new article 1195 of the *Code civil*: a 'closed' remedy would have stayed closer to the current 'closed' legal system. The former French proposal of 2015 thus had the chance of becoming a living institution – contrary to the Dutch transplant of the German 'open' remedy, which has remained a dead letter. This makes one pessimistic for the chances of the new Article 1195 of the *Code civil* becoming a living institution, although the experience with the 'open' remedy of *imprévision* in French administrative law may increase the chances somewhat.[47] Moreover, a 'closed' remedy might even be the more efficient solution, and that brings me to the practical implications.

4. Practical implications: which remedy is more efficient?

17. Lutzi points to essentially three practical implications of the German commercial impracticability excuse: (i) reduction of transaction costs *ex ante* (during the initial contracting);[48] (ii) contractual fairness *ex post* (after the occurrence of the unforeseen circumstance;[49] and (iii) reduction of transaction costs *ex post* (the renegotiation or modification of the contract by the parties or the court respectively).[50] These practical implications are dealt with rather briefly in Lutzi's paper, and that gives me the

45 The ADHGB appeared to be well suited for its task. See J.W. Flume, Law and Commerce: The Evolution of Codified Business Law in Europe, 2 *Comparative Legal History* (2014), 43–83 (56–7); Oosterhuis (n 44), 1004–5.

46 Lutzi (n 4), 103 (n 128).

47 Hondius (n 24), 147. The new article 1195 of the *Code civil* resembles the concept of *imprévision*, see *Rapport au Président de la République relatif à l'ordonnance n° 2016-131 du 10 février 2016 portant réforme du droit des contrats, du régime général et de la preuve des obligations* (2016), 14: *'L'article 1195 constitue quant à lui l'une des innovations importantes de l'ordonnance, puisqu'il introduit l'imprévision dans le droit des contrats français, notion bien connue en jurisprudence administrative.'*

48 Lutzi (n 4), 111 (no 59).

49 Lutzi (n 4), 90–1 (nos 3, 8), 111–2 (nos 61, 64).

50 Lutzi (n 4), 110–1 (nos 55–9).

opportunity to expand a bit more on them. I would like to discuss the practical implications from a law and economics perspective, or, in other words, use efficiency as a standard to compare 'open' and 'closed' remedies.

4.1. Efficient contracting: reduction of transaction costs ex ante

18. A preliminary question is whether an impracticability excuse is efficient in itself. Here the traditional law and economics argument can be made that an impracticability excuse reduces transaction costs *ex ante*, and Lutzi also refers to this argument.[51]

19. The content of a contract that the parties will conclude in the situation *ex ante* will be somewhere between two extremes, a totally open or unspecified contract on the one hand and a fully specified contract on the other. If a contract is rather simple and there are many market-mimicking default rules, then it will be less specified. Buying groceries in the supermarket is an example of a very simple, unspecified contract. Almost everything is solved by default rules in these kinds of contracts. But when a contract has a very long life span, deals with complex projects, and when the parties cannot rely on default rules, then the contract will be highly specified. Huge investments in developing countries without reliable legal systems will result in highly detailed, specified contracts. The circumstances dictate when it is efficient to have a highly specified contract.

20. But in all situations the parties will reach a certain point at which the marginal costs of additional contract clauses will exceed the marginal benefits. At that point it is no longer efficient to add new clauses. This is the case when the probability that a situation will occur is so low that it is economically inefficient to allocate the risk of that situation.[52] In addition, when transaction costs *ex post* are low, which is typically the case when default rules exist, it becomes at a certain point inefficient to add more clauses, precisely because the subject of those clauses are dealt with by existing default rules.[53]

21. A distinction can be made between the above-mentioned contingencies, of which the probability that they will occur is so low that reasonable parties will not negotiate over those circumstances,[54] and real unforeseeable circumstances. According to Sykes, there is a different rationale for both situations. In the first case, the impracticability excuse works as a default rule enhancing the welfare of the parties *ex ante*. But in the second case, when a situation really could not be foreseen, the impracticability rule is

51 Lutzi (n 4), 111 (no 59).

52 R. Cooter & T. Ulen, *Law and Economics*, London 2014, 284–6.

53 Schäfer & Ott (n 31), 455–6.

54 According to A. Sykes, The doctrine of commercial impracticability in a second-best world, 19 *Journal of Legal Studies* (1990), 43–94 (45), parties have made an informed choice not to include the possibility of such an event in the contract but to use the impracticability excuse as a default rule.

only important insofar as it improves welfare *ex post*.[55] The commercial impracticability excuse as a default rule is thus not only designed to improve welfare *ex ante*, but also welfare *ex post*. And it makes sense to analyse the *ex post* implications on total welfare of the impracticability excuse as well.[56] In any case, there is room for an impracticability excuse *ex ante*, not only from a doctrinal perspective, but also from an efficiency perspective. Even so, that does not say too much about what a remedy based on such excuse should look like.

4.2. *Contractual fairness, efficiency and financial loss*

22. Contracts normally lead to a Pareto improvement for both parties, that is when the monetary value to the buyer (V) exceeds the contract price (p), and when the latter exceeds the seller's production costs (c). Both seller and buyer make a profit by concluding such a contract. This mutual profit seems to be what Lutzi means when he touches upon the idea of contractual fairness[57] – and not for instance the idea of *laesio enormis* and a just price.[58] Such Pareto improvement will change in a Kaldor-Hicks improvement when increasing production costs (c*) exceed the contract price (p) but remain below the value to the buyer (V). The seller's loss (p – c*) can hypothetically be compensated by the buyer's profit (V – p = V – c* + c* – p). Obviously, in this situation one could argue that a contract is less 'fair', in the sense that one party, here the buyer, reaps all benefits, whereas the other party, the seller, ends up with a loss – even if such loss could hypothetically be offset by the buyer's profit. However, this 'unfairness' should only be addressed if performance has become impracticable.[59]

23. The sole increase of production costs (c to c*) is normally an event which concerns an individual producer, such as a fire or a strike in a particular plant. Those events normally do not influence the value of the good to the buyer (V). But with large supervening events such as a war, an oil crisis[60] or a shortage of raw materials, the increase in costs for the seller will also be reflected in an increase in value to the buyer (V

55 Sykes (n 54), 91. Admittedly, the two cases are basically the same. Parties with enough imagination can think over all possible situations. Some assumptions are so basic, that parties will not negotiate over all the variances on those assumptions. If that is because it is almost impossible to imagine them or because the chance that a particular variance will occur, is impossibly small, is not a fundamental difference.

56 See below, 4.3. Reduction of transaction costs ex post: discharge or adjustment?

57 Lutzi (n 4), 90–1 (nos 3, 8), 111–2 (nos 61, 64)].

58 Indeed, fairness in exchange or contractual fairness had its heydays in early modern scholasticism, on which W. Decock, *Theologians and Contract Law, The Moral Transformation of the Ius Commune (ca. 1500–1650)*, Leiden 2013, 507–604, but since then gradually lost terrain and was for instance rejected by the drafters of the BGB, see Hondius (n 24), 61.

59 This will be discussed below, 4.3. Reduction of transaction costs ex post: discharge or adjustment?, no 30.

60 See for example BGH 8 February 1978, VII ZR 221/76, JZ 1978, 235; *Aluminium Company of America v. Essex Group Inc.*, 499 F. Supp. 53 (W.D. Pa. 1980).

to V*): rather, generally the seller's increase in costs will run roughly parallel to a buyer's increase in value in case of large supervening events.[61]

24. An efficient allocation of resources is reached as long as the seller's production costs remain below the value to the buyer ($c^* < V$ or $c^* < V^*$). Under those circumstances, resources are put to their highest valued use. As already mentioned above, such allocation does not always reflect a Pareto efficient solution, for the seller's costs can indeed rise above the original contract price. But it is in all circumstances a Kaldor-Hicks improvement, because the buyer can, at least hypothetically, compensate the seller, as the seller's costs remain below the value of the goods to the buyer.[62] This allocation can be reached when the perfect expectation damage rule applies.[63] Performance is efficient as long as the seller's costs remain below the value to the buyer.[64] In this way the price has disappeared completely from the analysis.[65] The relationship between the increased production costs and the contract price (c^* and p) is not important as long as the total welfare of seller and buyer increases.[66]

25. However, when the seller's costs exceed the value to the buyer, breach, that is paying expectation damages, is more efficient: paying damages is then less expensive than performance.[67] This result can also be reached when the perfect expectation damage rule applies[68] – not with specific performance as primary remedy, for that matter.[69] Under the expectation damage rule, the losses of a seller can hypothetically always be offset by the profit of a buyer, by way of zero-sum transfer.[70]

26. However, when the increased production costs dramatically exceed the contract price, this is not just a zero-sum game.[71] The financial organisation of a company is the

61 V will then increase to V*, an increase normally similar to the increase from c to c*, which also happened for instance in *Florida Power & Light Co. v. Westinghouse Electric Corp.*, 826 F.2d 239 (4th Cir. 1987), because a certain production process appeared to be unavailable. See P. Trimarchi, Commercial Impracticability in contract law: an economic analysis, 11 *International Review of Law and Economics* (1991), 63–82 (66).

62 That c* exceeds p is not important in this analysis as long as $c^* - p < V(^*) - p$.

63 See Cooter & Ulen (n 52), 272–3, 279–81.

64 Performance is efficient when $c^* < V$ or $c^* < V^*$, for in case of a breach the seller has to pay $V - p$ or $(V - p) + (V^* - V)$. This is more expensive than performance by the seller, for this will cost him $c^* - p$ instead of $V - p$ or $V^* - p$.

65 Trimarchi (n 61), 74.

66 When there is a Kaldor-Hicks improvement, in other words.

67 Performance is inefficient when $c^* > V$ or $c^* > V^*$, for in case of a breach the seller has to pay $V - p$ or $(V - p) + (V^* - V)$. This is less expensive than performance, for this will cost the seller $c^* - p$ instead of $V^* - p$. Recently on efficient breach in contract law, W. Liao, *The Application of the Theory of Efficient Breach in Contract Law, A Comparative Law and Economics Perspective*, Cambridge 2015, particularly 45–62.

68 See Cooter & Ulen (n 52), 272–3, 279–81.

69 See Liao (n 67), 93–101; Shavell (n 1), 833, 841–6.

70 Sykes, for instance, states that the commercial impracticability rule is not relevant as far as *ex post* welfare improvement is concerned. He sees the *ex post* consequences only as a division of the losses. See Sykes (n 54), 92.

71 Trimarchi (n 61), 73–5.

result of information and planning, which has a cost and therefore represents a value. A considerable unexpected loss will damage that organisation and thus impair real value without justification.[72] The shock of such financial loss to the seller will at some point exceed the financial benefit to the buyer. Therefore, it is not only the *ex ante* incentives on welfare that matter, but also the *ex post* consequences of the impracticability rule.

4.3. Reduction of transaction costs ex post: discharge or adjustment?

27. After the occurrence of an unforeseen event, several steps have to be taken to decide whether an excuse of commercial impracticability should be granted or not, and what kind of remedy – discharge or adjustment – should be used. I generally assume that the losses fall on a seller, for he is typically the one who has to bear an increase in costs.

28. First it has to be decided that the risk will not, after all, be explicitly allocated to one of the parties. Because if the risk is allocated to one of parties – and the circumstances were thus not unforeseen after all – the contract should be performed or damages should be paid: this is efficient, for the contract still represents an *ex ante* Pareto improvement.[73] Triantis has even argued that there are no really unforeseen circumstances, because all risks can be put into a broader framework and managed within this framework.[74] Some risks, however, cannot be insured against because they do not conform to statistical rules. And even if it were possible, however small the probability of the occurrence, to insure against all those risks, this would make insurance far too costly. The costs involved in the allocation of all risks of all dramatic price increases due to all possible unforeseen circumstances, even though the probability of most of those circumstances is very low, will be prohibitively high.[75]

29. If the risk is not explicitly allocated to one of the parties, it still might be implicitly allocated to one of them. To decide whether or not the risk of a certain event is implicitly allocated to one of the parties depends on the interpretation of the contract,[76] so one of the conventional doctrines of contract law applies.[77] Important criteria to decide if and

72 Trimarchi (n 61), 74.

73 Schäfer & Ott (n 31), 433, 445.

74 G. Triantis, Contractual allocation of unknown risks: a critique of the doctrine of commercial impracticability, 42 *University of Toronto Law Journal* (1992), 450–83 (464–8).

75 Trimarchi (n 61), 66–7.

76 If a contract price is much higher than usual, this is an indication that a seller has taken over the risk of certain price increases. Obviously a judge should never go beyond the parties' intention. This means for instance that a judge cannot place the risk of all possible price increases on a seller, simply because he is getting a higher price than usual for his product. In addition, an implicit risk allocation still concerns specific risks, not the risk of something in general. A high contract price can mean that a seller has to bear the losses of an increase in costs of 100%, but this does not necessarily mean that he has to bear every possible increase in costs, even if this amounts to 600%.

77 Hondius & Grigoleit (n 23), 3, 5–6.

how parties have implicitly allocated a risk are the cheapest cost avoider,[78] the cheapest insurer,[79] and the superior risk bearer.[80] Because of this preliminary step, the impracticability doctrine remains in practice rather close to a constructive interpretation of a contract, to which similarity Lutzi refers as well.[81] In addition, the party to which the risk has been allocated implicitly should bear the losses of the unforeseen circumstances.

30. Only when a risk is not implicitly allocated should it be decided whether the increase in costs is impracticable for the seller, which means that his financial losses should be unacceptably large and performance thus economically impossible. This is the real impracticability excuse and here a threshold should be introduced. Such threshold should be set at a theoretically efficient level, which means that the marginal benefits of the commercial impracticability excuse should equal the marginal costs. The benefit of the impracticability excuse to the seller should be equal to the loss, including those incurred inter alia by litigation and renegotiation costs. When the threshold is set too low, efficient contracts will be discharged or modified, and the rate of litigation will be inefficiently high. On the other hand, if the threshold is set too high, parties will have to carry out inefficient contracts and any efficiency of the impracticability excuse disappears.

31. Unfortunately, the vagueness of the criteria used to decide whether a risk has been implicitly allocated or whether performance is impracticable or not is problematic. The cheapest cost avoider, the cheapest insurer, and the superior risk bearer, but also the threshold after which performance becomes impracticable, are all more or less factors that courts cannot observe. Such factors give judges a large discretion in deciding a case on commercial impracticability. The outcome of commercial impracticability cases is therefore highly unpredictable. And when the outcome is unpredictable, parties may be tempted to spend the whole amount at stake in the conflict on litigation. Indeed, the costs spent on litigation may vary more or less directly in line with the value of the contested performance. If a lot of money is involved, parties might spent the entire amount on litigation, because they simply do not know the probability of success. In this

[78] The cheapest cost avoider is the party who can avoid the event which causes the increase in costs, at the lowest cost. To avoid the event is efficient when the costs of avoiding are smaller than the expected increase in costs itself, the so-called Learned Hand formula. In the *ex ante* situation this party would have taken over the risk of a cost increase. See Schäfer & Ott (n 31), 434–7.

[79] The cheapest insurer is the party who can insure an increase in costs at the lowest price. And this party typically would have taken over the risk of a cost increase at the time when the contract is concluded. This criterion does not work properly in an impracticability case, for unforeseen circumstances cannot be insured. Those circumstances do not respond to statistical rules, and it will be too costly for insurance companies to insure the risks involved in those kind of cases. Therefore this criterion is not very helpful in deciding an implicit risk allocation of the parties in case of unforeseen circumstances. See Schäfer & Ott (n 31), 437–41.

[80] The superior risk bearer is the party who can bear the risk that the losses will occur at the lowest costs. This capacity depends mainly on the ability of a party to gather information and the use of economies of scale. The advantages of the economies of scale are unaffected in a case of unforeseen events, but the advantage of being better informed is getting less important in such circumstances. See Schäfer & Ott (n 31), 442–4.

[81] Lutzi (n 4), 93–4 (no 13). See also Schäfer & Ott (n 31), 457–68.

way those unobservable factors will lead to directly unproductive profit-seeking.[82] This may help to explain why courts are generally quite reluctant to grant an impracticability excuse in the first place,[83] and if they do, why a very high threshold is set.[84]

32. Thus, if the losses remain under this threshold, those losses should remain where they have fallen, in this case with the seller. And when the losses are above the threshold the contract should be discharged or adjusted.

33. Obviously, when performance is no longer efficient, that is, no longer a Kaldor-Hicks improvement, the contract should be discharged. This result is reached in most 'closed' legal systems, such as the English system and the former French proposal. However, in 'open' legal systems too, courts can and probably will discharge an impracticable contract, performance of which will cost a seller more than it will benefit the buyer.

34. Especially as regards whether to adjust or to discharge a contract that still is efficient and therefore should be upheld, legal systems – both common law and civil law – differ substantially, as Lutzi's paper also shows. For each point of view there are economic arguments.

35. When courts adjust the contract, like German courts – and in the future maybe also French courts – they can remain close to the preference order of the parties in the *ex ante* situation. For in the *ex ante* situation the parties would also have concluded the contract, just with a different allocation of the risk of unforeseen circumstances. However, if a contract is adjusted, the model of the fully specified contract should be applied. The court has to allocate the risks in the way the parties themselves would have done in the *ex ante* situation, at the conclusion of the contract.[85] Three important criteria to decide how the parties would have allocated a risk in the *ex ante* situation are the cheapest cost avoider,[86] the cheapest insurer[87] and the superior risk bearer.[88]

82 See D. Vandegrift, Decision Costs, Contract Excuse and the Westinghouse Commercial Impracticability Case, 4 *European Journal of Law and Economics* (1997), 41–54 (42–5).

83 No excuse was for example granted in BGH 8 February 1978, VII ZR 221/76, JZ 1978, 235; BGH 16 February 2000, XII ZR 279/97, NJW 2000, Heft 23, 1714–1718.

84 See for example *Florida Power & Light Co. v. Westinghouse Electric Corp.*, 826 F.2d 239 (4th Cir. 1987); *Aluminium Company of America v. Essex Group Inc.*, 499 F. Supp. 53 (W.D. Pa. 1980).

85 Schäfer & Ott (n 31), 433.

86 On the cheapest cost avoider, see above, n 77. The problem is that the probability of unforeseen circumstances, even when they are foreseeable in the strict sense of the word, is so low that the costs of avoiding the unforeseen circumstance will easily exceed the expected return of the lower increase in costs. Or put it another way, you cannot avoid an event which is unforeseen. Moreover, in most cases of commercial impracticability, none of the parties can influence or avoid the events. See Schäfer & Ott (n 31), 434–7.

87 On the cheapest insurer, see above, n 79. Also in deciding the *ex ante* risk allocation of the parties in case of unforeseen circumstances this criterion is not very helpful. See Schäfer & Ott (n 31), 437–41.

88 On the superior risk bearer, see above, n 80. See also Schäfer & Ott (n 31), 442–4.

36. When the seller is the cheapest cost avoider, the cheapest insurer and the superior risk bearer, the losses due to the increase in costs should be allocated to him, so the losses will remain where they have fallen. When the buyer is the cheapest cost avoider, the cheapest insurer and superior risk bearer, the cost increase should be allocated to him, but he will only have to bear the losses when they have become impracticable for the seller. If the seller and the buyer could both have avoided the cost at the same price, or could have insured the risk at the same effort and are also equal risk bearers, they will have to share the losses if performance has become economically impossible for the seller. The same happens when both parties have generally been in equal positions to avoid the losses. For instance, the seller is the cheapest cost avoider, but the buyer is the cheapest insurer and the superior risk bearer. And if the parties, which is often the case, are in an equal position to bear the risks, then the losses also should be shared between the parties.

37. That a court has to find out how unforeseen circumstances would have been allocated by the parties in the *ex ante* situation is a clear disadvantage of a remedy allowing a court to adjust a contract. Allocating risks according to the *ex ante* situation is difficult and costly: the cheapest cost avoider, the cheapest insurer, and the superior risk bearer are factors that courts more or less cannot observe, or factors that can only be observed at very high cost. It is certainly possible that a court will make errors in this allocation.[89]

38. Discharging the contract has the disadvantage that this is clearly not in accordance with the preference of the parties in the *ex ante* situation, for performance of the contract is still efficient, even in the *ex post* situation. On the other hand, because the contract is still efficient, the parties will probably renegotiate the discharged contract and conclude a new one that is perfectly in line with their preferences. Indeed, many legal systems, including the former French proposal of 2015 and the new Article 1195 of the *Code civil*, have a duty to renegotiate, which gives parties the possibility of sticking to their preferred order *ex ante*. There are some additional costs involved in this process, but the possibility of a court error is excluded.

39. Problematically, if the parties fail to respect the duty renegotiate under the new article 1195 of the *Code civil*, the court can be asked to adjust the contract.[90] The possibility of the court eventually adjusting the contract might result in strategic behaviour of the parties: a party might frustrate the renegotiation of a still efficient contract because he or she would prefer the court to adjust the contract, in the hope of getting a higher profit or a smaller loss. Such strategic behaviour – frustrating the renegotiation of still efficient contracts – obviously leads to higher costs, inter alia in litigation, while such behaviour

89 Trimarchi (n 61), 78–9.

90 *Ordonnance n° 2016-131* (n 3), Article 1195: *(1) … (2) En cas de refus ou d'échec de la renégociation, les parties peuvent convenir de la résolution du contrat, à la date et aux conditions qu'elles déterminent, ou demander d'un commun accord au juge de procéder à son adaptation. A défaut d'accord dans un délai raisonnable, le juge peut, à la demande d'une partie, réviser le contrat ou y mettre fin, à la date et aux conditions qu'il fixe.*

will be probably hard to observe by courts. And if a court discharges the contract when parties fail to renegotiate a still efficient contract, a new contract can be renegotiated anyway. On the other hand, if the parties' failure to renegotiate is followed by the discharge of the contract – as in the former French proposal of 2015[91] – such strategic behaviour is excluded, as well as the chance of wrongly adjusted contracts, discussed above.

40. It is hard to assess whether the benefits of adjusting contracts in accordance with the preferences of the parties exceed the costs of wrongly adjusted contracts. Therefore, it cannot be determined upfront which remedy is the more efficient one: the 'open' German remedy (still) without a duty to renegotiate, the new 'open' French remedy including a prior duty to renegotiate, or the former 'closed' French proposal of 2015 only introducing a duty to renegotiate prior to discharge.

5. Conclusion

41. According to Lutzi, the 'open' German impracticability excuse is dogmatically superior to the English and the current and proposed French exception. Although admittedly the English common law system can be hardly compared to the German and French civil law systems, I do agree that having an exception as such, ultimately based on good faith, like the German exception, is indeed dogmatically superior than essentially having no impracticability excuse at all. However, in my opinion legal doctrine does not dictate the content of the remedy – 'open' or 'closed' – based on such exception.

42. Moreover, comparative legal history shows that only in legal systems that have experienced massive economic upheaval, such as the hyperinflation in Germany after the First World War, can an 'open' remedy have a lasting effect. The proposed 'closed' French remedy would indeed have had a chance of survival, as it would have remained similar to the current 'closed' system of French private law unlike the 'open' remedy in Article 6:258 of the *Burgerlijk Wetboek*, which remained a virtually dead letter as it was transplanted into the traditionally 'closed' Dutch legal system. This makes one somewhat pessimistic for the chances of the new Article 1195 of the *Code civil* – ultimately an 'open' remedy despite its prior duty to renegotiate – becoming a living institution. It might be that the new Article 1195 of the *Code civil* will remain a virtually dead letter because of its transplant into a traditionally 'closed' legal system – French private law. And a dead letter certainly does not make the French remedy on unforeseen circumstances more attractive for commercial parties. The fact that French administrative law has quite a lot of experience with the concept of *imprévision* gives some reason for hope, however.

43. Finally, law and economics presents a strong case for an impracticability excuse as such, both *ex ante* and in respect of contractual equality *ex post*. In respect of a remedy

91 *Projet d'ordonnance* (n 2), Art 1196: *(1)... (2) En cas de refus ou d'échec de la renégociation, les parties peuvent demander d'un commun accord au juge de procéder à l'adaptation du contrat. A défaut, une partie peut demander au juge d'y mettre fin, à la date et aux conditions qu'il fixe.*

based on such impracticability excuse, there are economic arguments for both adjustment and discharge. When performance is still efficient, courts should stick to the parties' preferred order *ex ante*; however, courts might wrongly adjust a contract as the relevant economic factors are hard to observe for courts. Although discharging a still efficient contract is clearly not in line with parties' preferences, this disadvantage can nevertheless be partly met by a duty to renegotiate before parties can ask a court for relief – as in the former French proposal and the new Article 1195 of the *Code civil*.

44. However, for the new 'open' remedy in Article 1195 of the *Code civil* it remains to be seen whether the prior duty to renegotiate will make the remedy less prone to wrongly adjusted contracts. Strategic behaviour of the parties – hoping that a court will eventually adjust the contract in their favour – might frustrate the renegotiation of still efficient contracts, as a result of which the parties will end up in court anyway. Apart from additional costs, this strategic behaviour again increases the chance of wrongly adjusted contracts. Therefore, it might very well be that the former French proposal of 2015 had the best of both worlds: a dogmatically sound and also viable impracticability excuse, with an efficient 'closed' remedy, including a duty to renegotiate.

Sanne Jansen*

PRICE REDUCTION UNDER THE FRENCH CONTRACT LAW REFORM

"Ainsi, la variété des sanctions permet-elle l'adaptation des techniques à la diversité des sanctions. C'est signe de richesse et de raffinement d'un système juridique qui ne se contente pas de sanctions brutales, à l'emporte-pièce."
J. Deprez[1]

1. Introduction

1. The French Civil Code (hereinafter 'CC') does not (yet) recognise price reduction as a general remedy of contract law. Under French contract law the creditor has merely the choice between forced execution (primarily in kind, or subsidiary, by equivalent) and termination of the contract.[2] However, some applications of price reduction are recognised by means of a custom (e.g. the *réfaction* in internal commercial sales contracts) or legislation (for example Article 1644 CC: *actio quanti minoris*, Articles 1617 and 1619 CC,[3] Articles 1722, 1724 and 1726 CC, price reduction under consumer sales contracts,[4] price reduction under the Vienna Sales Convention[5] ...).[6] All these applications can be

* Postdoctoral researcher and fellow (aspirant) of the Research Foundation – Flanders (FWO), KU Leuven, Institute for the Law of Obligations.

1 J. Deprez, "Rapport sur les sanctions qui s'attachent à l'inexécution des obligations contractuelles en droit civil et commercial français", *Les sanctions attachées à l'inexécution des obligations contractuelles*, Paris, Dalloz, 1968, (28) 30.

2 P. Grosser, "La réforme en pratique. La réduction du prix comme remède général à l'exécution imparfaite du contrat", *AJCA* 2014, (219) after footnote 1.

3 See also for a price reduction in case of a shortcoming in the surface with regard to bigger building projects with private and communal parts: Article 46 of the Loi no.65–556 du 10 juillet fixant le statut de la copropriété des immeubles bâtis. See also Cass. Fr. civ. 10 December 2015, no. 14–13.832.

4 See Article L.211–10 du Code de Consommation.

5 See Article 50 of the United Nations Convention on Contracts for the International Sale of Goods of 1980 (hereinafter also 'CISG').

6 See also for some examples: P. Grosser, "La réforme en pratique. La réduction du prix comme remède général à l'exécution imparfaite du contrat", *AJCA* 2014, (219) between footnote 1 and 8; P. Lemay, "L'inexécution du contrat: la réduction du prix (Projet, art. 1223)" in M. Latina and G. Chantepie (eds.), *Projet de réforme du droit des contrats, du régime général et de la preuve des obligations. Analyses et propositions*, Paris, Dalloz, 2015, (78) 78.

situated in special contracts (such as sale contracts, tenancy contracts ...) but do not imply a general recognition of price reduction. Nevertheless, there is a growing body of opinion that the remedy of price reduction deserves more attention.[7] As a result of some remarkable judgements of the Court of Cassation,[8] the question whether price reduction has to be recognised as a general and autonomous remedy has been the subject of much debate in doctrine.[9, 10] The influential scholar Mestre ended an overview of jurisprudence that price reduction has to be considered as "*un mode d'intervention plus général, une véritable technique du droit commun des contrats*".[11] De La Ascuncion Planes undertook in 2006 an extensive research about this topic.[12] She considers '*la réfaction du contrat*' to be an autonomous judicial and an extrajudicial remedy. The aim of the price reduction is, according to her, to correct contractual imbalances and illegalities.[13]

7 See e.g. J. Deprez, "Rapport sur les sanctions qui s'attachent à l'inexécution des obligations contractuelles en droit civil et commercial français", *Les sanctions attachées à l'inexécution des obligations contractuelles*, Paris, Dalloz, 1968, (28) 50 *et seq.*; J. Ghestin, *Conformité et garanties dans la vente*, Paris, LGDJ, 1983, no. 183 (*réfaction* in sale contracts); J. Scioldo-Zurcher, *La résolution des contrats au cas d'inexécution partielle*, Lyon, Bosc Frères M. et L. Riou, 1934, 133–142 (price reduction as '*résolution partielle*').

8 See Cass. Fr. 25 March 1997, no. 95–11.995, *Bull.* 1997, I, no. 111, 73 (implicit recognition of the *réfaction* in case of a non-conforming delivery in ordinary sale contracts); Cass. Fr. 2 March 1993, no. 90–20.289, *Bull.* 1993, IV, no. 83, 57 (solution between termination and execution in kind in case of a building contract). Unclear: Cass. Fr. 16 September 2009, no. 08–10487, www.legifrance.gouv.fr, (tenancy case: damages in case of a loss of enjoyment does not equal a reduction for changes to the rented ground). See nevertheless *contra* Cass. Fr. civ. 10 March 2015, no. 13–27660, www.legifrance.gouv.fr (no price reduction in civil sales contracts in case of non-conform delivery; see also D. Houtcieff, "Chronique de jurisprudence de droit des contrats", *Gazette du Palais* 2015, issue 190, (18) no. 231z0).

9 *Pro* a general remedy: C. Albiges, "Le développement discret de la réfaction du contrat", *Mélanges Michel Cabrillac*, Paris, Litec, 1999, (3) 3–21; P. Grosser, "La réforme en pratique. La réduction du prix comme remède général à l'exécution imparfaite du contrat", *AJCA* 2014, (219) between footnote 8 and 13 (based on an analysis of case law); Grosser dans J. Ghestin, A.-S. Barthez, P. Grosser *et al.*, "Droit des contrats", *La Semaine Juridique Edition Générale* 2015, issue 46–47, (1261) no. 10; P. Jourdain, "A la recherche de la réfaction du contrat, sanction méconnue de l'inexécution", *Mélanges en l'honneur de Philippe le Tourneau*, Paris, Dalloz, 2008, (449) 463; V. Lasbordes, *Les contrats déséquilibrés*, Aix-en-Provence, PUAM, 2000, no. 713–716; C. Malecki, *L'exception de l'inexécution*, Paris, LGDJ, 1999, 77–101; C. Malecki, *Histoire de la réfaction des contrats*, Paris, Mémoire, Paris II, 1991, 63 p.; G. Piette, *La correction du contrat*, Aix-en-Provence, PUAM, 2004, no. 98–105; C. Popineau-Dehaullon, *Les remèdes de justice privée à l'inexécution du contrat*, Paris, LGDJ, 2008, 133–148.

10 *Contra* a general remedy: S. Le Gac-Pech, *La proportionnalité en droit privé des contrats*, Paris, LGDJ, 2000, no. 1157. Not enthusiastic: T. Genicon, *La résolution du contrat pour inexécution*, Paris, LGDJ, 2007, 568–578; C.P. Wilson, "Les remèdes à l'inexécution contractuelle dans la réforme du droit des contrats en France: regard d'un juriste chilien", *Revue des contrats* 2015, issue 3, (706) II.B (partial termination will render this remedy superfluous).

11 J. Mestre, "Jurisprudence française en matière de droit civil, B., Obligations et contrats spéciaux", *RTD Civ.* 1988, (519) 538.

12 K. De La Asuncion Planes, *La réfaction du contrat*, Paris, LGDJ, 2006, 499 p.

13 K. De La Asuncion Planes, *La réfaction du contrat*, Paris, LGDJ, 2006, 271–348 (as a judicial remedy) and 349–396 (as an extrajudicial remedy).

2. Road-map to price reduction: projet Catala, projet de la Chancellerie and projet Terré

2. A few years before the thesis of De la Ascuncion Planes appeared, there was a growing awareness about the modernisation of the 200-year-old Civil Code.[14] The first attempts to modernise the Civil Code were mainly academic and prudent. The first (academic) project is called '*Projet Catala*' of 2005 and treats the law of obligations and the law of prescription.[15] The second project '*Projet de la Chancellerie*' of 2008 about contract law, is the first of different versions issued by the Chancellerie.[16] Finally, the progressive and academic '*Projet Terré pour une réforme du droit des contrats*' appeared in 2009.[17] Although the first two projects omit to introduce an (autonomous) price reduction remedy, the drafters of the last project came around and included explicitly this proportional remedy. Nevertheless, it is still interesting to examine the first two projects – although they do not include a price reduction remedy – to seek for similar mechanisms (such as partial termination).

2.1. No price reduction under the Catala project, but a partial termination

3. The Catala project (hereafter also 'pr. C.') does not recognise the proportional price reduction as an autonomous and general remedy for (un)excused non-performances. Nevertheless, we must point to a similar proportional mechanism that can be found in the Catala project: partial termination.

4. It is for instance striking that termination of a contract will only be for the future (and not *ex tunc*, which is the general rule today), with an exception for contracts which are executed immediately (see Article 1160-1, second part pr. C.).[18]

> Article 1160-1: '*La résolution du contrat libère les parties de leurs obligations.*
> *Dans les contrats à exécution successive ou échelonnée, la résolution vaut résiliation; l'engagement des parties prend fin pour l'avenir, à compter de l'assignation en résolution ou de la notification de la résolution unilatérale.*[19]

14 Explains the details for the French recodification movement (European soft law instruments that are considered to be a threat, a severe report of the world bank that condemns the lack of competitiveness of French law and the renewed recodification thoughts after the "*Bicentenaire*" of the 200th birthday of the Civil Code): S. Van Loock, "Hervorming van het Frans verbintenissenrecht uit de startblokken. Le nouveau droit des obligations est presque arrivé", *TBH* 2015, (619) no. 2. See also C.M.D.S. Pavillon, "Een nieuw contractenrecht voor Frankrijk", *NTBR* 2015, (11) title 1.

15 Www.justice.gouv.fr/art_pix/RAPPORTCATALASEPTEMBRE2005.pdf. P. Catala, *Avant-projet de réforme du droit des obligations et de la prescription*, La Documentation française, 2006, 208 p.

16 Projet de réforme du droit des contrats, juillet 2008.

17 F. Terré (ed.), *Pour une réforme du droit des contrats*, Paris, Dalloz, 2009, 310 p.

18 J. Rochfeld, "La proposition de réforme des sanctions de l'inexécution du contrat dans l'Avant-projet de réforme du Code civil français et l'influence européenne" in R. Schulze (ed.), *New Features in Contract Law*, Munich, Sellier, 2007, (197) 202.

19 Emphasis added.

> *Si le contrat a été partiellement exécuté, les prestations échangées ne donnent pas lieu à restitution ni indemnité lorsque leur exécution a été conforme aux obligations respectives des parties*'.

Consequently, termination will have an *ex tunc* effect in case of contracts which are executed immediately. In case of contracts with continuous or successive performances Article 1160–1, third part pr. C. prescribes: '*Si le contrat a été partiellement exécuté les prestations échangées ne donnent pas lieu à restitution ni indemnité lorsque leur exécution a été conforme aux obligations respectives des parties*'. Consequently, this (*ex nunc*-effect) rule introduces a *de facto* temporal partial termination of the contract.

5. Furthermore, and this is even more important with regard to the recognition of price reduction, the project introduces a general criterion to adapt the consequences of termination, taking into account the divisibility of the performance of the contract (see Article 1160 pr. C.).

> Article 1160: '*La résolution peut avoir lieu pour une partie seulement du contrat, lorsque son exécution est divisible*'.[20]

As a consequence, this project recognises price reduction, not as an autonomous remedy, but as a kind of partial termination. If the project would recognise this partial termination for material divisible performances, price reduction could potentially be recognised under the 'umbrella' of partial termination.

6. Finally, it is interesting that this project proposes to integrate the 'theory of risk' in the concept of 'termination'. This means that termination will be the remedy for excused and unexcused non-performances (see Article 1158 pr. C.).[21] Consequently, the drafters do not differentiate anymore between unexcused or excused (force majeure) non-performances, with regard to termination. This shift has already been announced by the jurisprudence of the French Court of Cassation that bases the consequences of *force majeure* on termination under Article 1184 CC and not on an independent 'theory of risk' (which is for example the case in Belgium).[22]

2.2. *No price reduction under the project of the Chancellerie (2008)*

7. The Catala project and the project of the Chancellerie (hereafer: 'pr. Ch.') overlap with regard to the introduction of the *ex-nunc* effect of termination. The project of the Chancellerie

20 See also J. Rochfeld in P. Catala (ed.), *Avant-projet de réforme du droit des obligations et de la prescription*, Paris, La Documentation française, 2005, 55.

21 See also J. Rochfeld in P. Catala (ed.), *Avant-projet de réforme du droit des obligations et de la prescription*, Paris, La Documentation française, 2005, 54; J. Rochfeld, "La proposition de réforme des sanctions de l'inexécution du contrat dans l'Avant-projet de réforme du Code civil français et l'influence européenne" in R. Schulze (ed.), *New Features in Contract Law*, Munich, Sellier, 2007, (197) 201.

22 See also C. Popineau-Dehaullon, *Les remèdes de justice privée à l'inexécution du contrat*, Paris, LGDJ, 2008, no. 519.

also differentiates between contracts which are executed immediately and contracts that imply continuous or successive performances. On the one hand, the termination has *ex tunc* (or retroactive) effect in case of the first kind of contracts (Article 166, first part pr. Ch.).

> Article 166, first part: '*Dans les contrats à execution instantanée, la resolution s'entend de l'anéantissement rétroactif d'un contra ten raison de son inexécution. Elle libère les parties de leurs obligations*'.

On the other hand, termination has *ex nunc*-effect in case of contracts implying continuous or successive performances (Article 166, second part and Article 171, second part pr. Ch.)

> Article 166, second part: '*Dans les contrats à execution successive ou échelonnée, l'engagement des parties prend fin pour l'avenir, à compter de l'assignation ou de la notification de la resolution unilatérale*'.

> Article 171, second part: '*Toutefois, dans les contrats à exécution successive ou échelonnée, les prestations échangés ne donnent pas lieu à restitution lorsque leur exécution a été conforme aux obligations respectives des parties*'.

We can conclude that 'temporal partial termination' has been introduced because of the *ex nunc*-effect of termination.

8. However, 'material partial termination' of the Catala project has not been included in the project of the Chancellerie. At first sight, we must conclude that the project does not recognise price reduction, not even under the 'umbrella' of partial termination.

2.3. *Price reduction and partial termination under the Terré project*

2.3.1. Price reduction

9. The Catala project provoked the Terré project (hereafter: 'pr. T.'), which is also dedicated to contract law.[23] Article 97 pr. T. prescribes the creditor's choice between different remedies if their respective conditions of application are fulfilled: performance in kind, suspension, price reduction, termination and damages. It is striking that the Terré project – contrary to the Catala project and the project of the Chancellerie – recognises explicitly the price reduction remedy in Articles 97 and 107 pr. T.[24]

> Article 107: '*Le créancier peut accepter une execution non conforme du débiteur et réduire proportionnelement le prix.*

[23] F. Terré (ed.), *Pour une réforme du droit des contrats*, Paris, Dalloz, 2009, 310 p.

[24] This remedy is based on Article 9:401 of the Principles of European Contract Law (hereinafter also 'PECL') and Article III. – 3:601 of the Draft Common Frame of Reference (hereinafter also 'DCFR'): P. Remy-Corlay in F. Terré (ed.), *Pour une réforme du droit des contrats*, Paris, Dalloz, 2009, 267.

Il peut, s'il a déjà payé, obtenir remboursement du surplus.
Il peut demander des dommages et intérêts pour tout autre préjudice'.

10. The accompanying text of Remy-Corlay makes clear that the *judicial* as well as the *extrajudicial* ("*réduction du prix par notification*") application of this price reduction remedy is possible.[25] Moreover, the fact that a price reduction can be invoked without the prior intervention of a judge is in accordance with the possibility of an extrajudicial termination by notification.[26]

11. The calculation method of the price reduction is not fully elaborated in Article 107 pr. T., it merely mentions in its first part that price reduction has to be calculated proportionally. The accompanying text proposes that the party that deducts a part of the price, has to take into account the 'purpose of the contract' ('*l'économie du contrat*'). This purpose entails that the reduction of the price has to be reasonable in comparison with the (partially) executed performance and in accordance with the price that would have been paid for this (partial) performance.[27] Remy-Corlay adds that if the judge[28] has to calculate the price reduction he can autonomously decide on the amount of the price reduction.[29]

12. Furthermore, Article 107 pr. T. makes clear that price reduction can be applied before and after payment of the price. If the creditor has not yet paid, he can withhold a part of the price and if he has already paid he will receive a part of the price he has already paid back (Article 107, second part pr. T.).

13. The third part of Article 107 pr. T. indicates that a price reduction can be cumulated with damages. The wording of the third part elucidates that damages can only be claimed in combination with a price reduction if they bear upon other losses than those compensated by a price reduction.

14. Finally, the question rises whether price reduction can also be applied in case of an unexcused non-performance (*force majeure*). It is difficult to determine whether the drafters of the project differentiate between remedies for excused and unexcused non-

25 P. Remy-Corlay in F. Terré (ed.), *Pour une réforme du droit des contrats*, Paris, Dalloz, 2009, 267–268.

26 C. Aubert de Vincelles in F. Terré (ed.), *Pour une réforme du droit des contrats*, Paris, Dalloz, 2009, 270–271. See also about the extrajudicial price reduction under the Terré project: P. Lemay, *Le principe de la force obligatoire du contrat à l'épreuve du développement de l'unilatéralisme*, inédit, Université Lille Nord de France 2, 2012, no. 68.

27 P. Remy-Corlay in F. Terré (ed.), *Pour une réforme du droit des contrats*, Paris, Dalloz, 2009, 268.

28 The judge can exercise an *a posteriori* examination if the debtor contests the unilaterally enforced price reduction. He can exercise an *a priori* control if the creditor claims a part of the price (already paid) back by means of court proceedings.

29 He deduces this because the Court of Cassation required an expert opinion with regard to the calculation of the price reduction in case of hidden defects (Article 1644 CC; but the law has recently been changed with this regard): P. Remy-Corlay in F. Terré (ed.), *Pour une réforme du droit des contrats*, Paris, Dalloz, 2009, 268.

performances.[30] Although Article 101 pr. T. only mentions the remedies of termination and suspension in case of *force majeure*, an *a contrario* interpretation of Article 117 pr. T. (about damages) shows that all remedies can be applied in case of *force majeure* except for damages.[31] Of course, the remedy of performance in kind is also not applicable, because performance is, in case of *force majeure*, impossible (see Article 105 pr. T.).[32] This would mean that price reduction is also applicable in case of *force majeure*. Nevertheless, Article 107 pr. T. does not mention the applicability of this remedy in case of *force majeure* (but does not rule it out explicitly). If this remedy would be applicable in case of an excused non-performance, it is advisable to indicate that a combination of a price reduction *with damages* is ruled out in case of an excused non-performance (see also Article 117 pr. T.).

2.3.2. Partial termination

15. Notwithstanding the explicit recognition of price reduction as a general remedy of contract law, we must also point at some important changes to the remedy of termination. As we have seen, price reduction can also potentially be recognised under the 'umbrella' of partial termination.

16. First and foremost, the Terré project opts in favour for the *ex nunc* effect of the termination of the contract. The drafters do not differentiate between contracts that are executed immediately and contracts that imply continuous or successive performances (Article 115 pr. T.).[33] This means that a temporal partial termination has been introduced by means of the *ex nunc* effect of termination.

> Article 115: '*La résolution du contrat libère les parties pour l'avenir. Elle prend effet, selon les cas, soit dans les conditions prévues par la clause résolutoire, soit au jour où la notification prend effet, soit au jour de la décision de justice. (...)*'.

17. The drafters of the Terré project also chose to introduce the remedy of material partial termination by means of Article 114 pr. T.[34]

30 See also the confusing passage of P. Remy in F. Terré (ed.), *Pour une réforme du droit des contrats*, Paris, Dalloz, 2009, 259: '*Le traitement, à cette place, de la résolution pour impossibilité d'exécution, la distingue clairement de la résolution pour une défaillance imputable à l'une des parties, qui est réglée aux articles 108 s. projet Terré*'.

31 See Article 117 pr. T.: '*Le débiteur est condamné, s'il y a lieu, au paiement de dommages et intérêts, soit à raison de l'inexécution, totale ou partielle, du contrat, soit à raison du retard dans l'exécution, sauf à établir qu'il a été empêché d'exécuter par suite d'une force majeure*' (emphasis added). See also P. Remy in F. Terré (ed.), *Pour une réforme du droit des contrats*, Paris, Dalloz, 2009, 259.

32 See also P. Remy in F. Terré (ed.), *Pour une réforme du droit des contrats*, Paris, Dalloz, 2009, 259.

33 See extensively: C. Aubert de Vincelles in F. Terré (ed.), *Pour une réforme du droit des contrats*, Paris, Dalloz, 2009, 275–276.

34 See Article 114 pr. T.: '*Lorsque l'exécution est divisible, la résolution peut avoir lieu pour une partie seulement du contrat, s'il n'en résulte aucun déséquilibre significatif*'.

Article 114: *'Lorsque l'exécution est divisible, la résolution peut avoir lieu pour une partie seulement du contrat, s'il n'en résulte aucun déséquilibre significatif'*.

The accompanying text clarifies the scope of application of the partial termination. Article 114 pr. T. refers to a material or substantial partial termination and not to a temporal termination.[35] Moreover, two conditions have to be fulfilled to apply this remedy: (1) the obligations must be severable (in several obligations or stages) and (2) the partial termination may not create a significant contractual imbalance.[36] Both the Terré and the Catala project use the criterion of the 'severability' or 'divisibility'. The Terré project adds to this requirement that the partial termination may not create an important imbalance between the performances of the parties.

18. It is striking that the drafters of the Terré project chose to introduce a (material and temporal) partial termination next to an autonomous price reduction remedy in Article 107 pr. T. It is clear that price reduction, as described under Article 107 pr. T., could be applied, under certain circumstances, under the wings of partial termination. It is revealing that the accompanying text already points to the partial termination when commenting on the price reduction remedy: *'[La réduction du prix] répond à la perspective "remédiale" qui a été choisie de manière générale en permettant une sorte de "résolution partielle" du contrat (c'est d'ailleurs ainsi que le droit néerlandais le présente) [...]'*. Indeed, partial termination and price reduction might potentially overlap. Nevertheless, I believe that price reduction does not require a 'material severability', which is required for (material) partial termination. An abstract severability will suffice. This means that the remaining contract (after carrying out a price reduction) must retain its (economic) usefulness for both contractual parties. This means that a price reduction can easily be applied in case of a defect in quality, which is not the case for partial termination. It is clear that in case of a defect in quality the contract will not be materially severable, but the contract can still retain its usefulness for both contractual parties.

3. Price reduction under the *ordonnance*

3.1. General

19. The above described projects were not written in vain. In 2013, the French government took action. On 27 November 2013 a bill was introduced to allow the government to amend book III of the *Code Civil* to modernise the law of obligations and the law of proof by means of an *'edict'* (*'ordonnance'*).[37] This procedure means an acceleration of the legislative process and a serious reduction of parliamentary

35 C. Aubert de Vincelles in F. Terré (ed.), *Pour une réforme du droit des contrats*, Paris, Dalloz, 2009, 276.

36 C. Aubert de Vincelles in F. Terré (ed.), *Pour une réforme du droit des contrats*, Paris, Dalloz, 2009, 276.

37 *Projet de loi relatif à la modernisation et à la simplification du droit et des procédures dans les domaines de la justice et des affaires* of 27 November 2013 (www.senat.fr/leg/pjl13-175.html).

involvement.[38] In the meanwhile, the document that had been prepared by the ministry of Justice (*Chancellerie*) leaked in the press on 15 January 2014: the '*avant-projet de réforme du droit des obligations*' of 23 October 2013.[39] Moreover, the 'undemocratic' choice for an '*ordonnance*' provoked critical reactions of the *Sénat* and slowed down the whole process. Consequently, the bill that allows the government to modernise the law of obligations by means of an *ordonnance*, was only approved on 28 January 2015 by the *Assemblée nationale*.[40] On 12 February 2015, the *Conseil Constitutionnel* approved this method of working.[41] On 16 February 2015 the bill was finally enacted officially.[42] On 26 February the ministry of Justice launched a public consultation until 30 April 2015 and published on its website a slightly modified version of the working document of 23 October 2013: '*projet d'ordonnance n° (...) du (...) portant réforme du droit des contrats, du régime général et de la preuve des obligations*'.[43] The final '*ordonnance*' was promulgated and presented to the Council of ministers the 10th of February 2016.[44] Has the *ordonnance* (hereafter also: 'Ord.') retained the price reduction remedy, such as in the Terré project, or did the drafters consider this remedy superfluous?

20. The *ordonnance* of 2016 explicitly prescribes a price reduction as a contractual remedy in Article 1223. It slightly differs from the Article 1223 of the *projet d'ordonnance* of 2015.[45] We will examine these differences when assessing the characteristics of the price reduction.

> Article 1223 *projet d'ordonnance* 2015: '*Le créancier peut accepter une exécution imparfaite du contrat et réduire proportionnellement le prix. S'il n'a pas encore payé, le créancier notifie sa décision dans les meilleurs délais*'.

38 This way of proceeding provoked a lot of critical reactions: J.-L. Harouel, G. Teboul and O. Tournafond, "Le droit des contrats réformé par *ordonnance*?", *Dalloz* 2014, (1099) 1099–1100 (are concerned about the fundamental character of the reform with a direct impact on daily and business life and about the lack of preparatory works).

39 Www.lesechos.fr/15/01/2014/lesechos.fr/0203242436733_document---avant-projet-de-reforme-du-droit-des-contrats.htm.

40 Loi no. 2015–177 du 16 février 2015 relative à la modernisation et à la simplification du droit et des procédures dans les domaines de la justice et des affaires intérieures, *JORF* 17 February 2015, 2961. See also www.assemblee-nationale.fr/14/ta/ta0467.asp.

41 Decision by the Conseil Constitutionnel of 12 February 2015, no. 2015–710 DC, www.conseil-constitutionnel.fr/conseil-constitutionnel/francais/les-decisions/acces-par-date/decisions-depuis-1959/2015/2015–710-dc/decision-n-2015–710-dc-du-12-fevrier-2015.143268.html.

42 Loi no. 2015–177 du 16 février 2015 relative à la modernisation et à la simplification du droit et des procédures dans les domaines de la justice et des affaires intérieures, *JORF* no. 0040 du 17 février 2015, 2961. See www.legifrance.gouv.fr/affichTexte.do?cidTexte=JORFTEXT000030248562&categorieLien=id.

43 See for the launch of the public consultation: www.textes.justice.gouv.fr/textes-soumis-a-concertation-10179/reforme-du-droit-des-contrats-27897.html. See for the proposed text: www.justice.gouv.fr/publication/j21_projet_ord_reforme_contrats_2015.pdf.

44 *Ordonnance* no. 2016–131 du 10 février 2016 portant réforme du droit des contrats, du régime général et de la preuve des obligations, NOR: JUSC1522466R, *JORF* no. 0035 du 11 février 2016 (https://www.legifrance.gouv.fr/eli/*ordonnance*/2016/2/10/JUSC1522466R/jo/texte).

45 Hereafter also: 'pr. Ord.' and 'the 2015 project' or '*projet d'ordonannce*'.

> Article 1223 *ordonnance* 2016: '*Le créancier peut, après mise en demeure, accepter une exécution imparfaite du contrat et solliciter une réduction proportionnelle du prix. S'il n'a pas encore payé, le créancier notifie sa décision de réduire le prix dans les meilleurs délais.*'[46]

On the other hand, the remedy of material partial termination – which was introduced by the Catala and the Terré project – has been left out. Article 1217 Ord. introduces a whole range of possible remedies such as price reduction ('*solliciter une reduction du prix*') and termination ('*provoquer la resolution du contrat*').

> Article 1217: '*La partie envers laquelle l'engagement n'a pas été exécuté, ou l'a été imparfaitement, peut:*
> - *poursuivre l'exécution forcée en nature de l'obligation;*
> - *solliciter une réduction du prix;*[47]
> - *provoquer la résolution du contrat;*
> - *demander réparation des conséquences de l'inexécution.*
>
> *Les sanctions qui ne sont pas incompatibles peuvent être cumulées; des dommages et intérêts peuvent toujours s'y ajouter*'.

21. In what follows, we will evaluate in detail the price reduction remedy under the *ordonnance* taking into account: the conditions of application (3.2); the role of the judge and the parties (3.3); the calculation method (3.4); some other characteristics (3.5); and the interplay with a possible recognition of partial termination (3.6).

3.2. *Conditions of application*

3.2.1. Contracts and the meaning of 'price'

22. The fact that the remedy of price reduction has been introduced in '*Sous-Titre I: le contrat*' means that this remedy is restricted to '*reciprocal*' or '*multiparty*' *contracts*. Indeed, Article 1101 Ord. defines 'contract' as every agreement between two or more persons intended to create legal effects. There is no explicit possibility to expand the scope of application to connected and interdependent obligations outside the borders of a contract (as defined by Article 1101 Ord.). Under Dutch law, for example, (partial) termination is not only applicable in case of reciprocal contracts, because the second part of Article 6:261 Dutch Civil Code extends it also to 'other legal relations that imply an interdependent exchange of performances, unless in case of incompatibility with the nature of the disposition(s)'.[48] The same holds true for the price reduction remedy under

46 Emphasis added.

47 Emphasis added.

48 See also C. Asser, A.S. Hartkamp and C.H. Sieburgh, *v° Algemeen overeenkomstenrecht, Asser-serie*, 6-III, 2014, no. 680; F.B. Bakels, *Ontbinding van wederkerige overeenkomsten*, Deventer, Kluwer, 2011, no. 22; C.J.H. Brunner, G.T. de Jong, H.B. Krans, *et al.*, *Verbintenissenrecht algemeen*, Deventer, Kluwer, 2011, no. 224–225; R.J.Q. Klomp, *v° Artikel 261 Boek 6 BW, Groene Serie Verbintenissenrecht*, 2007, no. 7; M.M. Olthof, *v° Artikel 261 Boek 6 BW, Tekst en Commentaar Burgerlijk Wetboek*, 2013, no. 3; M.M.

the Draft Common Frame of Reference (DCFR).[49] Article III.-3:601 DCFR states that the creditor can invoke a price reduction in case of a non-conforming 'obligation' ('*not conforming to the terms regulating the obligation*').[50] The application of price reduction requires that the reciprocal obligations are clearly connected or interdependent.[51]

23. More ambiguous is the meaning of the concept *'price'* when applying a price reduction under Article 1223 Ord. Can this price only be expressed in money or can it also be another performance? Article 1223 Ord. does not provide for a clear answer. Some special contracts, such as sales contracts require a price expressed in money,[52] otherwise the contract would be requalified as a 'barter' contract.[53] Nevertheless, in case of for example tenancy-contracts the price must not necessarily be expressed in money and can exist out of other performances such as services...[54] Consequently, the concept 'price' cannot be restricted to a price in money.[55] The DCFR and the Acquis Principles[56] also apply a price reduction in case of other performances than a price in money. Paragraph 4 of Article III.-3:601 DCFR states: '*This Article* [about price reduction] *applies with appropriate adaptations to a reciprocal obligation of the creditor other than an obligation to pay a price*'. In the Acquis principles the remedy is not called a 'price

Olthof, *v° Artikel 265 Boek 6 BW, Tekst en Commentaar Burgerlijk Wetboek*, 2013, no. 1 (partial termination is in principle not applicable in case of a "*schenking onder last*").

49 C. Von Bar and E. Clive, *Draft Common Frame of Reference (DCFR)*, Munich, Sellier, 2009, 6v.

50 The remedies for non-performance in the DCFR are applicable to all obligations in a contract or other juridical acts: C. Von Bar and E. Clive, *Draft Common Frame of Reference (DCFR)*, I, Munich, Sellier, 2009, 669–672.

51 See also the fourth paragraph of Article III.-3:601 DCFR: '*This Article applies with appropriate adaptations to a reciprocal obligation of the creditor other than an obligation to pay a price*'. According to Article III.-1:102 DCFR 'reciprocal obligation' means: '(a) performance of the obligation is due in exchange for performance of the other obligation; (b) it is an obligation to facilitate or accept performance of the other obligation; or (c) it is so clearly connected to the other obligation or its subject matter that performance of the one can reasonably be regarded as dependent on performance of the other'.

52 See Article 1582 *juncto* 1702 CC. G. Baudry-Lacantinerie and L. Barde, *Traité théorique et pratique de droit civil. Des obligations*, XIX, Paris, Larose, 1908, no. 128; E. Gardounis, *La détermination du prix dans le contrat. Etude comparée entre le droit Français et le droit Hellénique*, Brussels-Athens, Bruylant-Sakkoulas, 2007, no. 9–10 (refines his opinion in no. 12 *et seq.*); H. Narayan-Fourment, *L'approche concurrentielle et contractuelle de la détermination du prix (dans les ventes commerciales et les contrats-cadres)*, Aix-en-Provence, PUAM, 2003, no. 2.

53 See e.g. M. Thioye, *Recherches sur la conception du prix dans les contrats*, I, Aix-en-Provence, PUAM, 2004, no. 13.

54 E. Gardounis, *La détermination du prix dans le contrat. Etude comparée entre le droit Français et le droit Hellénique*, Brussels-Athens, Bruylant-Sakkoulas, 2007, no. 26; M. Thioye, *Recherches sur la conception du prix dans les contrats*, I, Aix-en-Provence, PUAM, 2004, no. 8.

55 *Contra* with regard to the 2015 project: E. Savaux, "Article 1223: la réduction du prix", *Revue des contrats* 2015, (786) no. 5. *Contra* with regard to the *ordonnance* of 2016: M. Mignot, "Commentaire article par article de l'*ordonnance* du 10 février 2016 portant réforme du droit des contrats, du régime général et de la preuve des obligations (IV)", *Petites Affiches* 2016, (5) Article 1223.

56 Acquis Group. Research group on the existing EC private law, *Contract II, General Provisions, Delivery of Goods, Package Travel and Payment Services in Principles of the Existing EC Contract Law (Acquis Principles)*, Munich, Sellier, 2009, xii.

reduction' but a 'wider remedy of reduction of performance'. The reduction can accordingly be applied on other obligations '*which are capable of being reduced or diminished*'.[57] We have to stress that it is not self-evident to apply a price reduction remedy in case of non-monetary performances. Nevertheless, price reduction should not be restricted to merely prices expressed in money. Other performances can only be the subject of price reduction if they can be reduced (see also the Acquis Principles for this expression). According to me, this means that a reduction can only be applied if both performances are comparable and/or divisible.[58]

3.2.2. Partial non-performance and seriousness of the non-performance

24. Article 1223 Ord. prescribes a price reduction with a wide scope of application in case of '*une exécution imparfaite*'. We can derive from this three important aspects of the price reduction remedy.

25. Notwithstanding Article 1217 Ord. seems to enable a price reduction in case of a total and a partial non-performance ('*n'a pas été exécuté, ou l'a été imparfaitement*'),[59] it is clear that the drafters of the *ordonnance* restrict the remedy of price reduction to a *partial* non-performance. Indeed, according to Article 1223 Ord. price reduction can only be applied in case of '*une exécution imparfaite*'.[60] A price reduction up to zero has clearly not been envisaged in the *ordonnance* (see also *infra*, no. 43), which is the case for Article 50 of the Vienna Sales Convention.[61] I also wonder whether this remedy can be applied for a (temporal) rent reduction up to zero and how to apply it in this case.

57 J. Pisulinski, F. Zoll and M. Szpunar, "Termination and Reduction of Performance" in Acquis Group (ed.), *Contract II: General Provisions, Delivery of Goods, Package Travel and Payment Services in Acquis Principles*, Munich, Sellier, 2009, (411) 414.

58 The German remedy of *Minderung* in sales law is, however, also applicable in case of non-severable performances. See e.g. A. Matusche-Beckmann, "§441" in M. Martinek (ed.), *von Staudingers Kommentar zum BGB*, Berlin, Sellier-de Gruyter, 2013, no. 35.

59 Points correctly to this lack of clarity of the 2015 project (because of the wording of Article 1217 pr. Ord.): E. Savaux, "Article 1223: la réduction du prix", *Revue des contrats* 2015, (786) no. 3.

60 See similarly with regard to the 2015 project: C. Asfar-Cazenave, "La réforme du droit français des contrats", *Revue Thémis* 2016, (1) 17 (not yet appeared); E. Savaux, "Article 1223: la réduction du prix", *Revue des contrats* 2015, (786) no. 3.

61 See e.g. I. Bach, "Art. 50" in S. Kröll, L. Mistelis and P.P. Viscasillas (eds.), *CISG*, Munich, Beck, 2011, (748) 761; C. Liu, *Remedies in International Sales*, New York, Juris Net, 2007, 135–138; U. Magnus, "Art. 50 CISG" in M. Martinek (ed.), *von Staudingers Kommentar zum BGB, Wiener UN-Kaufrecht*, III, Munich, Sellier - de Gruyter, 2013, no. 23; M. Müller-Chen, "Art. 50 CISG" in I. Schwenzer (ed.), *Commentary on the CISG*, Oxford, OUP, 2010, (770) no. 13; P. Schlechtriem and P. Butler, *UN Law on International Sales*, Berlin, Springer, 2009, no. 202; A.K. Schnyder and R.M. Straub, "Art. 50" in H. Honsell (ed.), *Kommentar zum UN-Kaufrecht*, Heidelberg, Springer, 2010, (641) no. 45–46 (defended another opinion in the version of 1997). See also extensively: Austria Oberster Gerichtshof 23 May 2005, http://cisgw3.law.pace.edu/cases/050523a3.html. This jurisprudence has often been confirmed in different Member States of the convention.

26. Secondly, the wording "*exécution imparfaite*" points at a very wide scope of application with regard to the different kinds of shortcomings that can be covered.[62] According to me, the price reduction under Article 1223 Ord. can be applied in case of: a defect in quality, a defect in quantity, a legal defect (such as legal claims, hidden servitudes, ...), a late performance, a performance at the wrong place, a divergence with the description of the goods/services, a defect in packaging and documents, ...

27. Finally, this means that, according to me, the application of a price reduction *does not require any degree of 'seriousness'*,[63] which is in principle the case for the application of termination (requirement of '*une inexécution suffisamment grave*').[64] Nevertheless, I do believe that the application of a price reduction requires inherently that the remaining contract must retain some usefulness for both contracting parties. It is self-evident that the remaining contract retains its usefulness for the creditor if he chooses to apply this remedy. The creditor would not ask for a price reduction if the remaining contract would not be useful to him anymore. How to protect the interests of the debtor if the creditor chooses a price reduction remedy? According to me, the creditor has also to take into account the remaining usefulness for the debtor. If the creditor insists unreasonably on applying a price reduction remedy when the remaining contract is useless to the debtor, he might, under some circumstances, violate the prohibition of abuse of rights[65] (which is also known under French contract law).

3.2.3. Excused and (un)excused non-performance?

28. The specific applications of price reduction in the current French Civil Code are not restricted to unexcused non performances. Indeed, Article 1722 CC explicitly prescribes a price reduction remedy in tenancy contracts if a part of the rented good is destroyed in case of *force majeure*.

29. Similarly to the Terré project, the drafters of *ordonnance* do not clearly indicate whether the general price reduction remedy can also be applied in case of *force majeure*. Article 1218 Ord. about *force majeure* merely prescribes suspension of the contract (in case of a temporary shortcoming) or the termination of the contract (in case of a permanent shortcoming).[66] One author even mentioned that Article 1218 of the *projet*

62 See similarly with regard to the 2015 project: E. Savaux, "Article 1223: la réduction du prix", *Revue des contrats* 2015, (786) no. 3.

63 See also with regard to the 2015 project: E. Savaux, "Article 1223: la réduction du prix", *Revue des contrats* 2015, (786) no. 3.

64 See for the requirement of '*une inexéuction suffisamment grave*' in case of termination: Article 1224 Ord.

65 See for the same reasoning with regard to the 2015 project: E. Savaux, "Article 1223: la réduction du prix", *Revue des contrats* 2015, (786) no. 3 ('*Aucun degré de gravité n'est exigé, un manquement minime suffisant, à moins de considérer que le créancier manque à la bonne foi en l'invoquant*').

66 See about this Article with regard to the 2015 project: H. Boucard, "Article 1218: la force majeure contractuelle", *RDC* 2015, (779) no. 1–8.

d'Ordonnace was 'incomplete' because it omits to include a price reduction remedy in case of *force majeure*.[67] The same holds true for article 1218 under the current *ordonannce*. Furthermore, Article 1223 Ord. about price reduction does not refer to the liability for shortcomings. However, and this opinion has to be welcomed, some authors, consider the price reduction remedy applicable in case of excused and unexcused shortcomings to the contract.[68] Nevertheless, we have seen that the wording from Article 1223 *projet d'ordonnance* slightly differs from Article 1223 Ord. The new article clearly indicates that a '*mise en demeure*' is required. This means that the creditor is obliged to put his debtor formally in delay. The *mise en demeure* is only required in case of remedies for unexcused non-performance of a contract. Implicitly, this might signify – much to my regret – that price reduction is only considered a remedy in case of an unexcused failure to perform, and not in case of *force majeure* (excused non-performance). A lack of a price reduction remedy in case of *force majeure* would be a missed opportunity for a coherent remedial system.

30. One exception must be made in any case. Unfortunately, the *projet d'ordonnance* does not modernise with regard to its old fashioned system concerning the transfer of risk in case of contracts that imply a transfer of property or another right (such as a sale contract). Article 1196 Ord. states in its first part that the transfer of property (or another right) takes place at the moment of the conclusion of the contract ('*consensus*'), in contracts implying transfer of property (or another right). The third paragraph proceeds that the transfer of property implies the transfer of risk. This means that, in principle, the conclusion of the contract brings about the transfer of risk. Thus, the buyer in a sales contract will bear the risk as from the moment of the conclusion of the contract (*res perit domino* rule). This means that if the transferred good or right has been affected by *force majeure* after the conclusion of the contract and before delivery, the buyer will bear the risk and still has to pay the complete price that the contractual parties agreed upon. This means that a price reduction (in case of a partial destruction of the transferred goods or rights) cannot be applied, because the buyer will always have to pay the full price. Of course, this system can be criticised in light of the new developments in European private law (and especially for example in the Netherlands, Germany, and the DCFR). In the German[69] and the Dutch[70] system, the risk is in principle transferred at the moment of delivery (and not at

[67] H. Boucard, "Article 1218: la force majeure contractuelle", *RDC* 2015, (779) no. 7 (with regard to the 2015 project).

[68] See (with regard to the 2015 project): Y.-M. Laithier, "Les règles relatives à l'inexécution des obligations contractuelles", *La Semaine Juridique Edition Générale* 2015, (47) 51 and 53. See also S. Jansen, "De hervorming van het Franse verbintenissenrecht: le renouveau de la grande dame", *Contracteren* 2015, (96) 103. The following author is uncertain about its applicability in case of *force majeure* (with regard to the 2015 project): E. Savaux, "Article 1223: la réduction du prix", *Revue des contrats* 2015, (786) no. 3 *in fine*.

[69] §446 BGB specifies that, independently from the transfer of property, the risk is transferred to the buyer upon delivery of the good.

[70] Article 7:10 Dutch Civil Code states that the buyer bears the risk as from the delivery, even if property is not yet transferred.

the moment of the *consensus*). The same holds true for the DCFR.[71] This means that a remedy, such as price reduction and termination, can be applied in case that the transferred goods or rights have been affected by *force majeure* after the conclusion of the contract and before delivery.

3.2.4. Relation between price reduction and other remedies

31. It is unclear how price reduction under Article 1223 Ord. fits into the *hierarchy of remedies*. Because of the lack of preparatory works it is difficult to retrieve the exact implication of each provision in the project. As far as I understand the new provisions, nothing radical has happened.

32. Article 1217 Ord. merely gives an overview of all possible remedies (*cf.* no. 20). Nevertheless, this article mentions *in fine* that remedies that are not incompatible with each other can be combined ('*cumuler*') and that damages can always be combined with all the other remedies. This means that the price reduction remedy of Article 1223 Ord. can be combined with damages (in case of an unexcused non-performance).[72, 73] Of course, this combination is only possible in as far that damages will not be available for the part that has already been covered by the price reduction.[74]

If price reduction and damages are combined, what would be the amount of the additional damages? Two possible approaches can be taken: the expectation interests (*dommages-intérêts positifs*) or the reliance interests (*dommages-intérêts négatifs*).[75] The first option means that the creditor has to be put in the situation wherein he would be if the contract would have been performed correctly; the second means that the creditor has to be replaced in the situation wherein he would be if he would not have concluded the contract.[76] According to me, price reduction has the aim to continue the contract, but in a reduced form. The contract will be partially performed and therefore additional

71 See Article IV.A. – 5:102 (1) DCFR.

72 See also with regard to the 2015 project: P. Grosser, "La réforme en pratique. La réduction du prix comme remède général à l'exécution imparfaite du contrat", *AJCA* 2014, (219) between footnotes 21 and 24 (this means that price reduction and damages can not be assimilated and are considered seperate remedies). Wonders whether price reduction an damages can be combined: A. Bénabent, "Les nouveau mécanismes", *Revue des contrats* 2016, (17) *in fine*.

73 Article 107 projet Terré about price reduction explicitly prescribes the possibility to combine a price reduction with damages, whilst the drafters of the *ordonnance* consider it sufficient to mention this possibility in the general Article 1217 and do not repeat it in Article 1223, specifically about price reduction.

74 See also with regard to the 2015 project: E. Savaux, "Article 1223: la réduction du prix", *Revue des contrats* 2015, (786) no. 6.

75 See also about reliance and expectation interests: Y.-M. Laithier, "Les sanctions de l'inexécution du contrat", *Revue des contrats* 2016, (39) after footnote 31.

76 See e.g. Y.-M. Laithier, *Etude comparative des sanctions de l'inexécution du contrat*, Paris, LGDJ, 2007, 157 *et seq.* See also L.L. Fuller and W.R. Perdue, "The Reliance Interest in Contract Damages: 1", *The Yale Law Journal* 1936, 52 *et seq.* and "The Reliance Interest in Contract Damages: 2", *The Yale Law Journal* 1936, 373 *et seq.*

damages should be calculated taking into account the expectation interests (*dommages-intérêts positifs*).[77]

Of course, parties can also stipulate the amount of damages that can be combined with a price reduction in a liquidated damages clauses.[78]

33. If we would have to conclude that price reduction could also be applied in case of an excused non-performance (*force majeure*) (which is highly uncertain, see *supra,* 3.2.3), this would mean that in the case of a definitive 'imperfect performance' due to *force majeure* the creditor can also appeal to a price reduction remedy (next to the termination of the contract). Of course, it would be impossible to cumulate price reduction with damages in case of an excused non-performance (such as indicated by Article 1217 *in fine* Ord., see also *supra*). It would be then advisable to indicate this somewhere in Article 1223 Ord.

34. Performance in kind (Articles 1221–1222 Ord.) is, according to many authors, the primary remedy, unless performance is impossible or – and this is new and controversial[79] – if there would be a manifest imbalance between the cost of performance for the debtor and its interest for the creditor.[80] The question rises whether performance in kind takes precedence to the price reduction remedy. However, the remedy of price reduction seems not to be subject to any restrictions or hierarchy: '*Le créancier peut [...]accepter une execution imparfaite du contrat et solliciter une réduciton proportionnelle du prix*'. The creditor may choose to make an appeal to a price reduction remedy by accepting the 'imperfect' performance. The debtor has, according to Laithier, no 'right to cure' even if he can perform in kind.[81] The only restrictions that apply to the price reduction remedy are the previously described conditions of application.

77 S. Jansen, *Prijsvermindering: remedie tot bijsturing van contracten*, Antwerp, Intersentia, 2015, no. 1109–1110. *Contra*: E. Savaux, "Article 1223: la réduction du prix", *Revue des contrats* 2015, (786) no. 6.

78 Wonders whether price reduction can be combined with a liquidated damages clause: A. Bénabent, "Les nouveau mécanismes", *Revue des contrats* 2016, (17) *in fine*.

79 The terms have been changed from '*si son coût est manifestement déraisonnable*' (*projet d'ordonnance*) to '*s'il existe une disproportion manifeste entre son coût pour le débiteur et son intérêt pour le créancier*' (*ordonnance* of 2016). See about this controversy (*projet d'ordonnance*): D. Mainguy, "Du "coût manifestement déraisonnable" à la reconnaissance d'un "droit d'option"", *Droit et Patrimoine* 2014, (60) 60–62. See against this change: T. Genicon, "Contre l'introduction du "coût manifestement déraisonnable" comme exception à l'exéctuion forcée en nature", *Droit et Patrimoine* 2014, (63) 63–66 (this will go further than a mere prohibition of abuse of rights). See for an alternative: P. Lemay, "L'inexécution du contrat: l'exécution forcée en nature (Projet, art. 1221)" in M. Latina and G. Chantepie (eds.), *Projet de réforme du droit des contrats, du régime général et de la preuve des obligations. Analyses et propositions*, Paris, Dalloz, 2015, (76) 76–77. See also about this topic: Y.-M. Laithier, "Les règles relatives à l'inexécution des obligations contractuelles", *La Semaine Juridique Edition Générale* 2015, (47) 52 (with regard to the 2015 project).

80 Some authors also propose to restrict performance in kind if it breaches the fundamental freedoms of a person: J. Le Bourg and C. Quézel-Ambrunaz, "Article 1221: l'exécution forcée en nature des obligations", *Revue des contrats* 2015, (782) after footnote 20 (with regard to the 2015 project).

81 Y.-M. Laithier, "Les sanctions de l'inexécution du contrat", *Revue des contrats* 2016, (39) after footnote 39.

3.3. *Role of the judge and of the parties*

3.3.1. Role of the parties

35. According to what we have seen before, the creditor has *a right to choose*[82] a price reduction remedy if all the conditions of application are complied with and if he accepts the 'imperfect' performance of the contract. According to us, price reduction is not subordinated to some hierarchy of remedies or priority of performance in kind (or a 'right to cure').[83] Indeed, Article 1223 states: '*Le créancier peut, [...], accepter une exécution imparfaite du contrat et solliciter une réduction proportionnelle du prix* '.[84]

36. Secondly, the former *projet d'ordonnance* did not clarify the obligation to put the debtor in delay ('*mise en demeure*') by the creditor in case of a price reduction.[85] I was convinced that, even if the *projet* did not refer to the *mise en demeure*, that it would be required in case a price reduction was applied when remedying an *unexcused* non-performance. Indeed, the application of contractual sanctions in case of unexcused non-performances generally require such a communication. The new *ordonnance* of 2016 has clarified this issue. The new Article 1223 requires explicitly the *mise en demeure*: '*Le créancier peut, après mise en demeure, accepter une exécution imparfaite du contrat et solliciter une réduction proportionnelle du prix*'. Nevertheless, as already mentioned, this clarification brings about a new problem. Does the mentioning of the duty to put ones debtor in delay in Article 1223 Ord. mean that a price reduction cannot be applied in case of *force majeure* (*cf. supra*, 3.2.3)?

37. Next to a *mise en demeure*, the question arises whether one must notify the intention to apply the price reduction remedy. Article 1223 Ord. explicitly prescribes this notification duty by the creditor. It is interesting that Article 1223 Ord. merely stipulates that the application of the price reduction remedy has to be notified if the creditor *has not yet been paid*. It is unclear why the drafters only envisage the situation 'when the price is not yet paid by the creditor' and not the situation in which the price has already been paid by the creditor. According to some authors, there is no reason to restrict the notification of the price reduction to cases in which the price has not yet been paid.[86] I agree and it has to be stressed that this 'notification' is merely necessary if one wants to

82 Y.-M. Laithier, "Les sanctions de l'inexécution du contrat", *Revue des contrats* 2016, (39) before footnote 37 (the creditor may choose the sanction in case of non-performance).

83 Y.-M. Laithier, "Les sanctions de l'inexécution du contrat", *Revue des contrats* 2016, (39) around footnote 30 ('*L'ordonnance n'instaure pas de hiérarchie*').

84 Emphasis added.

85 See e.g. E. Savaux, "Article 1223: la réduction du prix", *Revue des contrats* 2015, (786) no. 4 (did not consider the *mise en demeure* to be applicable and was worried about this).

86 Y.-M. Laithier, "Les règles relatives à l'inexécution des obligations contractuelles", *La Semaine Juridique Edition Générale* 2015, (47) 53 (with regard to the 2015 project); M. Mignot, "Commentaire article par article de l'*ordonnance* du 10 février 2016 portant réforme du droit des contrats, du régime général et de la preuve des obligations (IV)", *Petites Affiches* 2016, (5) Article 1223. Compare: E. Savaux, "Article 1223: la réduction du prix", *Revue des contrats* 2015, (786) no. 4 (wonders with regard to the 2015 project

apply the price reduction *extrajudicially* (see also *infra*, n° 38).[87] The notification of a unilateral price reduction is necessary because it is a unilateral juridical act implying a notification for its validity[88] ('*acte unilatéral réceptice*').[89, 90] This notification is required 1) to inform the debtor about the application of the price reduction remedy and 2) to enable the judge to examine the application of the price reduction remedy *a posteriori*. Therefore, this notification should also contain a motivation.[91] Savaux indicated that the *projet d'ordonnance* did not prescribe a sanction if the price reduction has not been notified (nor does the final version of the *ordonannce* prescribe a sanction).[92] Nevertheless, one must bear into mind that a notification is required for the *validity* of the unilateral application of the price reduction, because it is an *acte unilatéral réceptice*. This means that if an extrajudicial price reduction has not been notified, it will have no effect.

3.3.2. Role of the judge

38. The wording of the project[93] (and of the final *ordonnance*) is not clear with regard to the question whether a price reduction requires a prior intervention of the judge. Article 1217 Ord. – which enumerates all the different remedies – specifies ambiguously that the creditor can, amongst others, '*solliciter une réduction du prix*' in case of an

whether the creditor can reduce the price without notification if the price has already been paid or whether price reduction is ruled out if the price has already been paid).

87 The extrajudicial application of the price reduction under the Vienna Sales convention requires also a notification by the creditor. The mere payment of a reduced amount will not make clear whether the buyer wants to apply a price reduction or wants to exercise a temporary suspension: I. Bach, "Art. 50" in S. Kröll, L. Mistelis and P.P. Viscasillas (eds.), *CISG*, Munich, Beck, 2011, (748) 756–757; M. Müller-Chen, "Art. 50 CISG" in I. Schwenzer (ed.), *Commentary on the CISG*, Oxford, OUP, 2010, (770) no. 4. See also A.K. Schnyder and R.M. Straub, "Art. 50" in H. Honsell (ed.), *Kommentar zum UN-Kaufrecht*, Heidelberg, Springer, 2010, (641) no. 27.

88 R. Encinas de Munagorri, *L'acte unilatéral dans les rapports contractuels*, Paris, LGDJ, 1996, no. 267 (this author is of the opinion that every unilateral 'dissolution' of a contract has be considered an *acte juridique unilatéral réceptice*, implying a notification for its validity).

89 J. Martin de la Moutte, *L'acte juridique unilatéral*, Paris, Sirey, 1951, no. 178–187. See also R. Encinas de Munagorri, *L'acte unilatéral dans les rapports contractuels*, Paris, LGDJ, 1996, no. 267.

90 M. Mignot, "Commentaire article par article de l'*ordonnance* du 10 février 2016 portant réforme du droit des contrats, du régime général et de la preuve des obligations (IV)", *Petites Affiches* 2016, (5) Article 1223.

91 Are of the opinion that this is not required under the 2015 project and deplores it: P. Lemay, "L'inexécution du contrat: la réduction du prix (Projet, art. 1223)" in M. Latina and G. Chantepie (eds.), *Projet de réforme du droit des contrats, du régime général et de la preuve des obligations. Analyses et propositions*, Paris, Dalloz, 2015, (78) 79; E. Savaux, "Article 1223: la réduction du prix", *Revue des contrats* 2015, (786) no. 4.

92 E. Savaux, "Article 1223: la réduction du prix", *Revue des contrats* 2015, (786) no. 4.

93 See with regard to the 2015 project: P. Grosser, "La réforme en pratique. La réduction du prix comme remède général à l'exécution imparfaite du contrat", *AJCA* 2014, (219) between footnote 25 and 29; M. Mekki, "Les remèdes à l'inexécution dans le projet d'*ordonnance* portant réforme du droit des obligations", *Gazette du Palais* 2015, issue 120, (37) no. 13; E. Savaux, "Article 1223: la réduction du prix", *Revue des contrats* 2015, (786) no. 3.

imperfect performance or a non-performance. '*Solliciter*' means 'request', but can also be translated as 'make an appeal on'. If a creditor may 'request' a price reduction, this would imply – according to me – a prior intervention by a judge.[94] But if a creditor can 'make an appeal on' price reduction this does not necessarily exclude an extrajudicial price reduction. We can conclude that the wording of Article 1217 pr. Ord. is not decisive.

The former wording of Article 1223 in the *projet d'ordonnace* made it is clear that a creditor could invoke the price reduction extrajudicially.[95] Indeed, it stated '*Le créancier peut accepter une exécution imparfaite du contrat et réduire proportionnellement le prix*'.[96] This means that the creditor can choose to apply a price reduction. The wording of this Article clearly pointed at a possibility to reduce the price extrajudicially. Unfortunately, Article 1223 Ord. has changed: '*Le créancier peut, après mise en demeure, accepter une exécution imparfaite du contrat et solliciter une réduction proportionnelle du prix*'. The ambiguous term '*solliciter*' pops up again. As we have seen before (*supra*), this term is not conclusive with regard to the question whether or not the price reduction can be applied extrajudicially.

Nevertheless, the second part of Article 1223 remains the same. It stipulates that the creditor has to notify *its decision* in due time if he has not yet paid the price.[97] This means, according to me, that a creditor can, without prior intervention of a judge, decide upon a price reduction.[98] Of course, an extrajudicial price reduction can always give rise to an *a posteriori* examination by the judge of e.g. the conditions of application and the

94 The following author thinks that the verb 'solliciter' means that the other party has to agree with the price reduction (consequently, price reduction would be contractual and not a unilateral remedy): M. Mignot, "Commentaire article par article de l'*ordonnance* du 10 février 2016 portant réforme du droit des contrats, du régime général et de la preuve des obligations (IV)", *Petites Affiches* 2016, (5) Article 1223. Is not sure whether 'solliciter' means that the other party has to agree or that price reduction requires a prior intervention of a judge: Y.-M. Laithier, "Les sanctions de l'inexécution du contrat", *Revue des contrats* 2016, (39) between footnotes 20 and 24.

95 Y.-M. Laithier, "Les sanctions de l'inexécution du contrat", *Revue des contrats* 2016, (39) before footnote 20. Are of the opinion that article 1223 pr. Ord. prescribed an extrajudicial price reduction remedy: C. Asfar-Cazenave, "La réforme du droit français des contrats", *Revue Thémis* 2016, (1) 16 (will appear in 2016); P. Grosser, "La réforme en pratique. La réduction du prix comme remède général à l'exécution imparfaite du contrat", *AJCA* 2014, (219) before footnote 25; S. Jansen, "De hervorming van het Franse verbintenissenrecht: le renouveau de la grande dame", *Contracteren* 2015, (96) 103; Y.-M. Laithier, "Les règles relatives à l'inexécution des obligations contractuelles", *La Semaine Juridique Edition Générale* 2015, (47) 53; P. Lemay, "L'inexécution du contrat: la réduction du prix (Projet, art. 1223)" in M. Latina and G. Chantepie (eds.), *Projet de réforme du droit des contrats, du régime général et de la preuve des obligations. Analyses et propositions*, Paris, Dalloz, 2015, (78) 78; C.M.D.S. Pavillon, "Een nieuw contractenrecht voor Frankrijk", *NTBR* 2015, (11) before footnote 57. Is critical towards an extrajudicial price reduction: E. Savaux, "Article 1223: la réduction du prix", *Revue des contrats* 2015, (786) no. 3.

96 Emphasis added.

97 As we have indicated before, there is, however, no reason to restrict the notification of the price reduction to cases in which the price has not yet been paid: Y.-M. Laithier, "Les règles relatives à l'inexécution des obligations contractuelles", *La Semaine Juridique Edition Générale* 2015, (47) 53 (with regard to the 2015 project).

98 See also for the same opinion (with regard to the project of 2015) Y.-M. Laithier, "Les règles relatives à l'inexécution des obligations contractuelles", *La Semaine Juridique Edition Générale* 2015, (47) 53. See also with regard to the *ordonnance* of 2016: M. Mignot, "Commentaire article par article de l'*ordonnance* du 10 février 2016 portant réforme du droit des contrats, du régime général et de la preuve des obligations

effectuated reduction of the price.[99] One author also points at the ambiguity of Article 1223, but he nonetheless believes that the price reduction remedy can be applied extrajudicially because of the general idea of unilateralism of the text of the *ordonnance*.[100]

Moreover, the acceptance of an extrajudicial price reduction does not rule out the possibility to make an appeal upon a judge. Parties may always invoke the price reduction judicially.[101] A judicial application of a price reduction will be necessary if the creditor has already paid the price and the debtor does not want to cooperate with the application of a price reduction. If the creditor is not certain about the amount he has to reduce the price, he can also call upon a judge to apply and calculate the price reduction. It is also possible that the creditor only calls upon the price reduction as a defence during court proceedings. In the three aforementioned situations a prior intervention of a judge will be desirable and necessary.

39. As we have already pointed out, an *extrajudicial* price reduction requires, according to me, a price reduction declaration or a notification (*supra*, no. 37). A *judicial* price reduction merely requires (in case of an unexcused non-performance) a *mise en demeure*. Afterwards, it is sufficient to invoke the price reduction in a writ of summons or in the pleadings.

3.4. Calculation method

40. Luckily, Article 1223 Ord. prescribes clearly that the price reduction has to be calculated proportionally. This means that the price has to be reduced in proportion with the shortcoming (which is the reduction in value or the reduction of enjoyment).[102] The calculation of a price reduction will be a rather easy exercise if there is a quantitative shortcoming.[103] However, it has to be admitted that the calculation of a price reduction will be more difficult in case of a shortcoming in the quality.[104]

(IV)", *Petites Affiches* 2016, (5) Article 1223 (the second part of Article 1223 makes clear that the price can be reduced unilaterally, but the first part of Article 1223 blurs this by using the verb 'solliciter').

99 See also M. Mignot, "Commentaire article par article de l'*ordonnance* du 10 février 2016 portant réforme du droit des contrats, du régime général et de la preuve des obligations (IV)", *Petites Affiches* 2016, (5) Article 1223.

100 O. Sabart, "Les sanctions de l'inexécution du contrat (suite): résolution/réduction du prix", *L'essentiel. Droit des contrats* 2016, (7) *in fine*.

101 Y.-M. Laithier, "Les règles relatives à l'inexécution des obligations contractuelles", *La Semaine Juridique Edition Générale* 2015, (47) 53.

102 Criticises the calculation method of the 2015 project: P. Lemay, "L'inexécution du contrat: la réduction du prix (Projet, art. 1223)" in M. Latina and G. Chantepie (eds.), *Projet de réforme du droit des contrats, du régime général et de la preuve des obligations. Analyses et propositions*, Paris, Dalloz, 2015, (78) 79.

103 It is true that this calculation method is easily applicable in case of a quantitative shortcoming but is more difficult to apply in case of qualitative shortcomings (with regard to the 2015 project): E. Savaux, "Article 1223: la réduction du prix", *Revue des contrats* 2015, (786) no. 5. See also M. Mignot, "Commentaire article par article de l'*ordonnance* du 10 février 2016 portant réforme du droit des contrats, du régime général et de la preuve des obligations (IV)", *Petites Affiches* 2016, (5) Article 1223.

104 Proposes two ways of calcultating the price reduction in case of a shortcoming in quality: M. Mignot, "Commentaire article par article de l'*ordonnance* du 10 février 2016 portant réforme du droit des contrats, du régime général et de la preuve des obligations (IV)", *Petites Affiches* 2016, (5) Article 1223.

In any case, the following formula will apply:[105]

$$\frac{\text{stipulated price}}{\text{reduced price}} = \frac{\text{value of the conforming performance}}{\text{value of the imperfect performance}}$$

$$\text{reduced price} = \frac{\text{value of the imperfect performance} \times \text{stipulated price}}{\text{value of the conforming performance}}$$

41. However, Article 1223 Ord. does not specify the time for calculating the values of the conforming and imperfect performance: the time of the conclusion[106] of the contract or the moment of delivery or performance[107] of the goods/services. We have already stated in previous contributions that the moment of calculation can have an important effect upon the outcome of the calculation.[108]

In case of a calculation on the *moment* of delivery (performance) a rise or fall of the good/services will, under certain circumstances, play a role. If the value of conforming goods/services and imperfect good/services rise or fall equally, this will not affect the end result (because it is a fraction).

$$\text{reduced price} = \frac{\overset{\nearrow +10\%}{\text{value of the imperfect performance}} \times \text{stipulated price}}{\underset{\nearrow +10\%}{\text{value of the conforming performance}}}$$

But a *difference* in the rise/fall in value between the conforming and imperfect performance will of course influence the reduction in price.

$$\text{reduced price} = \frac{\overset{\searrow -70\%}{\text{value of the imperfect performance}} \times \text{stipulated price}}{\underset{\nearrow +10\%}{\text{value of the conforming performance}}}$$

105 This is the same formula as the one proposed by Will for Article 50 of the Vienna Sales Convention: M.R. Will, "Art. 50" in M.C. Bianca and M.J. Bonell (eds.), *Bianca-Bonell Commentary on the International Sales Law*, Milan, Giuffrè, 1987, (368) 372.

106 See for this method: Article 46 ULIS ('Convention relating to a Uniform Law on the International Sale of Goods, of 1964), §441 BGB, the *réfaction* in case of non-conforming delivery in commercial sales contracts (S. Jansen, "De "*réfaction*" in de handelskoop", *TBH* 2014, (127) no. 45; see also M. Alter, note under Cass. Fr. com. 23 March 1971, *D.* 1974, (40) 42).

107 See for this method: Article 50 CISG and the price reduction under the PECL, the DCFR and the CESL (Common European Sales Law proposal).

108 See e.g. S. Jansen, "Price Reduction as a Remedy in European Contract Law and the Consumer Acquis" in A. Keirse and M. Loos (eds.), *Alternative Ways to Ius Commune. The Europeanisation of Private Law*, Antwerp, Intersentia, 2012, (169) 206–207; S. Jansen, Prijsvermindering: remedie tot bijsturing van contracten, Antwerp, Intersentia, 2015, no. 1194–1199.

If a price reduction would be calculated on the moment of the conclusion of the contract, a rise of fall of the value of the goods of services after the conclusion of the contract will not play a role and will not affect the calculation of the price reduction. This means that it is advisable that the French legislator chooses for one of both moments of calculation, otherwise there will be legal uncertainty about this aspect.

42. Which method should the French legislator choose? Will defends the system that calculates the price reduction at the moment of delivery.[109] He points out that chances and risks are distributed fairly by this method. On the one hand, if the market price of the non-conforming goods rises compared to the conform goods, the buyer has goods of a higher market value and inferior of quality, because the buyer chooses to profit from the higher market value, the price reduction is lesser or even nothing. On the other hand, if the market price of the non-conforming goods falls compared to the conforming goods, he has not only goods of a lower quality, but also goods of a lower market-value. If the buyer accepts the non-conforming goods, it is only fair that the price reduction will be more. Nevertheless, there are more arguments to adopt the calculation method at the moment of the conclusion of the contract. First and foremost it respects the aim of a price reduction remedy: a quick and simple remedy to adjust a contract. Because one has not to take into account a rise/fall of values of the conforming and imperfect goods/services, price reduction will be easy to calculate. Another argument can be deduced from an interesting remark from Van Der Velden.[110] He argues that if one takes into account the *difference* in the rise/fall in value between the conforming and imperfect performance (which is the case if the price reduction is calculated at the moment of performance or delivery), price reduction resembles more and more to damages. Moreover, it is striking that the systems that use the method of calculation at the moment of delivery/performance are modern international and/or European instruments (such as the PECL, the DCFR, the CESL and the CISG). I believe that the CISG-drafters' choice for this method severely influenced the drafters of the European soft law instruments. Furthermore, the CISG-drafters chose to deviate from the former ULIS-rule which calculated the price reduction at the moment of the conclusion of the contract. While drafting the CISG, the Norwegian delegation proposed to change the moment of calculation to 'the moment of delivery'.[111] One of the most important reasons therefore was that the same numbers could then be used for the calculation of price reduction and of damages, both are calculated (under the CISG) at the moment of delivery. The American representative (Mr. Honnold) approved this reasoning and added that this would simplify his task to explain this

109 M. Will, 'Article 50' in C.M. Bianca and M.J. Bonell (eds.), *Bianca-Bonell Commentary on the International Sales Law*, Milan, Giuffrè, 1987, (368) 370.

110 F.J.A. Van Der Velden, *Het Weense Koopverdrag 1980 en zijn rechtsmiddelen*, Deventer, Kluwer, 1988, 351.

111 UN Doc. A/CONF.97/C.1/L.167. See also Official Records, Summary records of meetings of the First Committee, 23rd meeting, 357–358 and www.cisg.law.pace.edu/cisg/firstcommittee/Meeting23.html. See also Report of the First Committee, UN. Doc. A/CONF.97/11, www.cisg.law.pace.edu/cisg/1stcommittee/summaries50.html.

remedy to the lawyers in his country.[112] This means that the choice for a calculation at the moment of delivery/performance indeed results in a price reduction that resembles more to damages, but does not coincide with it. In sum, a pure and simple price reduction remedy should be calculated at the moment of the conclusion of the contract and not at the moment of delivery/performance.

43. Another question is whether or not price reduction until zero can be accepted. With regard to Article 50 CISG, a part of doctrine and case law defends that if the delivered goods are worthless, the seller should, within the framework of price reduction, reimburse the entire price.[113] Mignot also raises this question with regard to the *ordonnance*, but does not give any answer.[114] However, we have to repeat that according to Article 1223 Ord., price reduction can only be applied in case of '*une exécution imparfaite*' (see also *supra*, no. 25). A price reduction up to zero has clearly not been envisaged in the *ordonnance*.

3.5. *Other characteristics*

44. Finally, we will address some other characteristics of the price reduction remedy as conceived in Article 1223 Ord.

3.5.1. Price reduction before and after the payment of the price

45. Article 1223 Ord. indicates that it does not matter whether the price has already been paid by the creditor. We can implicitly draw this conclusion from the second part of this Article because it specifies: '*s'il n'a pas encore payé*'. This means that if the creditor has not yet paid the price, he will have to deduce a proportional part of the price. Notwithstanding the fact that the project does not explicitly regulates it, I believe that in case the creditor has already paid the price, he will have the possibility to claim a part of the price he has paid back.[115] The latter was better regulated in Article 107 *projet* Terré,

[112] Www.cisg.law.pace.edu/cisg/firstcommittee/Meeting23.html.

[113] I. Bach, "Art. 50" in S. Kröll, L. Mistelis and P.P. Viscasillas (eds.), *CISG*, München, Beck, 2011, (748) 761; C. Liu, *Remedies in International Sales*, New York, Juris Net, 2007, 135–138; U. Magnus, "Art. 50 CISG" in M. Martinek (ed.), *von Staudingers Kommentar zum BGB, Wiener UN-Kaufrecht*, III, Berlin, Sellier - de Gruyter, 2004, (530) no. 23; M. Müller-Chen, "Art. 50 CISG" in I. Schwenzer (ed.), *Commentary on the CISG*, Oxford, OUP, 2010, (770) 777, no. 13; P. Schlechtriem and P. Butler, *UN Law on International Sales*, Berlin, Springer, 2009, no. 202. See also extensively: Austria Oberster Gerichtshof 23 May 2005, http://cisgw3.law.pace.edu/cases/050523a3.html. This jurisprudence has often been confirmed in different Member States of the convention.

[114] M. Mignot, "Commentaire article par article de l'*ordonnance* du 10 février 2016 portant réforme du droit des contrats, du régime général et de la preuve des obligations (IV)", *Petites Affiches* 2016, (5) Article 1223.

[115] Considers the new *ordonnance* unclear with regard to this point: O. Sabart, "Les sanctions de l'inexécution du contrat (suite): résolution/réduction du prix", *L'essentiel. Droit des contrats* 2016, (7) *in fine* (the *ordonnance* only regulates the situation in which the creditor has not yet paid the price). Considered the 2015 project unclear with regard to this point: M. Mekki, "Les remèdes à l'inexécution

which explicitly states that the creditor who has already paid the price can '*obtenir remboursement du surplus*' (*cf. supra*, no. 12).

3.5.2. Price reduction as a defence and as a claim of the creditor

46. Because we have concluded that the price reduction under Article 1223 pr. Ord. implies that it can be applied before and after the payment of the price, this also means that price reduction can be used as a defence and a claim by the creditor. If the creditor has already paid the full price, he will have to *claim* a proportional part of the price back. If the creditor has not yet paid the (full) price, he can use the price reduction *defence* to assert that he does not have to pay the full price.[116]

3.5.3. Combination with damages

47. Finally, we have already noticed that price reduction can be combined with damages in case of an unexcused non-performance (Article 1217 *in fine* Ord. and *supra*, no. 32).[117] Of course, this combination is only possible in as far that damages are not available for the part that has already been covered by the price reduction. The combination with damages is evidently ruled out in case we would accept a price reduction in case of an excused non-performance (*force majeure*) because damages are not available in case of *force majeure* (Article 1231–1 Ord.).[118]

3.5.4. No restitution

48. An important question is whether the price reduction under Article 1223 Ord. can imply restitution[119] by the creditor. Imagine for example that a buyer orders 80 bottles of vintage port wine for his shop and he receives 60 conforming bottles and 20 bottles which are fundamentally affected because the corks have leaked. Can the buyer accept the 60 conforming bottles and apply a price reduction for the 20 affected bottled

dans le projet d'*ordonnance* portant réforme du droit des obligations", *Gazette du Palais* 2015, issue 120, (37) no. 13.

116 *Cf.* also (with regard to the 2015 project): P. Lemay, "L'inexécution du contrat: la réduction du prix (Projet, art. 1223)" in M. Latina and G. Chantepie (eds.), *Projet de réforme du droit des contrats, du régime général et de la preuve des obligations. Analyses et propositions*, Paris, Dalloz, 2015, (78) 79 (urges the legislator to explicitly mention this possibility in Article 1223 pr. Ord., such as in the Terré project in Article 107, al 2). Compare: E. Savaux, "Article 1223: la réduction du prix", *Revue des contrats* 2015, (786) no. 4 (seems to consider that the price reduction remedy under the 2015 project might not be invoked in case the creditor has already paid the price).

117 See with regard to the 2015 project: Y.-M. Laithier, "Les règles relatives à l'inexécution des obligations contractuelles", *La Semaine Juridique Edition Générale* 2015, (47) 53.

118 Article 1231–1 Ord.: '*Le débiteur est condamné, s'il y a lieu, au paiement de dommages et intérêts soit à raison de l'inexécution de l'obligation, soit à raison du retard dans l'exécution, s'il ne justifie pas que l'exécution a été empêchée par la force majeure*' (emphasis added).

119 Note that 'restitution' under French contract law is an effect or a consequence of the remedies that are applied (such as termination of the contract).

and send them back? In other words, can the creditor make restitution of the last 20 bottles?

49. Article 1223 Ord. is quite clear. It states: '*Le créancier peut, après mise en demeure, accepter une exécution imparfaite du contrat et solliciter une réduction proportionnelle du prix*'.[120] Applying a price reduction means that the totality of the imperfect performance is accepted by the creditor. This means that this Article does not imply any restitution by the creditor. The goods/services are accepted but under the condition that the creditor can proportionally reduce the price. The situation as described above (of the 80 bottles of old port wine) will not be covered by Article 1223 Ord. because it implies a (partial) restitution by the creditor. In some systems this situation would be covered by the additional recognition of a material partial termination, which would imply (partial) restitution(s). Therefore, it is important to check whether the *ordonnance* also introduces a material partial termination remedy. If it does not recognise such a remedy, this would mean that the situation described above (of the 80 bottles of old port wine) will not be covered at all. In that case, I would suggest to the drafters of the project to open up Article 1223 Ord. for (partial) restitution, to be able to cover the situation described above.

3.6. *Material partial termination*

50. The *projet d'ordonnance* does not prescribe a wide material partial termination which can cover the situation as described above.[121] It recognises a kind of temporal partial termination by means of a termination with *ex nunc* effect. The judge has a wide margin of appreciation to determine the starting point of the *ex nunc* termination. Article 1229 Ord. states:

> Article 1229: '*La résolution prend effet, selon les cas, soit dans les conditions prévues par la clause résolutoire, soit à la date de la réception par le débiteur de la notification faite par le créancier, soit à la date fixée par le juge ou, à défaut, au jour de l'assignation en justice.*
>
> *Lorsque les prestations échangées ne pouvaient trouver leur utilité que par l'exécution complète du contrat résolu, les parties doivent restituer l'intégralité de ce qu'elles se sont procuré l'une à l'autre. Lorsque les prestations échangées ont trouvé leur utilité au fur et à mesure de l'exécution réciproque du contrat, il n'y a pas lieu à restitution pour la période antérieure à la dernière prestation n'ayant pas reçu sa contrepartie; dans ce cas, la résolution est qualifiée de résiliation.*'

This means that the remedy of partial termination will not absorb the price reduction, since material partial termination is not recognised.

120 Emphasis added.

121 Article 1230 Ord. merely states that termination will not affect clauses such as e.g. confidentiality and non-competition clauses.

4. Conclusion

51. I have to conclude that many important aspects of the price reduction remedy have not been fledged out by the drafters of the *ordonnance* (for example the applicability in case of *force majeure*, the notification duty in case the creditor has already paid the price, the concept of 'price', the way how price reduction fits into the hierarchy of remedies, its extrajudicial application, ...). Moreover, the lack of preparatory works makes it even more difficult to grasp all the subtle aspects of the price reduction remedy. The hasty introduction of the price reduction remedy without clarity about its relation with other remedies, its condition of application, and the role of the judge and the parties seems a lost opportunity. A balanced-out, well-described price reduction remedy could indeed be the suitable and proportionate answer in case of a partial non-performance.

Brecht Verkempinck

THE MEASURE OF DAMAGES IN THE FRENCH CONTRACT LAW REFORM – LESSONS FROM FAR MORE INSPIRING SYSTEMS

1. Belgian Civil Code

1.1. Need for innovation

1. Necessity of modification of rules on contractual damages – The Belgian Civil Code can still be used by creative case law, but is somewhat out of date. This seems to be particularly the case as regards the measure of damages for breach of contract. In a recent comparative study on contractual remedies, however, an Australian professor praised French contract law as it stood in 1804: "*Whereas French contract law was extremely well developed by 1804 when the Code civil was first published, English contract law in contrast was still astonishingly undeveloped.*"[1] Would this again be valid as of 1 October 2016, with the entry into force of the new French contract law[2] as regards the rules on the quantification of damages for breach of contract? Should the Belgian legislator draw inspiration from the new French legal framework on damages for breach of contract?

2. Current provisions on the measure of damages for breach of contract (Articles 1149–1153 CC) – In Belgium the ordinary measure of damages for breach of contract is still governed by the Articles 1149–1153 of the *Code civil*. Article 1149 CC only provides a vague guideline for the basic measure of compensation: the aggrieved party is entitled to compensation for the loss suffered, including loss of profit. In addition, the Civil Code recognises some limits on that liability. However, those limits of unforeseeability (Article 1150 CC) and indirectness (Article 1151 CC) of harm caused by a breach of contract have been hollowed out in practice. Do these articles still serve any purpose? In this context the subsequent question arises as to why the duty to mitigate and the recoverability of non-pecuniary loss and lost chances are not yet enshrined in

1 T.D. Musgrave, "Comparative Contractual Remedies", *University of Western Australia Law Review* 2009 (www.austlii.edu.au), (300) 355.

2 *Ordonnance* n° 2016–131 du 10 février 2016 portant réforme du droit des contrats, du régime général et de la preuve des obligations, *JORF* n° 0035 du 11 février 2016.

this Civil Code. Could the new French legal framework be suitable as a model for new Belgian provisions on the measure of damages for breach of contract? With Belgium swiftly moving closer to a new Belgian Civil Code, the French reform should be considered in detail from the perspective of contractual damages.

1.2. New French legal framework as a godsend?

3. Does the new French reform have the potential to provoke tectonic legislative shifts as regards the measure of contractual damages? – The current unclear legislative framework can jeopardise legal certainty. For that reason, it seems astonishing that it took more than two centuries to undertake any modifications. Propelled by recent French legislative initiatives, the Belgian legislator finally awoke in 2015.[3] The run-up to a reform of the Belgian Civil Code begs the question as to the convincing nature of the new French legal framework. What message is to be delivered to the drafting committee as regards that quantification of contractual damages? Is that reform so superbly engineered that this new framework has grown into such a promising model that it could contribute to facing the challenge of drafting new Belgian provisions in this field? This question of whether the French reform is a godsend is without any doubt on the minds of a myriad of Belgian legal writers. The answer to that question will prove to be, however, rather uncomplicated. The French reform is speeding up the Belgian timetable for reforms, but has not provided any substantial relief. This article aims to flesh out the French reform and explores several ways of avoiding its deficiencies.

2. French Contract Law Reform

2.1. A lost chance

4. French contract law reform 2016: a lost chance – The upcoming examination by Belgian legal scholars of the new French legal framework on contract law are the beginning of an arduous journey towards new Belgian provisions on the measure of contractual damages. The key element for setting out on this odyssey seems to be whether the Belgian legislator could just copy what its French counterpart has just hammered out. The answer to this question should be "no". The new French provisions will most probably leave many disenchanted. Such pithy sayings as "*quand il pleut à Paris, il bruine à Bruxelles*"[4] should cause some alarm bells to ring, at least in relation to the measure of contractual damages. The truth is the new French legal framework does not result in progress comparative to that of the Napoleonic Code. As a whole, it might be welcomed by some of the academic world, but will undoubtedly be struck down by damages specialists. From the viewpoint of contractual damages, the general feeling is therefore

3 K. Geens, "Woord vooraf" in *Het Justitieplan. Een efficiëntere justitie voor meer rechtvaardigheid*, available on: justitie.belgium.be/nl/binaries/Plan%20justitie_18maart_NL_tcm265-264636.pdf.

4 E.g. rightly mentioned in E. Dirix and P. Wéry, "Pour une modernisation du Code civil", *JT* 2015, (625) 625, No 2, referring to the incentive given to the Belgian legislator to adopt a new Civil Code.

one of a lost chance. One could strongly advise against reproduction of the new provisions.

5. Overview of objections – The new French legal framework fails to ease the strenuous trip to be undertaken by the Belgian legislator. Its deficiencies seem quite obvious. Its fairly uninteresting-looking nature mainly results from the fact that the French legislator, as regards contract damages, did not even codify the established compensation principles as meanwhile developed by legal scholars and evolved in case law. He merely repeated existing provisions without going beyond the rules laid down in 1804 by Napoléon's draftsmen. The major drawback is hence that it does not even fulfil its basic task: fixing the law as it stands. That reform does not give formal expression to solutions which have been worked out in the case law to complete the elliptical Napoleonic Code nor does it expunge legal provisions which appeared outdated, such as Article 1151 CC (*infra* §7).

2.2. *Lack of innovation*

6. New French Civil Code identical to Napoleonic Code as regards the basic measure of contractual damages (Article 1149 CC) – That the French reform should not be welcomed has first of all to do with the poorly conceived articles on the basic measure of damages. An unmistakable warning sign for the pessimism sparked by the new provisions is the wording of the new Article 1231–2 CC. This Article only underscores the recoverability of loss suffered[5], including lost profits[6]: "*Les dommages et intérêts dus au créancier sont, en général, de la perte qu'il a faite et du gain dont il a été privé, sauf les exceptions et modifications ci-après.*" This provision could be translated into English as follows: "*Damages due to the creditor are, as a rule, for the loss which he has suffered and the profit which he has been deprived of, subject to the exceptions and modifications below.*" That Article disregards innovative theories on the prominence of expectation damages by merely reproducing Article 1149 CC. Just like the current Article 1149 CC, Article 1231–2 CC does not explicitly mention the generally accepted principle of full compensation.[7] It only mentions that compensation principle implicitly.[8] So far, there is no alteration of the status quo.

5 The French notion "*perte subie*" is generally translated into English as *loss sustained, loss incurred* or *loss suffered, erlittenen Schaden* in German, *danno emergente* or *perdita subita* in Italian, *pérdida sufrida* in Spanish, and *prejuízo causado* in Portuguese.

6 The French notion "*gain manqué*" is generally translated into English as *lost gain, gain deprived* or *loss of profits, entgangener Gewinn* in German, *lucro cessante* or *mancato guadagno* in Italian, and *lucro cesante* in Spanish.

7 Cour de cassation belge, "Le droit belge" in P. Pierre and F. Leduc (eds.), *La réparation intégrale en Europe. Études comparatives des droits nationaux*, Brussels, Larcier, 2012, (225) 225–226 ("*S'il est généralement considéré comme gisant dans les articles 1149 (responsabilité contractuelle) et 1382 (responsabilité quasi délictuelle) du Code civil, ces dispositions ne comportent toutefois aucune référence explicite au caractère intégral (ou complet) de la réparation.*"); I. Durant, "La réparation dite intégrale du dommage. Rapport belge" in B. Dubuisson and P. Jourdain (eds.), *Le dommage et sa réparation dans la responsabilité contractuelle et extracontractuelle*, Brussels, Bruylant, 2015, (441) 442.

8 Italy: V. Roppo, *Trattato del contratto. V. Rimedi. 2*, Milan, Giuffrè, 2006, 894–895 ("*L'art. 1223 [...] enunciando la necessità di far fronte sia alla "perdita subita", sia al "mancato guadagno", offre la base*

7. New French Civil Code identical to Napoleonic Code as regards the limitations on the principle of full compensation (Articles 1150–1151 CC) – Admittedly, the evidence of poorly crafted provisions piles up when looking further on in the new legal framework. The current Articles providing for limitations on the principle of full compensation have been reproduced. The foreseeability limitation is now enshrined in Article 1231-3 CC. This Article is almost identical to Article 1150 CC: "*A debtor is liable only for damages which were foreseen or could have been foreseen at the time of the conclusion of the contract, unless the breach of contract is caused by intentional or gross fault.*"[9] The directness limit on contractual damages is laid down in the new Article 1231-4 CC. This provision is also almost an identical reproduction of the current Article 1151 CC: "*Even in the case where the non-performance of the contract is due to a intentional or gross fault, damages include only what is an immediate and direct consequence of the non-performance.*"[10]

2.3. *Non-inclusion of several basic compensation principles*

8. Non-inclusion of dominant target position of contract damages: expectation interest – Another notable reason why the French contract law reform is unlikely to seduce Belgian legal scholars is the fact that it does not even look at the bigger picture of the award of contractual damages. In fact, it conceals the main target position of contract damages. A new Civil Code should unquestionably put a strong emphasis on the requirement that damages for breach of contractual obligations – even in the case of termination of the contract – protect the so-called expectation interest. According to this originally German measure criterion, damages are to be ascertained by comparing the position of the victim after the breach with the hypothetical situation in which he would have been had the contract been duly performed. When facing the challenge of drafting of a provision in this regard, the legislator could, however, draw inspiration from Article III.-3:702 DCFR, which reads: "*The general measure of damages for loss caused by non-performance of an obligation is such sum as will put the creditor as nearly as possible into the position in which the creditor would have been if the obligation had been duly performed*" (*infra* §32).

9. Non-inclusion of subsidiary target position of reliance interest – Aside from the non-inclusion of the expectation interest as the main target position for

testuale a cui ricollegare il principio del risarcimento integrale."); C. Salvi, *La responsabilità civile*, Milan, Giuffrè, 2005, 250 ("*È dal principio della riparazione integrale come compensazione economica che discende la regola (espressamente posta dall'art. 1223) per la quale il lucro cessante è componente del danno risarcibile alla stessa stregua del danno emergente.*").

9 New Article 1231-3 CC states in French: "*Le débiteur n'est tenu que des dommages et intérêts qui ont été prévus ou qui pouvaient être prévus lors de la conclusion du contrat, sauf lorsque l'inexécution est due à une faute lourde ou dolosive.*"

10 New Article 1231-4 CC states in French: "*Dans le cas même où l'inexécution du contrat résulte d'une faute lourde ou dolosive, les dommages et intérêts ne comprennent que ce qui est une suite immédiate et directe de l'inexécution.*"

contractual damages, the newest French reform should not be endorsed because it also fails to emphasise that, when deemed appropriate, it is open to the aggrieved party to seek compensation for his reliance interest. A brief look at our American and German counterparts could already contribute to the drafting of a relevant provision. In the United States, §349 Second Restatement of Contracts provides for the following: "*the injured party may, if he chooses, ignore the element of profit and recover as damages his expenditures in reliance.*" In Germany §284 BGB also lays down this possibility: "*In place of damages in lieu of performance, the obligee may demand reimbursement of the expenses which he has made and in all fairness was entitled to make in reliance on receiving performance*" (*infra* §43).[11]

10. Non-inclusion of the recoverability of non-pecuniary loss and lost chances – As to the recoverable types of loss, the French reform could also be vehemently opposed in that it merely reproduces (in Article 1231-2) Article 1149 of the Napoleonic Code. This article will most likely mortify damages specialists by not providing for the recoverability of non-pecuniary loss resulting from a breach of contract. The DCFR looks more developed in this respect, since Article III.-3:701 (3) thereof defines loss in such a broad sense that it encompasses non-pecuniary loss: "*'Loss' includes economic and non-economic loss.*" Article 1607 Civil Code of Québec could serve as an alternative drafting strategy, as it explicitly provides for the recoverability of non-pecuniary loss: "*The creditor is entitled to damages for bodily, moral or material injury which is an immediate and direct consequence of the debtor's default.*" In sharp contrast with the Catala proposal, the French reform neither mentions the recoverability of lost chances. The Catala proposal was more convincing, since Article 1346 stated: "*Loss of a chance constitutes a reparable loss distinct from the advantage which would have inured to the claimant's benefit if the chance had materialised.*"[12]

11. Non-inclusion of the possibility of equitable assessment – The newest French provisions seem to amass one grievance after another. In the context of lost profits, future loss, non-pecuniary loss and lost chances, the Belgian legislator should also explicitly allow equitable assessment of contract damages. Other legal systems seem more persuasive in this regard. In Louisiana, Article 1999 of the Civil Code states: "*When damages are insusceptible of precise measurement, much discretion shall be left to the court for the reasonable assessment of these damages.*" In Italy, Article 1226 CCI also speaks volumes: "*Se il danno non può essere provato nel suo preciso ammontare, è liquidato dal giudice con valutazione equitativa.*" The latter provision could be translated as follows: "*If the precise amount of loss cannot be proved, the judge assesses this loss equitably.*"

11 §284 BGB states in German: "*Anstelle des Schadensersatzes statt der Leistung kann der Gläubiger Ersatz der Aufwendungen verlangen, die er im Vertrauen auf den Erhalt der Leistung gemacht hat und billigerweise machen durfte, es sei denn, deren Zweck wäre auch ohne die Pflichtverletzung des Schuldners nicht erreicht worden.*" Translation: www.gesetze-im-internet.de/englisch_bgb/german_civil_code.pdf.

12 Article 1346 PC stated in the French original version: "*La perte d'une chance constitue un préjudice réparable distinct de l'avantage qu'aurait procuré cette chance si elle s'était réalisée.*"

12. Non-inclusion of the duty to mitigate – There are more major reasons why the Belgian legislator should not embrace the new French legal framework: the well-known and widely accepted duty to mitigate has been overlooked. In 2005, the Catala reform proposal seemed to bring the French law on contract damages into the 21st century by mentioning this *Obliegenheit* and its consequences in the case of non-compliance: "*Where the victim had the possibility of taking reliable, reasonable and proportionate measures to reduce the extent of his loss or to avoid its getting worse, the court shall take account of his failure to do so by reducing his compensation*" (Article 1373 APC).[13] This provision was seamlessly aligned with the well-known soft law instruments. A clear example is the DCFR, where the first paragraph of Article III.3:705 states: "*The debtor is not liable for loss suffered by the creditor to the extent that the creditor could have reduced the loss by taking reasonable steps.*" Also for that reason, the new French reform implies a relapse by keeping silent about this duty. This seems all the more striking as that mitigation limit was already present in the works of Dumoulin (*Tractatus de eo quod interest,* 1546, nr. 61), Domat (*Les lois civiles dans leur ordre naturel,* 1689, 254) and Pothier (*Traité des Obligations,* 1761, nr. 167). Why did the French drafting committee not join the ranks of the civil codes admitting that *incombance*?

3. Drafting prerequisites

3.1. Necessity

13. Necessity of pre-establishment of drafting prerequisites – The above-mentioned non-inclusion examples should suffice to persuade the future Belgian drafting committee that following the new French reform will inevitably imply lagging behind other legal systems. Before suggesting other provisions on the measure of damages for breach of contract, it seems useful to take a look at some basic drafting rules. In order for new legislation to be correctly understood, it is vital that it is well drafted. Legislation should be drawn up in a consistent and understandable way in order to ensure that citizens can identify their rights and obligations.[14]

14. Source of inspiration: quality requirements and checks at Union level – For good law-making at national level, inspiration could be drawn from various French and English textbooks[15] or from the elaborate principles of legal technique drawn up by

13 Article 1373 PC stated in French: "*Lorsque la victime avait la possibilité, par des moyens sûrs, raisonnables et proportionnés, de réduire l'étendue de son préjudice ou d'en éviter l'aggravation, il sera tenu compte de son abstention par une réduction de son indemnisation, sauf lorsque les mesures seraient de nature à porter atteinte à son intégrité physique.*"

14 Point 4 of Council Resolution of 8 June 1993 on the quality of drafting of Community legislation (OJ C 166, 17.6.1993, p. 1) states: "*the rights and obligations of those to whom the act is to apply should be clearly defined*".

15 C. Bergeal, *Rédiger un texte normatif: manuel de légistique,* Paris, Le point sur, 2012, 433 p.; P. Butt, *Modern Legal Drafting. A Guide to Using Clearer Language,* Cambridge, Cambridge University Press,

the Belgian Council of State.[16] Most inspiring seem to be the experiences at Union level. The European Council acknowledged the need for clearer and simpler legislation at its Edinburgh meeting in 1992, which led to the adoption of a Resolution on the quality of drafting of Community legislation.[17] This Resolution clearly stated: "the wording of the act should be clear, simple, concise and unambiguous". Five years later, the Amsterdam Intergovernmental Conference adopted Declaration No 39 on the quality of the drafting of Community legislation, annexed to the Final Act of the Amsterdam Treaty.[18] This Declaration called on the European Parliament, the Council and the Commission to "establish by common accord guidelines for improving the quality of the drafting of Community legislation". To comply with this declaration, those institutions adopted an Interinstitutional Agreement on common guidelines for the quality of drafting of Community legislation.[19] Following this agreement, they adopted a Joint Practical Guide for persons involved in the drafting of European Union legislation.[20]

3.2. *Clear, simple and precise rules*

15. Clear, simple and precise rules – When it comes to drafting legislation, the legislator should first of all bear in mind that the wording must be clear, simple and precise.[21] The suggested provision must be *clear*, in the sense that it must be easy to understand and leave no room for ambiguity. No less essential is the requirement of *simpleness*. Unnecessary elements should be avoided. This does not mean that the provision should not be *precise*. There should be no uncertainty in the mind of the reader. This is in line with the principle of legal certainty, in that it should be possible to foresee how the law will be applied. At Union level, the Court of Justice specifies regularly that this principle of legal certainty requires in particular that rules involving negative consequences for individuals should be

2013, 379 p.; H. Xanthaki, *Thornton's Legislative Drafting*, Haywards Heath, Bloomsbury Professional, 2013, 590 p.

16 The legislative drafting manual of the Belgian Council of State is available at: www.raadvst-consetat.be/?page=technique_legislative&lang=fr. For French law: Guide de légistique at: www.legifrance.gouv.fr/Droit-francais/Guide-de-legistique. For English law: Drafting guidance at: www.gov.uk/government/collections/the-office-of-the-parliamentary-counsel-guidance.

17 Council Resolution of 8 June 1993 on the quality of drafting of Community legislation (OJ C 166, 17.6.1993, p. 1).

18 Treaty of Amsterdam amending the Treaty on European Union, the Treaties establishing the European Communities and certain related acts – Declarations adopted by the Conference – Declaration on the quality of the drafting of Community legislation (OJ C 340, 10.11.1997, p. 139).

19 Interinstitutional Agreement of 22 December 1998 on common guidelines for the quality of drafting of Community legislation (OJ C 073, 17.3.1999, p. 1).

20 Necessity: point a of the Interinstitutional Agreement of 22 December 1998 on common guidelines for the quality of drafting of Community legislation (OJ C 073, 17.3.1999, p. 1): "*In particular, the institutions: (a) shall instruct their legal services to draw up, within one year after the publication of these guidelines, a joint practical guide for persons involved in the drafting of legislation.*" Version of 2013: http://eur-lex.europa.eu/content/pdf/techleg/joint-practical-guide-2013-en.pdf.

21 Point 1 of the Interinstitutional Agreement of 22 December 1998 on common guidelines for the quality of drafting of Community legislation (OJ C 073, 17.3.1999, p. 1): "*Community legislative acts shall be drafted clearly, simply and precisely.*"

clear and precise and their application predictable for those subject to them.[22] The aim is to render acts more comprehensible and to avoid disputes resulting from poor drafting. This goal can for instance sometimes be reached by avoiding the passive voice and thus clearly identifying who is under the specific obligation[23] (e.g. Article 1150–1 CC; *infra* §53), or by correctly applying the punctuation rules (including the rules on the use of commas[24]).

16. Rule of a thumb: one idea per sentence – A chief characteristic of a good legislative style seems to be the succinct expression of the key ideas of a text. A sentence should express only one idea. Texts must therefore be broken down into easily comprehensible subdivisions. An excessively compact block of text is hard for the mind to take in. In general, it seems easier to draft complicated sentences than to make the effort of summarising content which results in clear wording. However, such attempts at simplification are imperative in order to create a provision which can be easily understood.

17. Illustration of by-passing complicated provisions – A hypothetical but unfortunately not unrealistic example of an avoidable provision which is too complicated is the following provision on the duty to mitigate and its consequences: "*The victim of a breach of contract has a duty to mitigate, which implies that the non-performing party is not liable for loss suffered by the aggrieved party to the extent that this victim could have mitigated this loss by taking reasonable measures, whereby the victim of a breach of contract is, in accordance with Article 1149–1 (1), entitled to full compensation for the expenses he incurred in reasonably attempting to mitigate his loss, principle which shall also apply when those measures have not effectively led to prevention or mitigation of losses.*" A clearer way of drafting this Article is breaking it up into two paragraphs. A first paragraph can specify the principle of non-recoverability of avoidable loss: "*The non-performing party is not liable for loss suffered by the victim of a breach of contract to the extent that this victim could have mitigated this loss by taking reasonable measures.*" A second paragraph can clarify the requirement of compensation for expenses incurred in reasonable mitigation efforts: "*The victim of a breach of contract is, in accordance with Article 1149–1 (1), entitled to full compensation for the expenses he incurred in reasonably attempting to mitigate his loss*" (*infra* §64). The avoidable use of the synonyms "victim of a breach of contract" and "aggrieved party" brings us to the next point: the requirement of legal and linguistic consistency of legal acts.

3.3. *Legal-linguistic consistency*

18. Legal and linguistic consistency: "1-term-1-concept rule" – When drafting legal provisions, the legislator should pay particular attention to this legal and linguistic

[22] Case 325/85 *Ireland* v *Commission* [1987] ECR 5041, Case C-143/93 *Van Es Douane Agenten* [1996] ECR I-431, paragraph 27; and Case C-63/93 *Duff and Others* [1996] ECR I-569, paragraph 20.

[23] As a rule, the passive voice should only be used when the emphasis is on the action rather than on the person or when the subject cannot be easily identified.

[24] For Belgium: J. Waelkens, "Komma's in juridische teksten", *TBBR* 2015, 235–244.

consistency. The same terms are to be used to express identical concepts.[25] The legislator should refrain from using synonyms and different expressions to convey the same idea. For example, the legislator should avoid expressing "non-pecuniary loss" by also using synonyms such as "immaterial loss" or "non-economic loss". Aside from that, identical terms must not be used to express different concepts. "Damages" should be used to indicate the compensation concerned ("*dommages-intérêts*") and not as a plural of "damage" in the sense of loss or harm ("*dommages*" or "*préjudices*").

19. Use of words in their ordinary sense – Furthermore, in legislative texts words should be used in their ordinary sense.[26] One illustration is the term "loss", which in its ordinary sense also covers non-pecuniary loss.[27] If the meaning remains controversial, however, defining the term could pay off.[28] A notable example is the definition of loss in the DCFR. Article 3:701 (3) DCFR provides for the recoverability of non-pecuniary loss by defining the term "loss" in a wide sense, as including both economic and non-economic loss: "*'Loss' includes economic and non-economic loss.*"

3.4. *References*

20. Precise internal references – In addition to the requirements of clear, simple, precise and legally and linguistically consistent rules, there is a requirement that internal references should be used to simplify the text. When the legislator is not repeating the

25 Point 3 of Council Resolution of 8 June 1993 on the quality of drafting of Community legislation (OJ C 166, 17.6.1993, p. 1) states: "*the various provisions of the acts should be consistent with each other; the same term should be used throughout to express a given concept*"; point 6 of the Interinstitutional Agreement of 22 December 1998 on common guidelines for the quality of drafting of Community legislation (OJ C 073, 17.3.1999, p. 1) states: "*Identical concepts shall be expressed in the same terms, as far as possible without departing from their meaning in ordinary, legal or technical language.*"

26 Point 6 of the Interinstitutional Agreement of 22 December 1998 on common guidelines for the quality of drafting of Community legislation (OJ C 073, 17.3.1999, p. 1) states: "*Identical concepts shall be expressed in the same terms, as far as possible without departing from their meaning in ordinary, legal or technical language.*" Belgium: Cass. 15 December 1983, *Arr.Cass.* 1983–84, 449 (tax law: "Overwegende dat het Hof, wanneer de wet een term niet omschrijft, moet nagaan of de feitenrechter die term in zijn gebruikelijke betekenis heeft gehanteerd, die de wet, bij ontstentenis van een andere wilsuitdrukking, moet geacht worden bedoeld te hebben."); Cass. 4 December 1985, *Arr.Cass.* 1985–86, 493 ("Overwegende dat het woord 'vis' in de gebruikelijke en wetenschappelijke betekenis [...]"); Cass. 15 April 1992, *Arr.Cass.* 1991–92, 788 ("Overwegende dat de betekenis van de woorden 'uitoefening van de veeartsenijkunde' in de wet niet verschilt van de betekenis ervan in het gewone taalgebruik [...]"); C. Parmentier, "Les dits et les non-dits d'un arrêt de cassation" (annotation on Cass. 25 September 2014), *JLMB* 2015, (64) 65 (tax law: "*L'on sait, en effet, que lorsque la loi, notamment la loi fiscale, utilise un terme sans en donner de définition, ce terme doit être entendu dans son sens usuel.*").

27 Cass. 17 March 1881, *Pas.* 1881, I, 163 (non-pecuniary loss for the death of a family member because of a train accident in 1877: "*[...] le mot dommage dont se sert le législateur dans les articles 1382 et suivants du code civil est un terme général qui s'applique au dommage moral comme au dommage matériel [...]*").

28 Point 14 of the Interinstitutional Agreement of 22 December 1998 on common guidelines for the quality of drafting of Community legislation (OJ C 073, 17.3.1999, p. 1) stipulates in this regard: "*Where the terms used in the act are not unambiguous, they should be defined together in a single article at the beginning of the act. The definitions shall not contain autonomous normative provisions.*"

content of a provision by simply referring to it, that reference should be sufficiently precise in order to enable the reader to consult the provision to which reference is made.[29] He should, however, avoid making a reference by merely citing another provision. For instance, if he wants to express that the principle of full compensation also applies to non-pecuniary loss, he should not reproduce the wording of the provision on that principle. Rather than "*The aggrieved party is entitled to full compensation of the non-pecuniary loss incurred as a result of the non-performance*" he should state "*Compensation for non-pecuniary loss falls within the scope of the principle of full compensation as set out in paragraph 1*" (*infra* §37).

21. No unnecessary internal references – Ideally, the reader should be able to understand a provision without consulting too many other provisions. In addition, a reference should be worded in such a way that the key element of the provision to which reference is made can be understood without consulting that provision. Rather than "*Paragraph 1 applies to non-pecuniary loss*", use "*The principle of full compensation as set out in paragraph 1 applies to non-pecuniary loss*" (*infra* §37).[30] With these principles in mind, we can attempt to draft other provisions on contractual damages.

4. Belgium 2020: new provisions on contractual damages

4.1. Basic structure of legal framework

22. Preliminary remark: possibility of general provisions common to contractual and non-contractual liability, supplemented by specific provisions on contractual liability – Now that the new French reform has been diagnosed with fragility, the Belgian legislator should be supported in his attempts to draft a proposal from scratch. When coping with this ordeal, he should first decide on the respective places to be assigned to provisions on contractual and non-contractual liability. In this regard, it is essential to note that there is a tendency to advocate an advanced unification of the rules on contractual and non-contractual liability.[31] As early as in 1892,

[29] Point 2 of Council Resolution of 8 June 1993 on the quality of drafting of Community legislation (OJ C 166, 17.6.1993, p. 1) states: "*imprecise references to other texts should be avoided as should too many cross-references which make the text difficult to understand*".

[30] See also Rule 16.7 of the Joint Practical Guide of the European Parliament, the Council and the Commission: http://eur-lex.europa.eu/content/pdf/techleg/joint-practical-guide-2013-en.pdf.

[31] L. Cornelis, *Algemene theorie van de verbintenis,* Antwerp, Intersentia, 2000, 575–576; L. Cornelis, "Verkeerd verbonden" in V. Sagaert and D. Lambrecht (eds.), *Actuele ontwikkelingen inzake verbintenissenrecht,* Antwerp, Intersentia, 2009, (259) 272 (title: "Er was eens… een contractueel aansprakelijkheidsrecht"; "Op het vlak van het (contractuele) schade- en causaliteitsbegrip is evenwel op de merkwaardige jurisprudentiële ontwikkeling *contra legem* te wijzen waardoor aan die begrippen een inhoud is toebedeeld of opgedrongen, die van het buitencontractuele schade- en causaliteitsbegrip is overgenomen.") and 300 ("Uit dat alles blijkt dat het contractueel aansprakelijkheidsrecht zo goed als volledig door het buitencontractueel aansprakelijkheidsrecht werd gekoloniseerd."); L. Cornelis, "Over samenloop, schade en overbodig causaal verband: roemloos aansprakelijkheidsrecht (partim)", *TBH* 2013, (989) 993 ("[d]e weinige verschillen die beide aansprakelijkheidsregimes nog onderscheiden

the French author Grandmoulin called for this fusion of both regimes.[32] In the Netherlands, Ribbius launched a similar proposal in 1906.[33] Five years later this reasoning resulted in that merger in Switzerland. Since then, the Swiss *Code des obligations*, as regards contractual liability, merely contains a cross-reference to the rules governing non-contractual liability. Article 99 (3) CO reads: "*Les règles relatives à la responsabilité dérivant d'actes illicites s'appliquent par analogie aux effets de la faute contractuelle*" ("*The provisions governing liability in tort apply mutatis mutandis to a breach of contract*").

23. Approach adopted in the French reform proposals – Is it advisable to maintain separate rules governing the measure of contractual damages or should the legislator bring all those provisions under a single heading governing "liability" in general? After having drafted rules covering the whole area, the Catala working group came to the conclusion that the rules common to the two branches of liability prevailed over all. Subsequently, the Catala working group opted for the latter strategy by proposing a chapter with introductory provisions as to govern the relationship between the two branches of liability (Articles 1340–1342), followed by two chapters relating to the conditions (Chapter II) and the effects (Chapter III) of liability. As regards the effects of liability, §2 of Chapter III (Articles 1370–1377) dealt with the assessment of damages in general, without special provisions on damages for breach of contract. The only exception was the foreseeability limit, characteristic for contractual liability, which was enshrined in Article 1366. Both the Terré proposal (2009) and the French proposal of 2015 did not follow this line of thoughts and remained faithful to their Napoleonic heritage. As a consequence, the new French law of obligations also clearly delimitates both liability regimes by providing for a specific part on the measure of damages for breach of contract ("*La réparation du préjudice résultant de l'inexécution du contrat*": Article 1231–1231-7).[34] The fact that damages for breach of contract aim at placing the victim of a breach in the position of hypothetical due performance seems to justify this reasoning.[35]

4.2. Introductory provision on the location of contractual damages

24. Introductory provision relating to the location of damages within the system of remedies for breach of contract – It seems logical to begin by locating

[kunnen] niet meer [...] verhinderen dat zij zo goed als versmolten zijn geraakt [...]"). More background: S. Stijns and P. Wéry (eds.), *De raakvlakken tussen de contractuele en de buitencontractuele aansprakelijkheid*, Bruges, die Keure, 2010, 290 p.

32 J. Grandmoulin, *De l'unité de la responsabilité ou nature délictuelle de la responsabilité pour violation des obligations contractuelles*, Rennes, Alphonse Le Roy, 1892, 176 p.

33 H.R. Ribbius, *De omvang van de te vergoeden schade bij niet-nakoming van verbintenissen en bij onrechtmatige daad*, doctoral thesis, Leiden, 1906, 268 p.

34 Against this unification: M. Fabre-Magnan, "Réforme du droit des contrats: 'un très bon projet'", *JCP* 2008, N° 43, answer to the third question ("*Il est en outre artificiel de traiter ensemble le régime des deux responsabilités*").

35 Ph. Rémy, "Les dommages et intérêts" in F. Terré, *Pour une réforme du droit des contrats. Réflexions et propositions d'un groupe de travail sous la direction de François Terré*, Parijs, LGDJ, (281) 2009, (281) 281–282.

the remedy of damages for breach of contract within the broader framework of the available remedies for breach of contract. At present, Article 1147 CC merely provides for the availability of damages for breach of contract: "*A debtor shall be ordered to pay damages, if there is occasion, either by reason of the non-performance of the obligation, or by reason of delay in performing, whenever he does not prove that the non-performance comes from an external cause which may not be ascribed to him, although there is no bad faith on his part.*"[36] Being limited to that Article, the actual Civil Code fails to give an outline of all available contractual remedies. Such an overview would, however, enhance the accessibility of the relevant provisions. Only to this end can the French reform be a source of inspiration, since Article 1217 states: "*The victim of the breach of contract can: refuse to perform or withhold performance of its own obligation; seek specific performance, request price reduction, provoke the termination of the contract; seek compensation for the consequences of the non-performance.*"[37]

25. Coherence between remedies? – Ideally, the legislator should complement that Article on the remedies which are available to the victim of a breach of contract with a provision on the coherence between those remedies. At the same time, he could stress the dominance of specific performance, the possibility of choosing between termination and damages and the possibility of combining termination and damages for breach of contract.[38] For this purpose, Article III.-3:102 DCFR (cf. Article 8:102 PECL) can give some inspiration: "*Remedies which are not incompatible may be cumulated. In particular, a creditor is not deprived of the right to damages by resorting any other remedy.*"

4.3. *Basic measure of contractual damages*

4.3.1. Principle of full compensation

26. Principle of full compensation – After positioning the damages within the system of remedies for breach of contract, it seems appropriate to highlight the leading principle of the measure of such contractual damages: the entitlement of the aggrieved party to full compensation of the loss he has suffered because of the breach of contract. This seems all the more necessary given that this principle also applies to contractual liability and serves as an indication for the measure of damages.[39] The current Article 1149

36 Article 1147 CC reads in French: "*Le débiteur est condamné, s'il y a lieu, au paiement de dommages et intérêts, soit à raison de l'inexécution de l'obligation, soit à raison du retard dans l'exécution, toutes les fois qu'il ne justifie pas que l'inexécution provient d'une cause étrangère qui ne peut lui être imputée, encore qu'il n'y ait aucune mauvaise foi de sa part.*"

37 New Article 1217 PO states in French: "*La partie envers laquelle l'engagement n'a pas été exécuté, ou l'a été imparfaitement, peut: refuser d'exécuter ou suspendre l'exécution de sa propre obligation; poursuivre l'exécution forcée en nature de l'obligation; solliciter une réduction du prix; provoquer la résolution du contrat; demander réparation des conséquences de l'inexécution.*"

38 Overview: P. Wéry, "L'agencement des sanctions applicables à un manquement contract" in *Liber amicorum François Glansdorff et Pierre Legros*, Brussels, Bruylant, 2014, 441–460.

39 Italy: A. Pinori and E. Corradi, "Il principio della riparazione integrale dei danni" in G. Visintini (ed.), *Il risarcimento del danno contrattuale ed extracontrattuale*, Milan, Giuffrè, 1999, (41) 43 and 49 ("*[è]*

CC does not mention that generally accepted principle of full compensation.[40] Nonetheless, Belgian case law frequently refers to this requirement within this specific context.[41] In his speech of 7 February 1804 to the *Corps législatif*, Mouricault labelled this principle of full compensation of loss caused by a breach of contract already as an obvious rule: "*Ces dommages et intérêts, à adjuger au créancier, doivent naturellement l'indemniser de tout le tort qu'il éprouve par l'inexécution ou le retard.*"[42] This basic idea is deemed to be in line with the common sense of justice[43] and fairness.[44]

27. Sources of inspiration and wording of a new provision on the principle of full compensation (Article 1149-1 (1) CC) – The wording of a new Article on the desideratum of full compensation[45] can be based on the corresponding provisions of

una regola capace di caratterizzare la disciplina del risarcimento nel suo complesso e di trovare concreta applicazione nella prassi giurisprudenziale [...] tale principio [...] è suscettibile di guidare i giudici nella decisione e di constituire la direttiva fondamentale [...]"); G. Visintini, *Trattato della responsabilità contrattuale. Volume terzo. Il risarcimento del danno contrattuale. La responsabilità per ritardo e per fatto degli ausiliari*, Padua, Cedam, 2009, 58 ("*il carattere assorbente che il principio della riparazione integrale presenta negli ordinamenti di civil law, condiziona il modo in cui il danno viene calcolato*"). Portugal: N.M. Pinto Oliveira, *Princípios de direito dos contratos*, Coimbra, Kluwer, 2011, 686 ("*A teoria da diferença contribuiria [em primeiro lugar] para resolver um problema de fundamentação do dever de indemnizar [e em segundo lugar] para resolver um problema de extensão (de "medida") do dever de indemnizar.*"). Switzerland: H.-U. Brunner, *Die Anwendung deliktsrechtlicher Regeln auf die Vertragshaftung*, Freiburg, Universitätsverlag, 1991, 61 ("*Die Differenzhypothese umschreibt zwar den äusseren Rahmen der Schadensberechnung.*").

40 Cour de cassation belge, "Le droit belge" in P. Pierre and F. Leduc (eds.), *La réparation intégrale en Europe. Études comparatives des droits nationaux*, Brussels, Larcier, 2012, (225) 225–226 ("*S'il est généralement considéré comme gisant dans les articles 1149 (responsabilité contractuelle) et 1382 (responsabilité quasi délictuelle) du Code civil, ces dispositions ne comportent toutefois aucune référence explicite au caractère intégral (ou complet) de la réparation.*"); I. Durant, "La réparation dite intégrale du dommage. Rapport belge" in B. Dubuisson and P. Jourdain (eds.), *Le dommage et sa réparation dans la responsabilité contractuelle et extracontractuelle*, Brussels, Bruylant, 2015, (441) 442.

41 Recently: Antwerp 27 October 2014, *RABG* 2015, (776) 777 (concerning liability of a lawyer: "Degene door wiens contractuele wanprestatie aan een ander schade werd veroorzaakt, is verplicht deze schade integraal te vergoeden, door de benadeelde terug te plaatsen in de toestand waarin hij zou gebleven zijn indien de contractuele wanprestatie niet was gepleegd.").

42 Mouricault, "Prononcé au Corps législatif par le citoyen Mouricault [Séance du 17 Pluviose an XII)" in *Recueil des lois composant le code civil. Cinquième volume. Livre IIIe*, Paris, Rondonneau, 1804, books.google.be, 257.

43 B. Weyts, "Punitieve elementen in het buitencontractueel aansprakelijkheidsrecht" in J. Rozie, A. Van Oevelen and S. Rutten (eds.), *Toetsing van sancties door de rechter*, Antwerp, Intersentia, 2011, (173) 200–201.

44 C. Demolombe, *Cours de code Napoléon. XXIV. Traité des contrats ou des obligations conventionnelles en général*, Paris, Hachette, 1868, 583 ("*Ce que veut l'équité véritable et juridique, c'est que le créancier soit indemnisé de la perte qu'il éprouve comme du gain qu'il manque, et sur lequel il devait compter, d'après le contrat qu'il avait fait.*"); T. Huc, *Commentaire théorique et pratique du code civil*, VII, Paris, Cotillon, 1894, 212–13 ("*Or, que veut l'équité quand l'inexécution provient de la fraude du débiteur? L'équité veut que le débiteur soit tenu de réparer le dommage dans toute son étendue, quelles qu'aient été ses prévisions.*").

45 Spain: E. Vicente Domingo, "El daño" in L.F. Reglero Campos, *Tratado de responsabilidad civil*, Cizur Menor, Aranzadi, 2002, (201) 261 ("*Se trata de un 'desideratum', algo que se ve como deseable aun a sabiendas de la imposibilidad de hacerlo realidad.*").

the Romanian Civil Code of 2011 and the Argentinian Civil and Commercial Code, which entered into force in 2015. In Romania, Article 1531 (1) of the Civil Code conclusively underscores the general requirement of full compensation of loss incurred because of a breach of contract: "*The creditor is entitled to full compensation for the loss suffered because of the non-performance.*"[46] The Belgian legislator could also favour the Argentinian solution. Article 1740 of the brand new *Código Civil y Comercial* provides for that principle as follows: "*La reparación del daño debe ser plena. Consiste en la restitución de la situación del damnificado al estado anterior al hecho dañoso, sea por el pago en dinero o en especie.*" The Unidroit Principles are also in the running as a model for a new provision in this regard. The first paragraph of Article 7.4.2 of these Principles recalls that leading liability principle: "*The aggrieved party is entitled to full compensation for harm sustained as a result of the non-performance.*" Following those models, a new Belgian Article 1149-1 (1) CC could stipulate: "*The victim of breach of contract is, in principle, entitled to full compensation of the loss he incurred as a result of the non-performance.*"

4.3.2. Date of assessment

28. Date of assessment of the loss – Unfortunately, the new French reform does not include any provision on the date of assessment of the loss suffered as a result of the breach of contract. The entitlement to damages arises at the moment the loss occurs.[47] Several months or years can nonetheless elapse between this date and the date on which damages are awarded to the victim. For this reason, it seems fundamental to clearly establish the date of assessment of the loss. Contrary to the common law, where case law traditionally follows the breach-date rule,[48] in Roman civil law the relevant date for this evaluation is the date which is as close as possible to the moment of the payment of compensation.[49]

29. Date of the final judgment (Article 1149-1 (2) CC) – As a general rule, the date which is as close as possible to the payment of compensation is the date of delivery

46 Article 1531 (1) of the Romanian Civil Code states: "*Creditorul are dreptul la repararea integrala a prejudiciului pe care l-a suferit din faptul neexecutarii.*"

47 D. Simoens, "Latere gebeurtenissen, al dan niet vreemd aan de schade: alternatieven voor de vaste cassatieregel" (annotation on Cass. 2 May 2001), *TBBR* 2003, (46) 47.

48 There are some exceptions to this rule: *Golden Strait Corporation v Nippon Yusen Kubishika Kaisha ('The Golden Victory')* [2007] UKHL 12; [2007] 2 AC 353.

49 Belgium: Cass. 28 May 1931, *Pas.* 1931, I, 180; Cass. 7 February 1946, *Pas.* 1946, I, 60; Cass. 27 June 1974, *Pas.* 1974, I, 1128; Cass. 28 September 1995, *Pas.* 1995, I, 860; Cass. 2 May 2001, *Pas.* 2003, 749; Cass. 4 March 2010, *Pas.* 2010, 691. France: Cass.Req.fr. 23 March 1942, *D.* 1942, 118; Cass.civ.fr. 18 June 1953, *Gaz. Pal.* 1953, II, 240; Cass.com.fr. 16 February 1954, *D.* 1954, 534, annotation R. Rodière; Cass.civ.III.fr. 5 April 1978, *Bul.civ.* III, No. 155; Cass.com.fr. 2 November 1993, *Bull.civ.* IV, No. 380; Cass.civ.I.fr. 6 October 1998, *Bull.civ.* 1998, I, 191, No. 275. Luxembourg: Cour de cassation luxembourgeoise, "Le droit luxembourgeois" in P. Pierre and F. Leduc (eds.), *La réparation intégrale en Europe. Études comparatives des droits nationaux*, Brussels, Larcier, 2012, (247) 254 ("*Le juge évalue le dommage à la date la plus proche du jugement qui alloue l'indemnité.*"). Spain: STS 9 February 1998, *RJ* 1998, 907, No. 607.

of the judgment on the damages to be awarded to the aggrieved party. On this date, the judge seized can take into account all the circumstances which could affect the constituent elements of the victim's loss.[50] This requires some specification. It is the date of the final judgment which is decisive,[51] such as the date of the appeal decision.[52] It seems appropriate to incorporate this rule in the Article on the basic measure of damages, immediately after the principle of full compensation, since this date of assessment is particularly justified by this requirement.[53] In this context, the Belgian Court of Cassation ruled for instance that "the court, in order to ensure full compensation of the loss suffered, has to assess damages as at the date of its final judgment".[54] For the purpose of drafting this new provision, the legislator could capitalise on Article 1372 of the Catala proposal, which stated: "*The court must assess the victim's loss as at the date of its judgment, taking into account all the circumstances which could affect its constituent elements, their value and its reasonably foreseeable future development.*"[55] The second paragraph of a new Article 1149-1 CC could take that Article as a model.

4.3.3. Expectation interest

30. Expectation interest as dominant target position for damages for breach of contract – Following the mention of the principle of full compensation and the subsequent date of assessment of the loss, the legislator should lay down the dominant target position for the measure of damages for breach of contract, since this target position specifies the requirement of full compensation.[56] The distinction between

50 J. Ronse, *Aanspraak op schadeloosstelling uit onrechtmatige daad*, Brussels, Larcier, 1954, 323.

51 Cass. 19 January 1993, Pas, I, 64; Cass. 22 November 2005, *Pas.* 2005, 2321; Cass. 23 April 2012, *Pas.* 2012, 875.

52 Belgium: Cass. 23 April 2012, *Pas.* 2012, 875. France: Cass.civ.fr. 18 February 1952, *D.* 1952, 323.

53 Belgium: Cass. 28 September 1995, *Pas.* 1995, I, 860; Cass. 4 March 2010, *Pas.* 2010, 691. France: Cass. civ.fr. 18 February 1952, *D.* 1952, 323; Cass.com.fr. 16 February 1954, *D.* 1954, 534, annotation R. Rodière; Cass.civ.III.fr. 5 April 1978, *Bul.civ.* III, No. 155; Cass.com.fr. 2 November 1993, *Bull.civ.* IV, No. 380.

54 Cass. 28 September 1995, *Pas.* 1995, I, 860.

55 In its original French version, Article 1372 PC stated: "*Le juge évalue le préjudice au jour où il rend sa décision, en tenant compte de toutes les circonstances qui ont pu l'affecter dans sa consistance comme dans sa valeur, ainsi que de son évolution raisonnablement prévisible.*"

56 Germany: T. Dreier, *Kompensation und Prävention*, Tübingen, Mohr Siebeck, 2002, 28 ("*Denn die von Mommsen formulierte Differenzmethode [...] vermeidet [...] die Gefahr sich überlappender einzelner Schadensposten.*"). Sweden: J. Ramberg and J. Herre, *Köplagen. En Kommentar*, Stockholm, Norstedts Juridik, 2013, 15.1.1 (first paragraph: "*Utgångspunkten med reglerna att den skadelidande parten genom skadeståndet skall försättas i samma ekonomiska situation som om avtal har fullgjorts på riktigt sätt (ersättning enligt det positiva kontraktsintresset)*". England: H. McGregor, *McGregor on Damages*, London, Sweet & Maxwell, 2014, 14 ("*The statement of the general rule from which one must always start in resolving a problem as to the measure of damages [is] defined [...] as 'that sum of money which will put the party who has been injured, or who has suffered, in the same position as he would have been in if he had not sustained the wrong for which he is now getting his compensation or reparation.*"). South Africa: J.S. McLennan, "Positive and negative damages for breach of contract: the confusion of labels", *South African Law Journal* 1999, (521) 521 and 529 ("*The distinction between concepts such as expectation*

the positive and the negative interest goes back to the German author Von Jhering.[57] Taken from that precontractual context, this paradigm was extrapolated to contractual damages by the American authors Fuller and Perdue in "The Reliance Interest in Contract Damages", which was published in the *Yale Law Journal* in 1936.[58] Three decades later Corbin already clearly highlighted the importance of this distinction in his treatise on the working rules of contract law: "*The use of this newer analysis is gaining acceptance as it often permits a clearer way of determining the actual economic harm.*"[59] As regards contractual liability, the Belgian legislator should be urged to use this "*clearer way of determining the actual economic harm*" by specifying that the party in breach has to put the victim as nearly as possible into the situation in which he would have been if the contract as a whole had been duly performed. This target position of the so-called expectation interest[60] or performance interest[61] (*Erfüllungsinteresse*) – also called the positive interest[62] (*intérêt positif*) – prevails in a contractual context.

31. Some reasons for the dominance of the expectation interest – The linguistic intuition of Belgian academic writers already seems to dictate the primacy of the positive interest. When debating contractual liability, Belgian legal scholars very often reason in terms of "equivalent performance" ("*exécution par équivalent*" / "*uitvoering bij equivalent*"). To be *equivalent* to *performance*, damages can only be

damages and reliance damages serves, in my view, only one function, and that is to prevent a plaintiff from […] obtaining 'double compensation' or 'double damages' through incompatible remedies.").

57 R. von Jhering, *Culpa in contrahendo oder Schadensersatz bei nichtigen oder nicht zur Perfektion gelangten Verträgen* in *Jahrbücher für die Dogmatik des heutigen römischen und deutschen Privatrechts*, IV, Jena, Friedrich Mauke, 1861, 16 ("*Das Interesse des Käufers läßt sich in doppelter Weise denken: einmal nämlich als ein Interesse an der Aufrechterhaltung des Contracts, also an der Erfüllung – hier würde der Käufer in einem Geldäquivalent alles erhalten, was er im Fall der Gültigkeit des Contracts haben würde – und sodann als ein Interesse am Nichtabschluß des Contracts – hier würde er erhalten, was er haben würde, wenn die äußere Tatsache des Contractsabschlusses gar nicht vorgekommen wäre. Einige Beispiele werden diesen Unterschied, den ich der Kürze wegen positivem und negativem Vertragsinteresse bezeichnen will, klar machen.*").

58 L.L. Fuller and W.R. Perdue, "The Reliance Interest in Contract Damages", *Yale Law Journal* 1936, 52–96. Importance of their article: T.D. Rakoff, "Fuller and Perdue's *The Reliance Interest* as a work of legal scholarship", *Wisconsin Law Review* 1991, (203) 203 ("*[…] some articles have proven more enduring than spats on the Nehru jacket. Concerning the law of contracts, the preeminent example is The Reliance Interest in Contract Damages.*").

59 A.L. Corbin, *Corbin on Contracts. A comprehensive treatise on the working rules of contract law. Volume 5. Sections 990–1121*, St. Paul, West Publishing, 1964, 592.

60 L.L. Fuller and W.R. Perdue, "The Reliance Interest in Contract Damages", *Yale Law Journal* 1936, 52–96.

61 D. Friedmann, "The Performance Interest in Contract Damages", *Law Quarterly Review* 1995, (628) 632 ("*The expectation interest is simply an inappropriate term describing the performance interest.*" and 635: "*Indeed, the term 'expectation' may be more appropriate in this context, in which the expectation is not based upon a legal right, than in the contractual context, in which the plaintiff has a legal right to receive that which was promised to him.*").

62 The term "positive interest" seems of a rather common use in South African contract law. E.g. J.S. McLennan, "Positive and negative damages for breach of contract: the confusion of labels", *South African Law Journal* 1999, (521) 521. This term is also used in Austria: P. Apathy and A. Riedler, *Bürgerliches Recht. III. Schuldrecht. Besonderer Teil*, Wenen, Springer, 2002, 117.

measured on the basis of the expectation interest.[63] But what are the main justifications for the dominance of the expectation interest in the context of damages for breach of contract? Above all, this approach seems to be in line with the subjective intention of the parties, who conclude contracts for the purpose of obtaining performance, and thus in order to obtain expectation damages when being a victim of a breach of contract. Dogmatically, this primacy of the expectation interest stems from the binding force of the contract between parties (Article 1134 (1) CC). As soon as the contract acquires binding force, the parties are virtually entitled to expectation damages if their contractual partner fails to comply with his contractual obligations. This implies, for instance, that the aggrieved party seeking expectation damages, cannot obtain reimbursement of expenses made in performance or in preparation of performance of his obligations. In the case of performance, the now aggrieved party would have borne those expenses anyway. As a consequence, they are not recoverable under the positive interest. Reimbursement would lead to overcompensation and would subsequently impair the upper limit set by the principle of full compensation.

32. SOURCES OF INSPIRATION AND WORDING OF THE PROVISION ON THE RECOVERABILITY OF THE EXPECTATION INTEREST (ARTICLE 1149-1 (3), FIRST SENTENCE CC) – For the wording of a provision on the contractual interest, the new Russian Civil Code – which entered into force in 2015 – can give some guidance. It can be read in Article 393 (1) of this Code that "*full compensation entails a recovery that places the aggrieved party in the position it would have been in had the contract been properly performed*".[64] In France, only the Terré proposal contained a reference to the expectation interest: "*Les dommages et intérêts sont, en règle générale, d'un montant qui place le créancier dans la situation où il se trouverait si le contrat avait été dûment exécuté, en considérant la perte qu'il a faite et le gain dont il a été privé.*" (Article 118 (1)). This provision was possibly inspired by Article III.-3:702 DCFR, which reproduces Article 9:502 PECL, and stipulates under the heading "General measure of damages": "*The general measure of damages for loss caused by non-performance of an obligation is such sum as will put the creditor as nearly as possible into the position in which the creditor would have been if the obligation had been duly performed.*" At Union level, the European Commission intended to lay down this same general measure in a Common European Sales Law. The first sentence of the proposed Article 160 of the CESL stated: "*The general measure of damages for loss caused by non-performance of an obligation is such sum as will put the creditor into the position in which the creditor would have been if the obligation had been duly performed, or, where that is not possible, as nearly as possible into that position.*" Despite the recent withdrawal of this

63 B. Fauvarque-Cosson, *Projet de cadre commun de référence. Terminologie contractuelle commune. Volume 6*, Paris, Société de législation comparée, 2008, 382 ("*[L']intérêt positif [...] correspond très exactement à l'expression plus familière aux juristes français, d'exécution par équivalent dont on perçoit tout le sens. À proprement parler, l'exécution par équivalent désigne les dommages-intérêts évalués en fonction de l'intérêt du créancier à l'exécution de l'obligation, par opposition aux dommages-intérêts évalués en fonction de l'intérêt à la non-conclusion du contrat.*").

64 Translation based on: A. Dontsov, M. Kobzev and P. Boulatov, "Civil Code Reform: New Provisions on Contracts and Obligations", *White & Case* 2015, August, www.whitecase.com, (1) 5.

proposal[65], this provision could be taken as a model for a new Article 1149-1 (3) CC. This new provision can also be entitled "General measure of damages" and could state the following: "*The general measure of damages for breach of contract is such sum as will put the victim of a breach of contract, as nearly as possible, into the position in which he would have been if the contract had been performed.*"

33. Entitlement to the expectation interest in the case of termination for breach of contract (Article 1149-1 (3), second sentence CC) – Furthermore, the Belgian legislator could also put an end to the academic debates on whether damages awarded in case of retroactive termination for breach of contract should protect the expectation interest or should rather put the victim of a breach of contract into the position in which he would have been had the contract never been concluded (reliance interest).[66] As the Belgian Court of Cassation has already ruled quite explicitly on several occasions, the expectation interest should also dominate the measure of damages in the case of retroactive termination for breach of contract.[67] The retroactive effect does not eliminate all traces of the terminated contract. Retroactivity can explain the measure of the restitutions resulting from the termination, but does not influence the measure of damages awarded as a complement to this remedy. Mere protection of the reliance interest would undeniably impair the legitimate expectations of the victim of the breach of contract. Therefore, a second sentence of Article 1149-1 (3) CC could clarify this still controversial question: "*This general measure of damages also applies when that victim seeks termination for breach of contract.*"

4.3.4. Non-pecuniary loss

34. Specification of main recoverable heads of loss – In a next paragraph of the new Article on the basic measure of damages for breach of contract, the legislator could specify the main recoverable heads of loss. The new provision can repeat the beginning of the actual Article 1149 CC by stating: "*Damages due to a victim of a breach of contract*

65 Point 60 of the Annex to the Communication from the Commission to the European Parliament, the Council, The European Economic and Social Committee and the Committee of the Regions. Commission Work Programme 2015. A New Start (COM(2014) 910 final) of 16 December 2014 (ec.europa.eu/atwork/pdf/cwp_2015_withdrawals_en.pdf). In the meanwhile, the Commission did two new proposals: a proposal for a Directive of the European Parliament and of the Council on certain aspects concerning contracts for the supply of digital content (COM(2015) 635 final) and a proposal for a Directive of the European Parliament and of the Council on certain aspects concerning contracts for the online and other distance sales of goods (COM(2015) 635 final).

66 Reliance interest: J. Baeck, *Restitutie na vernietiging of ontbinding van overeenkomsten*, Antwerp, Intersentia, 2012, 294–300. Expectation interest: R. Jafferali, *La rétroactivité dans le contrat*, Brussels, Bruylant, 2014, 903.

67 Cass. 9 May 1986, *Pas.* 1986, I, 1100; Cass. 7 November 1988, *Pas.* 1989, I, 243; Cass. 5 March 1993, *Pas.* 1993, I, 253; Cass. 15 April 1996, *Pas.* 1996, I, 342; Cass. 15 November 2002, *Pas.* 2002, 2180, *RABG* 2003, 656; Cass. 16 April 2004, *Pas.* 2004, 641; Cass. 26 January 2007, *Pas.* 2007, 193; Cass. 26 January 2007, *Pas.* 2007, 183, *TBBR* 2009, 45, *TBO* 2008, 8; Cass. 13 October 2011, *Pas.* 2011, 2237; Cass. 5 December 2014, *RABG* 2015, 411, point 14.

are, as a rule, for the loss which he has suffered and the profit which he has been deprived of". This specification of the principle of full compensation, in conjunction with the scope of the expectation interest, as set out in the previous paragraphs of the new Article 1149-1 CC, still falls somehow short of legal reality.

35. Principle of recoverability of non-pecuniary loss – In fact, contractual damages are not only due for the loss which the creditor has suffered and the profit which he has been deprived of, but also for the non-pecuniary harm he has suffered as a result of the breach of contract. Even if it could be argued that "loss suffered", as referred to in the current Article 1149 CC, also covers non-economic loss, codification of the recoverability of this specific type of loss could enhance legal certainty in this respect. As regards non-contractual liability, the French Court of Cassation recognised the recoverability of immaterial loss as early as in 1833.[68] The Belgian Court of Cassation followed half a century later by considering that "damage", for the purposes of Article 1382 CC, also covers immaterial loss.[69] This paved the way for the acceptance of the recoverability of non-pecuniary loss in a contractual context.[70] Planiol declared that contract law should take into account the moral interest and damage of the creditor.[71] In 1924 Demogue caused the breakthrough by stating that the non-recoverability of non-pecuniary loss originating from a breach of contract leads to unacceptable results: "*Nous concluons donc nettement en faveur du dommage moral comme nous l'avons fait en matière de contrats en admettant des conventions de nature morale.*"[72]

36. Sources of inspiration and wording of the provision on the recoverability of non-pecuniary loss (Article 1149-1 (4), first sentence CC) – The quest for a

68 Cass.fr. 15 June 1833, *S.* 1833, I, (458) 461 ("*la difficulté d'apprécier un dommage ne rend pas non recevable l'action en réparation de ce dommage*"; "*dans l'espèce soumise à la Cour, l'action des pharmaciens [...] poursuit la réparation d'un préjudice tout moral, la conservation de l'honneur et de l'exercice consciencieux de la profession [...]*").

69 Cass. 17 March 1881, *Pas.* 1881, I, 163 (non-pecuniary loss for the death of a family member because of a train accident: "*Considérant que le mot dommage dont se sert le législateur dans les articles 1382 et suivants du code civil est un terme général qui s'applique au dommage moral comme au dommage matériel et qu'il appartient au juge du fond de vérifier si le dommage moral est appréciable.*").

70 Some Belgian applications: Cass. 4 January 1984, *RW* 1986-87, 546; Cass. 26 October 2006, *Arr.Cass.* 2000, 1663; Antwerp 8 September 2003, *NJW* 2004, 558; Antwerp 21 March 2005, *RW* 2007-08, 489; Antwerp 27 October 2014, *RABG* 2015, (776) 780; Brussels 4 December 1987, *JLMB* 1989, 394; Brussels 19 September 2002, *RGAR* 2003, nr. 13743; Ghent 6 May 1959, *RW* 1960-61, 183; Ghent 19 October 2012, *RW* 2014, 32, annotation R. Steennot; Liège 4 April 1996, *JLMB* 1999, 5; Liège 17 April 2008, *RRD* 2008, 34, annotation Q. Van Enis.

71 M. Planiol, *Traité élémentaire de droit civil*, II, Paris, LGDJ, 1923, 91-92 ("*Presque tous les auteurs proclament à l'envi que l'inexécution d'une obligation contractuelle ne donne pas lieu à des dommages-intérêts lorsqu'il n'en résulte qu'un préjudice moral. [...] Cependant on obtient tous les jours de nos tribunaux la réparation pécuniaire de préjudices non matériels dans les matières les plus diverses. [...] On pourrait donc hardiment renverser le principe et dire que la jurisprudence française tient compte, et avec grande raison, de l'intérêt moral du créancier et du préjudice immatériel qu'il peut éprouver. [...] Mais on le fait tous les jours en matière de délit; pourquoi agir autrement en matière de contrat? Il n'y en a pas de raison [...]*").

72 R. Demogue, *Traité des obligations en général. I. Sources des obligations.* IV, Paris, Rousseau, 1924, 55.

good model provision on the recoverability of non-pecuniary loss leads us straight to Article 1741 of the Argentinian *Código Civil y Comercial*, which entered into force in 2015. Under the heading "*Indemnización de las consecuencias no patrimoniales*" (*compensation for non-pecuniary consequences*), that Article clearly provides for the recoverability of non-pecuniary loss: "*Está legitimado para reclamar la indemnización de las consecuencias no patrimoniales el damnificado directo*" (*The directly affected party is entitled to seek compensation for non-pecuniary consequences*). Another technique is found in the DCFR, which provides, in Article 3:701 (3), for the recoverability of non-pecuniary loss by defining "loss" in a wide sense, as including both economic and non-economic loss: "*'Loss' includes economic and non-economic loss. [...] 'Non-economic loss' includes pain and suffering and impairment of the quality of life.*" In line with this provision, the Unidroit Principles enshrine the recoverability of non-pecuniary loss in the Article on the principle of full compensation, by defining "harm", a type of loss which has to be fully compensated, in Article 7.4.2 (2) as follows: "*Such harm may be non-pecuniary and includes, for instance, physical suffering or emotional distress.*" The same approach is applied by the PECL (Article 9:501 (2), a) and the CESL (Article 2, a). The Belgian legislator could follow that strategy by defining "loss" in a broad sense in an introductory Article or by wording a new Article 1149–1 (4) CC as follows: "*Damages due to a victim of a breach of contract are, as a rule, for the loss which he has suffered, including non-pecuniary loss, as well as the profit which he has been deprived of.*"

37. Applicability of the principle of full compensation to non-pecuniary loss (Article 1149–1 (4), second sentence CC) – In order to enhance legal certainty, the Belgian legislator could, in a second sentence of this provision, recall the applicability of the compensation principle to non-pecuniary loss. The English approach was adopted in *Hayes v James & Charles Dodd* (1990), where it was declared that "*The English courts should be wary of adopting what he [the trial judge] called 'the United States practice of huge awards.*"[73] In line with this, the Belgian Court of Cassation explicitly ruled, in a non-contractual context, that damages awarded for non-pecuniary loss do not aim at punishing the party causing harm, and that those damages should not be proportionate to the gravity of the fault committed.[74] As a consequence, in Belgium, contractual damages for non-pecuniary harm fall entirely within the scope of the above-mentioned principle of full compensation. This idea is reflected, on the international level, in an official comment on Article 7.4.2 (2) Unidroit Principles, which states: "*The compensation of non-material harm may assume different forms and it is for the court to decide which of them, whether taken alone or together, best assures full compensation.*"[75] A second sentence of Article 1149–1 (4) CC could thus make a reference to that principle of full compensation: "*Compensation of non-pecuniary loss falls within the scope of the principle of full compensation as set out in paragraph 1.*"

73 *Hayes v James & Charles Dodd* [1990] 2 All ER 815.
74 Cass. 10 October 1972, *Arr.Cass.* 1973, 146.
75 Unidroit, *Unidroit principles of international commercial contracts*, Rome, International Institute for the Unification of Private Law, 2010, www.unidroit.org, 269.

38. Possibility of equitable assessment of non-pecuniary loss (Article 1149–1 (4), third sentence CC) – The required application of this principle of full compensation to non-pecuniary loss should be put into perspective. For this purpose, a third sentence of Article 1149–1 (4) could underscore the possibility of equitable assessment, as it is widely accepted by Belgian case law.[76] To this end, the Belgian lawmaker could take lessons from his Dutch and Portuguese colleagues. In Portugal, Article 496 (3) of the *Código civil* – entitled "*Danos não patrimoniais*" (non-pecuniary loss) – clearly provides for this possibility of equitable assessment: "*O montante da indemnização será fixado equitativamente pelo tribunal*". The same observation applies to the relevant Dutch provision. Article 6:106 (1) of the Dutch Civil Code also indicates this possibility, by stating: "*The injured person has a right of compensation for damage that does not consist of material loss, assessed in conformity with the standards of reasonableness and fairness*".[77] In conformity with those provisions, a third sentence of Article 1149–1 (4) CC could lay down: "*With due regard to the previous sentence, the seized court can assess non-pecuniary loss in conformity with the standards of reasonableness and fairness, as set out in Article 1149–3.*"

4.3.5. Lost chances

39. Principle of recoverability of lost chances – Following the provision on non-pecuniary loss, the legislator should also lay down the principle of recoverability of lost chances. In the common law, the Court of Appeals of New York approved the recoverability of such lost chances in 1868, by deciding: "*His damages are what he lost by being deprived of his chance of profit.*"[78] However, the ultimate reference point for that recovery came in 1911 with the English case *Chaplin v Hicks*, where the claimant was entitled to recover damages for her loss of a chance of gaining employment after a beauty contest where she was wrongly not invited for the final job interview. Lord Justice Vaughan Williams ruled that "*the fact that damages cannot be assessed with certainty does not relieve the wrongdoer of the necessity of paying damages for his breach of contract*".[79] In Roman civil law, this so-called chance theory dates back to the end of the nineteenth century. In 1889, the French Court of Cassation recognised the recoverability of lost chances, in a case where a plaintiff lost a chance of winning his case because of the negligence of a bailiff.[80] Belgium followed four decades later with an arbitral award recognising that doctrine: "*Le docteur C. a néanmoins fait preuve en l'occurrence d'un optimisme exagéré qui a fait perdre à la blessée les chances de guérison ou de limitation de*

76 Cass. 17 March 1881, *Pas.* 1881, I, (163) 165 (non-pecuniary loss for the death of a family member because of a train accident); Antwerp 21 March 2005, *RW* 2007–08, 489 (lost holidays); Brussels 4 December 1987, *JLMB* 1989, 394 (non-pecuniary loss suffered by the irregular and sudden termination by the bank of rental agreement).

77 Article 6:106 (1) of the Dutch Civil Code reads in Dutch: "Voor nadeel dat niet in vermogensschade bestaat, heeft de benadeelde recht op een naar billijkheid vast te stellen schadevergoeding […]" Translation: www.dutchcivillaw.com/ civilcodebook066.htm.

78 *Taylor v Bradley*, 39 NY 129 (1868).

79 *Chaplin v Hicks* [1911] 2 KB 786.

80 Cass.Req. 17 July 1889, S. 1891, I, 399.

son mal qui pouvaient exister."[81] Belgian lawyers had to wait until 1984 for the "final" green light. In that year, the Belgian Court of Cassation formally accepted damages for lost chances in the well-known amputation case.[82] Even though this theory remained somewhat controversial for a certain period of time[83] and is from time to time still contested,[84] it has repeatedly been clearly confirmed at the highest judicial level that an aggrieved party is eligible to obtain damages for lost chances.[85]

40. Sources of inspiration and wording of a provision on the recoverability of lost chances (Article 1149-1 (5) CC) – Taking due account of that widely accepted chance theory, how should the Belgian legislator provide for the recoverability of chances lost because of a breach of contract? Could he benefit from the new French legal framework? Unfortunately, the answer to this question can again not be in the affirmative. The new French provisions do not mention this head of loss. In terms of lost chances, the former Catala reform proposal was more precise, since it clearly stressed that possibility. It was stated in proposed Article 1346: "*Loss of a chance constitutes a reparable loss distinct from the advantage which would have inured to the claimant's benefit if the chance had materialised.*"[86] In line with this provision, Article 7.4.3 (2) of the Unidroit Principles states the following: "*Compensation may be due for the loss of a chance in proportion to the probability of its occurrence.*" Hence, a new Belgian Article 1149–1 (5) CC could read as follows: "*Damages due to a victim of a breach of contract can also cover the loss of a chance to obtain an advantage or to avoid a disadvantage.*" In conformity with those models, this provision could further mention the way in which courts should measure lost chances: "*Compensation may be due for the loss of a chance in proportion to the probability of its occurrence*" (Article 7.4.3 (2) Unidroit Principles).

4.3.6. Reliance interest

41. Provision on the subsidiary protection of the reliance interest – The expectation interest clearly prevails in the context of damages for breach of contract. It is therefore called the "*contract measure of damages*"[87], the "*contractual interest*"[88], or even

[81] Arbitral Award 10 October 1927, *RGAR* 1928, No. 292, annotation HVL.
[82] Cass. 19 January 1984, *Arr.Cass.* 1983–84, 585.
[83] Cass. 19 June 1998, *Arr.Cass.* 1998, 721; Cass. 1 April 2004, *Arr.Cass.* 2004, 549, concl. T. Werquin.
[84] Cass. 6 December 2013, *RW* 2014–15, 790.
[85] Cass. 23 February 2005, *Pas.* 2005, 442; Cass. 27 February 2008, *Pas.* 2008, 539; Cass. 5 June 2008, *Pas.* 2008, 1425.
[86] Article 1346 PC stated in the original French version: "*La perte d'une chance constitue un préjudice réparable distinct de l'avantage qu'aurait procuré cette chance si elle s'était réalisée.*"
[87] R. Halson, "Remedies for breach of contract" in A. Grubb and M. Furmston, *The law of contract*, London, LexisNexis Butterworths, 2007, (1573) 1577; G.H. Treitel, *Remedies for Breach of Contract. A Comparative Account*, Oxford, Clarendon, 1991, 82 ("*It is the protection of the expectation interest which is a characteristic feature of an action based on contractual default.*"); G.H. Treitel, *The law of contract*, London, Sweet & Maxwell, 1995, 846.
[88] E. McKendrick, *Contract Law: Text, cases and materials*, Oxford, OUP, 2008, 420; C. Webb, "Performance and compensation: an analysis of contract damages and contractual obligation", *OJLS* 2006, 42.

"*the cornerstone of damages in contract law*".[89] Yet primacy does not necessarily stand synonym for exclusivity. The reliance interest (negative interest; *Vertrauensinteresse*) could be relevant as a proxy for the expectation measure in cases in which this expectation interest seems hard to prove.[90] In a subsidiary alternative, the victim of a breach can ask to be put as nearly as possible in the position in which he would have been had the contract never been concluded. His reliance interest serves as a subsidiary mechanism for measuring his expectation interest. The claimant's reliance can only occasionally be awarded as evidence of his expectation loss. This expectation loss remains even then the ultimate goal of the contractual damages. Compensation for the reliance interest could therefore be considered as a means of ensuring minimum protection for the aggrieved party. When drafting a provision on the availability of the reliance interest, the legislator should, as a consequence, clearly stress the subsidiary nature of this protection. The expectation interest controls the reliance interest.[91]

42. Justification? Presumption of breaking even – Awarding the reliance interest is only the best approximation of the expectation interest which is hard to prove. Compensation (under the reliance interest) of expenses made in preparation for performance or in performance, which are not recoverable under the expectation interest, constitutes such an approximation. This alternative measure could be based on the so-called *presumption of breaking even*, which is the assumption that expectation would at least equal expenditure.[92] Legal scholars both in the common law and in Germany presume that the victim, in the hypothetical situation of performance, would have recouped these costs.[93] When it is very difficult for a victim of a breach of contract

89 M.G. Bridge, "Expectation Damages and Uncertain Future Losses" in J. Beatson and D. Friedmann (eds.), *Good Faith and Fault in Contract Law*, Oxford, Clarendon Press, 1995, (427) 429.

90 Common Law: A. Kramer, *The law of contract damages*, Oxford, Hart Publishing, 2014, 482 ("*it is important to understand that there is in contract law no 'reliance' measure [...] it is a proxy for the expectation measure where profits are hard to prove [...]*"). Switzerland: Kantonsgericht St. Gallen, III. Zivilkamer 5 February 2008, swisslex, punt II.4.a ("*Es wird im allgemeinen Zusammenhang auch die Meinung vertreten, der Gläubiger könne, soweit er zur Geltendmachung des positiven Interesses berechtigt sei, stattdessen generell auch das negative Interesse wählen. Eine solche Option müsste aber mit der Ausübung eines Rücktritts- bzw. Auflösungsrechts verbunden sein.*").

91 R. Halson, "Remedies for breach of contract" in A. Grubb and M. Furmston, *The law of contract*, London, LexisNexis Butterworths, 2007, (1573) 1578 and 1661 ("*the expectation interest controls the reliance interest*").

92 Belgium: R. Jafferali, *La rétroactivité dans le contrat*, Brussels, Bruylant, 2014, 917–918 ("*Si l'on accepte, en effet, de présumer que l'opération conclue était normalement rentable pour le créancier ou devait, au minimum, s'avérer neutre pour celui-ci, alors il pourra toujours réclamer après résolution des dommages-intérêts égaux, à tout le moins, aux frais et aux pertes subies du fait du contrat, c'est-à-dire à l'intérêt négatif s.s. On parviendrait ainsi à éviter les difficultés rencontrées dans la preuve de l'étendue de l'intérêt positif.*").

93 Common Law: E. Peel, *Treitel – The law of contract*, London, Sweet & Maxwell, 2011, 1005–1006 ("*While the claimant has the option of claiming damages on the basis of his reliance loss, this is only on the basis that such loss is presumed to represent his expectation loss, i.e. that if the contract had been performed, the claimant would, at least, have recouped his expenditure.*"). Germany: H. Unberath, *Die Vertragsverletzung*, Tübingen, Mohr Siebeck, 2007, 351 ("*Der Ersatz der frustrierten Aufwendungen dient als alternative Berechnungsmethode dem Ersatz des positives Interesses, die bei Beweisschwierigkeiten*

to prove what position he would have been in had the contract been properly performed, he can overcome this evidence difficulty by assuming that his expectation interest would at least have been equal to his expenditure in reliance upon the contract.[94]

43. Sources of inspiration and wording of a provision on the possibility of subsidiary protection of the reliance interest (Article 1149-2 CC) – How could we assist the Belgian legislator with drafting a provision enabling the victim of a breach of contract to seek protection for his reliance interest? German law might provide some inspiration in this regard. §284 BGB provides victims of a breach of contract with protection for their so-called expenditure measure (*Aufwendungsersatz*) or limited reliance interest.[95] §284 BGB states: "*In place of damages in lieu of performance, the obligee may demand reimbursement of the expenses which he has made and in all fairness was entitled to make in reliance on receiving performance*".[96] Characteristic of this provision is the fact that it fails to mention the widely accepted recoverability of lost opportunities, the gain of which the aggrieved party has been deprived of as result of the conclusion of the contract.[97] In the USA, §349 of the Second Restatement of Contracts

dem Glaübiger einen durchaus Zweckmäßigen Weg eröffnet, sein Leistungsinteresse zumindest annäherungsweise geltend zu machen."). With nuance: Bundesgerichtshof 10 December 1986, *NJW DE* 1987, (831) 834 ("*In Erwartung der Durchführung des Vertrages gemachte Aufwendungen könnten in solchen Fällen nach der Rechtsprechung nur ersetzt verlangt werden, soweit die Vermutung begründet sei, dass der Gläubiger sie bei Vollzug des Vertrages warscheinlich wieder erwirtschaftet hätte. Von einer solchen Vermutung könne aber im Falle der Kläger nicht ausgegangen werden, weil sie mit der Verantstaltung nur ideelle Zwecke verfolgt habe und ihre Kosten deshalb auch bei Durchführung des Mietvertrages nicht wieder hereinbekommen hätte.*").

94 Recently: M. Chen-Wishart, *Contract Law*, Oxford, OUP, 2015, 506.

95 B. Markesinis, H. Unberath and A. Johnston (eds.), *The German Law of Contract. A Comparative Treatise*, Oregon, Hart Publishing, 2006, 469 ("*[...] the Second Commission [...] came down in favour of an 'amputated' version of the right to claim for the negative interest in §284 BGB*"); H. Unberath, *Die Vertragsverletzung*, Tübingen, Mohr Siebeck, 2007, 351 ("*Der Ersatz der frustrierten Aufwendungen dient als alternative Berechnungsmethode dem Ersatz des positives Interesses, die bei Beweisschwierigkeiten dem Glaübiger einen durchaus Zweckmäßigen Weg eröffnet, sein Leistungsinteresse zumindest annäherungsweise geltend zu machen.*"); C. Bittner, M. Löwisch and H. Otto, *J. von Staudingers Kommentar zum Bürgerlichen Gesetzbuch mit Einführungsgesetz und Nebengesetzen*, Berlin, Sellier, 2004, 689 ("*Wirtschaftlich bedeutet die Schadlosstellung bezogen auf getätigte Aufwendungen den Ersatz des negativen Interesses, weil der Gläubiger so gestellt wird, als wäre es überhaupt nicht zu einem Vertragsschluß gekommen.*").

96 §284 BGB states in German: "*Anstelle des Schadensersatzes statt der Leistung kann der Gläubiger Ersatz der Aufwendungen verlangen, die er im Vertrauen auf den Erhalt der Leistung gemacht hat und billigerweise machen durfte, es sei denn, deren Zweck wäre auch ohne die Pflichtverletzung des Schuldners nicht erreicht worden.*" Translation: www.gesetze-im-internet.de/englisch_bgb/german_civil_code.pdf.

97 B. Dauner-Lieb, T. Heidel, M. Lepa and G. Ring, *Schuldrecht*, Bonn, Deutscher AnwaltVerlag, 2002, 296 ("*Der Aufwendungsersatz gemäß §284 ist nicht identisch mit einem Ersatz des Vertrauensschadens, sondern kann dahinter zurückbleiben.*"); B. Markesinis, H. Unberath and A. Johnston (eds.), *The German Law of Contract. A Comparative Treatise*, Oregon, Hart Publishing, 2006, 469 ('*amputated' version of the right to claim for the negative interest*"); P. Bassenge e.a., *Palandt Bürgerliches Gesetzbuch*, München, Beck, 2005, 387 ("*Der Gläubiger hat einen Anspruch auf Aufwendungsersatz, keinen Anspruch auf Ersatz des negativen Interesses.*"); J.F. Stoppel, *Der Ersatz frustrierter Aufwendungen nach*

offers a similar right to victims: "*As an alternative to the measure of damages stated in §347, the injured party has a right to damages based on his reliance interest, including expenditures made in preparation for performance or in performance, less any loss that the party in breach can prove with reasonable certainty the injured party would have suffered had the contract been performed.*" Somewhat inspired by these articles, but leaving the way open for protection of lost opportunities, a possible new provision on the availability of reliance damages for breach of contract could therefore be: "*Inasmuch as he encounters major difficulties in proving his expectation interest within the meaning of Article 1149-1 (3), the victim of a breach of contract can opt for protection of his reliance interest. This reliance interest aims at putting him in the position in which he would have been had the contract never been concluded.*" A second paragraph could specify: "*This reliance interest allows recovery of both expenses made in preparation for performance or in performance and opportunities lost because of the conclusion of the contract.*"

4.3.7. Equitable assessment of damages

44. Subsidiary possibility of equitable assessment of damages – Following the mentioning of the possibility of awarding reliance damages as an alternative to expectation damages, which are hard to prove, the legislator could codify the possibility, generally accepted under Belgian law, of equitable assessment of damages. Reference was already made to this measuring method in the Article on the recoverability of non-pecuniary loss (Article 1149-1 (4) third sentence CC; *supra* §38). As a matter of fact, it is often the case in respect of lost chances, future loss, non-pecuniary loss and even lost profits that the existence of those losses cannot be disputed, but that they are difficult to quantify. How can a court measure the loss of a chance to win a competition or the detriment to someone's reputation or even the pain and suffering because of a breach of contract? In such a situation in which the amount of damages cannot be established with a sufficient degree of certainty, the court should be empowered, rather than refuse any compensation, to make an equitable quantification of the loss sustained. Difficulty in assessing damages does not disentitle a claimant from having an attempt to assess them.[98] According to well-established Belgian case law, the seized court can only make use of this measuring method by demonstrating that it has no precise calculation elements at its disposal[99], and by establishing that the loss incurred cannot be measured

§284 BGB, doctoral thesis, Cologne, 2003, kups.ub.uni-koeln.de, 35 ("*Eingeschränkt würde dieses negative Interesse im Ergebnis dahingehend, dass lediglich die frustrierten Aufwendungen, nicht jedoch der entgangene Gewinn und damit ausschließlich bereits entstandene Vermögenseinbußen ersatzfähig sind.*").

98 Belgium: Cass. 16 April 1998, *AJT* 1999–00, 301. France: Cass.fr. 15 June 1833, S. 1833, I, (458) 461 ("*la difficulté d'apprécier un dommage ne rend pas non recevable l'action en réparation de ce dommage*"). Common law: J. Beatson, *Anson's Law of Contract*, Oxford, OUP, 2010, 535 ("*Difficulty in assessing damages does not disentitle a claimant from having an attempt to assess them, unless they depend on entirely speculative possibilities.*"); J.H. Drake, "The rule of certainty in damage and the value of a chance", *Michigan Law Review* 1913, (392) 394 ("*mere difficulty in assessing damages is no reason for denying them.*").

99 Cass. 22 November 1972, *Arr.Cass.* 1973, 297; Cass. 9 October 2009, *Pas.* 2009, 2204.

with (mathematical) certainty.[100] This court should also clearly state the reasons why it can only use this method for measuring the loss suffered.[101]

45. Sources of inspiration and wording of a provision on the subsidiary possibility of equitable assessment of damages (Article 1149-3 CC) – Other legal systems have established provisions allowing the possibility of measuring damages with the standards of reasonableness and fairness. Clearly drafted is Article 42 (2) of the Swiss *Code des obligations*: "*Where the exact value of the loss cannot be quantified, the court shall estimate the value at its discretion in the light of the normal course of events and the steps taken by the injured party.*"[102] Equally straightforward are Article 1226 of the Italian Civil Code ("*Se il danno non può essere provato nel suo preciso ammontare, è liquidato dal giudice con valutazione equitativa*") and Article 566 (3) of the Portuguese Civil Code ("*Se não puder ser averiguado o valor exacto dos danos, o tribunal julgará equitativamente dentro dos limites que tiver por provados*"). A new Belgian provision in this context could be based on the Unidroit Principles or even on the relevant provision of the Civil Code of Louisiana. In the Unidroit Principles, Article 7.4.3 (3) states: "*Where the amount of damages cannot be established with a sufficient degree of certainty, the assessment is at the discretion of the court.*" In Louisiana, Article 1999 of Civil Code states accordingly: "*When damages are insusceptible of precise measurement, much discretion shall be left to the court for the reasonable assessment of these damages.*" Inspired by those provisions, the Belgian legislator could draft Article 1149-3 CC as follows: "*When damages are insusceptible of precise measurement, the assessment is at the discretion of the court.*"

4.3.8. Gain-based measure of damages

46. Possibility of gain-based measure of damages – A final, but no less important provision on the basic measure of damages for breach of contract could relate to the rather exceptional possibility of disgorgement of the profits made by the non-performing party by failing to comply with his contractual obligations. Taking into account the amount of literature on this subject,[103] gain-based damages are likely to be the next

[100] Cass. 26 October 2000, *Arr.Cass.* 2000, 1663.

[101] Cass. 20 November 2012, *Pas.* 2012, 2268; Commercial Court Dendermonde 16 June 2011, *TRV* 2013, (274) 278; Commercial Court Dendermonde 27 June 2013, *DAOR* 2013, (277) 282.

[102] Original version: "*Der nicht ziffernmässig nachweisbare Schaden ist nach Ermessen des Richters mit Rücksicht auf den gewöhnlichen Lauf der Dinge und auf die vom Geschädigten getroffenen Massnahmen abzuschätzen.*" Translation: www.admin.ch/opc/en/classified-compilation/19110009/201507010000/220.pdf.

[103] More on this topic: A.-F. Bock, *Gewinnherausgabe als Folge einer Vertragsverletzung*, Basel, Helbing, 2010, 340 p.; D. Campbell, "A relational critique of the Third Restatement of Restitution §39", *Washington and Lee Law Review* 2011, 1063–1131; C. Chappuis, "Violation contractuelle et remise du gain" in P. Gauch, F. Werro and P. Pichonnaz (eds.), *Mélanges en l'honneur de Pierre Tercier*, Freiburg, Schulthess, 2008, 153–172; T.E. Deurvorst, "Is winstafdracht een bruikbare sanctie?" in *Privaatrecht en Gros*, Antwerp, Intersentia, 1999, 147–159; J. Edelman, *Gain-Based Damages*, Oxford, Hart Publishing, 2002, 320 p.; M.A. Eisenberg, "The disgorgement interest in contract law", *Michigan Law*

remedy to become mainstream. In the Netherlands, Article 6:104 NBW seems to provide for this remedy: "*If someone, who is liable towards another person on the basis of tort or a default of complying with an obligation, has gained a profit because of this tort or non-performance, then the court may, upon the request of the injured person, estimate that damage in line with the amount of this profit or a part of it.*"[104]

47. Sources of inspiration and wording of a provision on gain-based damages (Article 1149-4 CC) – In France, only the Terré reform proposal laid down the possibility of gain-based damages. Article 120 of this proposal reads: "*Toutefois, en cas de dol, le créancier de l'obligation inexécutée peut préférer demander au juge que le débiteur soit condamné à lui verser tout ou partie du profit retiré de l'inexécution.*" The comments on this suggested provision clarify that "*dol*" refers in this context to opportunistic breaches of contract.[105] This is in line with the reasoning behind §39(1) of the (American) Third Restatement of the law of restitution and unjust enrichment: "*If a breach of contract is both material and opportunistic, the injured promisee has a claim in restitution to the profit realized by the defaulting promisor as a result of the breach. Liability in restitution with disgorgement of profit is an alternative to liability for contract*

Review 2006, 559–602; J.-L. Fagnart, "La peine privée: une réalité qui dérange?" in E. Van den Hautte (ed.), *Liber Amicorum François Glansdorff et Pierre Legros*, Brussels, Bruylant 2013, 133–167; D. Fox, "Restitutionary damages to deter breach of contract", *Cambridge Law Journal* 2001, 33–35; A. Gray, "Disgorgement damages", *Journal of Business Law* 2013, 657–678; T. Helms, *Gewinnherausgabe als haftungsrechtliches Problem*, Tübingen, Mohr Siebeck, 2007, 526 p.; S. Hocquet-Berg, "Caractère indemnitaire ou punitif des dommages-intérêts. Rapport français" in B. Dubuisson and P. Jourdain (eds.), *Le dommage et sa réparation dans la responsabilité contractuelle et extracontractuelle*, Brussels, Bruylant, 2015, 215–236; E. Hondius and A. Janssen (eds.), *Disgorgement of Profits. Gain-based remedies throughout the world*, Basel, Springer, 2015, 507 p.; T. Kah Leng and S.H.S. Leong, "Contractual protection of business confidence", *Journal of Business Law* 2002, 513–538; J.G.A. Linssen, *Voordeelsafgifte en ongerechtvaardigde verrijking*, Tilburg, Boom, 2001, 884 p.; C.L. Roberts, "A Commonwealth perspective on restitutionary disgorgement for breach of contract", *Washington and Lee University School of Law* 2008, 945–991; C.L. Roberts, "Restitutionary disgorgement for opportunistic breach of contract and mitigation of damages", *Loyola of Los Angeles Law Review* 2008, 131–176; C.L. Roberts, "Restitutionary disgorgement as a moral compass for breach of contract", *University of Cincinnati Law Review* 2009, 991–1026; M. Siems, "Disgorgement of profits for breach of contract: a comparative analysis", *Edinburgh Law Review* 2003, 27–59; A. Temple, "Disgorgement damages for breach of contract", *Denning Law Journal* 2008, 87–110; X. Thunis and B. Fosséprez, "Caractère indemnitaire ou punitif des dommages et intérêts. Rapport belge" in B. Dubuisson and P. Jourdain (eds.), *Le dommage et sa réparation dans la responsabilité contractuelle et extracontractuelle*, Brussels, Bruylant, 2015, 237–310; W.H. van Boom, "Twee arresten over 'winstafroming' ex artikel 6:104 BW", *AA* 2011, 118–125; N.J. van der Graaff, "Restitutionary damages: schadevergoeding zonder schade?" in W.H. van Boom, J.H. van Dam-Lely and S.D. Lindenbergh, *Rake remedies*, The Hague, BJU, 2011, 87–104.

104 Article 6:104 NBW states in the Dutch version: "*Indien iemand die op grond van onrechtmatige daad of een tekortkoming in de nakoming van een verbintenis jegens een ander aansprakelijk is, door die daad of tekortkoming winst heeft genoten, kan de rechter op vordering van die ander de schade begroten op het bedrag van die winst of op een gedeelte daarvan.*" Translation: www.dutchcivillaw.com/civilcodebook066.htm.

105 Ph. Rémy, "Les dommages et intérêts" in F. Terré, *Pour une réforme du droit des contrats. Réflexions et propositions d'un groupe de travail sous la direction de François Terré*, Parijs, LGDJ, 2009, (281) 286.

damages measured by injury to the promisee." Following these examples, a new Article 1149-4 CC could stipulate: "*If a breach of contract is both material and opportunistic, the victim may request disgorgement of the profits realized by the non-performing party as a result of the breach of contract.*" In a next subparagraph, this Article could specify that disgorgement of profits serves as an alternative to expectation damages: "*Disgorgement of profits is an alternative to protection of the expectation interest within the meaning of Article 1149-1 (3), when those expectation damages do not offer adequate protection for the contractual claims of the victim of the breach of contract.*"[106]

4.4. *Limits on principle of full compensation*

48. Limits on the principle of full compensation – The English reference work *McGregor on Damages* puts the scope of the principle of full compensation in contract law rightly into perspective: "*Rigorously to insist upon such full compensation would be too harsh upon defendants. The loss for which the claimant will be compensated is cut down by a variety of factors.*"[107] This nuance of the requirement of full compensation also applies to Belgian contract law. The assessment of compensatory damages may therefore be regarded as a two stage process.[108] In the first stage, the prima facie measure is ascertained (new Article 1149 CC). In the second stage, a number of limiting factors are considered (new Article 1150 CC).

4.4.1. Foreseeability

49. Maintenance of foreseeability limitation (Article 1150-1 CC) – The current Article 1150 CC states: "*A debtor is liable only for damages which were foreseen or which could have been foreseen at the time of the contract, where it is not through his own intentional breach that the obligation is not fulfilled.*"[109] Nevertheless, this Article has been hollowed out by the Belgian Court of Cassation. It has frequently ruled, since 1928, that unforeseeability of the amount of loss is irrelevant.[110] Since then, that Article has proved difficult to implement. Notwithstanding that case law, it seems appropriate to

106 The outlines of the proposed provision may reasonably be expected to become sharper with a forthcoming doctoral thesis on disgorgement damages (T. Gladinez, KUL).

107 H. McGregor, *McGregor on Damages*, London, Sweet & Maxwell, 2014, 16.

108 R. Halson, "Remedies for breach of contract" in A. Grubb and M. Furmston, *The law of contract*, London, LexisNexis Butterworths, 2007, (1573) 1573.

109 Article 1150 CC states in French: "*Le débiteur n'est tenu que des dommages et intérêts qui ont été prévus ou qu'on a pu prévoir lors du contrat, lorsque ce n'est point par son dol que l'obligation n'est point exécutée.*"

110 Cass. 23 February 1928, *Pas.* 1928, I, 85; Cass. 5 January 1962, *Pas.* 1962, I, 531; Cass. 20 October 1983, *Arr.Cass.* 1983-84, 193, *Bull.* 1984, 182, *Pas.* 1984, I, 182; Cass. 11 April 1986, *Arr.Cass.* 1985-86, 1091, *RW* 1986-87, 1963, *RCJB* 1990, 79, annotation L. Cornelis ("*Overwegende [...] dat immers, opdat de schuldenaar wegens wanprestatie kan worden veroordeeld tot vergoeding van de schade die was voorzien of die men heeft kunnen voorzien ten tijde van het aangaan van het contract, niet vereist is dat reeds de omvang van de schade was voorzien of kon worden voorzien.*"); Cass. 23 October 1987, *Arr.Cass.* 1987-88, 228 ("Overwegende dat de artikelen 1150 en 1151 van het Burgerlijk Wetboek alleen betrekking

maintain the foreseeability limitation. The usefulness of this limit has recently been confirmed by rulings of the French Court of Cassation applying this limitation.[111] This statement is also borne out by the fact that new codifications strictly maintain this requirement. This is true for Québec (1994; Article 1613 CCQ), Moldova (2002; Article 610 CCM), Slovenia (2002; §243 (1) OZ), Romania (2011; Article 1533 CCR), Hungary (2014; Article 6:143 (2) CCH), Argentina (2015; Article 1728 CCCA) and France (2016; new Article 1231-3 CC). In both the Netherlands and in Switzerland, various legal scholars even regret the abolition of this limit.[112] Also reflective of this solid basis of the limitation on contractual damages is its incorporation in all international harmonization initiatives: the CISG (Article 74 CISG), the Unidroit Principles (Article 7.4.4), the PECL (Article 9:503), the DCFR (Article III-3:703) and the CESL (Article 161). Having regard to this universal confirmation, the foreseeability limit should definitely be maintained in Article 1150-1 CC. The drafting of Article 1150-1 CC is quite straightforward and can be aligned with the actual Article 1150 CC. Nevertheless, some minor issues should be dealt with.

50. MAINTENANCE OF THE EXCEPTION FOR INTENTIONAL BREACHES (ARTICLE 1150-1 CC) – First of all, there is the question of the exception for intentional breaches ("*dol*"). Whereas this exception is unknown to the common law – in the leading case *Hadley v Baxendale* (1854), Baron Alderson did not make a distinction between intentional and non-intentional breaches[113] – it is widespread in Roman civil law. The intention-related character of this provision is present in Belgium and Luxembourg (Article 1150 CC). The law in Italy (Article 1225 CCI) and Spain (Article 1107 CCE) is to the same extent imbued with this thought. Even the above-mentioned new codifications – Québec (1994; Article 1613 CCQ), Moldova (2002; Article 610 CCM), Slovenia (2002; §243 (1) OZ), Romania (2011; Article 1533 CCR), Hungary (2014; Article 6:143 CCH), Argentina (2015; Article 1728 CCCA) and France (2016; Article 1231-3 CC) – remain faithful to that idea. This clash between civil law and common law created a division among the international instruments. While the PECL (Article 9:503 PECL) and the DCFR (Article III-3:703) follow Roman civil law by laying down a similar exception, the CISG (Article 74), the

hebben op de oorzaak van de schade en niets uit te staan hebben met de omvang ervan"); Cass. 4 February 2010, *TBH* 2010, 498.

111 Cass.civ.I.fr. 28 April 2011, No. 10-15056, *JurisData* No. 2011-007612; Cass.civ.III.fr. 14 March 2012, No. 11-10695, *JurisData* No. 2012-004329; Cass.civ.I.fr. 2 October 2013, No. 12-26.975, *JurisData* No. 2013-021573 (train passenger misses flight because of a 5 hours train delay).

112 NETHERLANDS: R.J. Tjittes, "Viva voorzienbaarheid", *Themis* 2008, (1) 1-2 ("Wat mij betreft zou daarom bij schadevergoeding wegens wanprestatie ons recht meer mogen aansluiten bij dat van andere landen door de voorzienbaarheid als begrenzing van het recht op schadevergoeding de prominente plaats te geven die haar toekomt."). SWITZERLAND: H.-U. Brunner, *Die Anwendung deliktsrechtlicher Regeln auf die Vertragshaftung*, Freiburg, Universitätsverlag, 1991, 103 ("*Diese Lücken vermag die Voraussehbarkeitsregel Maynes Erachtens zu füllen, nicht nur weil sie rechtspolitisch und in ihre Wertungen begründet ist, sondern auch weil sie dogmatisch überzeugt.*"); P. Pichonnaz, "Le dommage contractuel et la question de la prévisibilité" in F. Werro and P. Pichonnaz (eds.), *Le dommage dans tous ses états. Sans le dommage corporel ni le tort moral*, Bern, Stämpfli, 2013, (33) 37 ("*On peut dès lors se demander si en droit suisse également l'étendue de la responsabilité contractuelle ne devrait pas être limitée à ce que les parties considéraient comme prévisible au moment de la conclusion du contrat.*").

113 *Hadley v Baxendale* [1854] 9 *Exch* 354.

Unidroit Principles (Article 7.4.4) and the CESL (Article 161) make use of the Anglo-American rule. In line with the other Roman legal systems, a new Article 1150-1 CC could preserve that exception.

51. Impact of grossly negligent breaches of contract on contractual damages – Should the intention-based exception to the foreseeability limitation on contractual damages be extended to gross negligence? In France, in line with the case law of the Court of Cassation[114], as of 1 October 2016[115], the maxim *culpa lata dolo equiparatur* is codified in the French Civil code: "*A debtor is liable only for damages which were foreseen or could have been foreseen at the time of the conclusion of the contract, unless the breach of contract is caused by intentional or gross fault.*" (Article 1231-3 CC).[116] On the international level, the PECL (Article 9:503 PECL) and the DCFR (Article III-3:703) make grossly negligent breaches equal to intentional breaches for the purpose of precluding the non-performing party from the benefit of the foreseeability limit. According to Belgian law, that limitation on damages is, however, not to be extended to grossly negligent breaches.[117] Grossly negligent contract parties should, as a consequence, not be debarred from the unforeseeability limit under Belgian law.

52. Date of assessment of foreseeability of loss – Some other thorny issues to deal with when redrafting Article 1150 CC are the date of assessment of the foreseeability of loss, the foreseeability addressee and the burden of proof. As to the date of assessment of foreseeability of loss, the Slovenian legislator opted in 2002 for the date of the breach of contract.[118] This seems utterly questionable. The date of conclusion of the contract fits better in with the underlying grounds of party autonomy[119] and risk allocation.[120] The

114 Cass.civ.I.fr. 29 October 2014, No. 13-21.980, *JurisData* No. 2014-025744.

115 *Ordonnance* n° 2016-131 du 10 février 2016 portant réforme du droit des contrats, du régime général et de la preuve des obligations, *JORF* n° 0035 du 11 février 2016.

116 New Article 1231-3 CC states in French: "*Le débiteur n'est tenu que des dommages et intérêts qui ont été prévus ou qui pouvaient être prévus lors de la conclusion du contrat, sauf lorsque l'inexécution est due à une faute lourde ou dolosive.*"

117 Cass. 25 September 1959, *Pas.* 1960, I, 112; Cass. 18 May 1987, *Arr.Cass.* 1986-87, 1250; Cass. 27 January 1995, *Arr.Cass.* 1995, 93.

118 §243, (1) OZ, as quoted in A. Vodicar, *Schadensersatz bei Vertragsverletzungen. Eine rechtsvergleichende Betrachtung des deutschen Rechts und der Rechtsordnung der Nachfolgestaaten Ex-Jugoslawiens*, Hamburg, Kovac, 2008, 151.

119 Belgium: E. Picard, N. d'Hoffschmidt and J. De le Court, *Pandectes belges. Encyclopédie de législation, de doctrine et de jurisprudence belges. Tome 32*, Brussels, Larcier, 1889, 134 ("*La raison de cette disposition réside dans une clause tacite de la convention*"). France: Bordeaux 24 May 1858, *Pas.* 1859, II, 146 ("*un contrat ne se formant que par le consentement mutuel des parties, l'une d'elles ne peut être engagée à son insu et au delà de ce qu'elle a prévu ou dû prévoir*").

120 D. Možina, "Damages and interest" in R. Schulze (e.a.), *Common European Sales Law (CESL). Commentary*, Baden-Baden, Nomos, 2012, art. 159-171 CESL, 645 ("*Its purpose is to limit the liability of parties to the risks that they were able to take into account when they were considering entering the contract and could have taken out insurance against liability.*"); P. Schlechtriem, *Uniform Sales Law. The UN-Convention on Contracts for the International Sale of Goods*, Wenen, Manz, 1986, cisgw3.law.pace.edu, 96 ("*The underlying idea is that the parties, at the conclusion of the contract, should be able to calculate the risks and potential liability they assume by their agreement.*").

date of conclusion of the contract seems more logical since it is the only time when the contracting parties had an opportunity to protect themselves by raising the contract price, excluding or limiting liability, procuring insurance or even by giving up the transaction.[121] As a consequence, it would be unfair to increase contractual liability by accepting the foreseeability of facts communicated after that specific moment.[122] In addition, that assessment date is followed by both the Roman law family – e.g. Belgium and Luxembourg (Article 1150 CC), France (new Article 1231–3 CC), Spain (Article 1107 CCE) and Italy (Article 1225 CCI) – and the common law[123], as well by harmonization initiatives such as the CISG (Article 74), the Unidroit Principles (Article 7.4.4), the PECL (Article 9:503), the DCFR (Article III.-3:703) and the CESL (Article 161). With a view to align with its neighbouring legal systems[124], the Belgian legislator should not depart from this rule.

53. Foreseeability addressee – Furthermore there is the question as to the addressee of the foreseeability requirement. Which party has to foresee the loss – the non-performing party, the victim of the breach, or both of them? Both the civil law and the common law adopt the view that the non-performing party is the only addressee.[125] The creditor's point of view is completely irrelevant. This is also supported by the official

121 V. Di Gravio, *Prevedibilità del danno e inadempimento doloso*, Milan, Giuffrè, 1999, 148 ("*È, infatti, quello il momento in cui il (futuro) debitore decide se assumere l'obbligo ed in quale misura accollarsi il rischio.*"); A. Kramer, "Remoteness: new problems with the old test" in D. Saidov and R. Cunnington, *Contract Damages. Domestic and International Perspectives*, Oxford, Hart Publishing, 2008, (276) 294–295 ("*[T]he time of contracting rule is the correct time if one holds the view [...] that remoteness is actually about the implied assumption of risk by the promisor.*"); D. Saidov, *The law of damages in international sales: the CISG and other international instruments*, Oxford, Hart Publishing, 2008, 119 ("*the rule is generally fair: only the risk assumed by the party at the conclusion of the contract should, as a rule, be of legal significance because the time of making the contract is the only time when the party has an opportunity to protect itself (for example, by raising the price, excluding or limiting liability, or by procuring insurance).*").

122 D. Saidov, *The law of damages in international sales: the CISG and other international instruments*, Oxford, Hart Publishing, 2008, 119.

123 *Hadley v Baxendale* [1854] 9 *Exch* 354. Background: M.A. Eisenberg, "The principle of Hadley v. Baxendale", *California Law Review* 1992, (563) 571–572.

124 Spain: Comisión General de Codificación, "*Propuesta de Modernización del Código Civil en materia de Obligaciones y Contratos*", *Boletín de Información* 2009, (1) 11–12 ("*Una segunda finalidad, esta evidente, habrá de ser buscar la mayor aproximación posible del Derecho español a los ordenamientos europeos, tal y como estos son concebidos hoy. No es discutible que la existencia de diferencias no muy grandes entre unos y otros ordenamientos dentro de la Unión Europea, puede facilitar lo que reiteradamente se denominan operaciones transfronterizas. Y todo ello, en espera de una unificación de las normas de Derecho Europeo de Contratos que, en algún momento, podrá producirse.*").

125 Belgium: H. De Page, *Traité élémentaire de droit civil belge*, III, Brussels, Bruylant, 1942, 141 ("*[...] le juge, pour apprécier les dommages-intérêts prévus et imprévus, doit se mettre à la place du débiteur et voir quelles sont les conséquences de l'inexécution [...] qu'il a pu prévoir ou qu'il était possible de prévoir [...]*"). France: Cass.civ.fr. 27 June 1928, *Gaz.Pal.* 1928, II, 520 ("*d'après l'art. 1150, qui ne fait aucune allusion à la prévision de la cause du dommage, le débiteur, hors le cas de dol [...], n'est tenu que des dommages-intérêts dont la quotité a pu être prévue par lui lors du contrat.*"); Cass.civ.I.fr. 28 April 2011, No. 10–15056, *JurisData* No. 2011–007612; Cass.civ.I.fr. 2 October 2013, No. 12–26.975, *JurisData* No. 2013–021573.

comment on §351 (1) of the (American) Second Restatement of Contracts: "*There is no requirement of foreseeability with respect to the injured party.*"[126] The avoidance of the passive voice in Article 1150 CC could clarify this point. In the current Article 1150 CC, the use of the passive voice in "*damages which were foreseen or which could have been foreseen*" needlessly causes uncertainty as to the person who has to foresee the loss at the time of concluding the contract. In order to break with this reprehensible practice of passive sentences, the legislator should redraft the foreseeability limit as follows: "*loss which the party in breach foresaw or ought to have foreseen*" (cf. Article 74 CISG, Article 7.4.4 Unidroit Principles, Article 9:503 PECL and Article 161 CESL).

54. Burden of proof – The common law fiercely debates the question as to the burden of proof relating to the foreseeability of losses incurred as a result of a breach of contract.[127] Who carries this burden of proof? The actual Article 1150 CC fails to solve this question. It merely stipulates that "*[a] debtor is liable only for damages which were foreseen or which could have been foreseen at the time of the contract, where it is not through his own intentional breach that the obligation is not fulfilled*". Under Belgian law, the victim of a breach has to prove the existence and the extent of loss suffered (Article 870 Belgian Code of Civil Procedure and Article 1315 (1) CC).[128] Is this aggrieved party, in accordance with the maxim *actori incumbit probatio*, also under the obligation of proving the foreseeability of loss as at the conclusion of the contract? The common law and some CISG case law tend to answer this question in the affirmative.[129] This approach, however, puts an excessively heavy burden of proof on the victim of the breach and could accordingly impair his claim for damages. More convincing is therefore the point of view that unforeseeability of loss constitutes a means of defence for the non-performing party. Unforeseeability benefits this party in breach. For this reason, it is up to him to demonstrate the possible unforeseeability of a specific head of loss.

55. Wording of a provision taking due account of burden of proof – How could the Belgian legislator now rephrase Article 1150 CC in such a way that it becomes apparent that the onus of proof rests with the defaulting party? The new Article 1150-1

126 Consultation: www.lexinter.net/LOTWVers4/unforeseeability_and_related_limitations_on_damages .htm.

127 H. McGregor, *McGregor on Damages*, London, Sweet & Maxwell, 2014, 113; J.E. Stannard, *Delay in the performance of contractual obligations*, Oxford, OUP, 2007, 228–229.

128 Belgium: Cass. 10 October 1984, *Arr.Cass.* 1984–85, 235; Cass. 28 November 1984, *Arr.Cass.* 1984–85, 432; Cass. 6 January 2005, *Pas.* 2005, 24; Cass. 13 October 2011, *Pas.* 2011, 2237. France: Cass.civ.II.fr. 8 July 1987, No. 85-14.052, *JurisData* No. 1987-701245.

129 Common Law: *Singleton Abbey v S.S. Paludina* [1927] A.C. 16, points 25–26; H. McGregor, *McGregor on Damages*, London, Sweet & Maxwell, 2014, 113; J.E. Stannard, *Delay in the performance of contractual obligations*, Oxford, OUP, 2007, 228–229. CISG: Oberlandesgericht Bamberg 13 January 1999, 3 U 83/98, CISG-online No. 516, point 2c ("*Die Darlegungs- und Beweislast für die Voraussehbarkeit des Schadens bei Vertragsabschluß obliegt dem Geschädigten.*"); Handelsgericht Zürich 26 April 1995, CISG-online No. 248, point 6e ("*According to this, it is [seller] who has to prove the damage and the causality between the breach of contract and the damage as well as the foreseeability of the damage pursuant to Art. 74 sentence two CISG.*").

CC could be formulated in a negative way. Only the Moldavian Civil Code seems to adopt this particular approach. Article 610 (4) CCMD states: "*Damages do not cover the loss which, according to the experience of the debtor, could not reasonably have been foreseen.*"[130] Even though this provision also makes use of the avoidable passive voice, it clearly indicates the person carrying the burden of proof. Whereas the victim of the breach has to prove his actual loss, it is for the non-performing party to establish that he did not or could not reasonably foresee that type[131] (or amount[132]) of loss at the time of concluding the contract. Taking into account this remark, a new Article 1150-1 CC could be worded as follows: "*The non-performing party is not liable for losses which he did not or could not reasonably foresee at the date of the conclusion of the contract.*" A second paragraph can then specify the non-applicability of that limit in case of intentional breaches of contract: "*Paragraph 1, however, shall not apply in case of an intentional breach of contract.*"

4.4.2. Avoidability

56. NON-RECOVERABILITY OF AVOIDABLE LOSS – Unlike most new civil codes, the new French law keeps silent about the widely accepted duty to mitigate. This seems all the more surprising given that the Catala proposal already clearly indicated the consequences of non-compliance with this *Obliegenheit*: "*Where the victim had the possibility of taking reliable, reasonable and proportionate measures to reduce the extent of his loss or to avoid its getting worse, the court shall take account of his failure to do so by reducing his compensation*" (Article 1373).[133] The Terré proposal laid down a similar provision.[134] Feelings of disappointment with the new French legal framework increase when realising

130 Romanian version (lex.justice.md): "*Despăgubirea nu se extinde asupra prejudiciului care, conform experienţei debitorului, nu putea fi prevăzut în mod raţional în cazul unei aprecieri obiective.*"

131 According to Belgian law the unforeseeability of the amount of loss is irrelevant: Cass. 23 February 1928, *Pas.* 1928, I, 85; Cass. 5 January 1962, *Pas.* 1962, I, 531; Cass. 20 October 1983, *Arr.Cass.* 1983–84, 193, *Bull.* 1984, 182, *Pas.* 1984, I, 182; Cass. 11 April 1986, *Arr.Cass.* 1985–86, 1091, *RW* 1986–87, 1963, *RCJB* 1990, 79, annotation L. Cornelis ("*Overwegende [...] dat immers, opdat de schuldenaar wegens wanprestatie kan worden veroordeeld tot vergoeding van de schade die was voorzien of die men heeft kunnen voorzien ten tijde van het aangaan van het contract, niet vereist is dat reeds de omvang van de schade was voorzien of kon worden voorzien.*"); Cass. 23 October 1987, *Arr.Cass.* 1987–88, 228 ("*Overwegende dat de artikelen 1150 en 1151 van het Burgerlijk Wetboek alleen betrekking hebben op de oorzaak van de schade en niets uit te staan hebben met de omvang ervan*"); Cass. 4 February 2010, *TBH* 2010, 498.

132 Under French law, the unforeseeability of the amount of the loss is also relevant: Cass.civ.fr. 7 July 1924, *D.* 1927, I, 119; Cass.civ.fr. 27 June 1928, *Gaz.Pal.* 1928, II, 520 ("*le débiteur, hors le cas de dol [...], n'est tenu que des dommages-intérêts dont la quotité a pu être prévue par lui lors du contrat.*").

133 Article 1373 PC stated in French: "*Lorsque la victime avait la possibilité, par des moyens sûrs, raisonnables et proportionnés, de réduire l'étendue de son préjudice ou d'en éviter l'aggravation, il sera tenu compte de son abstention par une réduction de son indemnisation, sauf lorsque les mesures seraient de nature à porter atteinte à son intégrité physique.*"

134 Article 121 (2) of the Terré proposal laid down: "*Il en va de même si le créancier n'a point pris les mesures sûres et raisonnables, propres à éviter, à modérer ou à supprimer son préjudice. Le créancier sera remboursé de tous les frais raisonnablement engagés à cet effet.*"

that this mitigation limit was already present in the Treaties of the founding fathers of the Napoleonic Code. In his *Tractatus de eo quod interest* (1546, no. 61) Dumoulin declared that a buyer should refrain from aggravating the duty, incumbent on the non-performing party, to pay damages in case of a breach of contract.[135] Following this line of reasoning, Domat specified, in *Les lois civiles dans leur ordre naturel* (1689, 254), that a winegrower who eventually lost his harvest because of the non-delivery of carriages, was not entitled to damages for those losses resulting from a hailstorm "*if one could get other carriages elsewhere*".[136] In his *Traité des Obligations* (1761) Pothier alluded to that same principle by stating that a non-performing party shall not be deemed liable for loss which the victim of the breach could have avoided by concluding cover transactions.[137]

57. Belgian acceptance of principle of duty to mitigate – The duty to mitigate was concealed in the cases which the founding fathers of the Napoleonic Code gave as illustrations of damages for breach of contract, but was decidedly not formulated as an autonomous and general principle. In the heat of moment, that duty incumbent on the non-performing party escaped the attention of Napoleon's draftsmen and was eventually not codified as such in 1804. Yet nowadays this duty constitutes a widely acknowledged principle under Belgian law.[138] First of all, it is common to construe Article 1760 CC as containing an application of that principle. Article 1760 CC states: "*In case of termination owing to the fault of the tenant, the latter is bound to pay the rental price during the time necessary for re-letting, without prejudice to damages which may have resulted from the abuse.*"[139] The wording "*the time necessary for re-letting*" is generally understood as "*the time objectively speaking as necessary for re-letting*", implying the necessity of reasonable mitigating measures to be taken by the landlord by seeking a new tenant.[140] Furthermore,

135 C. Dumoulin, *Tractatus de eo quod interest*, Cologne, Coloniae Agrippinae, 1598, www.bsb-muenchen-digital.de, 78, No. 61 ("*Quemadmodum ob culpam emptoris non debet obligatio venditoris aggravari, ita ob culpam emptoris non purgatur culpa venditoris.*").

136 Version: J. Domat, *Les loix civiles dans leur ordre naturel*, The Hague, Adrian Moetjens, 1703, books.google.be, 254 ("*si on pouvait avoir d'ailleurs d'autres voitures*").

137 R.J. Pothier, *Traité des obligations. Tome premier*, as re-edited by M. Siffrein, *Oeuvres de Pothier*, Paris, Didot l'ainé, 1821, gallica.bnf.fr, 190, No. 167.

138 Cass. 7 February 1946, *Pas.* 1946, I, 60; Cass. 8 May 1952, *Pas.* 1952, I, (570) 577; Cass. 17 May 2001, *Pas.* 2001, 889; Antwerp 10 April 2000, *Huur* 2000, 148; Brussels 19 September 2002, *RGAR* 2003, No. 13743; Brussels 20 December 2011, *TBH* 2012, 314; Ghent 29 October 1993, *TGR* 1994, 143, annotation I. Geers; Ghent 10 October 1997, *RW* 1999–00, 502; Liège 25 May 1990, *RRD* 1990, 507; Liège 4 April 1996, *JLMB* 1999, (5) 9; Liège 20 March 2001, *JLMB* 2001, (1698) 1701; Mons 29 June 1993, *JLMB* 1994, 61, annotation M. Vandermersch; Mons 4 December 2006, *JLMB* 2007, 357; Court of first instance Antwerp 26 February 1992, *TBBR* 1993, (401) 402; Court of first instance Bruges 16 May 2012, *Huur* 2012, 194, annotation S. Caeyers; Court of first instance Veurne 10 October 2007, *T.Verz.* 2008, 440.

139 Article 1760 CC states in French: "*En cas de résiliation par la faute du locataire, celui-ci est tenu de payer le prix du bail pendant le temps nécessaire à la relocation, sans préjudice des dommages et intérêts qui ont pu résulter de l'abus.*"

140 F. Laurent, *Principes de droit civil français*, XXV, Paris, Durand, 1877, 424, nr. 379 ("*La loi ne dit pas que le preneur doit payer le prix du bail jusqu'à ce que la chose soit relouée; elle restreint cette obligation au temps nécessaire à la relocation. Aller plus loin, c'eût été mettre le preneur à la merci du mauvais vouloir ou de la négligence du bailleur; celui-ci n'a aucun intérêt à relouer tant qu'il touche son prix.*); S. Stijns, K. Vanderschot and F. Vermander, "Schorsing en beëindiging van de huurovereenkomst naar gemeen

as regards insurance, a codification of that principle can also be found in Article 75 of the new Insurance Act (old Article 17 of the former Insurance Act of 1874 and old Article 20 of the former Insurance Act of 1992). For liability in general, the Belgian Court of Cassation accepted this principle in 1952, by ruling that the damages to be paid can be influenced by the mitigating steps taken by the victim.[141] In 2001, the same Court reiterated this principle in a contractual context on the basis of the requirement of performance in good faith (Article 1134 (3) CC). More specifically, it ruled that Article 1134 (3) CC requires the creditor to take reasonable measures in order to mitigate or limit his loss.[142]

58. Sources of inspiration for a new provision on the duty to mitigate – It seems logical that the most coherent approach would be to codify the well-established mitigation principle. A quick glance at neighbouring legal systems could be of great help when drafting this provision. The acceptance of the duty to mitigate is hardly an exclusively Belgian phenomenon. Article 1227 (2) of the Italian Civil Code could serve as a model provision: "*Compensation is not due for losses that the creditor could have avoided by using ordinary diligence.*"[143] Louisiana may take part in this competition, thanks to Article 2002 of its Civil Code: "*An obligee must make reasonable efforts to mitigate the damage caused by the obligor's failure to perform. When an obligee fails to make these efforts, the obligor may demand that the damages be accordingly reduced.*" Québec has a similar provision (Article 1479 CCQ).[144] In Spain, a proposal to reform the law of obligations and contracts of 2009 intends to head in a similar direction: "*No responderá el deudor del daño que el acreedor hubiera podido evitar o reducir adoptando para ello las medidas requeridas por la buena fe*".[145] For the common law, *British Westinghouse Electric Co Ltd v Underground Electric Rys* (1912) marked a milestone. In that case, Viscount Haldane LC highlighted a principle "*which imposes on a plaintiff the duty of taking all reasonable steps to mitigate the loss consequent on the breach, and debars him from claiming in respect of any part of the damage which is due to his neglect to take such*

recht" in M. Dambre, B. Hubeau and S. Stijns (eds.), *Handboek Algemeen Huurrecht*, Bruges, die Keure, 2006, (529) 585 ("De wederverhuringsvergoeding vergoedt de verhuurder voor het verlies aan huurgelden gedurende de periode die *nodig wordt geacht* om een nieuwe huurder te zoeken.").

141 Cass. 8 May 1952, *Pas.* 1952, I, (570) 577 ("*l'évaluation de la réparation par le juge peut être influencée par la circonstance que la victime, en raison de la carence de l'auteur responsable, a elle-même, antérieurement au jugement, procédé au remplacement de la chose dont elle fut dépouillée ou qu'elle a commis une négligence en n'y procédant pas*").

142 Cass. 17 May 2001, *Pas.* 2001, 889 ("*[...] l'article 1134, alinéa 3, du Code civil dispose que les conventions doivent être exécutées de bonne foi; [...] si cette règle n'impose pas au créancier de restreindre son dommage dans toute la mesure du possible, elle lui commande de prendre, avec loyauté, les mesures raisonnables qui permettent de modérer ou de limiter son préjudice.*").

143 Article 1227 (2) CCI states: "*Il risarcimento non è dovuto per i danni che il creditore avrebbe potuto evitare usando l'ordinaria diligenza.*"

144 Article 1479 CCQ states: "*La personne qui est tenue de réparer un préjudice ne répond pas de l'aggravation de ce préjudice que la victime pouvait éviter.*"

145 Comisión General de Codificación, "*Propuesta de Modernización del Código Civil en materia de Obligaciones y Contratos*", *Boletín de Información* 2009.

steps".[146] For the USA, that reasoning was later laid down in §350 of Second Restatement of Contracts: "*damages are not recoverable for loss that the injured party could have avoided without undue risk, burden, or humiliation*". Given the universal nature of the duty to mitigate, it is actually not surprising that this duty has also found its way into the international harmonization initiatives, such as the CISG (Article 77 CISG), the Unidroit Principles (Article 7.4.8), the PECL (Article 9:505), the DCFR (Article III.-3:705) and the CESL (Article 163 (1)).

59. Codification of the duty to mitigate (Article 1150–2 (1) CC) – How should the Belgian legislator enshrine that duty to mitigate and its consequences in a new provision? In a first paragraph the drafting committee could stress the obligation to mitigate loss as such. For this purpose, he could at first sight draw inspiration from Article 1710 of the new Argentinian Civil and Commercial Code, which states under the heading "duty to prevent losses" ("*deber de prevención del daño*") that everyone has the obligation, in accordance with the requirements of good faith and where appropriate, to take reasonable measures to avoid the occurrence or the aggravation of harm.[147] Should the Belgian legislator follow this example? The answer to this question is not in the affirmative inasmuch as he intends to follow recent academic developments. Under the influence of German civil law, Roman civil law acknowledges that the duty to mitigate is in fact an *Obliegenheit* (*incombance*) rather than a classical obligation.[148] For this specific reason, it seems more beneficial to phrase the new provision in a negative way while clearly stressing the possible repercussions of non-performance of this (creditor-free) *Obliegenheit*. In this regard, the Belgian legislator could take advantage of what the Union legislator laid down in the CESL. Article 163 CESL – which is entitled "Reduction of loss" – stipulates in its first paragraph: "*The debtor is not liable for loss suffered by the creditor to the extent that the creditor could have reduced the loss by taking*

146 *British Westinghouse Electric Co Ltd v Underground Electric Rys* [1912] AC 673, 689 ("*The first is that, as far as possible, he who has proved a breach of a bargain to supply what he contracted to get is to be placed, as far as money can do it, in as good a situation as if the contract had been performed. The fundamental basis is thus compensation for pecuniary loss naturally flowing from the breach; but this first principle is qualified by a second, which imposes on a plaintiff the duty of taking all reasonable steps to mitigate the loss consequent on the breach, and debars him from claiming in respect of any part of the damage which is due to his neglect to take such steps.*").

147 Article 1710 CCCA stipulates: "*Deber de prevención del daño. Toda persona tiene el deber, en cuanto de ella dependa, de [...] b) adoptar, de buena fe y conforme a las circunstancias, las medidas razonables para evitar que se produzca un daño, o disminuir su magnitud.*"

148 Belgium: M. Fontaine, "Le droit des contrats à l'écoute du droit comparé" in Y. Poulet, P. Wéry and P. Wynants (eds.), *Liber amicorum Michel Coipel*, Brussels, Kluwer, 2004, (301) 306 ("*L'"obligation" de plus en plus souvent reconnue à charge du créancier de minimiser le dommage, sous peine de ne pouvoir réclamer réparation du préjudice qu'il aurait pu éviter, relève également de l'incombance.*"); P. Wéry, "Mutations et défis du droit belge des obligations", *Rev.dr.ULg* 2015, (203) 212; K. Willems, *De natuurlijke verbintenis*, Bruges, die Keure, 2011, 19. France: A. Mettetal, "L'obligation de modérer le préjudice en droit privé français", *RRJ* 2005, (1889) 1934. Spain: J.P. Pérez Velázquez, "La carga de evitar o mitigar el daño derivado del incumplimiento del contrato", *InDret* 2015, (1) 21 ("*no se trata de una obligación jurídicamente exigible, sino de una carga – onere o eine blosse Obliegenheit – que tiene el acreedor [...]*").

reasonable steps." A first paragraph of a new Article 1150-2 CC could consequently state: "*The non-performing party is not liable for loss suffered by the victim of the breach of contract to the extent that this victim could have mitigated this loss by taking reasonable measures.*"

60. Possible criticism on the application of the avoidable loss rule – This is not the place to dwell too long on the extent of the non-recoverability of avoidable loss. Nonetheless, it should be pointed out that the so-called avoidable loss rule, according to which the aggrieved party is deprived of any entitlement to damages for loss he could reasonably have avoided, is increasingly under fire. To date, most legal systems follow that guiding principle. In Italy, for instance, Article 1227 (2) CCI states: "*Il risarcimento non è dovuto per i danni che il creditore avrebbe potuto evitare usando l'ordinaria diligenza.*" Probably influenced by a critical article written by the Austrian author Koziol (H. Koziol, "Rechtsfolgen der Verletzung einer Schadensminderungspflicht - Rückkehr der archaischen Kulpakompensation", *ZEuP* 1998, 593–601), the German Bundesgerichtshof advocated another approach by ruling: "*Die in der Literatur [...] vereinzelt vertretene Ansicht, dass der Geschädigte den vermeidbaren Schadensteil stets in vollem Umfang zu tragen habe [...] stellt überdies einen teilweisen Rückfall in das durch §254 BGB überwundene Alles-oder-nichts-Prinzip dar.*"[149] The avoidable loss rule thus implies a relapse to the so-called all-or-nothing approach. For the extra loss arising out of the non-compliance with the duty to mitigate, the victim of the breach loses his entire entitlement to compensation, even though that extra harm was also partially but definitely caused by the conduct of the non-performing party. In this regard, the legislator should bear in mind the aggrieved party's contribution to the fact giving rise to the loss does on the contrary not entirely debar him from his claim for damages, but does so only in proportion to his causal contribution. From that perspective, precluding a victim of any claim for damages for extra loss caused by the non-compliance with the duty to mitigate seems inconsistent.

61. Codification of the recoverability of expenses incurred in mitigating the loss – Complementary to the duty to mitigate is the recoverability of expenses which the aggrieved party made in mitigating this loss. When the victim of a breach of contract takes reasonable measures to mitigate the loss resulting from a breach of contract, he should definitely be provided with a claim to recover the expenses incurred in taking those measures. The non-performing party is obliged to reimburse those costs. He is the one benefiting from the mitigating steps undertaken by his contract partner. The Belgian Court of Cassation recognised this approach in 1985 by deciding: "*les frais exposés par le contractant lésé pour limiter ou éviter le dommage sont à charge du contractant en défaut d'exécuter*".[150]

149 Bundesgerichtshof 24 July 2001, *NJW DE* 2001, 3257.
150 Cass. 22 March 1985, *Pas.* 1985, I, 929, *RCJB* 1989, 7, annotation Kruithof.

62. Sources of inspiration for codification of the recoverability of expenses incurred in mitigating the loss (Article 1150-2 (2) CC) – The international harmonization initiatives also provide for this recoverability (Article 9:505 (2) PECL; Article III.-3:705 (2) DCFR; Article 163(2) CESL). Illustrative in this respect is Article III.-3:705 (2) DCFR, which states: "*The creditor is entitled to recover any expenses reasonably incurred in attempting to reduce the loss.*" The Dutch Article 6:96 (2) CC also looks influential: "*The following damages also qualify for compensation as material loss: reasonable costs to prevent or limit the loss which could be expected as a result of the event which makes someone liable.*"[151] The Catala and the Terré reform proposals rightly allowed the reimbursement of that type of costs.[152] Article 1344 of the Catala proposal stated: "*Expenses incurred in order to prevent the imminent occurrence of harm, to avoid its aggravation, or to reduce its consequences, constitute a reparable loss as long as they were reasonably undertaken.*"[153] The new French legal framework, however, falls short of codifying this compensation rule. This undoubtedly shows again that the French reform is, also in this regard, to be considered as a lost opportunity.

63. Contemplation of reasonable *attempts* to mitigate the loss – When finalising the drafting of Article 1150-2 (2) CC, the legislator should pay particular attention to another sensitive issue. In some cases, a victim takes what at the time seems to be a reasonable measure to mitigate his loss, but in fact he increases it. How should Belgian law deal with this situation? Whose interest should prevail? In the Czech Republic, §419 of the former Civil Code stipulated that anyone who avoids imminent loss is entitled to compensation of *usefully* spent costs.[154] This will probably remind Belgian legal scholars of Article 1375 of the Napoleonic Code, which limits the compensation to be awarded to the manager in case of *negotiorum gestio* (*gestion d'affaires*; "*management of business*") to "all the useful or necessary expenses" ("*dépenses utiles ou nécessaires*"). This is, however, no more than a false analogy, since management of business is not the legal basis for the duty to mitigate. To date, the duty to perform in good faith (Article 1134 (3) CC) takes up that task. As a consequence, the costs incurred by the victim in order to limit or to avoid extra losses should be covered by the principle of full compensation. The Czech legislator finally corrected that aberration in 2014 when adopting a new Civil Code. A new §2908 now enshrines the right of anyone who avoids imminent loss to reimbursement of expenses reasonably incurred.[155] Hence, compensation of losses incurred in mitigating the loss is not limited to those expenses

151 Article 6:96 (2) CC states in the Dutch version: "*Is vermogensschade komen mede voor vergoeding in aanmerking: redelijke kosten ter voorkoming of beperking van schade die als gevolg van de gebeurtenis waarop de aansprakelijkheid berust, mocht worden verwacht.*"

152 Article 121 (2) of the Terré proposal stated in French: "*Il en va de même si le créancier n'a point pris les mesures sûres et raisonnables, propres à éviter, à modérer ou à supprimer son préjudice. Le créancier sera remboursé de tous les frais raisonnablement engagés à cet effet.*"

153 Article 1344 of the Catala proposal stated in French: "*Les dépenses exposées pour prévenir la réalisation imminente d'un dommage ou pour éviter son aggravation, ainsi que pour en réduire les conséquences, constituent un préjudice réparable, dès lors qu'elles ont été raisonnablement engagées.*"

154 Translation based on: www.evropskyspotrebitel.cz/files/civil-code.pdf.

155 Translation based on: www.czechlegislation.com/en/89-2012-sb.

which lead to a positive outcome. The aggrieved party is entitled to reimbursement of his expenses if he took reasonable mitigating measures, even though they appeared to be useless afterwards.

64. Codification of contemplation of reasonable *attempts* to mitigate the loss (Article 1150–2 (2) CC) – For the common law, the American Second Restatement of Contracts stresses this principle in the second paragraph of §350: "*The injured party is not precluded from recovery [...] to the extent that he has made reasonable but unsuccessful efforts to avoid loss.*" How could the legislator implement this thought? Instructive to this end are the relevant provisions of the PECL (Article 9:505[156]) and the DCFR (Article III.-3:705). Article III.-3:705 (2) DCFR states: "*The creditor is entitled to recover any expenses reasonably incurred in attempting to reduce the loss.*" Any reasonable attempt or effort to reduce the loss appears to be sufficient for the entitlement to full compensation of expenses incurred. Taking due account of these findings, the second paragraph of Article 1150–2 CC could be phrased as follows: "*The victim of a breach of contract is, in accordance with Article 1149–1 (1), entitled to full compensation for the expenses he incurred in reasonably attempting to mitigate his loss.*"

4.4.3. Indirectness

65. Future of the directness limitation (current Article 1151 CC)? – A last step which the legislator could undertake is the abolition of Article 1151 CC. This Article currently contains the so-called directness limit. The French legislator reproduces this limitation on contractual damages in the new Article 1231–4: "*Even in the case where the non-performance of the contract is due to a intentional or gross fault, damages include only what is an immediate and direct consequence of the non-performance.*"[157] This directness limitation on contractual damages has, however, been totally hollowed out by the Belgian Court of Cassation. As a logical consequence, it never puts a real limit on the extent of contractual damages. By conceiving this Article as a mere expression of the theory of causal equivalence, the scope of the principle of full compensation was even broadened to indirect loss.[158] Abolitionists therefore rightly state that Article 1151 CC is no longer of any use.

66. Conclusion: abolition of the directness limitation (current Article 1151 CC) – The conclusion that Article 1151 CC should be abolished is wrongly not supported by the new French reform.[159] The abolition idea was nonetheless luckily embraced by the

[156] Article 9:505 (2) PECL states: "*The aggrieved party is entitled to recover any expenses reasonably incurred in attempting to reduce the loss.*"

[157] New Article 1231–4 CC states in French: "*Dans le cas même où l'inexécution du contrat résulte d'une faute lourde ou dolosive, les dommages et intérêts ne comprennent que ce qui est une suite immédiate et directe de l'inexécution.*"

[158] Cass. 24 June 1977, *Arr.Cass.* 1977, 1101, *RW* 1977–78, 775, *Pas.* 1977, I, 1087; Cass. 9 May 1986, *Pas.* 1986, I, 1100; Cass. 2 September 2004, *Arr.Cass.* 2004, 1271.

[159] The Terré proposal of 2009 also maintained the indirectness limit, in particular in Article 119.

Catala proposal. Article 1347 of the Catala proposal abolished the directness limit and recalled the causality requirement for contractual liability: "*Liability rests on a causal connection between an action attributable to the defendant and the loss.*"[160] Switzerland and the Netherlands abandoned this Napoleonic directness limitation in 1911 and 1992 respectively.[161] The international harmonization initiatives do not make use of any directness limit. The qualification of a type of loss as "indirect loss" is therefore irrelevant under the CISG, the Unidroit Principles, the PECL, the DCFR, and the CESL. The overall conclusion in this respect should hence be that Article 1151 CC is no longer useful.[162] As a replacement for Article 1151 CC, the legislator could set out a provision, common to contractual and non-contractual liability, pointing out the necessity of a causal link between the action attributable to the defendant and the loss. Such a provision is however related to the conditions of liability and should therefore not be incorporated in the chapter on the effects of liability. When drafting a provision on causality, the Belgian lawmaker could draw inspiration from the Catala proposal (Article 1347), which would without any doubt have provided a far better reform than the reform adopted in 2016.

5. Conclusion

67. The Belgian legislator should not follow the French reform as regards contractual damages – The overall conclusion is saturated in disappointment. The Belgian legislator clearly has to refrain from spiralling into the French reform, at least from the perspective of the quantification of contractual damages. The new provisions in that regard – and this is not glass-half-empty thinking – give rise to a fair amount of legitimate grounds of pessimism. It appears from the titles of recent articles – "*Le jour de gloire, est-il arrivé?*"[163] / "*Le nouveau droit des obligations est presque arrivé*"[164] – that some Belgian legal scholars seemed to be anxiously waiting for the new French contract law.[165] Regarding the measure of contractual damages, the new legal framework is verging on unmemorable. From the viewpoint of the measure of contractual damages, it still carries no more than the fingerprints of Napoléon's drafting committee.

68. There are potentially far more inspiring models for new provisions on the measure of damages for breach of contract – The Belgian legislator should

160 Article 1347 PC stated in the French version: "*La responsabilité suppose établi un lien de causalité entre le fait imputé au défendeur et le dommage.*"

161 Switzerland: J. Anex, *L'intérêt négatif, sa nature et son étendue*, Lausanne, Vaudoise, 1977, 117. Netherlands: Article 1284 CC as a reproduction of Article 1151 CCF.

162 J. Ronse and L. De Wilde, *Schade en schadeloosstelling*, Ghent, Story-Scientia, 1988, 171 ("Hierbij kan onderstreept worden hoe in moderne wetboeken de verwarrende splitsing van het schadebegrip in middellijke en onmiddellijke schade bewust werd verworpen.").

163 S. Van Loock, "De hervorming van het Franse verbintenissenrecht: Le jour de gloire, est-il arrivé?", *RW* 2014–15, 1562–1572.

164 S. Van Loock, "Hervorming van het Frans verbintenissenrecht uit de startblokken. Le nouveau droit des obligations est presque arrivé", *TBH* 2015, 619–622.

165 To some extent: E. Dirix and P. Wéry, "Pour une modernisation du Code civil", *JT* 2015, 625–626; P. Wéry, "Mutations et défis du droit belge des obligations", *Rev.dr.ULg* 2015, 203–230.

develop a new mindset of looking at less studied civil codes of Europe and far beyond.[166] The new French Civil Code is competing with much more persuasive models. Quite a few less examined new civil codes of Europe – Moldova (2002), Slovenia (2002), Romania (2011), Czech Republic (2014) and Hungary (2014) – could be vastly more inspiring.[167] In all fairness, its chief merit rests in the fact that it spurs the Belgian legislator to adopt a new Civil Code himself.[168] Despite more than two centuries of a happy marriage, this seems however the perfect moment for Napoléon's most loyal subjects[169] to say goodbye. Bearing this in mind, let damages specialists not waste time, money or energy on seminars on getting to know the French contract law reform. Belgian legal scholars could start focusing on other legal systems with a more persuasive legal framework, in order to make sure that one day their French counterparts can organise a series of seminars on getting to know the new Belgian Civil Code. The onus now rests on the Belgian legislator to proceed in a well-considered way when drafting provisions on damages. The following overview may somewhat help the legislator to face this challenge:[170]

Article 1149-1
Basic measure of damages for breach of contract

1. **Principle of full compensation.** The victim of a breach of contract is, in principle, entitled to full compensation of the loss incurred as a result of the non-performance.

166 On the rulings of the French Court of Cassation: S. Le Pautremat, "Mitigation of damage: a French perspective", *International and Comparative Law Quarterly* 2006, (205) 213 ("*One difficulty with the decisions of the Cour de cassation of 19 June 2003 is that they set French law apart from the approaches of other European countries, conventions regulating international trade and international principles of contract law.*").

167 On the necessity of looking at other legal systems of Europe: Comisión General de Codificación, "*Propuesta de Modernización del Código Civil en materia de Obligaciones y Contratos*", *Boletín de Información* 2009, (1) 11–12 (Spain: "*Una segunda finalidad, esta evidente, habrá de ser buscar la mayor aproximación posible del Derecho español a los ordenamientos europeos, tal y como estos son concebidos hoy. No es discutible que la existencia de diferencias no muy grandes entre unos y otros ordenamientos dentro de la Unión Europea, puede facilitar lo que reiteradamente se denominan operaciones transfronterizas. Y todo ello, en espera de una unificación de las normas de Derecho Europeo de Contratos que, en algún momento, podrá producirse.*").

168 E. Dirix and P. Wéry, "Pour une modernisation du Code civil", *JT* 2015, 625–626; D. Philippe, "Pour un nouveau Code civil?", *Justement*, 11 February 2015; S. Van Loock, "De hervorming van het Franse verbintenissenrecht: Le jour de gloire, est-il arrivé?", *RW* 2014–15, 1562–1572; S. Van Loock, "Hervorming van het Frans verbintenissenrecht uit de startblokken. Le nouveau droit des obligations est presque arrivé", *TBH* 2015, 619–622; P. Wéry, "Mutations et défis du droit belge des obligations", *Rev.dr.ULg* 2015, 203–230.

169 D. Heirbaut, "Napoleons trouwste onderdanen, of waarom de *Code civil* na tweehonderd jaar nog steeds overeind staat in België" in D. Heirbaut and G. Martyn (eds.), *Napoleons nalatenschap. Tweehonderd jaar Burgerlijk Wetboek in België*, Mechelen, Kluwer, 2005, 77–95; S. Van Loock, "De hervorming van het Franse verbintenissenrecht: Le jour de gloire, est-il arrivé?", *RW* 2014–15, (1562) 1569; S. Van Loock, "Hervorming van het Frans verbintenissenrecht uit de startblokken. Le nouveau droit des obligations est presque arrivé", *TBH* 2015, (619) 622.

170 More detailed provisions and more background can be found in my forthcoming doctoral thesis on the measure of damages for breach of contract.

2. **Date of assessment.** The court must assess the victim's loss as at the date of its judgment, taking into account all the circumstances which could affect its constituent elements, their value and its reasonably foreseeable future development.
3. **Target position.** The general measure of damages for breach of contract is such sum as will put the victim of a breach of contract, as nearly as possible, into the position in which he would have been if the contract had been performed. This general measure of damages also applies when that victim seeks termination for breach of contract.
4. **Compensation for loss, including lost profits and non-pecuniary loss.** Damages due to a victim of a breach of contract are, as a rule, for the loss which he has suffered, including non-pecuniary loss, as well as the profit which he has been deprived of. Compensation for non-pecuniary loss falls within the scope of the principle of full compensation as set out in paragraph 1. With due regard to the previous sentence, the seized court can assess non-pecuniary loss in conformity with the standards of reasonableness and fairness, as set out in Article 1149–3.
5. **Compensation for lost chances.** Damages due to a victim of a breach of contract can also cover the loss of a chance to obtain an advantage or to avoid a disadvantage. This compensation is due in proportion to the probability of its occurrence.

Article 1149–2

Subsidiary target position of the reliance interest

1. **Reliance interest.** Inasmuch as he encounters major difficulties in proving his expectation interest within the meaning of Article 1149–1 (3), the victim of a breach of contract can opt for protection of his reliance interest. This reliance interest aims at putting him in the position in which he would have been had the contract never been concluded.
2. **Extent.** This reliance interest allows recovery of both expenses made in preparation for performance or in performance and opportunities lost because of the conclusion of the contract.

Article 1149–3

Subsidiary possibility of equitable assessment

When damages are insusceptible of precise measurement, the assessment is at the discretion of the court.

Article 1149–4

Subsidiary possibility of gain-based assessment of damages

1. **Possibility of disgorgement of profits.** If a breach of contract is both material and opportunistic, the victim may request disgorgement of the profits realized by the non-performing party as a result of the breach of contract.
2. **Alternative for expectation damages.** Disgorgement of profits is an alternative to protection of the expectation interest within the meaning of Article 1149–1 (3), when those expectation damages do not offer adequate protection for the contractual claims of the victim of the breach of contract.

Article 1150-1
Unforeseeable loss

1. **Non-recovery of unforeseeable loss.** The non-performing party is not liable for losses which he did not or could not reasonably foresee at the date of the conclusion of the contract.
2. **Exception for intentional breaches of contract.** Paragraph 1, however, shall not apply in case of an intentional breach of contract.

Article 1150-2
Avoidable loss

1. **Non-recovery of avoidable loss.** The non-performing party is not liable for loss suffered by the victim of a breach of contract to the extent that this victim could have mitigated this loss by taking reasonable measures.
2. **Compensation for expenses incurred in reasonable mitigation efforts.** The victim of a breach of contract is, in accordance with Article 1149-1 (1), entitled to full compensation for the expenses he incurred in reasonably attempting to mitigate his loss.

Matthias E. Storme*

SET-OFF IN THE FRENCH REFORM OF THE LAW OF OBLIGATIONS: A TALE OF MISSED OPPORTUNITIES?

1. In this short paper, I would like to explain why the rules on set-off in the reformed French Civil Code (published 11 February 2016), are in many respects a missed opportunity to modernise the French law on that topic, even if some interesting innovations have taken place.

1. The role and definition of set-off

2. Whereas the old Code civil did classify set-off as a mode of extinction of obligations by its position in Chapter V (of Title III) entitled "*De l'extinction des obligations*", the new provisions start with an article containing a definition of set-off as the simultaneous extinction of reciprocal obligations between two parties (new Article 1347 CC).

3. First of all, it is unfortunate to add another definition instead of directly formulating the rule as the old Article 1289 CC did. Codes should contain as few definitions as possible; the task of codes is not to define things that are by their nature only instances of rules and not a description of facts; their task is to contain good, operative rules. Definitions only make sense in order to avoid having to repeat certain things over and over again in rules.[1]

4. Secondly, the definition is, as nearly all definitions in French codes, incomplete. It does not include the different elements and it does not spell-out the different roles of set-off. Modern doctrine stresses that set-off is not merely a mode of payment, i.e. extinction of obligations, but also a mode of getting paid, i.e. of enforcement of a right to payment and in anticipation thereof a security for the creditor. The security function of set-off is completely missing. If we turn e.g. to the EU Insolvency Regulation, that role is precisely

* Prof. ord. KU Leuven, director Institute for commercial and insolvency law.

1 Comp. my contribution "Une question de principe(s)? Réponse à quelques critiques à l'égard du projet provisoire de "Cadre commun de référence"", 9. *ERA-Forum* 2008 Supplement 1, p. S65 ff., also @ www.academia.edu/11544965/_Une_question_de_principe_s_R%C3%A9ponse_%C3%A0_quelques_critiques_%C3%A0_l_%C3%A9gard_du_projet_provisoire_de_Cadre_commun_de_r%C3%A9f%C3%A9rence.

stressed, esp. in consideration (70): "*If a set-off of claims is not permitted under the law of the State of the opening of proceedings, a creditor should nevertheless be entitled to the set-off if it is possible under the law applicable to the claim of the insolvent debtor. In this way, set-off would acquire a kind of guarantee function based on legal provisions on which the creditor concerned can rely at the time when the claim arises*".

5. The fact that the guarantee function is missing, goes together with the absence of any rules of property law in connection with set-off. However, when set-off is extinguishing two rights to performance, it affects two objects of incorporeal property (more precisely two rights to payment). There are a series of property law questions swept under the carpet by defining set-off as an extinction of obligations "between two persons" and adding that set-off "does not prejudice rights acquired by third parties", a vague principle without any further details (new Article 1347–7 CC). Yet, it is really not so difficult to formulate precise rules as to the property aspects of set-off, as we will try to demonstrate below (5.).

2. The requirements for set-off: failure to distinguish the requirements for the active and the passive claim

6. Modern doctrine of set-off, as well as modern codifications or statutes, deal separately with both rights to performance, thus distinguishing the "active" right and the "passive" right, i.e. the right on the basis of which the right to set-off is asserted *c.q.* the right against which the right to set-off is asserted.

This is also very clearly the case in European law, esp. conflicts of law. Thus, Article 17 of the Rome I Regulation stipulates that "*Where the right to set-off is not agreed by the parties, set-off shall be governed by the law applicable to the claim against which the right to set-off is asserted*", and Article 9 of the Insolvency-Regulation that: "*The opening of insolvency proceedings shall not affect the right of creditors to demand the set-off of their claims against the claims of a debtor, where such a set-off is permitted by the law applicable to the insolvent debtor's claim*".

Traditional French and Belgian doctrine does not make that distinction because it erroneously believes that the requirements for set-off are the same for the active and the passive right. To some extent, this is understandable given the rule that set-off automatically takes place when certain requirements are met, that in this perspective are largely the same for the active and passive claim.

3. Automatic set-off?

7. Where the old Article 1290 CC declared that set-off takes place automatically, by operation of law, when certain requirements are fulfilled, this expression is no longer found in the new CC. It follows basically, however, from the new Article 1347 II, stipulating that set-off takes place at the date at which the requirements are fulfilled.

Most other legal systems have introduced the rule that set-off does not take place by operation of law, but only when one of the parties invokes it. From a practical perspective, this rule clearly makes more sense. If no party invokes set-off, it is not relevant; French law tends to reply that when one party pays after that moment, it implies a waiver of the (already acquired) right to set-off.

8. Attacking the artificial character of the automatic set-off, however, may obscure the real question to be answered, namely whether a declaration of set-off by one of the parties has retrospective effect or not. The real meaning of the French rule is that the declaration of set-off has retrospective effect until the moment at which the requirements to declare set-off were met, and later circumstances (such as e.g. insolvency of the debtor of the passive claim, assignment of the passive claim) do not deprive it of its effects. The French rule is thus an understandable answer to explain an operative rule, be it that that operative rule could be construed in a more coherent way.

Alternative rules are not necessarily better formulated: they are right to stress that it makes no sense to recognise set-off when none of the parties invokes it, but do not always deal satisfactorily with the effect of set-off when circumstances such as those named have meanwhile taken place. Whether this is the case or not, mainly depends on the rules applied in case of insolvency of one of the parties before set-off has been declared.

In my view, the French rule should have been supplemented by a second possibility, recognising set-off by declaration as soon as the passive claim is, although not due, already payable. See *infra* 4.2, no. 16.

4. Obligational aspects and requirements

9. Before turning to the question how French law deals with the proprietary aspects of set-off – and how it should deal with them – we look at the purely obligational aspects: which requirements do the active and the passive claim have to meet?

As said, French law does still not distinguish both, and dictates the same requirements for both claims: bot should be fungible (*fongible*), ascertained (*liquide*) and due (*exigible*). See the new Article 1347–1 CC.

10. It is quite evident that both debts should be fungible (old Article 1291 CC and new Article 1347–1 CC), and it is good that the Code now explicitly states that set-off may take place between debts in different currencies, provided they are convertible (new Article 1347–1 II, compare a slightly different rule on this point in Article III-6:104 DCFR on foreign currency set-off).

The new CC contains also, as the old one, a reference to the rules on imputation of payments (old 1297 CC, new Article 1347–4 CC; comp. Article III-6:106 (2) DCFR).

11. The requirements do not apply to so-called connected debts or claims (see Article 1348–1 CC); here, the set-off is in reality based on the interdependency of reciprocal obligations, also expressed in the right to suspend performance (*exception d'inexécution*); set-off is merely a further practical remedy added to the right to suspend and giving a final solution.

4.1. *Requirements for the active claim*

12. According to the general rule, the active claim must also be ascertained (*liquide*). Where the active claim is disputed by the party opposing set-off (and in that sense not *liquide*), set-off cannot take place according to Article 1347–1 CC, but only be effected by judicial decision according to Articles 1348 and 1348–1 CC. Article III-6:103 DCFR is with good reason less strict in this regard.

13. It is a standard requirement that the active claim must be due; one cannot require payment by set-off of a claim that is not yet due. However, as in the old CC, a 'grace period' allowed by the judge to the debtor, does not prevent set-off (Article 1292 old CC and Article 1347–3 new CC).

14. The requirement is traditionally understood as excluding set-off when the active claim is prescribed (and thus no longer due).[2]

4.2. *Requirements for the passive claim*

15. Further, there is no reason why the passive claim should be ascertained (*liquide*) when its debtor – namely by definition the party invoking set-off – invokes or declares set-off. Such declaration implies a recognition of the debt.

16. There is also no reason to exclude set-off when the passive claim is not yet due, but already payable, i.e. when the debtor of that claim (the party invoking set-off) is not yet obliged to pay, but may do so (comp. Article III-6:102 (a) DCFR). This is the case whenever a term of payment is stipulated to the benefit of the debtor (as is presumed by Article 1305–3 (new) CC, old Article 1187 CC). In such case, the debtor of the passive claim may waiver the term and declare set-off. True, such an anticipated set-off does not take place automatically, but only by declaration. It is nevertheless a pity that this is not regulated in the Civil Code, as such a rule could clarify whether such a declaration would effect set-off ex nunc or retroact to the moment from which on the debtor could have declared set-off.

17. Finally, as in the old law (old Article 1293 CC), certain passive claims are protected against set-off, namely certain restitutionary claims (Article 1347–2 CC) such as a right to restitution of things borrowed, deposited or wrongfully dispossessed and rights incapable of being seized because of the protection of their owner (esp. maintenance rights, old Article 1293, 3° CC and new Article 1347–2 CC). Article III-6:108 DCFR is more restrictive in regard to restitutionary claims (merely right to restitution from intentional wrongful act), but the wider French rule is perfectly legitimate.

2 Comp.: prescription with a prescribed claim is not possible under Belgian law: Cass. 13 juni 2014, *Immobilière Christiaens*, nr. C.11.0595.F, jure.juridat.just.fgov.be/pdfapp/download_blob?idpdf=N-2014 0613-3 = *RW* 2014–15, 1543.

18. The new rules do not clarify on the other hand whether other rights can be made incapable of set-off (protected against set-off) in advance by agreement (whereas they do clarify the autonomy of the parties in the opposite sense: Article 1348–2 CC allows the parties to agree in advance on set-off in cases where the conditions for set-off by operation of law are not fulfilled); there is, however, no reason to doubt that this is in principle possible, too (comp. DCFR Article III-6:108 (a)).

5. Property law aspects

19. No lawyer having a reasonable knowledge of French private law and one or more other legal systems will be surprised by the fact that the new CC deals with the proprietary aspects of set-off merely in a vague and indirect way; this is true for property law in general in the Civil Code, and especially for the property law of intangibles. As in the old CC, also in the new one the matter of assignment, e.g., is treated purely as a matter of the law of obligations, and proprietary questions are hidden behind rules on 'opposability' and dealt with only very fragmentarily. The same is true in relation to set-off, although set-off is clearly also a proprietary operation whereby a creditor seizes or at least uses a right of its debtor (the passive claim) to pay himself (or discharges his own debt by giving up his active right).

5.1. Requirements for the active claim

20. The DCFR (Article III-6:102) clarifies that a party can only declare set-off when it has authority to dispose over the active claim; indeed a set-off implies a waiver or disposition over that claim (that is used to pay one's debt). In the new French CC, this requirement is hidden behind the vague rule of Article 1347–7 new CC, namely that set-off cannot prejudice the rights of third parties. The latter rule is too general, as only third parties who have a right in the active claim (or the passive claim, *infra* 2.) should be protected. Further, French law has still not really developed the concept of authority to dispose, now well-known even in Belgian law. It is true, that the lack or restriction of authority to dispose always corresponds to some extent with a right of a third party protected by this lack of authority, but it is nevertheless very useful to have such a concept.

5.2. Requirements for the passive claim

21. As set-off includes also an execution in the passive claim, a way for a party to pay oneself with the passive claim, it is in principle required that the passive claim belongs to the estate or patrimony on which that party has recourse, thus in principle in the patrimony of the debtor, and that the claim is also capable of seizure or attachment. The new French CC, as the old one, explicitly mentions this latter requirement, now in Article 1347–2 CC (mentioning as exception the consent of the creditor of that claim). The text does, however, not clarify that this is relevant only for the passive claim.

22. The DCFR more generally requires that a creditor can only set-off its (active) right against a (passive) right of the other party, if that party has equally the authority to dispose of the (passive) claim (Article III-6:102). The requirement could be formulated more precisely by stating that the other party must have the authority to collect the claim and do so on own account. The French CC on the other hand has only the much vaguer rule that set-off cannot prejudice the rights of third parties (Article 1347–7 new CC).

Here, again this does not clarify in which cases a third party is protected. As said, the correct rule is that set-off can no longer take place when the other party does no longer have the authority to collect the claim on its own account. Article 1324 II new French CC clarifies that in case of assignment set-off can take place until the assignment is notified to or recognised by the party invoking set-off. This indeed corresponds with the idea that the assignor has authority to collect the assigned claim as long as the assignment is not notified to or recognised by the debtor. It would have been clearer if the rule were also clarified in other cases where a third party acquires a right in the passive claim (this was done in Article 1346–5 CC in relation to personal subrogation). It shows at least that the rule of Article 1347–7 new CC is too vague.

Another case where it could have been clarified which rights of third parties are protected against set-off, is the case of trust accounts or similar situations where the creditor of the passive claim has acquired the claim in its own name but for the account of a third party. The creditor of the active claim, such as e.g. the financial institution where the account is held, cannot invoke set-off with a claim against the holder of such trust account personally.

23. Despite the acquisition of rights in the passive claim by a third party, the debtor of that claim is still able to declare set-off with an active claim that is reciprocal or at least sufficiently connected with the passive claim. Again, this rule can be found for the case of assignment in the new Article 1324 II CC, but it is a more general rule deduced from the right to suspend performance of reciprocal or sufficiently connected debts (in the case of contractual obligations the *exceptio non adimpleti contractus*), right that can also be invoked against the assignee or other acquirer of the passive claim.

24. As to the important question whether set-off is still possible after the passive claim has been seized by another creditor of its owner, or after the opening of insolvency proceedings against that owner, the new CC is saying even less than the old one (leaving it to separate statutes on insolvency proceedings to regulate the matter).

25. The old Article 1298 CC stated that the debtor of a seized (passive) claim who acquired a right against the (insolvent) owner of that claim *after* the seizure cannot set-off. This seems nevertheless to have been understood *contra legem*, in the sense that set-off was excluded even if the active claim was acquired before the seizure or insolvency, but not yet due at that moment (again except in case of connected claims).

The new CC, however, does not indicate in any way whether the creditors of the owner of a passive claim are protected against set-off as acquirers of a right in the claim in case of seizure before the requirements for set-off by operation of law were met.

26. The effect on set-off of other insolvency proceedings than seizure, is as said regulated in special statutes (*Code de Commerce* for businesses insolvency, *Code de la consommation* for consumer insolvency). On the basis of these rules, set-off is traditionally excluded if the requirements are not met before the opening of the insolvency proceeding, though both claims did already exist at that moment, again with the exception of connected claims.

The new French law resists the clear tendency in modern law to allow set-off after insolvency where both claims were already in existence at the opening of the proceedings, even if they are not yet both due. The EU Collateral Directive imposes this solution, be it only within the limited scope of application *ratione materiae* of the Directive (see Article 7 *iuncto* the definition in Article 2 I n). The reform misses the opportunity to generalise this sound rule.

27. Finally, the new Article 1348–2 does neither clarify the proprietary effects of a netting agreement or contractual set-off.

Article 7 of the EU Collateral directive states that (again within the limited scope of application *ratione materiae* of the Directive) "*Member States shall ensure that a close-out netting provision can take effect in accordance with its terms: (a) notwithstanding the commencement or continuation of winding-up proceedings or reorganisation measures in respect of the collateral provider and/or the collateral taker; and/or (b) notwithstanding any purported assignment, judicial or other attachment or other disposition of or in respect of such rights*".

In the German, Dutch and – majority of – Belgian doctrine, a valid agreement between a creditor and debtor relating to the content of their relationship is binding upon third parties acquiring rights in one of the claims after that agreement. Any netting agreement relating to nominative claims should in that respect have proprietary effect. The French position in this regard was not clear under the old CC and remains unclear under the new CC.

Chantal Mahé

FUNDAMENTAL RIGHTS IN THE FRENCH CONTRACT LAW REFORM

Abbreviations

Af.	Aforementioned
Ass. Plén.	The Plenary Assembly of the *Cour de cassation*
Bull. civ.	Bulletin civil
Cass.	Cour de cassation
Civ. 1e	The First Civil Chamber of the *Cour de cassation*
Civ. 3e	The Third Civil Chamber of the *Cour de cassation*
C. civ.	Code civil
Com.	The Commercial Chamber of the *Cour de cassation*
Cons. Consti.	France's *Conseil Constitutionnel*
ECHR	European Convention on Human Rights
ECtHR	European Court of Human Rights
Nr.	Number
Par.	Paragraph
Soc.	The Social Chamber of the *Cour de cassation*

1. Introduction

On 10 February 2016, the French Government's *ordonnance* (hereafter: the 2016 *ordonnance*), leading to a comprehensive revision of Book III of the 1804 Civil Code on general contract law, was published in the *Journal Officiel*.[1] The new statutory rules should come into force on 1 October 2016,[2] without the First and the Second Chambers having either amended or adopted each single provision of the revised Book III, following lengthy and stormy debates. In February 2015, the Chambers entrusted the Government

1 *Ordonnance* nr. 2016-131 dated 10 February 2016 and entitled '*ordonnance (…) portant réforme du droit des contrats, du régime général et de la preuve des obligations*', *Journal Officiel de la République Française*, 11 février 2016, Texte 26, NOR: JUSC1522466R.

2 Art. 9 *ordonnance* nr. 2016-131 provided that the Parliament ratifies the text of *ordonnance* nr. 2016-131.

with the overall reform of French general contract law.[3] With this reform project, the French Government, more precisely the Ministry of Justice, pursued two major objectives, namely the strengthening of legal security and accessibility (respectively readability) of French contract law.[4] General contract law is currently overwhelmingly case law based. As even the Government itself has observed, French general contract law is on many issues rather unsystematic and unclear, at least for French laymen and foreign legal observers.[5] Regarding legal security, governmental drafters opted for a *codification à droit constant*,[6] which, besides continuity of the law, secures the French legal community's agreement to the revision of Book III of the Civil Code.

The final version of Book III as enacted by the 2016 *ordonnance* was preceded by several governmental drafts, the latest being the 2013 draft *ordonnance*.[7] The 2013 draft *ordonnance* was published and later submitted to public consultation by the Ministry of Justice, and was also translated into English.[8] The 2013 draft version of Book III and the 2016 *ordonnance* differ from each other. Some early comments already refer to the more conservative nature of the 2016 *ordonnance*.[9] One of the changes between the 2013 draft and the 2016 *ordonnance* is worth singling out, since it concerns the general principles of contract law, specifically the freedom of contract and one of its opposites, fundamental rights and liberties (hereafter: FR). While Article 1102 of the 2013 draft *ordonnance* (hereafter: Article 1102 D.O.) dealt with interpersonal effects of fundamental rights and freedoms within the contractual sphere, this issue has totally disappeared from the corresponding Article 1102 of the revised Civil Code (hereafter: Article 1102 C. civ. rev.). Article 1102 C. civ. rev. states the following:

> "Everyone is free to contract or not to contract, to choose the person with whom to contract, and to determine the content and form of the contract, within the limits imposed by legislation.

3 See Delegation Act no 2015–177 dated 16 February 2015 and entitled 'Loi (…) relative à la modernization et à la simplification du droit et des procédures dans les domaines de la justice et des affaires intérieures' *Journal Officiel de la République Française*, 17 février 2015, Texte 1, NOR: JUSX1326670L. In Art. 8 of Delegation Act nr. 2015–177, the Parliament delegated to the Government the task to reform Book III of the Civil code, who then proceeded to the reform by way of *ordonnance*, in accordance with the objectives set out by the Parliament in Delegation Act no 2015–177.

4 As article 8 of Delegation Act no 2015–177.

5 'Rapport au Président relatif à l'*ordonnance* no 2016–131 du 10 février 2016 portant réforme du droit des contrats, du régime général et de la preuve des obligations', *Journal Officiel de la République Française*, 11 février 2016, Texte 25, NOR: JUSC1522466P, p. 2–3.

6 Ibid.

7 Available at www.justice.gouv.fr/publication/j21_projet_ord_reforme_contrats_2015.pdf (last consulted on 15 March 2016).

8 *Draft ordonnance for the reform of the law of contract, the general regime of obligation, and proof of obligation*, Translation of the proposed new text by J. Cartwright, B. Fauvarque-Cosson and S. Whittaker, available at www.textes.justice.gouv.fr/art_pix/Draft-*ordonnance*-for-the-Reform-of-the-Civil-Codepdf.pdf (latest version dated 30 March 2016).

9 See M. Mignot, Commentaire article par article de l'*ordonnance* du 10 février 2016 portant réforme du droit des contrats, du régime général et de la preuve des obligations (I), *Petites affiches*, 26 février 2016 nr. 41, p. 8 ff.

> However, this contractual freedom does not allow the parties to derogate from rules which are an expression of public policy."[10]

By contrast, Article 1102 D.O. adds that freedom of contract does not allow a party

> "to infringe fundamental rights and freedoms recognized by a provision which applies to relationships between private parties, except where such infringement is indispensable to the protection of legitimate interests and proportionate to the intended purpose".[11]

Although both provisions spell out the principle of freedom of contract using exactly the same wording, they depart dramatically from each other as regards the limits they subsequently impose on contractual freedom. In line with Article 6 of the 1804 Civil Code (hereafter: Article 6 C. civ.), Article 1102 C. civ. rev. opts for a more conservative approach by only referring to public policy rules as a limit to contractual freedom whilst refraining from addressing the issue of interpersonal effects of FR. By contrast, Article 1102 D.O. prohibits a party from exercising its contractual freedom in such a way as to violate the other party's FR. It thereby clearly differentiates between the two categories of infringement, public policy and FR. With regard to the legal regime of both categories, derogation from public policy rules is prohibited, whereas a party's FR may be infringed provided that specific requirements are fulfilled. However, the reference in Article 1102 D.O. to FR "recognized by a provision which applies to relationships between private parties", limits its scope of application to contractual infringements of FR that are implemented into private law. But Article 1102 D.O. did not reach the finishing line. As a consequence, given that the revised Civil Code does not address that issue, the current (case) law on contractual infringements of FR retains its full authority.

Yet looking at current French law on contractual infringements of FR left unchanged by the revised Civil Code leads one to wonder why relinquishing Article 1102 D.O. took precedence over amending it, bearing in mind the Government's general objectives to strengthen legal security and accessibility of contract law rules. Current contract law forbids contractual violation of public policy rules (Article 6 C. civ.), but lacks a *general clause* prohibiting contractual infringements of FR (par. 2). Instead, the issue is dealt with in special enacted law (for example labour code) and case law. The ensuing overall picture is rather fragmented. Interpersonal effects of FR within the contractual area depend on the particular FR at stake. Freedom of religion for example is treated differently compared to other FR. Furthermore, the consequences of contractual infringements of FR remain

10 See fn 13 regarding the English translation of the French expression '*ordre public*'.

11 Draft *ordonnance* as translated by J. Cartwright, B. Fauvarque-Cosson and S. Whittaker, see fn 7. The French version of Art. 1102 D.O. reads:
"Chacun est libre de contracter ou de ne pas contracter, de choisir son cocontractant et de déterminer le contenu et la forme du contrat dans les limites fixées par la loi.
Toutefois, la liberté contractuelle ne permet pas de déroger aux règles qui intéressent l'ordre public, ou de porter atteinte aux droits et libertés fondamentaux reconnus dans un texte applicable aux relations entre personnes privées, à moins que cette atteinte soit indispensable à la protection d'intérêts légitimes et proportionnée au but recherché".

unsettled due to the differing case law of the several Chambers within the *Cour de cassation* (par. 3). The ensuing legal uncertainty clearly pleads in favour of codification, in particular with regard to the general goals targeted by the reform (par. 4). In contrast to these gaps and inconsistencies, convergences can nevertheless be detected. Enacted and case law have the common view that fundamental rights have interpersonal effects and yet are not absolute.[12]

2. The non-codification of a general clause on contractual infringements of any FR

The 2016 *ordonnance* restricts the parties' contractual freedom by prohibiting contractual violations of public policy rules,[13] but this prohibition does not extend to contractual infringements of parties' FR. As a result, the interpersonal effects of FR within the contractual area will not gain ultimate recognition through codification. However, neither French case law nor French enacted law are unfamiliar with the horizontal effects of FR.[14] Given the state of positive contract law, this codification strategy deprives French revised contract law of a general clause on contractual infringements of FR, which would have been common to *all types of contracts* (2.1) and would have applied *regardless of the fundamental rights and liberties involved* (2.2). Another outcome of the Government's sudden volte-face is the upholding of the *direct* effects of FR within contractual relations, as developed in case law (2.3).

2.1. The abandoning of a general clause common to all types of contracts

The principle of freedom of contract is not explicitly dealt with in the 1804 Civil Code. However, Article 6 C. civ. imposes a clear limit on the parties' contractual freedom by prohibiting them from violating public policy rules, these being rules from which parties may not derogate by way of contract.[15] Not surprisingly, the *Code civil* contains no

12 Provided that such infringement is indispensable to the protection of legitimate interests of the infringing party and is proportionate to that purpose, as also provided in Art. 1102 D.O.

13 Article 6 C. civ. states that "One may not by private agreement derogate from *laws that concern public order and good morals*" (ital. added). Translation available at https://www.legifrance.gouv.fr/Traductions/en-English/Legifrance-translations. This official translation of Art. 6 C. civ. translates the French expression *ordre public* with the terms 'public order', thus not with the wordings 'public policy' like Cartwright, Fauvarque-Cosson and Whittaker do in their translation of Art. 1102 D.O. Here, both expressions will be used.

14 With regard to the effects of FR in interpersonal relationships in French private law, see for example J.P. Marguénaud e.a., *L'influence de la jurisprudence de la Cour Européenne des droits de l'homme sur le droit privé français,* Observatoire des Mutations Institutionnelles et Juridiques, Limoges, 1999; J. Raynaud, *Les atteintes aux droits fondamentaux dans les actes juridiques privés,* Th. Univ. Limoges, 2001, B. Moutel, *L'"effet horizontal" de la Convention Européenne des Droits de l'Homme en droit privé français,* Th. Univ. Limoges, 2006, L. Maurin, *Contrat et droits fondamentaux*, Paris: L.G.D.J. 2013 (Th. Univ. Aix-Marseille Paul Cézanne, 9 décembre 2011, dir. E. Putman).

15 Art. 6 C. civ. prohibits the violation of rules pertaining to public policy and good morals. Because Art. 6 C. civ. is part of the Civil code's Preliminary Title, the scope of application of this prohibition therefore reaches beyond the sole field of contract law.

general limitation of the contractual freedom of parties, on the basis of fundamental rights and freedoms, as Book III has remained almost unchanged since 1804. Yet, several of the Code's provisions are dedicated to a specific fundamental right, the basis on which contractual infringements of FR are assessed, for example Article 9 C. civ. (right to private life) or Article 544 C. civ. (right to property).[16] In its rulings, the *Cour de cassation* referred to both Article 6 and 544 C. civ. as a combined ground for sanctioning a contractual infringement of a party's constitutional right to property.[17] The Highest Court's case law on contractual infringement of FR nevertheless reveals the Court's parsimonious use of Article 6 C. civ. in that context.

The *Cour de cassation* also did not rule in general terms that a clause in any type of contract that violates any FR of a contracting party is deemed to have no legal effect. Its decisions firstly relate to the type of contract under deliberation.

The Civil Code's silence on contractual infringements of FR contrasts with their prohibitions through legislation – outside of the 1804 *Code civil* – regarding specific contracts, for example labour contracts and housing rental contracts. Article L1121-1 of the French Labour Code provides that

> "No one can impose restrictions on human rights nor on individual and collective liberties, which are not justified by the nature of the task to be fulfilled, nor proportionate to the goal these restrictions pursue" (CM transl.).[18]

Act no. 89-462 on housing rental relations also declares the right to housing to be a fundamental right.[19] That Act further regards provisions in a house rental contract which infringe upon the lessee's right to exercise his political or religious freedom, or the lessee's right to (respect for) private and family life, as being invalid.[20] Both the French Labour Code and the Housing Rental Act contain a series of anti-discrimination provisions forbidding violations of an employee's, and respectively a lessee's, fundamental right to equal treatment.[21]

16 Art. 544 C. civ. on the right to property, which since 1982 has enjoyed the status of fundamental right, provides that "Ownership is the right to enjoy and dispose of things in the most absolute manner, provided they are not used in a way which is prohibited by statutes or regulations", see www.legifrance.gouv.fr/Traductions/Catalogue-des-traductions. Art. 9 C. civ. states that: "*Chacun a droit au respect de sa vie privée. Les juges peuvent, sans préjudice de la réparation du dommage subi, prescrire toutes mesures, telles que séquestre, saisie et autres, propres à empêcher ou faire cesser une atteinte à l'intimité de la vie privée: ces mesures peuvent, s'il y a urgence, être ordonnées en référé*".

17 See section 2.3.2 below.

18 The French version is as follow: "*Nul ne peut apporter aux droits des personnes et aux libertés individuelles et collectives de restrictions qui ne seraient pas justifiées par la nature de la tâche à accomplir ni proportionnées au but recherché*".

19 Article 1 of Act nr. 89-462 provides that: "Le droit au logement est un droit fondamental; il s'exerce dans le cadre des lois qui le régissent."

20 Article 4 of Act nr. 89-462 declares any housing rental clauses to be invalid (*non écrite*):
"j) Qui interdit au locataire l'exercice d'une activité politique, syndicale, associative ou confessionnelle; (...)
n) Qui interdit au locataire d'héberger des personnes ne vivant pas habituellement avec lui; (...)".

21 See for example Art. L1132-1 and following of the Labour Code and Article 1, 3rd par. of Act nr. 89-462.

Conclusively, although French legislation on certain contracts, as well as general contract case law, recognise the interpersonal effects of fundamental rights and liberties, the resulting prohibition of the contractual infringements of FR is nevertheless sectorial, as it is limited to certain contracts only. In that context, departing from Article 1102 D.O., which was designed to cover all contractual relationships without distinction frustrates a systematic legal approach to the issue. This potentially jeopardises legal security which the reform of Book III of the *Code civil* aims to reinforce, as well as the accessibility of the rule of law, and eventually the protection that FR offer.

2.2. *The departure from a general clause common to all fundamental rights*

Again, French (both general and specific) contract law contains limited provisions on which basis contractual infringements of FR can be tackled, these provisions also lack a general scope because they only concern certain FR. For example, prohibition according to Article 4 of Act nr. 89–462 of contractual infringements of FR is not only limited to the type of contract it covers (housing rental), but also to the FR concerned (e.g. right to family life).[22] A look at the *Cour de cassation*'s case law further brings to light the Court's varying treatment of fundamental rights and liberties, especially that of the freedom of religion.

In a 1978 decision by the *Cour de cassation* on the interpersonal effects of freedom of religion, the question under consideration was whether the firing of a teacher for religious motives was an abuse.[23]

> The employee was fired following her divorce and remarriage. Her employer, a Catholic school, put forward the school's adherence to the doctrine of the indissolubility of marriage, and invoked the employee's non-respect of the school's religious belief as a justification for the dismissal. The employee subsequently claimed higher damages, asserting the abusive nature of her sacking as it infringed her fundamental freedom of the right to marriage. The Court of Appeal (hereafter: CoA) observed that at the time of the conclusion of the employment contract, the teacher's religious beliefs were taken into account. The CoA derives from this circumstance that religious beliefs thus became an 'essential and decisive element' of the employment contract, and for that reason alone belonged to the contract content. As a result, it did not consider the dismissal, based on the breach of a *contractual* duty of abidance to a religious doctrine, as being abusive.

Having stressed that religious beliefs 'usually fall outside of labour relationships', the Highest Court, in Plenary Assembly, affirmed that parties may nevertheless willingly incorporate religious beliefs into their contract. The *Cour de cassation* subsequently confirmed the CoA's decision that the incorporation of religious beliefs into the contract, which imposed abidance by a religious doctrine on the employee, acquitted the dismissal of any abusive nature.[24]

22 See fn. 19.

23 Cour de cassation, Assemblée Plénière, 19 mai 1978, nr. 76–41211, *Bull. civ.* Ass. Plén. 1978, nr. 1, p. 1.

24 The restrictions on the employee's freedom of the right to marriage imposed by the school's religious beliefs were not considered abusive, as they were contractually embedded.

Two decades later,[25] the Highest Court's Social Chamber set forth this line of reasoning. In the 1998 case, it was by contrast the employee's freedom of religion which was at stake. In the Court's view, the non-incorporation of his religious beliefs into the contract made the employee's dismissal exempt from any abusive nature.

After eight years of employment, a Muslim supermarket employee was assigned to the butcher's counter. When he discovered he could come into contact with pork, the employee asked his employer if he could switch departments, upon explaining that his current post was not compatible with his religious beliefs. The employer rejected this request. The employee, appealing to his religious beliefs, refused to start work again and was subsequently fired. According to the CoA, the employer's rejection contravened his duty to respect his employee's religious beliefs. The CoA's decision was yet to be quashed.

Although the *Cour de cassation* acknowledges that an employer must respect his employees' religious beliefs, the Court attaches that duty to the more general obligation of employers to respect their employees' private life. Except when the employment contract expressly provides otherwise, religious beliefs, invoked here by the employee, remain outside of the contractual employee/employer relation.[26] Later legislative labour law reform would nevertheless overturn the Court's ruling.[27]

However, as later case law reveals, in relation to *other* contractual relations the Highest Court still abides to the line of reasoning it embarked on in 1978. In a 2002 ruling concerning a housing rental contract, the Court's Third Chamber reiterated that unless otherwise stipulated in the rental contract, religious beliefs of the lessee fall outside of its scope.[28]

The conflict in question here concerned a lessor, an investment company owning several buildings, which was renting apartments in these buildings to several Jewish lessees. The owner placed power door locks on all entries to these buildings, rendering the few mechanical door locks which were still in place unusable. The lessees asked the lessor to enable access through all building entrances using mechanical door locks, invoking their religious beliefs forbidding them to use powered objects on the Sabbath, and other Jewish holy days. The CoA – as in the 1998 decision – acceded to the lessees claim on the grounds that the lessor, by rejecting the lessees' request, infringed the latter's freedom of religion, which, as the CoA points out, is guaranteed by both the constitutional and conventional FR. In spite of this, the *Cour de cassation* once again quashed the CoA's decision.

25 Cass. Soc., 24 mars 1998, nr. 95–44738, *Bull. civ.* 1998 V, nr. 171.

26 Cass. Soc., 24 mars 1998, af.: "*S'il est exact que l'employeur est tenu de respecter les convictions religieuses de son salarié, celles-ci, sauf clause expresse, n'entrent pas dans le cadre du contrat de travail (...)*".

27 See prev. Art. L. 1121–1 Labour Code cited in section 2.1.

28 Cass. Civ. 3e, 18 décembre 2002, nr. 01–00519, *Bull. civ.* 2002 III, nr. 262, p. 227.

Unlike in its 1998 decision, the Highest Court first referred to Article 1134 C. civ. (*pacta sunt servanda* principle),[29] and subsequently reaffirmed the standard that, unless stipulated otherwise in the rental contract, the lessee's religious beliefs play no part in the contract. As a consequence, the Court's Third Chamber added, 'practices dictated by the lessees' religious beliefs (...) do not impose any new specific obligation on the lessor' (transl. CM).[30] Due to this latter addition, some authors tend to present the Court's decision as primarily affirming that FR do not insert new obligations into a contract that parties have not provided for.[31] Still, the Highest Court's different wordings in fact conceal the transparent extension to housing rental contracts of the Court's prior differing treatment of infringements of the freedom of religion. As, in the *Cour de cassation*'s view, the religious beliefs of parties primarily remain outside of the contractual sphere, FR may logically not impose 'new obligations' on contracting parties.[32] By contrast, the respect for parties' other FR, for instance the right to work, does not require parties to draw it explicitly into the contract, because parties may directly invoke an FR in proceedings against a contracting party before the *national* judge.[33] As a result, obligations deriving from respect for a contracting party's FR, other than freedom of religion, are not 'new' but are implied contractual obligations.

Four years later,[34] the same Chamber extended its different handling of contractual infringement of freedom of religion further to condominium rules, which, under French law, form a contract.

> A Jewish couple owning an apartment in a condominium built a temporary hut made of branches on their balcony, for the limited duration of the celebration of the Sukkot holy days. The co-owners of the apartment building demanded that the hut be immediately removed on the grounds that placing wooden constructions (as well as other objects) on the balconies of the building was forbidden by condominium rules. In response the couple claimed, in reference to Article 9 C. civ., that the condominium rules violated their right to the respect for private life, and respectively the duty to respect their religious beliefs. The CoA of Aix-en-Provence confirmed the judgment, ordering the hut to be removed.

Again, according to the *Cour de cassation*, the legal question under consideration was whether the contracting parties had willingly included the freedom of religion within the ambit of their contract, which they in fact had not. The Highest Court confirmed the

29 In addition to that reference, the Court further mentioned Art. 9 ECHR (freedom of religion): "*Vu l'article 1134 du Code civil, ensemble les articles 9-1 et 9-2 de la Convention européenne de sauvegarde des droits de l'homme et des libertés fondamentales et l'article 6 a et c de la loi du 6 juillet 1989*", in Cass. civ. 3e, 18 décembre 2002.

30 Cass. Civ. 3e, 18 décembre 2002: '*les pratiques dictées par les convictions religieuses des preneurs (...) ne font naître à la charge du bailleur aucune obligation spécifique*'.

31 See for example B. Fages, *Droits des obligations*, L.G.D.J.:Paris, 2015, par. 167.

32 For instance, a 'new' obligation for the lessor to periodically maintain the lessee's access to his apartment via the existing mechanical door locks.

33 See section 2.3.2 below.

34 Cass. Civ. 3e, 8 juin 2006, nr. 05-14774, *Bull. civ.* 2006 III, nr. 140, p. 115.

CoA's decision by reinstating once more that the starting point is that religious freedom, despite its fundamental character, does not yet belong to the contractual domain.

Many authors expressed criticism towards France's Highest Court's reluctance to break away from its traditional treatment of contractual infringements of a party's freedom of religion.[35] Furthermore, the *Cour de cassation*'s handling of religious beliefs strikingly contrasts with its concomitant rulings concerning other fundamental rights and liberties, the latter receiving direct application in private legal disputes involving contracts. Yet, notwithstanding the renewed criticisms from the doctrine and the resistance of several CoAs,[36] the Highest Court did not change its attitude.

The Court's case law is in clear contradiction to the ECtHR's Article 9 ECHR case law.[37] In pursuance of its general legal security objective, the Government missed, by departing from instead of amending Article 1102 D.O., an opportunity to overrule the *Cour de cassation*'s case law with the introduction of a general clause ensuring a uniform assessment of fundamental rights infringements, regardless of the FR and the type of contract involved.

2.3. *Upholding direct horizontal effects of FR in the contractual context*

By removing any reference to fundamental rights from Article 1102 C. civ. rev. (freedom of contract), the French Government arbitrated the conflict opposing those supportive of the *direct* interpersonal application of fundamental rights to those advocating their *indirect* horizontal effects (Article 1102 D.O.).[38] The Government settled this controversy in favour of the former. The approach of the drafters of Article 1102 D.O., which conditions interpersonal effects of FR to their incorporation in a private law rule, is abandoned (section 2.3.1). This entails the furtherance of the *Cour de cassation*'s case law, which has consistently affirmed the direct application of FR to contractual relationships (section 2.3.2).

35 See for example D. Fenouillet, 'Règlement de copropriété et liberté religieuse, ou la difficile cohabitation des consciences', *Petites Affiches*, 2006, nr. 133, p. 9 ff, J.P. Marguénaud 'La troisième chambre civile de la cour de la cassation à la croisée des chemins d'influence de la Convention EDH sur le droit des contrats', *Revue Trimestrielle de Droit Civil*, 2006, p. 722 ff, S. Chassagnard-Pinet, 'Les droits fondamentaux à l'épreuve du lien contractuel – Contrats et Convention européenne des droits de l'homme' in *Mélanges Le Tourneau*, Dalloz: Paris, 2007, pp. 225 ff (esp. p. 244–245), F. Marchadier, 'Le droit commun des contrats du point de vue du droit européen des droits de l'Homme', *Revue des Contrats* 2014, nr. 3, pp. 553 ff (par. II).

36 See for example the CoA's stance in Cass. Civ. 3e, 18 décembre 2002, af. and Cass. Soc. 24 mars 1998, af.

37 See for example Marchadier 2014, fn. 36, referring to ECtHR, 16 December 2008, nr. 23883/06, Kurshid Mustafa et Tarzibachi v. Sweden.

38 The expression "direct horizontal effect" in relation to FR is used here in the sense that an FR can be directly invoked by one contracting party against the other party, thus without the intercession of the national rules of private law, in the course of proceedings before national courts and result in the disclosure, modification or termination of obligations between these parties. See for example A.S. Hartkamp, " 'Horizontal effects' (or Effects in Relationships between individuals') of EU Law', in A.S. Hartkamp et al. *The Influence of EU Law on National Private Law*, Kluwer: Deventer, 2014, p. 57 ff. The term "indirect horizontal effects" on the other hand refers to the impact that FR exercise on interpersonal relationships via 'the mediation of private law, for instance through (...) the interpretation of rules of private law in light of fundamental rights', C. Mak, 'Unchart(er)ed Territory EU Fundamental Rights and National Private Law', ibid, p. 323 ff., esp. p. 327.

2.3.1. The implicit rejection of FR *indirect* interpersonal effects

In contrast to Article 1102 C. civ. rev., the last 2013 draft version (Article 1102 D.O.) expressly impeded direct horizontal effects of FR. Indeed, its prohibition of contractual FR infringements was restricted to those FR that would have been '*recognized by a provision which applies to relationships between private parties*'. Several private law provisions on fundamental rights and liberties can be found in the *Code civil*, for example Article 9 or 544 C. civ., and in specific contract law, for example Article L1121–1 Labour Code. However, the explicit incorporation of FR in current private law is scarce.[39] Ensuring the protection aimed at in Article 1102 O.D. thus required further legislative intervention. The expression '*recognized by a provision*' refers to a provision explicitly mentioning the FR concerned. This principle would have therefore not only blocked the direct effects of FR, but would also have prevented the judge from assessing an FR contractual infringement via general contract law principles interpreted in the light of the FR at stake (indirect horizontal effects). The restriction to FR '*recognized by a provision*' could in simple terms be summed up as 'No provision? No protection!'. By favouring the primacy of enacted law, Article 1102 D.O. would have annulled the case law on contractual infringements of FR, and the ensuing protection.

The legislator's involvement called for in Article 1102 D.O. suffered serious weaknesses. Firstly, it remained fractional as it introduced differences between FR that are 'privatized' and those that are not. Such divergences would have also jeopardised the uniform assessment of FR contractual infringements to the type of contract involved, and subsequently the equality of protection of the contracting parties against such infringements. Secondly, the attitude of the French legislator towards this particular issue is often reactive as opposed to proactive, as revealed by its initiatives regarding the privatization of FR over the last three decades,[40] and its dormancy in other fields of contractual law.[41] Lastly, in terms of legislative efficiency, drafting and adopting a series of provisions explicitly embedding a range of FR into private law is less efficient than drafting and adopting one single general clause ascribing direct interpersonal effects to FR as a whole.

In this confidential clash of powers, the French government implicitly favoured judicial over legislative power. With the obliteration of any reference to fundamental rights in Article 1102 C. civ. rev., the authority of the *Cour de cassation* rulings attributing *direct* horizontal effects to FR in the contractual sphere has been upheld.

39 See par. 2.1. above.

40 See for example par. n of Art. 4 Loi nr. 89–462 (housing rental contract) which was enacted no less than three months after the 2006 Zéline decision (the right to respect of private life), reiterating the 1996 Mel Y. ruling, see section 2.3.2 below. See also Art. L.1132–1 and ff. Labour Code (prohibition of discrimination), which is rooted in an initiative of the European rather than French legislator.

41 On the absence of governmental regulatory action subsequent to the 1978 Scrivener Act on unfair contract terms and its negative impact on the protection of consumers, see for example Fabre-Magnan 2004 nr. 131, pp. 337–338.

2.3.2. The upholding of the *direct* interpersonal effects of FR

Since the late 1970s, the growing affirmation by the *Cour de cassation* of the direct effects of fundamental rights and liberties in contractual relationships can be observed. The evolution concerns a broad spectrum of fundamental rights and liberties, ranging from the right to respect for private resp. family life to the freedom of association, the freedom of exercising a professional activity, the right to a fair trial and the right to protection of property, but excludes the freedom of religion.[42] The most demonstrative aspect of this evolution is the reference in the Highest civil Court's rulings to the FR at stake, especially its positioning and the wording, whilst references to, and application of, contract law provisions such as Article 6 C. civ. (parties' violation of public policy) or Article 1134 C. civ. (*pacta sunt servanda* and good faith principles) are progressively placed in the background, or totally absent.

A ground-breaking ruling of the *Cour de cassation* on the issue of direct interpersonal effects of FR, is the 1996 *Mel Y.* case.[43] At stake was the validity of the provision of a rental contract, preventing the lessee from housing anyone other than herself and her children in the apartment she was renting. The owner of the apartment, a public housing office, challenged the CoA's decision which declared the contractual provision to be illicit, by arguing that the Court violated Article 1134 C. civ. (*pacta sunt servanda* principle).[44] The *Cour de cassation* nevertheless confirmed the CoA's decision on the grounds that, as stated in the final paragraph of its ruling, Article 8 ECHR precludes that a contractual clause prevents a lessee from housing relatives.[45] Only three years later, the Highest Court made an additional symbolic step towards the clear affirmation of the direct interpersonal effect of the right to respect for private life:[46] on the sole basis of Article 8 ECHR, referred to at the very outset of its ruling, the Court quashed a CoA's decision on the contractual restriction of an employee's right to freely choose his domicile.

A similar move can be observed in the Highest Court's case law with respect to the freedom of association in a business-to-business contractual setting. The *Cour de cassation* ruled in a series of decisions that a contractual provision which makes it mandatory for a contracting party to join an association for an unlimited duration and to remain a contributing member, is void. In a 2001 ruling,[47] the Highest Court based its

[42] See section 2.2 above.

[43] Cass. Civ. 3e, 6 mars 1996, nr. 93–11113, *Bull. Civ.* 1996 III, nr. 60, p. 41.

[44] The lessee allegedly breached the rental contract by housing the father of two of her children, and her sister.

[45] Cass. Civ. 3e, 6 mars 1996: "[*Les*] *clauses d'un bail d'habitation ne [peuvent], en vertu de l'article 8.1 de la Convention de sauvegarde des droits de l'homme et des libertés fondamentales, avoir pour effet de priver le preneur de la possibilité d'héberger ses proches*". See also Civ. 3e, 22 mars 2006, nr. 04–19349, Bulletin 2006 III nr. 73, p. 61 (illicit provision in a housing rental contract in a conflict involving two co-lessees).

[46] Cass. Soc. 12 janvier 1999, nr. 96–40755, *Bull. Civ.* 1999 V, nr. 7 p. 4.

[47] Cass. Ass. Plén., 9 février 2001, nr. 99–17642, Bull. Civ. Ass. Plén. 2001, nr. 3. The conflict involved the provision in a sales contract for an individual housing lot, which obliged the buyer to subscribe, and remain subscribed, to an association in charge of managing the sports infrastructure built on the subdivision, and to pay a yearly contribution for the duration of ownership of his housing lot.

holding on Article 4 of the 1901 Association Act, an Act which has constitutional authority.[48] Only two years later, and once again in 2010,[49] the citation, once more at the outset of the ruling, of the 1901 Act gave way to a reference to Article 11 ECHR in order to censure a contractual clause which was considered to violate one of the parties' freedom of association. In 2004, the Court of Cassation also prominently favoured Article 6 §1 ECHR (right to a fair trial), to quash a CoA's decision upholding a contractual clause whereby an insurance company restricted the types of burglary evidence available to the policy holder.[50]

The increased reference to FR at the beginning of the Highest Court's decision does not only concern conventional – ECHR – fundamental rights. This shift also extends to other fundamental rights, as the contract case law involving the contractual non-observance of the 'freedom of exercising professional activity' (hereafter: freedom of work) demonstrates. The freedom of work is at the heart of a series of rulings on the qualified (in)validity of the non-competition clause (hereafter: NCC). In the mid-1990s NCCs were at first considered to impose 'restrictions on individual liberties'.[51] However, in 2002 the first signs of a change towards a clear reference to the freedom of work, came about. In July 2002, the Social Chamber of the *Cour de cassation* referred to the freedom of work as 'a fundamental principle' in an introductory paragraph, which it furthermore applied *ex officio* to confirm the CoA's setting aside of a disproportionate NCC.[52]

The *Cour de cassation* not only recognises the direct application of FR in contractual relationships, it eventually also rejected their indirect effects by way of general contract law rules. This implicit rejection can be deduced from the scarcity of rulings on contractual interferences of a party's FR, which are based on rules such as for example Article 6 C. civ. (violation of public order).[53] A 2005 decision of the *Cour de*

48 Art. 4 of the 'Loi du 1er juillet 1901 relative au contrat d'association' stipulates that any member of an association which is not formed for a limited period of time may unsubscribe at any point, following the payment of contributions owed for the year, notwithstanding any contrary provision. The 1901 Association Act forms part of the so-called 'bloc de constitutionnalité', see Cons. Consti. décision nr. 71-44 DC du 16 juillet 1971 at www.conseil-constitutionnel.fr/conseil-constitutionnel/english/case-law/decision/decision-no-71-44-dc-of-16-july-1971.135366.html.

49 Cass. Civ. 3e, 12 juin 2003, nr. 02-10778, *Bull. civ.* 2003 III, nr. 125. Cass. 1ère civ., 20 mai 2010, nr. 09-65045, *Bull. civ.* 2010 I, nr. 118. Both cases involved the unlawful infringement of a party's freedom of association by way of a contractual duty to join an association and to remain a member, as well as to subscribe for the duration of the rental contract. The clause was inserted in a commercial rental contract between a shop owner and a company owning the shopping mall where the shop was located, thus a business-to-business relationship. The association was entrusted with the commercial promotion for the entire shopping mall.

50 Cass. Civ. 2e, 10 mars 2004, prv. nr. 03-10154, *Bull. Civ.* 2004 II, nr. 101 p. 86, for comments see for example A. Debet, 'Les conventions en matière de preuve et le droit à un procès équitable', *Revue des Contrats,* 2004, nr. 4, p. 938 ff. resp. p. 1080 ff.

51 Cass. Com. 4 janvier 1994, nr. 92-14121, *Bull. Civ.* 1994 IV, nr. 4, p. 4.

52 Cass. Soc. 10 juillet 2002, n° 99-43334, 99-43336, *Bull. Civ.* 2002 V, nr. 239, p. 234, see also Cass. Soc., 18 sept. 2002, nr. 00-42904, *Bull. Civ.* 2002, V, nr. 272, p. 262, and more recently Cass. Com. 15 mars 2011, nr. 10.13824, *Bull. Civ.* IV, nr. 39, *Revue Trimestrielle de Droit Civil* 2011, 348, obs. Fages.

53 Cass. Civ. 1e, 13 décembre 2005, nr. 04-13772 (only accessible via www.legisfrance.gouv.fr). See Raynaud 2001, af., pp. 113 ff with regard to the inappropriateness of Art. 6 C. civ. (public policy) as a legal basis for the assessment of the contractual breach of FR.

cassation applying Article 6 C. Civ. is furthermore contradicted by a later ruling in 2007, which abandoned any reference to Article 6 C. Civ.[54] Both decisions dealt with the breach, by means of an inalienability clause, of a party's fundamental right to property.

In the unpublished 2005 decision,[55] the Highest Court's First Civil Chamber confirmed the CoA's decision that an inalienability clause is 'contrary to public policy' (Article 6 C. civ.), and as a result null (Article 1172 C. civ.),[56] due to the absolute nature of the right to property.[57] But in 2007, the First Chamber overturned its 2005 ruling: it abandoned any reference to Article 6 C. civ. and furthermore considered the inalienability clause to now be operative, thus not inherently null.[58]

A further consequence of the overall departure from Article 1102 par. 2 D.O. is that in revised Book III of the *Code civil* a rule on the legal consequences attached to contractual infringements of a party's FR is missing, whereas with regard to that very issue the Court of Cassation's case law turns out to be a battlefield of fundamentally incompatible rulings.

3. Legal consequences of contractual infringements of FR

Observing the rulings of France's Highest Court on the sanctioning of contractual breaches of FR can only puzzle the onlooker. Recent rulings involving the contractual breach of a party's freedom of association opt for systematic nullity, while longstanding,

54 Cass. Civ. 1e, 13 décembre 2005, af., comp. with Cass. Civ. 1e, 31 octobre 2007, nr. 05-14238, *Bull. civ.* 2007, I, nr. 337.

55 Cass. Civ. 1e, 13 décembre 2005, af. The inalienability clauses were inserted in a money loan contract between two borrowers (spouses) and the *Caisse des Dépôts et Consignations* (hereafter: CDC), notably a public entity supporting housing ownership, with a view to financing the borrowers' purchase of an immovable property. The litigious clauses forbade the borrowers from renting out their property without the loaner's prior consent. A breach of the clause entitles the CDC to request the immediate reimbursement of the financial loan. The Court of Appeal deemed that the litigious clauses provided no particular advantage to either of the parties whereas, in our view, insufficient attention has been paid to the general interest goals that the CDC pursues by way of its financial aid policies regarding access to housing ownership.

56 See par. 3.2 hereafter on the sanction of nullity.

57 Cass. Civ. 1e, 13 décembre 2005, af.: "*les clauses du contrat de prêt relatives à l'interdiction de location sans accord du prêteur sous la sanction de l'exigibilité anticipée de ce prêt (...) sont prohibées au regard des articles 6 et 1172 du Code civil en ce qu'elles constituent une atteinte au principe constitutionnellement reconnu et énoncé à l'article 544 du même Code de disposer de son bien de la manière la plus absolue*".

58 Cass. 1re civ., 31 octobre 2007, af.: The configuration of the 2007 case was quite different to the one in the 2005 ruling as a third party, a bank, as opposed to the contracting parties, a father and his son, claimed the litigious clause to be void. The inalienability clause was inserted, to the benefit of the father, in both the donation act between father and son and in a joint purchase contract of an immovable property. The clause was unfavourable towards the bank, which granted a credit to the son and secured the credit agreement by means of a mortgage on the father and son's immovable property. The infringement clause was submitted to a necessity and proportionality test, see par. 3.2 hereafter.

and partly concomitant, case law on contractual infringement of a party's freedom of work applies a necessity and proportionality test. Article 1102 par. 2 D.O. is a clear codification of the latter:

> "contractual freedom does not allow the parties (...) to infringe fundamental rights and freedoms (...) *except where such infringement is indispensable to the protection of legitimate interests and proportionate to the intended purpose*" (Ital. ad.).

That necessity and proportionality test is already embedded in positive law (par. 3.1). Its codification in Article 1102 par. 2 D.O., would have offered a systematic solution which could thereby ensure the continuity between current and revised contract law. The necessity and proportionality test is nevertheless not incorporated in the final version of Book III of the *Code civil*. As a result, the government's choice leaves case law inconsistencies unresolved, in spite of the deadlock that the absolute nullity rule leads to (§3.2).

3.1. *The Cour de cassation long-standing case law on proportionality*

The rule that infringements of a party's FR by way of contract are not permitted, except if they are necessary for the protection of legitimate interests of the intruding party, and are proportionate to the pursued protection (Article 1102 par. 2 D.O.), is not at all foreign to French law, as some writers may have suggested.[59] The necessity and proportionality rule is, on the contrary, a rule that the *Cour de cassation* has continued to develop over the past two decades, in parallel to the growing recognition of the direct application of FR in the contractual context.

The Court of Cassation first mentioned the proportionality test in connection with contractual infringements of FR in 1994.[60] It then quashed a CoA's decision on the grounds that it failed to assess whether the contractual provision infringing a contracting party's freedom of work, despite being limited in time and space, 'was not disproportionate with regard to the objective of the contract'.[61] The ruling made no mention of the constitutionality or conventionality of the infringed right, yet the CoA's decision referred to litigious provisions as '[restricting] individual liberties'.

59 On the reception of the proportionality principle in French law, see for example M. Behar-Touchais, 'Rapport introductif (Le principe de proportionnalité)', *Petites Affiches* 1998, nr. 117, pp. 3 ff., J.-B. Seube, 'Le contrôle de proportionnalité exercé par le juge judiciaire: Présentation générale', *Petites Affiches* 2009, nr. 46, pp. 86. For contra see for example J. Rochfeld, 'Contrat et Convention européenne des droits de l'homme', *Revue des Contrats* 2004, nr. 2, p. 232.

60 Cass. Com., 4 janvier 1994, nr. 92–14121, *Bull. Civ.* 1994 IV, nr. 4, p. 4. The NCC – part of a service contract between a radio call centre and an independent taxi driver – forbade the driver, upon termination of his service contract with the call centre, from exercising his activity within a certain periphery for a period of three years.

61 Ibid. The CoA's judges indeed considered the litigious clause to be valid because the FR infringement in question was *limited* in time and space.

The subsequent fine-tuning of the proportionality rule, and incorporation of the necessity criterion, began in 1999. The Highest Court's Social Chamber spelled out what the necessity and proportionality test entailed, this time on the grounds of Article 8 ECHR (right to respect for private life).[62] The validity of the infringing clause depends, as the Chamber states, on whether the breach of the employee's FR is strictly necessary (*'indispensable'*) to the protection of the company's legitimate interest, and proportionate to the goal pursued, thereby taking the employee's office into account.[63]

An NCC may be valid provided it complies with the necessity and proportionality requirements, either *ab initio* or *a posteriori*, as a result of the judge's adjustment.[64] The necessity and proportionality assessment of a contractual clause infringing FR implies therefore that the litigious clause is not as such automatically null and void (*nullité absolue*).

The necessity and proportionality rule relates primarily, but not exclusively, to non-competition clauses. It was recently applied, with some adjustments, to assess whether a non-re-affiliation clause inserted in a shareholders' agreement, disproportionately infringed a party's fundamental freedom to work.[65] Furthermore, the scope of application of the necessity and proportionality rule was eventually extended to the infringement of property rights, after some wavering in case law. In 2007, an inalienability clause was considered conditionally operative, implicitly meaning that such a clause is not intrinsically null as long as it is 'limited in time and justified by a serious and legitimate interest' of the infringing party.[66]

62 Cass. Soc. 12 janvier 1999, nr. 96–40755, *Bull. civ.* 1999 V, nr. 7, p. 4. The litigious domicile clause obliged the employee to transfer his domicile to Montpellier, where he should take up permanent residence.

63 Only three years later, the same Social Chamber mentioned in addition to the abovementioned conditions, the employer's obligation to indemnify the employee from the infringement, all these criteria being cumulative. See Cass. Soc. 10 juillet 2002, nr. 99–43334, 99–43336, *Bull. Civ.* 2002 V, nr. 239, p. 234: "*moyen relevé d'office, pris de la violation du principe fondamental de libre exercice d'une activité professionnelle, (...) une clause de non-concurrence n'est licite que si elle est indispensable à la protection des intérêts légitimes de l'entreprise, limitée dans le temps et dans l'espace, qu'elle tient compte des spécificités de l'emploi du salarié et comporte l' obligation pour l'employeur de verser au salarié une contrepartie financière, ces conditions étant cumulatives*".

64 Cass. Soc. 18 sept. 2002, nr. 00–42904, *Bull. Civ.* 2002 V, nr. 272, p. 262: "*la cour d'appel ayant relevé que la clause litigieuse constituait, en raison de la spécificité de l'activité professionnelle de M. X..., une entrave à sa liberté de travailler, a pu décider qu'il y avait lieu d'en* réduire le champ d'application *à l'interdiction faite au salarié de démarcher les clients de la société GAN-vie*".

65 See Cass. Com. 15 mars 2011, nr. 10.13824 (shareholders' agreement), *Bull. Civ.* 2011 IV, nr. 39, *RTDciv.* 2011, p. 348, obs. Fages, and Cass. Com. 31 janvier 2012, nr. 11–11071 (non-re-affiliation clause), *Bull. Civ.* 2012 IV, nr. 17.

66 Cass. Civ. 1e, 31 octobre 2007, nr. 05–14238, *Bull. civ.* 2007 I, nr. 337. Yet in 2005, the Highest Court's First Civil Chamber approved the CoA's decision that an inalienability clause was null (Art. 1172 C. civ.) as it was violating Art. 6 C. civ. (public policy): "*les clauses du contrat de prêt relatives à l'interdiction de location sans accord du prêteur sous la sanction de l'exigibilité anticipée de ce prêt (...) sont prohibées au regard des articles 6 et 1172 [nullity; add. CM] du Code civil en ce qu'elles constituent une atteinte au principe constitutionnellement reconnu et énoncé à l'article 544 du même Code de disposer de son bien de la manière la plus absolue*", Civ. 1e, 13 décembre 2005, af.

However, as the Highest Court's case law on fundamental freedom of association reveals, the rejection of an automatic nullity in favour of the necessity and proportionality rule, is not a legal consequence systematically linked by the Highest Court to contractual infringement of all FR.

3.2. *The deadlock of unqualified invalidity*

From 2003 to 2011,[67] the Court of Cassation handed down three decisions dealing with the sanctioning of commercial rental provisions which violated the lessee's freedom of association. A common thread which binds these rulings is the affirmation of the automatic and absolute nullity of the contested contract clause, first discussed in a decision of the Court dating from 2003.[68]

The sanction of nullity means that the contested clause is retrospectively invalid from the moment of its acceptance. The absolute nature of the nullity further prevents the judge from shaping the effects of the litigious clause: the infringing clause may not produce any effect.[69] As a result, when parties have nevertheless performed according to the void clause, the legal basis for their performance vanishes. The sanction of nullity thus requires the judge to handle the mutual restitution of the performances carried out, provided they benefited the other party. The settlement of the restitution issue is at the heart of the clash between the subsequent 2010 and 2011 decisions of the First and Third Chamber respectively. This opposition originates from the conflict between on the one hand, the right of the infringed party to an effective remedy advocated by the First Chamber,[70] and on the other hand, the primacy of the duty of reciprocal restitutions resulting from the nullity, endorsed by the Third Chamber.[71] The legal deadlock the Highest Court entered into clearly becomes apparent when looking at the facts and procedures of the cases under consideration.

67 Cass. Civ. 3e, 12 juin 2003, nr. 02–10778 af., Cass. Civ 1e, 20 mai 2010, nr. 09–65045 af. and Cass. Civ. 3e, 23 nov. 2011, nr. 10–23928, af.

68 Cass. Civ. 3e, 12 juin 2003, nr. 02–10778 af.: '*La clause d'un bail commercial faisant obligation au preneur d'adhérer à une association des commerçants et à maintenir son adhésion pendant la durée du bail est entachée d'une nullité absolue*'. The CoA's decision, which was quashed, considered the clause to be valid.

69 With regard to that issue, see for example A. Marais, 'La liberté de ne pas s'associer', *Revue des Contrats* 2004, nr. 2, pp. 465 ff., C. Pérès, 'Anéantissement du contrat et restitutions sous l'emprise de l'effectivité des droits fondamentaux', *Revue des Contrats* 2010, nr. 4, pp. 1185 ff., C. Grimaldi, 'Bail commercial et liberté d'association, nullité et restitutions', *Revue des Contrats* 2011, nr. 1, pp. 169 ff., C. Pérès, 'L'instrumentalisation du droit européen des droits de l'Homme par la Cour de cassation', *Revue des Contrats* 2013, nr. 1, pp. 36 ff., Y.M. Laithier, 'La nullité absolue du contrat, ou comment défendre son intérêt personnel au nom de l'intérêt général', *Revue des Contrats* 2013, nr. 2, pp. 537 ff., N. Bareït, *La liberté contractuelle sous la toise de la Convention européenne des droits de l'homme*, L.G.D.J.:Paris 2013, pp. 71 ff, available at https://hal.archives-ouvertes.fr/hal-01081666/document.

70 Cass. Civ. 1e, 20 mai 2010, nr. 09–65045, af.

71 Cass. Civ. 3e, 23 nov. 2011, nr. 10–23928, af.

All three instances concern a retailer who rents a shop from a shopping mall owner with whom he is in conflict. The rental contract requires the lessee to join and subscribe to the shopping mall's retailers association in charge of the commercial promotion for the whole shopping mall, and remain a member of it, for the entire duration of the rental period. The lessee remains a member and subscribes for a number of years until he quits the association, whilst still renting from the shopping mall. From that moment, he stops paying his contributions to the retailers association and claims reimbursement of the contributions he has already paid, arguing that the rental contract violates his freedom of association, and should therefore have no legal effects.

In the 2010 case, the CoA recognized, in line with the Highest Court's 2003 decision, the nullity of the contested provision but nevertheless rejected the lessee's restitution claim and even ordered him to pay a sum equivalent to the contributions he would have paid, had the contractual clause been valid, for the duration of the shop rental. Due to the retroactivity of the nullity, the performances mutually rendered by the lessee and the association should have been reciprocally undone. The Court of Appeal seemingly reasoned that if the lessee unduly paid contributions on the basis of an invalid clause, he nevertheless benefited, and continued to benefit from the advertising activities of the retailers association for the time he was renting a shop in the shopping mall. The CoA's reasoning seemed to be that if it would order on the one hand the reimbursement of the contributions the lessee paid, and would prevent on the other hand that the association be compensated for the activities the lessee *de facto* benefited from, such decision would lead to the unjustified enrichment of the lessee to the detriment of the association. As a result, the lessee's patrimonial position remained practically unchanged, despite the acknowledgment of the violation of his fundamental freedom of association and associated absolute nullity. The First Chamber ultimately quashed the Court of Appeal's decision on the grounds that it violated Article 6 §1 ECHR (right to effective protection). According to the First Chamber, the CoA's decision leads to 'a theoretical recognition, deprived of any effectivity, of the lessee's freedom not to be a member of an association'.[72] The protection lessees could expect, in reliance of the *Cour de cassation* 2003 ruling, seemed at that point in time to be guaranteed.

However, less than 18 months later, the Third Chamber of the *Cour de cassation* overturned a CoA's decision abiding by the First Chamber's 2010 ruling.[73] 'Nullity due to the infringement of the freedom not to adhere to an association, does not set aside reciprocal *restitution rules* that the nullity may infer' (ital. add., transl. CM), the Third Chamber states matter-of-factly.[74] The Third Chamber recognises the nullity of the clause, which violates Article 11 ECHR and the 1901 Act, but nevertheless orders the

72 Cass. Civ. 1e, 20 mai 2010, nr. 09-65045, af.

73 The CoA rejected the association's claim that the lessee be ordered to restitute the value of the advertising activities of the association from which he benefited, on the grounds of effectivity of the nullity of the clause infringing the lessee's FR.

74 Cass. Civ. 3e, 23 nov. 2011, nr. 10-23928 af.: "l'annulation à raison de l'atteinte à la liberté fondamentale de ne pas s'associer ne fait pas échec *au principe des restitutions réciproques* que peut impliquer l'annulation d'un contrat exécuté " (Ital. ad.).

lessee to basically compensate for the advertising activities he has benefited from. Again, the lessee ultimately remained in the very same position, as if he had not benefited from the protection offered by Article 11 ECHR and the 1901 Act, which the nullity of the litigious rental clause was supposed to achieve.

This paradoxical situation does not, in my view, primarily originate in the private law reasoning on restitutions, underpinning the 2010 and 2011 rulings. Nor is it the allegedly 'destructive power' of the effectivity principle[75] which is at stake. The cause of this showdown of legal appearances is rooted in the *Cour de cassation*'s 2003 decision which implies the systematic nullity of the litigious infringing clause. Indeed, if in 2003 the Highest Court had opted for the necessity and proportionality test it applied at that time to NCC's, if only for the sake of a systematic case law on the direct effects of fundamental rights on contract, it would have prevented the legal insecurity caused by the subsequent contradictory rulings in the first place. But most significantly, it would have led to an appropriate outcome for the conflicting interests at stake and the contracting parties' expectations.

Indeed, if applied to the lessee/lessor conflict previously described, the necessity and proportionality test would have firstly led to the acknowledgment of the contractual violation of the lessee's fundamental freedom of association. In order to decide whether the violating clause was nevertheless valid, the judge would have then assessed the necessity of the infringement, and examined the legitimacy of the interests the clause aimed to protect. The judge would have subsequently questioned the proportionality of the infringement of the lessee's individual interest in view of the pursued protection of the collective interest of all retailers.[76] The judge may have further considered whether the lessee should have received any form of compensation in return, and more specifically whether the lessee had benefited from the association's activities.[77] The necessity and proportionality rule could have thus prevented lessees from bringing further proceedings because of an imaginary rule of law, namely that of an absolute fundamental right. With regard to the readability of the rule of law, which the French governmental reform strives

75 Pérès criticised the 2010 decision to favour effectivity considerations in reference to Art. 6 par. 1 ECHR, over the application of restitution rules. In her view '*l'effectivité des droits peut ainsi devenir un outil de démentèllement extrèmement énergique du droit positif*'. She further states that '*Parce qu'elle est attachée au respect des droits fondamentaux dont elle favorise la promotion, elle accentue l'atomisation des solutions au détriment du maintien d'une cohérence d'ensemble et de la recherche de subtils équilibres dont la technicité n'occulte qu'en apparence la justice. Parce qu'enfin, l'effectivité des droits de l'un ne peut l'emporter que jusqu'à un certain point sur l'effectivité des droits de l'autre, elle n'est elle-même qu'une illusion. À ce titre, elle est sans issue*', in Pérès 2010, par. 4.

76 The interests of all retailers, including the litigating lessee, in sharing the costs of a collective promotional and advertising activities are of a collective nature. The obligation for all retailers to adhere to this is essential, as it guarantees the equal repartition of the burden of the cost between all retailers. The interest of all retailers in the promotional and advertising activities, and in sharing the related costs, is a legitimate matter. Lastly, the infringement is proportional if the association's activities benefit the lessee.

77 Lacking any benefit for the lessee, it is highly likely that the litigious clause would be deemed disproportionate and therefore invalid, and ultimately lead to a restitution of the contribution paid, as the reciprocal performance of the association is supposed to have no value.

for, the necessity and proportionality test as formulated in Article 1102 par. 2 D.O. is preferable to the current contradictions within the Highest Court's case law.

4. A missed opportunity to codify

The French Government's decision not to uphold the general clause on interpersonal effects of fundamental rights and liberties in the 2016 Governmental reform of Book III of the *Code civil* gives rise to several questions as to governmental motives, and the consequences of that omission.

The main consequence of the non-codification is that for the time being, current contract law on that issue remains unchanged and as a result its evident internal inconsistencies are left unresolved. One can only but wonder, all the more when considering the general goals of the recodification of Book III of the *Code civil*, why the Government, for this matter alone, did not grasp this codification opportunity to remedy the absence of any systematic approach which, with regard to that specific issue, jeopardises both the reform goals of legal security, and accessibility of the rule of law.

Codifying a *general* clause on interpersonal effects of FR, as the 2013 Draft *ordonnance* intended to do, was not redundant. Indeed, neither current enacted contract law, nor contract case law offer common guidelines according to which an alleged contractual infringement of a party's FR can be assessed and sanctioned, regardless of the type of contract concerned, and regardless of the fundamental right at stake.

Nor was introducing a general clause on interpersonal effects of FR in Book III of the *Code civil* irrelevant, due to the many internal contradictions observed in contract case law. Incoherencies first appear when examining the handling of contractual infringements of the freedom of religion. Since its first decision on contractual infringements of FR in 1978, the *Cour de cassation* consistently denies any direct horizontal effects on freedom of religion within the contractual sphere, despite criticisms from the doctrine. The Highest Court never departed from its different approach. However, it contradicts both its own recognition of not only horizontal but also direct effects of all other FR, the legislator's growing recognition of the horizontal effect of freedom of religion in certain specific contract relationships, and ultimately France's positive obligation to guarantee the respect of that freedom under the ECHR. How relevant the codification of interpersonal effects of FR is in Book III of the *Code civil*, furthermore comes to light when looking at the legal consequences currently attached to contractual FR infringements. The Court of Cassation has developed two conflicting approaches towards sanctioning such FR infringements, one of which (systematic absolute nullity) leads to a legal deadlock, causing reversals of case law, and thus endangering the internal coherence of the system.

This all endangers legal security, and the readability and accessibility of the rule of law which the Government's recodification endeavours. It also deprives litigants of the protection they are entitled to, and leads them to engage in unsuccessful litigations.[78]

When looking at this overall lack of systematic approach, one must unfortunately conclude that the French Government has missed an opportunity to codify a rule on

78 See par. 3.2 in particular.

contractual FR infringements by not improving Article 1102 D.O., both in continuity in terms of the current case law, and in line with other existing drafts, and suppressing it instead. Article 1102 D.O. spells out what freedom of contract entails, and restricts that freedom in the event that contractual freedom violates public policy rules, or infringes the other party's fundamental rights and liberties. Article 1102 D.O. would have applied regardless of the type of contract or the fundamental rights and liberties at stake.

Article 1102 D.O. is no exception. On the contrary, it echoes in part a similar provision in a prior reform draft, and actually originates in the Highest Court's rulings themselves. Article 1102 D.O. is in the first place comparable, in its scope of application and formulation, to Article 4 (freedom of contract and its limits) of the 2009 draft of Prof. Terré's drafting group (hereafter: Terré Draft), a private reform draft of Book III of the *Code civil*.[79] However, other than Article 1102 D.O., Article 4 of the Terré Draft recognises direct interpersonal effects to FR in general, regardless of the type of contract and FR involved, thereby putting an end to one of the two major inconsistencies of French current case law, this being the varying treatment of the freedom of religion, which has now been left unresolved.[80] For that reason, by not improving Article 1102 par. 2 D.O. in line with Article 4 of the Terré Draft, the Government let a chance slip through its fingers.

Regarding the legal consequences of FR infringements, the Article 1102 D.O. necessity and proportionality test is consistent with part of the current contract case law, as well as with Article 4 of the Terré Draft. It thus sets aside a series of rulings supporting a 'monolithic nullity' of clauses that infringe FR,[81] which has led to a legal impasse. The generalization of the necessity and proportionality test would have contributed to the restoration of the readability of the rule of law aimed at by the Government's reform, as it implicitly and nevertheless indisputably rejects the absolute nature of fundamental rights and liberties. Indeed, the qualified invalidity of contractual infringements of FR signifies to contracting parties nothing less than that one's fundamental (contractual) freedom and rights end where those of the other contracting party begin.

5. Lessons to be learned from the French experience

A central underlying thread of the present volume is whether neighbouring legal systems can draw lessons from the overall recodification of France's general contract law. Answering such a question would require an in-depth analysis of national contract law systems, an exercise that goes beyond the scope of the present contribution. Furthermore, one must conclude that learning from the French codification experience

79 F. Terré (dir.), *Pour une réforme du droit des contrats*, Dalloz:Paris, 2009. See also Art. 59 of the Terré Draft on contents of the contract in relation to public policy rules and FR. The 2013 Draft *ordonnance* and the Terré Draft both differ from other earlier private reform drafts of Book III of the *Code civil*, namely the 2004 *Catala* Draft and the 2008 *Chancellerie* Draft, which do not address the issue.

80 Art. 4 of the Terré Draft also conditions the validity of FR infringements to their necessity in view of the protection of legitimate interests, yet not to their proportionate character.

81 N. Bareït, af. nr. 26.

with regard to the issue of interpersonal effects of FR within the contractual sphere, is barely possible now that the Government has decided, despite its initial intention, not to codify that issue.[82] From a Dutch perspective, three general observations can nevertheless be made.

A first observation is that, just like its 1804 French counterpart, the 1992 Dutch Civil Code contains no general clause which, like Article 1102 D.O. or Article 4 of the Terré Draft, is specifically designed to address contractual infringements of FR. Furthermore, the Dutch legal system is, just like the French one, monistic: conventional FR form part of the national *corpus legis*, and a specific implementation is not required. Regarding Article 1102 par. 2 D.O., though it partly reflects the approach developed by the Dutch Highest Civil Court, the *Hoge Raad*, it seems less elaborated. The Dutch Highest Court adds a subsidiarity test (*subsidiariteitscriterium*) to the necessity (*noodzakelijkheidscriterium*) and proportionality (*proportionaliteitscriterium*) rule.[83] From a Dutch perspective, the comparison with Article 1102 D.O. questions the reason behind the *Hoge Raad's* distinction between, on the one hand, a necessity criterion and, on the other hand, a subsidiarity criterion. On the basis of the former, one assesses whether an FR infringement an 'appropriate means' (*geschikt middel*) is to ensure the protection of the legitimate interest of the infringing party. The subsidiarity criterion aims at assessing whether these latter interests could be properly secured via other means, other than violating the other party's FR. If such alternative measures are within reach (subsidiarity test), how can an FR infringement still be considered an 'appropriate' means (necessity test)? In effect the necessity criterion under Article 1102 D.O. combines the Dutch necessity and subsidiarity tests.[84]

Finally, the French Government's unsuccessful attempt to codify the issue of interpersonal effects of FR in a contractual setting also raises the question of the added value of codification as compared to judge-made laws. Indeed, the Government's major goals, when engaging with the recodification of Book III of the *Code civil*, were not only the reinforcement of legal security but also the enhancement of accessibility, readability, of the rule of law for the layman.[85] A key message conveyed by Article 1102 D.O. is that also in interpersonal relations fundamental rights and liberties are not absolute. That essential message may well have attracted the attention of the legal community in the Netherlands as well as other countries neighbouring France. The *Code civil*, France's

82 Even less so as no information is available as to the motives of the Government due to a legislative procedure by way of *ordonnance*. See the 2016 Rapport au Président.

83 See *Hoge Raad*, 14 september 2007, ECLI:NL:HR:2007:BA5802, cons. nr. 3.4.2: "*Bij de beantwoording van de vraag of een dergelijke inbreuk gerechtvaardigd is, dient te worden onderzocht of de inbreuk makende handeling een legitiem doel dient en of zij een geschikt middel is om dat doel te bereiken (het noodzakelijkheidscriterium); voorts moet worden onderzocht of de inbreuk op de persoonlijke levenssfeer van de werknemer evenredig is in verhouding tot het belang van de werkgever bij het bereiken van het beoogde doel (het proportionaliteitscriterium), en of de werkgever dat doel redelijkerwijs op een minder ingrijpende wijze kon bereiken (het subsidiariteitscriterium)*".

84 This observation concerns as well the Cour de cassation's rullings on NCC's and Art. 4 of the Terré Draft.

85 See Rapport au Président 2016, p. 2.

Civil Constitution in the words of Dean Carbonnier, would, in its revised form, have echoed Article 4 of the 1789 Human Rights Declaration stating that

'(...), the exercise of the [fundamental] rights of every [human] has no bounds other than those that ensure to the other (...) the enjoyment of these same rights'.

IUS COMMUNE EUROPAEUM

A peer-reviewed book series in which the common foundations of the legal systems of the Member States of the European Union are the central focus.

The *Ius Commune Europaeum* series includes horizontal comparative legal studies as well as studies on the effect of treaties within the national legal systems. All the classic fields of law are covered. The books are published in various European languages under the auspices of METRO, the Institute for Transnational Legal Research at Maastricht University.

Recently published:
Volume 143: *A European Legal Framework for Nuclear Liability. Rethinking Current Approaches*, T. Heldt
Volume 144: *The Development of European Private Law in a Multilevel Legal Order*, E.A.G. Van Schagen
Volume 145: *Property Law Perspectives IV*, D. Gruyaert, E. Ramaekers and L. Rostill (eds.)
Volume 146: *The Citizen in European Private Law: Norm-setting, Enforcement and Choice*, C. Cauffman and J. Smits (eds.)
Volume 147: *Legal Certainty in Real Estate Transactions: A Comparison of England and France*, B. Du Marais and D. Marrani (eds.)
Volume 148: *Scarcity and the State I. The Allocation of Limited Rights by the Administration*, P. Adriaanse, F. van Ommeren, W. den Ouden and J. Wolswinkel (eds.)
Volume 149: *Optional Instruments of the European Union. A Definitional, Normative and Explanatory Study*, W.A. Bull
Volume 150: *The European Union and National Civil Procedure. A Smooth Process or a Rocky Road for Member States?*, A. Nylund and B.H. Krans (eds.)
Volume 151: *Different Paths Towards Sustainable Biofuels? A Comparative Study of the International, EU, and Chinese Regulation of the Sustainability of Biofuels*, T. Yue
Volume 152: *Regulation of Cross-border Establishment in China and the EU. A Comparative Law and Economics Approach*, G. Shen

www.ingramcontent.com/pod-product-compliance
Ingram Content Group UK Ltd.
Pitfield, Milton Keynes, MK11 3LW, UK
UKHW051927100926
8556IPUK00022B/1411

9 781780 684192